SCREWBALL

Books by Larry Swindell

SCREWBALL: The Life of Carole Lombard
BODY AND SOUL: The Story of John Garfield
SPENCER TRACY: A Biography

SCREWBALL

The Life of
Carole Lombard

—◆—

by Larry Swindell

WILLIAM MORROW AND COMPANY, INC.
NEW YORK   1975

B

Lombard

Picture Acknowledgments

The first photo insert of family pictures is provided by Frederic Peters, Jr., with three exceptions: The photo of the grown Carole Lombard and her mother is by courtesy of Legrant Alvine; the John Abbe portrait of Carole with parasol is by arrangement with Mary Dawn Early; and the Mack Sennett production scene is from the Picture Collection of the Library for the Performing Arts, Lincoln Center.

All motion picture stills are provided by the Stills Archive of the Museum of Modern Art Film Library, with the exception of the scenes from *True Confession, Mr. and Mrs. Smith,* and *To Be or Not to Be,* from the library of *The Philadelphia Inquirer.*

All other photographs are from private collections, including the author's. The endpaper montage executed by Robert Epp is from photos loaned by *The Philadelphia Inquirer,* which also provided the front and back dust-jacket photos.

Copyright © 1975 by Larry Swindell

Printed in the United States of America.
1 2 3 4 5   79 78 77 76 75

Library of Congress Cataloging in Publication Data

Swindell, Larry.
  Screwball: the life of Carole Lombard.
  Filmography: p.
  Includes index.
  1. Lombard, Carole, 1908-1942.
I. Title.
PN2287.L625S9   791.43′028′0924   [B]   75-12536
ISBN 0-688-00287-0

IN MEMORIAM

Virginia Royce Munshin
1931–1962
Rita Montgomery Zakowski
1930–1974

Author's Note

SEVERAL years ago I confided to Garson Kanin that I was considering a biography of Carole Lombard. Kanin, himself a Lombard director, said, "Oh, you *must* do it . . . but for God's sake, hurry!" I know what he meant. Nowadays we are writing film biographies that should have been accomplished years ago, to have had the benefit of those who were there and who saw and knew. Many whose rich memories of Carole would have strengthened the overall perspective are long departed. I read Walter Lang's obituary on the very day that I had written to him, requesting an interview.

Still, I sense having acted in time's strategic nick. To have begun only now, say, would have been too late in a very real way. Many who aided this book during its years of preparation are no longer with us, and there is no way to express appreciation other than to hope that they know: particularly Billy Grady, William Haines, and two directors of primary importance to the Lombard career, Mitchell Leisen and Wesley Ruggles.

The "research" feasibly has ancient roots. Well over twenty years ago I was a teen-aged member of something called The Great Films Society in Beverly Hills. Following a screening of *My Man Godfrey*, Gregory LaCava talked about screwball comedy so vividly that I still remember the essence of all he said. Once Richard Barthelmess got to reminiscing about Carole Lombard's effort to help revive his career. Mack Sennett often was our guest, and there was the time Miriam Hopkins recalled Paramount without sentimentality. These things have a way of feeding inspiration for a book, then feeding the book as well. John Ford's recollection of the very young Carole Lombard is the issue of some oral meandering when I met with him in the capacity of Spencer Tracy's first biographer. Persons contacted in my attentions to other projects unknowingly were adding flesh to the portraits here attempted—Clark Gable's as well as Carole's. Surely it is significant that almost anyone who worked in Hollywood prior to World War II eventually gets around to talking about Carole Lombard. We must always pay attention to anything we hear from people who have participated in an exciting history.

I could enumerate many dozens who have been helpful in different ways. But inevitably a special few meetings have the effect of giving a biography its essential shape and scope. For the insights they conveyed directly and for the many other doors to information that each opened, I am most indebted to two persons: Fred Peters, a gentleman endowed with amazing memory as well as the good fortune of having been Bess Peters's son and Carole Lombard's brother; and Mrs. Phil Karlson, the friend of Carole's lifetime. Most individual contributions should be evident, but Edith Head's assistance was greater than she might suspect, and my meeting with Jean Garceau was more vital than might be apparent in the text. Carol Burnett did not know Carole Lombard but was enormously helpful in leading me to several persons who did, Miss Head among them.

The idea of a full-scale Carole Lombard biography actually was Howard Cady's, and it was in 1968 that he invited me to think about it. He is my editor and has given stability to the project over its full distance. I thank other friends for their roles in the mundane necessities of getting a book started and keeping it in motion: Pat McHugh; Joe Gradel; Ruth Zook; and the Museum of Modern Art's mistress of film stills, Mary Corliss. My daughter Julie has assisted in three film biographies without having been previously acknowledged, though always appreciated. My custom is to conclude with a salute to my wife, and I suspect that a multitude of wives are the unsung heroines and uncredited collaborators in their husbands' work. Theirs is such determined encouragement as husbands too often fail to give their wives' own ventures. So again, thank you, Ellie: I don't think I would ever finish anything without you, or do it well.

Richboro, Pennsylvania
March, 1975

Contents

*Photographs follow pages 32, 74,
100, 160, 190.*

SCREWBALL

❋ I ❋

Tomboy

SHE WAS always beautiful. She said it was a curse, that plainness would have been a thing more comfortable for her to endure. Yet she exploited glamour as her own weapon on the economic and political battlefields of Hollywood when glamour was at its highest premium. She disciplined every physical advantage until she attained the impossible dream that obsessed millions of girls and women in that singular era.

The dream they courted was threefold: to be beautiful; to become a famous movie star; and to marry Clark Gable. Untold thousands from the country over—raw novice girls and diversely experienced stage actresses—made the earnest effort, and a modest few dozen accomplished two of those objectives. But only Carole Lombard completed the course.

No one enjoyed being a movie star more than she, if only belatedly did she appreciate the likelihood that she was also an artist. It would have been her most personal triumph—no doubt, she would have issued great howling laughter—to have known that in death she would be celebrated for traits other than beauty. But what had she become, just before the airliner gnawed into that Nevada mountainside on January 16, 1942?

She was one of the foremost stars of a filmdom still inhaling its most confident glory, yet her national popularity had waned steadily since its apogee five years earlier, despite having legally sealed the famous union with Gable. Even that idealized marriage was tarnished by unsettling rumors that were refueled when Gable failed to accompany his wife to Indiana on her fateful mission to sell defense bonds.

But in Hollywood, intramural deification of Carole Lombard was accomplished even before it was magnified by her death. She was filmdom's best pal and good-time girl—the loudest laugher, the ripest talker, the least practical joker, the favorite guest, the busiest peacemaker, the most inventive hostess, wisely irreverent but generous and always humane: the one person in town whom everyone liked, the brightest and the best and no mistake.

"Without her, this place changed permanently," recalled Wesley Ruggles, once her director and companion. "When Irving Thalberg and then Jean Harlow both died too young, the whole community experienced a shock of loss, but it was more industrial than personal. Somehow you knew you'd adjust. But we couldn't comprehend losing Carole, and we never adjusted to it, either. She was irreplaceable, and we just kept on missing her."

The Japanese attack on Pearl Harbor had rudely plunged the United States into its greatest war only six weeks before her death. Yet it was Carole's death that would sober the film colony into awareness of wartime realities. The first eulogists sanctified her a national heroine, repeatedly stressing that she had given her life in the service of her country. Carole Lombard would have scoffed and said that was so much shit.

She was not Hollywood's first cussing woman, as legend has made her, but she was the first star whose profanity was honest and direct in a manner that nicely accommodated an irrepressible style. Her personality was an anthology of excesses that did not diminish her beauty so much as impart to it a giddy shading. This became more pronounced and more agreeable during her heady vogue as the screen's first mistress of screwball comedy, and as Clark Gable's raucous paramour and then wife. But she was always beautiful.

Hollywood embraced her as a hometown girl risen to its own definition of royalty, but her beauty and even a suggestion of her singular charm were already in evidence before she was a large-eyed new arrival in the filmland, just eight years old. She came from the settled American heartland in the company of her mother and two older brothers, and even as a high-school dropout she was not allowed to forget her advantage of breeding, nor would she understate her pedigree. The girl who was Jane Alice Peters before she was Carole Lombard had inherited a fierce pride.

One of America's oldest continuous settlements exists in northeastern Indiana at the confluence of three rivers. The French and then the British maintained military posts where the St. Joseph and St. Mary's rivers meet to form the Maumee. The Miami Indians occupied the deserted installations until Mad Anthony Wayne routed them in 1794 and built a stockade, around which a white settlement grew. The stockade was abandoned but the community of Fort Wayne flourished, and its population swelled during the industrially energetic years following the Civil War. In middle-sized, Middle-American cities such as Fort Wayne, Indiana, the populace was nourished primarily by pioneer American stock; and it was in the Fort Waynes that a true American class system asserted itself, with economic status as the primary measurement.

The Indiana novelist Booth Tarkington captured the roles of this society in *The Magnificent Ambersons* and *Alice Adams;* and if Mr. Tarkington had fashioned a "Fort Wayne novel," he could hardly have found a more appropriate focus than the Knights and the Peterses, two of the city's established "best" families. Elizabeth Knight and Frederic Peters had been remotely acquainted since childhood; but when they found romance in the ballroom, they were Fort Wayne's pleasured and privileged youth, giving themselves buoyantly to the kaleidoscopic gaiety of the Nineties.

The Knights were perhaps the more glamorous family. There were formidable banking connections in the East. Gentleman Jim Cheney, Elizabeth Knight's maternal grandfather, was a friend and confidential adviser to Jay Gould and had amassed his own personal fortune of mysterious dimensions. His favorite daughter married a successful Fort Wayne businessman, but the gossip in the river mansions was that Charlie Knight was the one who had married into the real money.

An interviewer once asked Carole Lombard if it was a fact that her grandfather had laid the first Atlantic Cable and acquired several lucrative patents. Carole said, "No, that was the older guy. The only thing my granddad laid was Grandmother Knight, but he acquired three luscious daughters."

The Knight sisters were a Fort Wayne legend, as desirable for their manifold charms as for their likely dowries. Elizabeth, or

Bess as she was always called, wasn't as pretty as her sisters but she was more vivacious. She was at the vortex of the local merriment, much as her famous daughter would be to a later Hollywood. Bess Knight had a scheming wit and worldly curiosity. Unlike her sisters, who both married well but pursued no horizon beyond the Fort Wayne social hierarchy, she courted adventure that might surpass the Hoosier definition of it. She settled for frequent travel to Indianapolis, where she acquired an independent circle of friends; but when love subdued her, the young man would not budge from Fort Wayne.

The Peters family symbolized the confidence and prosperity of McKinley's America. John Peters had a Midas touch for business, if on a somewhat parochial scale. He was first and last a hardware man and apprenticed his four sons in the ways of business through their association with the J. C. Peters Hardware Company, before each son pursued his own future under the father's guidance. There were also three beguiling Peters daughters, friends to the Knight girls, and all would make admirably conservative marriages.

Frederic Peters was charming in the manner of a favorite son, and favored because he was obviously smart and spectacularly handsome. Business ability came easily to him but it was less than a flair: he lacked real aggressiveness because his heart beat as a playboy's. Not in a rakish way, however. He was convivial, and had both appetite and capacity for enjoyment. He was an outdoorsman—hunting, fishing, boating—but he also liked music, dancing, and traditional indoor sports.

Of course it was said that he could have his pick of the prettiest and most eligible girls in town; and in abundant numbers they advertised their candidacy for his attentions. But Fred Peters was instinctively a hunter, not prey; and so Bess Knight became the objective of a long courtship. She was not above coquetry and teased him with a notion of leaving Fort Wayne, perhaps to pursue a career on the stage. She had appeared in some of the minor Fort Wayne theatricals, regaling playgoers with her effusive personality, which further incited Fred's interest.

Charles Knight wanted Bess's young man to prove himself in business before he would listen to talk of marriage, and Fred Peters met the demand. One of his father's shrewdest investments (besides lumber, hotels, and paper mills) had been in an early washing machine called the Horton, and he negotiated its manufacture in Fort Wayne. Fred was groomed for a managerial position with the Horton Company, but then he sustained a crippling injury in an elevator accident at the factory. Since he was "lucky to be alive," it was thought he had narrowly escaped real tragedy, although the lasting effects of the accident were not then suspected. The permanent impairment of a "bad leg" did not alter his and Bess Knight's marriage plans, and their wedding was a gala event of the new century. Then they took their assigned roles in the younger circle of the regimented Fort Wayne society, and after an agreeable period they began to raise a family.

Frederic Peters, Jr., was born in 1902 and a second son, Stuart, arrived in 1906. The younger boy was two and a half when Bess Knight Peters finally got her wished-for daughter on October 6, 1908. The baby girl was extremely fair, characteristic more of the Peters line than of the dark-eyed, brown-haired Knights. She was pronounced extraordinarily beautiful, and was named Jane Alice. Fred Peters had purchased a large, handsome house at the foot of Rockhill Street and that was where Carole Lombard was born—within a stone's throw of the St. Mary's River, in a then-fashionable section of Fort Wayne. She had her own room from infancy onward and also shared a large playroom with her brothers.

The Peters marriage was a good one in the consensus view, and to some of their friends it represented the ideal. In a later day a computer might have brought Fred and Bess Peters together, so neatly did they complement one another. Both enjoyed company and the festive atmosphere of a crowd, but Bess was animated and outgoing where her husband was a more contemplative sort, typically a pipe smoker. The gimpy leg, it was thought, had made him more introverted; yet he became even more aristocratic in appearance, going in for conservative but expensively tailored suits, and the full regalia of outdoorsmanship. On hunting expeditions he wore a colorful Tyrolean hat, and acquired the nickname of Lord Algie—its origin uncertain, but it held among family and friends for many years to come. He was a favorite with his nephews and cousins, and properly idolized by his young sons. But Fred Peters's latter-day jauntiness may have been achieved only with great effort, as a means of camouflaging a creeping affliction that could not immediately be diagnosed, but was in evidence before Jane Alice was born.

The little girl had worshipful affection for her daddy, but his headaches restricted the true closeness they might have achieved. The "spells"—irregular but gradually increasing in their frequency —also disrupted the serenity of his life with Bess. They were never quarrelsome, and continued to present a joyful family picture, scooting over Fort Wayne's unpaved streets and horse-and-buggy rural roads in a Franklin touring car they called the "Weed-burner." Jane Alice, always outfitted in some adorable frock, was a smiling but passive adornment to this scene. She would retain happy memories of family outings at nearby lake resorts or at the homes of her respective grandparents, but was not aware—as her older brothers were—of the change in their life that tension had wrought.

Bess Peters became a bundle of nerves, she told her mother, because she was so helpless when Fred's attacks came on. They were more than mere splitting headaches; they gave him real pain, against which even the wonderful new aspirin tablets were impotent. If they got any worse, there was real fear of what he might *do*. The uncertainty affected the entire family, and also muted Bess's and Fred's function in the community whirl that they both enjoyed. To her sisters Bess confided a fear of growing old before her time. Getting away from Fort Wayne, if only briefly, had renewed appeal for her.

Fred Peters earnestly sought the advice of the best doctors in the Midwest. Even when it was determined that his cerebral ailment was a product of the accident that had made him partially lame, the brain was largely a mystery to the medical science of that day. Eventually the physicians would be able to pacify his pain, but by that time Fred Peters would be alone in Fort Wayne —Lord Algie in solitude, still devoted to a wife and family who were permanently removed.

That had not been the original plan. In the fall of 1914, shortly after Jane Alice Peters had entered first grade, the decision was made that Bess should take an extended holiday. It was Grandmother Knight's idea. She was a widow now and living frugally, although the talk was that she had money enough for several lifetimes. But compassion sometimes brought out her generosity, and she insisted on underwriting an elaborate vacation for her daughter and grandchildren. Bess had always wanted to go to New York. There was even talk of Europe—London and Paris. Instead, Bess followed the advice of friends and decided on California. Fred

Peters thought it was a good idea for everyone concerned. When the children were withdrawn from school, it was with the knowledge that they would probably "lose" a semester. Certainly, they expected to return to Fort Wayne.

Jane Alice would return to her birthplace and early home only once, as a teen-aged Carol Lombard. Then she would be fussed over as a starlet, but still experience a stranger's discomfort. She was barely six when she left Fort Wayne, and most of her memories of living there were confined to the last year when she started school, learned to dance, discovered the movies, and fancied herself a courageous heroine in a great flood. Although not reported by her own memory, she also made her first appearance as an actress, of sorts, in Fort Wayne.

Indeed, the people who claim vivid memory of little Jane Alice Peters in Fort Wayne seem to number into the hundreds. Some have recalled specific events in which she was ten or even twelve years old, but somehow still in town. A popular but certainly a false notion is that she recited "The Night Before Christmas" for the entire school when she was in third grade. Still, there were chroniclers of likely reliability, such as Robert Pollock, a boyhood friend of Carole Lombard's brothers in Fort Wayne. Later as columnist for the Hyde Park *Herald,* Pollock recalled a backyard production of *Ivanhoe* staged by the boys, with garbage-can lids employed as knightly shields, and with a little girl's debut performance as handmaiden to Rebecca, the Jewess.

Pollock also remembered that in football games improvised by the older boys at the foot of Union Street, the blond Jane always wanted to play and eventually had to be accommodated. And he remembered escorting winsome Jane to Trier's Dancing Academy for their Saturday lessons. Graduated to screen fame, Carole Lombard would summon her own direct recall of mean, mean Mr. Trier; yet she had looked forward to every lesson because she loved to dance—and would continue to do so for hours on end following each lesson, whether in her playroom at home or on the sloping sidewalk out front.

She also remembered the long walk with her older brothers to the Colonial and Gaiety movie houses in downtown Fort Wayne— a Saturday habit because of the thrilling serials with Kathlyn Williams, the first screen personality of her awareness. Then it was Pearl White, even more exciting. To Jane Alice Peters, the most unsettling thing about the trip to California would be that it interrupted the Pearl White continuity in midperil. Even at age six, Jane had decided she'd like to be a movie star, ideally a serial queen.

Her indelible Fort Wayne memory, however, was the 1913 flood, when the Peters house became a reception center for refugees and an unofficial headquarters for the rescue units. Steady rain brought the waterline of the St. Mary's River over its banks and threatened scores of riverfront cottages. Actual devastation was slight, but there was a massive evacuation and a temporary fear that the water would continue to rise and possibly even dislodge the strong foundation of the Peters house, despite its advantage of elevation.

Bess Peters's fortitude during the flood made a permanent impression on her daughter. Amid chaos, Bess was a leader, masterminding the logistics of evacuating and accommodating the riverbank families. She made dramatic use of the family's brand-new telephone, instructing firemen and other rescue stalwarts on which persons were still missing. Bess gathered in extra bedding from the neighbors, and directed an around-the-clock coffee-making operation. Jane and her brothers performed chores to her demand, and were made to feel that they were saving Indiana from disaster. It was capital excitement, especially for a little girl who was always eager to participate with her brothers.

She was pest and pet to them. An exceptional rapport with her brothers was evident from Jane's precocious infancy onward. They were her preferred company, and if they would not play with her dolls, the dolls were abandoned while she petitioned to share their activities. While her mother pampered Jane's femininity with hair ribbons and pretty frocks, Jane was an instinctive tomboy, friendlier with her brothers' companions than with other girls in the neighborhood.

In kindergarten she was uncharacteristically reserved, apparently well-liked but not a mingler. She did not single out a "best friend" or form the kind of close friendships that enrich early memories. With her brothers she was aggressive, combative; but they were intimidated by her tenderness and she wasn't likely to get slugged.

Fred Peters, Jr., was Fritz to all his friends and relatives, while the younger brother became Tootie within the immediate family group, as a result of Jane's earliest attempts to pronounce the name Stuart. Tootie was unmistakably Jane's physical sibling, a "pretty" boy, Peters-fair, and an extroverted charmer. Fritz conveyed, instead, the seriousness and early maturity often found in eldest children—a boy for others to look up to. The Peters boys scrapped, but. Fritz was Tootie's lord and protector, and Jane's station was as a princess. For all of them, the trip to California augured royal adventure—of indefinite duration, for none foresaw its permanence.

The train ride from Fort Wayne to San Francisco took four days. The city by the Golden Gate, exhaling from one of its periodic expositions that had spanned the summer, was quite the most beautiful place they'd seen. Leveled by earthquake less than a decade earlier, San Francisco showed no scars and was indeed a new city. But in its dampness, a head cold Jane Alice had carried with her from Indiana became worse, and Bess curtailed their visit to the Bay Area. Southern California was their objective. There they had several friends—transplanted Fort Wayne folk who were zealous lobbyists for their new climate. Los Angeles was experiencing a heat wave when Bess arrived in October with her brood, welcomed by the Charles Pigeons—old friends who assured Bess that none of her children would ever catch cold there.

Sure enough, Jane's head was quickly unclogged by the first dry rays of the southland sun. Bess confided that despite her daughter's high energy quotient, she had poor resistance to germs. Tonsillitis, the flu—Jane was too easily subdued; and the likely healthfulness of the climate was an important factor in persuading Bess that they were not just visitors to southern California. Within only a few days after arriving there, she decided it was their new home. Later, perhaps, if her husband was effectively delivered from his own problems of health, they might resume a life together in Los Angeles—if he could be coaxed away from Fort Wayne. But right away, she put Indiana out of her mind altogether.

Many years later Fred Peters, Jr., would have clear recall of their first Los Angeles exposure, flavored unmistakably by adventure. His mother was the animated scene of attention—suddenly relaxed and high-spirited, shoring up old friendships and forming new and strong ones very quickly. Aside from the favorable climate, a very real enticement for Bess obviously was the very idea of California. It was a new vogue.

Los Angeles was a well-settled community, with an august society that was formally structured in the 1880s. But in a newer sense it was also a magnet for seekers of health or wealth or both, and apartment hotels couldn't be built quickly enough to absorb the adventurers who were now streaming into the town. Much of the excitement was contained in a real estate word that had not yet acquired its classic connotation, and the word was Hollywood.

It was the estate name given by Mrs. H. H. Wilcox to her husband's sprawling ranch, only a few miles from downtown Los Angeles. The Wilcox acreage was subdivided for the speculative sale of land parcels after the turn of the century, and when the California land boom accelerated in earnest, "Hollywood lots" were coveted for their abundance of shade trees, even if there was an almost total absence of holly bushes.

Contrary to later supposition, Bess Peters did not come to California to push her daughter into the movies. Indeed, she had not associated southern California with the fairly recent diversion of motion pictures in which, nevertheless, Bess had a pronounced interest. She had started attending the movie programs fairly regularly in Fort Wayne, once they acquired respectability by graduating from nickelodeon to picture palace. But she thought New York was where most of the movies were made, although she also had heard of the activity in Fort Lee, New Jersey.

The first motion pictures filmed in California dated only to 1908, the year Jane Peters was born. But Colonel William Selig, the first pioneer of West Coast production, did not exactly incite a geographical revolution within the fledgling industry. The Motion Picture Patents Company sent a unit to Edendale where almost 200 one-reel westerns were filmed in the first six months of 1910, but then the company packed and returned to the East. D. W. Griffith brought a Biograph unit to Los Angeles for several weeks of filming in 1911, but they also went home to New York. Broncho Billy Anderson arrived in California about the same time, but made his Essanay westerns at Niles, far to the north. David Horsley's Nestor Studio was the first one constructed on one of the original Hollywood lots (at Sunset and Gower), but it did not endure.

But in two frolicsome years before the Peters family took up California residence, the transition of the movies from an undisciplined East Coast novelty game to a regulated West Coast industry began in earnest. Adolf Zukor's Famous Players company delivered Mary Pickford to Los Angeles in 1912. Griffith returned that same year, and in 1913 Mack Sennett and Hal Roach initiated their respective comedy endeavors in California. Jesse Lasky, Cecil

B. DeMille, and Samuel Goldwyn—in those days the last surname was still Goldfish—abandoned their chosen site of Flagstaff, Arizona, and made *The Squaw Man,* the first feature-length picture shot in Hollywood.

"Picture people" was one of the first terms to captivate Jane Peters's young but willing imagination. The picture people were different and a romantic lot, sort of like gypsies. Charlie Pigeon explained that most of the picture people were moving into Hollywood because there was so much room there, and they could live as a kind of colony. The picture people gave Hollywood an identity that was primarily residential, before the industry was centralized there.

When Jane Peters started to school in Los Angeles, D. W. Griffith was filming *The Birth of a Nation* in far-off Santa Ana. Thomas Ince was building his first studio in Culver City, and it would be the ancestor of the Metro-Goldwyn-Mayer studios there. Carl Laemmle had purchased some vast acreage that he would call Universal City, after his company. William Fox had not yet arrived in California, nor had the brothers Warner.

The emergence of an important new industry and a way of life without an antecedent pattern would be for Jane Peters to witness and experience, as a hometown girl living always within easy reach of the film colony itself. It would become her culture, and her own growth would be its reflection. She was a beguiling little girl but hoydenishly spunky, and even as a rosebud her tomboy cheekiness would prove difficult to purge. By the time the motion picture business had stabilized as both an industry and a popular art, she would be a young lady of disarming blond beauty. The movies and the Peters girl were fated for one another.

Her first Los Angeles home was at the Alvarado Terrace, an apartment building at 1435 Hoover Street, near Venice Boulevard, where Bess rented a two-bedroom unit. Jane was a first grader at Hoover Elementary School, which Stuart also attended, while Fritz was already at junior-high level. Bess considered taking a job, and there were likely opportunities in the movie-making arteries, which were then wide open. But she ruled out the studios, allowing that too strong a scent of the movie environment might prove an undesirable influence on her children. Finally she decided against any kind of binding regular employment, sensing that raising three children in a sunny but pagan land would be challenge enough.

Fred Peters wrote often and sent money with unerring regularity. Grandmother Knight also continued to contribute to their support voluntarily, not in a planned manner but with sure rhythm. Still, Bess budgeted her household more cautiously, even frugally, very unlike the unpractical society wife she had been. Her daughter's garments still were selected tastefully, but Bess scouted the bargains and waited for things to go "on sale." The children could expect toys and games at Christmas time, and new clothes and other adornments afterward when the merchants inevitably advertised their January clearance. That California children needed only one set of year-round clothing was considered a major blessing.

In school Jane proved an able but not precocious pupil, a friendly girl but not yet a markedly outgoing one. There were no more dancing lessons, but Jane continued to dance, and she and Stuart won parlor applause for their own version of the Castle Walk. They also improvised their accounts of movies they would see, sometimes for a home audience. But such a pastime occupied kids everywhere, and to be commended (as Jane was) as "a good little actress" was a commonplace, equating with the "all-boy" description bestowed on both her brothers.

In 1916 they moved to South Catalina Street into an apartment slightly roomier and no less arresting, but decidedly more economical than the Alvarado Terrace. Jane was transferred to Cahuenga Elementary School, most of whose pupils had parents who were variously employed by the ever-growing number of film-producing companies. During the three years they lived on Catalina Street, Jane came gradually to realize that her parents' separation was a permanent thing.

Unlike her brothers, for whom absence of their idolized father was an unsettling adjustment, Jane was not aware of "missing" her dad even as she was drawing ever closer to her mother in a friendship way. The authoritarian Fritz now materialized as her surrogate father. When the senior Fred Peters made the first of his several visits to Los Angeles, the boys resumed their old relationship with him but Jane regarded her impeccable father as a fascinating near-stranger. The children speculated on the possibility of permanent reunion, yet there is no evidence to suggest that reconciliation, either in California or Indiana, was ever discussed by their parents. For her children's ears, Bess spoke of their father in the most respectful terms, and there is no doubt that he was the enduring love of her life, perhaps the only one. Her would-be Los Angeles suitors inevitably were given the option of a just-friends relationship or a fare-thee-well, but it was easily noted that romantic sparks ignited on those years-apart occasions when Fred and Bess Peters were again together, however briefly. Yet Fred always returned to Fort Wayne on schedule, and if he was once more categorized as a possibly eligible bachelor, he did not encourage the notion. To Bess he was faithful in his high fashion.

Confident that her children were growing in character as well as physically, Bess embarked on a more personal domestic style, emerging as a frequent hostess for small dinner parties with intimate friends, who became more numerous. The Pigeons were good companions for several years. There were also the Wises, who would become Uncle Claude and Aunt Lottie to Jane, with whom their relationship would accrue depth as well as closeness. And there were the Lombards, Harry and Etta, who were well-to-do and would take up residence in the new and spectacular Beverly Hills Hotel. Harry Lombard, a "relative of a distant relative" back in Indiana, had lost a leg, and that caused Jane to associate him with her father.

Among the new neighbors were the Thomas Platts, and Mrs. Platt would exercise considerable and increasing influence on Bess; and, by extension, on Carole Lombard. Mrs. Platt was in the vanguard of what would become a significant fad in California, and particularly within the film industry: the spooky, dubious science of numerology. Bess had her own serious reservations about numerology but found it a fascinating indoor game, a worthwhile hobby however fragile its scientific basis. But Mrs. Platt was also one of the people who introduced Bess to the Bahai Faith—the religious order founded in Persia barely half a century earlier.

Earnestly skeptical of Christianity and critical of organized religion in the United States generally, Bess had participated in church activities as one of the social conventions of Fort Wayne but had not acquired a churchgoing habit in California. She was also apprehensive about Bahai—logically enough, since southern California was aswarm with freakish and far-out religious cults. Initially she resisted the historical legacy embodying the prophecies of the Bab, but she was attracted by Bahai's relative absence of dogma. Mrs. Platt emphasized that it was a faith, not a religion, and therefore more adaptable to individual needs. Finally Bess embraced the faith because it incorporated her instinctive beliefs with other ideas she wanted to believe, and she thought it entirely commonsensical. Bahai followers accepted the spiritual unity of mankind and the immortality of the human soul. Bahai stressed the essential harmony of science and religion. But the tenet that captivated Bess was the total equality of men and women. She decided to raise her daughter in the light of that conviction, and the daughter's receptiveness would incite the essential Carole Lombard —a personality reflecting the feat of self-liberation.

Not until her maturity would that personality assert itself, however. As Jane Peters advanced into adolescence she was basically serious and without raucous accent, although she exploited an all-around athletic excellence. But her mother's adoption of a personalized religion appeared to encourage an independence in Jane as well.

With each passing season, the girl's beauty became a more frequent topic of conversation among Bess's circle of friends. It was never discussed in Jane's presence, and she seemed unaware of having been physically blessed. But increasingly her mother heard the urging: "Bess, you really should do something about getting that girl into pictures."

The thought had not escaped her mother, as indeed it had not escaped Jane Alice, who occasionally declared the intention of being "a movie star when I grow up." But Bess had stern reservations, based not so much on the suspected amorality of the movie environment as on her observations of the girls in ever-growing numbers who were trying to crash the movies.

Many of the girls brought their mamas with them, and Bess could see that too often it was a matter of mama bringing the girl. Reluctance was apparent in many of the girls, whether they were fully grown candidates for ingenue service, or children of Jane Peters's comparable station. They were submitted to mama's desperate ambition or her crassly projected sublimation.

Within only a year or two after the Peterses had arrived in the vicinity, Hollywood had become a national household word with a specific connotation. The promise of riches or fame or glamour sucked in thousands of girls from all over the country and even from beyond. The film colony was a beacon for collar-ad boys as well, but the country's social orientation was such that many a likely young matinee idol still pursued more conventional paths; and in any given year, the new girls in Hollywood outnumbered their male counterparts by perhaps ten to one. This helped convey a unique sociology to the filmland; in human history there had not been anything quite like it.

Occasionally a gutsy girl would arrive in town unescorted, but some form of chaperoning was more likely. Even the teen-agers who were running away from home, defying parental warnings against the monstrous morality of Hollywood, tended to arrive in twos, even in groups. But girls with their mothers had the highest visibility. And the hopeful movie mama had a barbaric pushiness or perhaps an insidious sweetness that translated into tenacious will. They were not easily given to discouragement.

Picture people came to abhor the easily recognized movie mama, but lecherous inhabitants of the industrial periphery found ways to exploit the mothers and daughters to their own advantage. Many a mama was taken in by what she supposed was a bona fide movie contract for her little girl. Sometimes mama paid cash on the line, and often enough the person pocketing the money had his well-known way with the girl in question, plying her with bogus promises of important movie exposure. Some of the darkling accounts involved prepubescent girls.

Some of the girls picked up occasional work as extras. A small percentage obtained valid contracts, which might result in walk-on roles that could as easily land on the cutting-room floor. The number making the actual climb into roles of consequence was negligible, but the effect was usually the same. Most of the girls soon were sleeping around, even those who had arrived in town as innocents. Sometimes the mamas encouraged a little whoredom as a necessary investment. Dreams faded: the girls moved as flotsam into tawdrier scenes. The overly painted women barkers at the Venice and Ocean Park amusement piers often betrayed the wreckage of movieland aspiration. Some of the failed starlets, and their mamas as well, drifted into the consolation of employment within the individual crafts of movie making—picture people after all. Most of the girls simply went back home, perhaps to marry the boys they'd left behind. But Hollywood's exit gate was never as crowded as its entrances. The accelerating popularity of the new fan magazines—*Photoplay* and its sleazier imitations—perpetuated the near-myth of rags-to-riches destiny. The girls kept believing, and kept coming.

When Jane Peters, at age ten or eleven, talked of being a star "like Constance Talmadge or Mary Miles Minter," Bess neither fortified nor discouraged her daughter's immature and altogether typical ambition. She had no thought of exploiting her as a child, but as Jane grew into womanhood she would support her daughter's pursuit with her every means, whatever Jane's goals were. But she confided an early hope that Jane would someday sparkle in pictures.

To friends Bess confessed her own abandoned dreams of theatrical eminence, but would chortle that even if she'd had the opportunity, she may have lacked the talent; and that if she had the talent, she certainly lacked the looks. Her own ego extracted satisfaction from Jane's beauty. If opportunity came for Jane, Bess wanted her to be prepared. She decided that dramatic lessons would be a worthwhile investment, even if it meant doing without some things of more immediate necessity. Bess was wary of the proliferation of "studio preparatory schools" in the film colony—mainly opportunistic ventures operated by teachers of dubious credentials, bilking and milking everything from moppets to wearily aging ingenues. Bess checked around and got generally favorable reports on the Miriam Nolkes Dramatic School for Girls, which was attended mainly by preteens, who were not out-of-towners but resident girls of good family.

Jane was enrolled at Mrs. Nolkes's school for once-weekly lessons. Some benefit must have been presumed, for she showed up regularly at Mrs. Nolkes's for three years during the normal school term, although the Peters family moved twice during that period. Many years afterward, a securely established Carole Lombard would doubt that the lessons had accomplished much beyond a certain poise they may have given her. But the lessons had been a lot of fun. Few of the girls took them seriously.

The Miriam Nolkes school emphasized good stage deportment, concentrating on posture, body movement (including correctness in walking and some attention to modern dance). Florid dramatic technique was advocated, but it was not simply a matter of rolling the eyes and waving arms about hysterically. Vocal projection and articulation were not understressed, as further indication that Mrs. Nolkes was pointing her young charges to the stage more than to the screen. The eventual possibility of talking pictures was then being discounted throughout the movie industry; the technological possibilities were acknowledged, but not their commercial feasibility.

There is no evidence that the Nolkes school ever delivered a comely graduate directly into the professional ranks on either stage or screen, but some of the girls would eventually receive at least some minor attention in films—Florine McKinney, Linda Watkins, and Pauline Norman. There was also Betty Jane Young, a year younger than Jane Peters but already a rival in the school's beauty sweepstakes, although they became good friends while attending the Nolkes classes together. Betty Jane had an older sister who also had aspirations for a movie career, and a younger sister named Gretchen, who would eventually be more successfully propelled by her mother into the Hollywood commerce. About the time that Jane Peters became Carol Lombard, Betty Jane Young got a professional foothold as Sally Blane; but a few years later little Gretchen would grow up in a hurry and outdistance her sister rather smartly, as Loretta Young.

Someone had to take the male roles in Mrs. Nolkes's playlets, and Jane Peters appeared often enough in men's clothing, bewigged and moustached to suggest a rakish city slicker or perhaps a reliable good provider. She fought to play such parts, for they were the most fun she could have. She recalled having reached a point of utter boredom in always being the princess; but a princess she easily suggested, with hair darkening to ash blond during her adolescence.

The Peterses moved first from Catalina Street to Harvard Boulevard between Sixth and Wilshire, then to the Bryson Apartments at Wilshire and Rampart. Bess's good furniture arrived from Fort Wayne one or two pieces at a time, months and years apart, each time necessitating more room. Jane shifted from Hoover to Cahuenga to Belmont elementary schools, and while she was easily assimilated socially, her movements prevented the formation of lasting friendships. She was drawn ever closer to her brothers, with whom she had contrasting relationships. Stuart was her approximate equal: they waged domestic war with neither showing to clear advantage, and Stuart was no less indulged than she. At age twelve Jane even briefly passed Stuart in height, before he started his own spurt. But Fritz already had taken on an adult identity in her eyes. He was a good funmaker, but in any kind of crisis he would yield to a serious side that was nowhere apparent in Stuart. Fritz dropped out of school on a purely practical consideration: he knew he could get and keep a job, and help support the family in a more agreeable style. Jane had a combative affection for the one brother, but a respect bordering on awe for the other.

During their stay in the Bryson Apartments, Jane finally found a really special friend. Margaret Nelson, called Dixie by one and all, was of her own age and disposition. She lived nearby on Wilton Place, and the two girls took up with one another when their mothers became friends. Only briefly, however, because the tubercular Mrs. Nelson died in 1918—a tragedy that affected Jane almost as seriously as it did her bereft friend. Each girl felt a responsibility to comfort the other. Dixie, who was also fatherless, soon disappeared with an abruptness that was further grievance to Jane, who logically assumed she had lost her friend forever.

More than fifty years later, Dixie would recall that the girl first encountered as Jane Peters was not a dominant personality in any way. She was exuberant, immediately responsive to the humors of her brothers and their friends, to the fancies of other girls, and to the foibles of adults. But as audience, not as performer: a high-spirited girl who would laugh at anything or anybody in a distinctively personal giggle, but did not promote jokes of her own. "Once she asked me what I wanted to be when I grew up. I said I wanted to get married and have a dozen babies. I meant it, but Carole had a way of visualizing whatever had been said, and she imagined me with a dozen babies and it became very funny to her. She got into a laughing spell on the sidewalk and Totsie came out, wanting to know what was so funny."

Totsie was a nickname applied later to Bess Peters, at about the time Jane was evolving into Carol. Its origin was uncertain, but it was employed almost prohibitively by Totsie's young friends. To her own circle she remained Bess, but to her consternation she became Bessie to more recent acquaintances, in whose number would be Allan Dwan. Already a well-experienced movie director, Dwan would be credited with "discovering" Jane Peters for pictures, when she was twelve.

There are several slightly varying acounts of the event, which occurred in the spring of 1921. Bess was visiting a family named Kaufman, whose own friend and neighbor was the great Benny

Leonard—then at his peak as king of the lightweights. Mr. Kaufman coaxed Benny Leonard into giving boxing lessons to Stuart Peters, and the tomboy stirred afresh in Jane. She also pleaded for lessons from the champ.

In the Kaufmans' backyard they were sparring away, Jane and Stuart both in boxing gloves, and the little girl reacting to Leonard's instructions somewhat more successfully than her brother. She danced rhythmically away from Stuart's reach, but she would move in smartly to pepper him with her own light jabs.

That was the scene Allan Dwan may have observed from an adjacent backyard. (Another version has him watching Jane Peters play baseball in the street.) Surely he was intrigued: he was about to begin a feature film for which a minor role had not been cast— the tomboy kid sister of the leading man. Dwan introduced himself and asked Jane if she'd like to be in his next picture. Most certainly, the little girl said, but first they'd have to ask her mother. Dwan did and Bess agreed, so it was all quickly arranged.

Allan Dwan was a pioneer Hollywood director, active even before the advent of the "feature" film and for many years afterward—a career actually spanning fifty years. By 1921 he was already an important director, if somewhat obscured by the personality of the senior Douglas Fairbanks, who starred in Dwan's best-known pictures. Dwan and Fairbanks were then preparing the massive *Robin Hood* production, but meanwhile Dwan was confronted by a routine assignment—a melodrama called *A Perfect Crime* for the minor Associated Producers company.

Without disputing the facts as outlined, it is feasible to suspect Bess Peters of a more aggressive machination. The star of *A Perfect Crime* was Monte Blue and Bess probably knew him better than any of the movie actors with whom she had become variously acquainted in California. They had been friends in Indianapolis when Monte Blue was a teen-aged boy with stage aspirations, before he got his start in pictures.

All of Jane's scenes were with Monte Blue. Only three scenes remained in the final print, and only one of those carried to substantial length. She was photographed with a dreamy back-lighting that revealed Allan Dwan's appreciation of her budding physical charm. The legacy of still photographs would suggest a mood more romantic than melodramatic. Within only a few years no print of

A Perfect Crime was known to exist, and it was entirely forgotten after having been barely noted at the time of its very limited circulation during the summer of 1921.

Small producers on the order of Associated Producers competed rather helplessly with the new breed of giants such as Paramount and First National, being mainly crimped by lack of theaters for important first-run exposure to their features. *A Perfect Crime* was distributed by Fox, another titan of the new industry, and shooting was completed at the Fox studio on Western Avenue—within walking distance from the Peters apartment. But as an independent production it did not command the Fox company's special interest and it quickly died, a victim of underexposure. *A Perfect Crime* was a proficient movie according to its few complimentary but unexciting reviews, none of which gave more than passing mention to Jane Peters's debut.

Her scenes were shot in just two days. Allan Dwan said she was very alert to direction, and probably clever enough to become an accomplished movie actress. Monte Blue was complimentary, and all of Jane's family and their friends thought her captivating on film. But the picture did not give her a professional foundation. Allan Dwan began directing a picture called *A Broken Doll* immediately upon completing *A Perfect Crime* and again needed a juvenile actress, this time for a slightly larger role. He had hinted that the little Peters girl would do the part but instead he hired another girl and Jane was disappointed, if less so than her mother. Bess submitted herself to the discomfiting role of a movie mama and escorted Jane on a round of interviews.

Since there were no takers, the screen career of Jane Peters was over at its beginning. Bess said it was too early to be thinking about a movie career anyway. But she may have sensed that her daughter and the movie camera were made for each other, and that a right time would come.

For Jane, the experience of seeing herself on the screen was anticlimactic. Her shadow image on the screen was someone foreign to her. But those two days she had given to the making of the picture—that had been fun! She knew it was something she wanted to do again.

Scion of one of Fort Wayne's "best" families: Frederic C. Peters, Sr., the father of Carole Lombard.

Elizabeth Knight Peters, mother and best friend to Carole—whose friend Lansing Brown made this lovely study in the '20s.

The baby Jane Alice Peters and her brothers, Frederic Jr. (left) and Stuart, pose with their mother in 1909.

Very early on, the camera begins to respond to an unmistakable "star" quality.

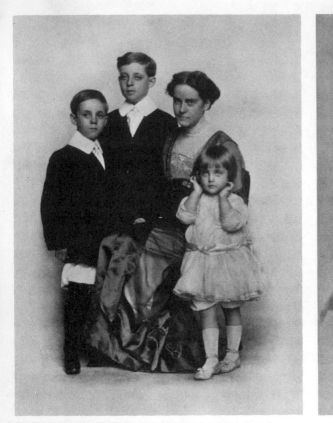

Still in Indiana, Bess Peters and her children show off their Sunday best.

Jane as a new Californian, at about age eight.

As jaunty a beach trio as you'd find: Jane went everywhere with her brothers and emulated them.

Already an ideal photographer's model, at age six.

Mother and daughter at the time of their return visit to Fort Wayne in 1930.

A hint of the impish Carole Lombard personality is given in this front-yard snapshot of Jane Peters at about age ten.

What a difference a few years could make! The mermaid at left grew into the formful creature at right. John Abbe's striking study of Carol Lombard with parasol, taken at the beginning of her tenure as a Sennett bathing beauty, was her favorite professional photo for several years.

Cutting up between takes of a Mack Sennett comedy romp: The rather large girl to Carol Lombard's right is Madalynne Fields —the companionable "Fieldsie" of Carol's bachelor-girl days.

❀ II ❀

Rosebud

ON THE threshold of her fourteenth year, Jane Peters had discarded a last faint trace of baby fat. Estimably contoured along feminine lines, without a hint of buxomness, she had attained her full height of five feet, four and one-half inches. She was a blond impala—a fleet thing, barely a hundred pounds, and ready to race.

The four Peterses were living at a better standard, living almost well. They had moved again, not to an apartment but into a house on South Manhattan Street—simple and modest but roomy, and affording Jane a comfortable, sun-filled room of her own. She could invite girl friends to spend the night at her house with no embarrassment over their accommodations; and in the autumn of 1921 she put away her dolls and began collecting friends.

Yet she was drawn ever closer to her family, even as their individual relationships changed. Religion had unleashed an eternal girlishness in her mother, and for Bess and Jane Peters a remarkable friendship flourished without the customary bickering to camouflage devotion. Diminished economic pressure also buoyed Bess: she continued to receive regular support checks from Indiana but was not entirely dependent on them. While she still shunned formal employment, she had a measure of independent income from little things she *did*. She was an active correspondent for the Bahai Faith, and for a clandestine vocation, she gave counseling in numerology for a small fee.

Fritz Peters, come to adulthood, was the breadwinner. Having started at the approximate janitorial-stockboy bottom with the Bullock's department store, he was working his way up in what would be a fifty-year successful association with the firm, as Bullock's became southern California's most prestigious department store chain. He assumed responsibility for the family's well-being, and Jane Peters would defer to her eldest brother in all matters of judgment for many years.

Still a contrast was Stuart—engaging, outgoing, confident of his good looks, endowed with a playboy's instincts if not the income. He was the object of many a romantic crush that afflicted Jane's growing circle of girl friends. The hope was that the advantages of higher education would compensate Stuart for his lack of such industriousness as Fritz possessed.

Jane entered Virgil Junior High School, on Vermont Avenue between Hollywood and downtown Los Angeles, as a seventh grader. Within only a few weeks she was transformed from a little girl into a precocious young lady. In the previous spring when she'd made *A Perfect Crime* with Monte Blue, she had been an elementary school senior coexisting with first graders on the same playground. Now she was in the company of eighth- and ninth-grade girls who wore makeup and roll-down hose, and talked mainly about boys.

She couldn't see what was so important about boys but she responded to other teen-age impulses. Her grooming, previously a matter of importance only to her mother, became her own concern. The new catchword was flapper, and that was what Jane wanted to be. The concept of flaming youth seduced her as it had the whole country.

Her years at Virgil Junior High were buoyant. A vibrant new friendship was with a vivacious blonde she resembled at least superficially: Sally Eilers, a grade ahead of Jane, and rated as the best actress in the school's tender theatricals. Sally had come from New York carrying her family's wishes for eventual success in motion pictures, soon enough to be attained. She would also be of minor but distinct importance to the shaping of the eventual Carole Lombard career.

Another blond girl, also an influence of sorts, was Carol Peterson, actually from Sweden and soon to return there, but not until she had introduced Jane to tennis. The Swedish girl shared a gym locker with Jane because their surnames were in alphabetical order, otherwise they might not have become acquainted. Carol Peterson was quite expert with a racquet. She idolized France's unbeatable Suzanne Lenglen, while Jane championed the young American star, Helen Wills. Suddenly tennis was right up there with dancing among Jane's primary passions, and a brief ambition—never realized —was to take the measure of Carol Peterson on the court. They never saw one another after the days at Virgil, but Jane wouldn't forget the girl whose very name, she thought, had a lilting loveliness.

Perhaps the happiest occurrence of Jane's stay at Virgil was the rediscovery of the girl who would be her best friend for life. An accidental hallway encounter reunited her with the girl she had once known as Dixie Nelson. Now her name was Dixie Pantages. As a child she had played with Carmen Pantages, a third-generation member of the wealthy California picture-palace family. When Dixie's mother died, the little girl was adopted by the Pantages family so Carmen would have a sister, and soon Dixie was living in a castle the size of a city block, and wearing smart, expensive dresses.

Jane's friendship with Dixie reignited instantly at Virgil and continued to flourish on the campus of Fairfax High School, where they pursued teen-age discovery to the urgent tempos of the Jazz Age. They were in the vortex of the high-school smart set, perhaps inordinately smart because the Fairfax rolls listed some of southern California's wealthiest young heirs, including many of the nouveau riche of the film colony. Most of Jane's friends enjoyed an affluence akin to Dixie's ("But they don't have your breeding," Bess Peters assured her daughter); yet while every yardstick for snobbery was employed, Jane easily won acceptance the way a really beautiful girl usually can. Another secret of her social success was her apparent inaccessibility, as the boys would find out.

Even while her plainer girl friends were acquiring their inevitable "steadies," Jane remained undated and unkissed, although there was no shortage of candidates. It was not a sheltered life, but she could hardly have been more protected. The watchful eyes of her brothers intimidated many a youthful swain. As Fred Peters explained, "Stuart and I couldn't trust ourselves with girls, so we weren't about to trust other boys with our sister. They were always around, like a swarm of hornets, but they just couldn't get anywhere. And she liked it that way—liked the attention, but wasn't boy crazy at all. Maybe living with Stuart and me sort of immunized her against falling for a boy, at least for a while."

Jane's first date was probably with Jack Hearst, the son of newspaper tycoon William Randolph Hearst. He was a boy her own age, and arrived at the Peters house in a chauffeured limousine merely because he was not old enough to have a driver's license. He escorted her to a high-school dance. They would remain sociable for several years, sometimes as a dating couple but more often as casual friends sharing a common crowd. Jane was not significantly impressed by the magnitude of the elder Hearst's newspaper empire, but Bess Peters was; and with some canniness she exploited the very tentative liaison into an acquaintance with Hearst's star reporter of filmland, Louella Parsons.

Another well-to-do high-school beau was a Jewish boy named George Rosenberg. One of the tenets of the Bahai Faith to which Jane was easily susceptible was its tolerance and respect for all religious beliefs, and she would grow up without awareness of ethnic differences. George Rosenberg could dance, and that was all that mattered. The Fairfax enrollment was becoming increasingly Jewish, but no distinctions were made in the Peters household, even if Jewish parental pressure prevented many a likely suitor from making an earnest pursuit of the fetching Miss Peters.

A sometime boyfriend was Bill Ince, son of movie pioneer Thomas Ince. In the fall of 1924 Jane found herself on the periphery of a curious Hollywood intrigue. At a time when she was juggling an Ince and a Hearst among her admirers, Thomas Ince died suddenly after a weekend party aboard W. R. Hearst's yacht. Although the death was officially attributed to heart failure following acute indigestion, rumors would persist (and the picture people would magnify them) that the whole story wasn't being told. That Hearst had somehow murdered Ince became a popular supposition, although without apparent foundation. Gradually the turbulent Hollywood society was becoming Jane's own.

Some of her close friends were a hereditary part of it, such as Jean Wood, whose father Sam was becoming an important screen director; and others would marry into it, such as Ann Boyar, who traded boyfriends with Jane several times before she finally consented to marry Jack of the picture-making Warner Brothers. Most of the girls Jane knew were dedicated to attaining some sort of Hollywood threshold. The customary objectives were fortune and fame, but for Jane the inducement was enjoyment itself. It wasn't the fact of the movies that thrilled her, but the giddiness of the environment in which they were made. In the Pantages home, among other places, she met movie stars and other princes of industry in the flesh and found them no bigger than life, but often more fun.

She thrived on competition, and at Fairfax High she had a lot of that. As a sophomore she tried out for the lead in the school play and predictably lost out to Sally Eilers. Undaunted, she asked to read for the character part of a white-haired grandmother, the role coveted by most of the girls who were less fortunately endowed. She won the part by spicing her audition with all of her Grandmother Knight's physical and vocal quirks. In a classroom exercise, with Sally Eilers again cast as the imperiled tender heroine in an old-fashioned melodrama, Jane took the part of the dastardly male villain, complete with moustache.

Her competitiveness flamed more spectacularly on the school-ground. She possessed a natural athletic grace more commonly evident in boys, and as a member of the girl's track team she excelled in both the sprints and the longer distance runs—the fleetest girl in school. She also scored in the broad jump and as a javelin hurler. Although still fairly new to tennis, she soon was unchallenged among the sophomores.

In the spring of 1924 she won for the first time a school competition that lacked masculine overtones. In what was unofficially a beauty contest, she was chosen Queen of the May—a title bestowed traditionally upon the prettiest girl in school, with the built-in restriction that the Queen of the May should always be blond. The school sponsored a May Day carnival for fund-raising purposes. Jane "reigned" over a winsome court, and all the girls were aflutter over reports that a movie talent scout was watching them.

It was more than a rumor, and the man in question was more than a talent scout. He was Alfred Reeves, not a well-known Hollywood personage because he was effectively upstaged by the celebrity of his employer; yet Reeves was general manager of Charlie Chaplin's independent producing operation. He talked with members of the queen's court and with the queen herself. Then Reeves conferred with Bess Peters on the schoolground, and Jane was appointed for a meeting with Charlie Chaplin himself, the very next day at the Chaplin studios on North La Brea Street.

Bess Peters had a way of maintaining calm during a consensus of excitement, and Jane's memory of her mother's steady behavior during the Fort Wayne flood inspired her to emulation. They were not visibly flustered by the prospect of confronting the most famous person in all moviedom, although it touched off a sensation among Jane's friends, and among Bess's confidants who had been insisting it was only a matter of short time before Hollywood would take notice of her daughter and put the incredibly beautiful girl to work. They also cautioned that Jane should not be even briefly alone with a Chaplin whose lasciviousness was popularly suspect, even though he was newly married to Lita Grey at the time.

So Bess again broke her vow against movie momism and accompanied Jane for an interview that must have gone well, since its result was Chaplin's decision to test the Peters girl for the film he was preparing. And that was *The Gold Rush,* destined for immortality as an unquestioned masterwork by one who at last had put short comedies and featurettes behind him.

By Carole Lombard's own recollection, Charlie Chaplin was "civil and polite to Mother without disguising his displeasure that she was there in the first place. He was sincerely committed to the picture he was going to make. It didn't sound like a comedy as he described it. If he tested a girl, it was for the leading role, but there were several other parts for girls—all of them entertainers at this fun house in the Klondike. Every girl that got a part had tested for the lead."

Screen-testing teen-aged girls was a favorite Chaplin pastime. He interviewed hundreds, would test dozens, and select a glamorous handful for the picture in question. Jane Peters was barely younger than most of the girls visible in *The Gold Rush,* prints of which are still in traffic. Nothing came of the Peters test, although rumor grew that Chaplin had scribbled "too pretty" on a card bearing her name. She never heard from him.

But film sometimes had a way of getting passed around in Hollywood. Arnold Wessel, a minor functionary with the Vitagraph company, smuggled the print of Jane's *Gold Rush* test into the office of his boss, J. Stuart Blackton, and that led to more meetings, more discussion, and a verbal agreement on a beginning player's contract with Vitagraph for the fifteen-year-old Jane Peters.

With summer coming on, Jane faced a decision that often confronted high-school girls in the reaches of Hollywood. Should she leave school to gamble on a movie career, or should she complete her lower education and gamble on a later "break"? Her notion was to drop out of school at the semester's end, when such action could go unnoticed and cause no fuss. Most advice was against her quitting school, but there was no pressure from her mother. Bess Peters had decided that her daughter would make her own important decisions —something Jane showed a healthy willingness to do—and that she would support her every whim. Jane returned to school in the fall, but possibly because Vitagraph had reneged on the agreement. No contract materialized with the company that was the sole survivor from the stone age of the movies. But then, the new criteria for movie making had passed Vitagraph by: in 1924 it was a struggling, debt-ridden weak sister, and its very survivability was suspect.

Yet Vitagraph gave Jane a new name she decided to retain. J. Stuart Blackton, one of the founders and the production chief throughout Vitagraph's long history, had a fancy for names that smacked of theatrical elegance. He thought Jane an entirely too common label for a budding movie player. He solicited suggestions for a substitute, and Jane's own idea was honored. Remembering the tennis-playing Carol Peterson, she proposed Carol Peters as an alternative and Blackton said it sounded just right. The Vitagraph adventure reached a dead end shortly afterward, but she liked her adopted name. When she enrolled at Fairfax for the fall 1924 semester she was still Jane in the formality of the class rolls, but she coached her friends to call her Carol. From that time onward, they did.

The near-brush with professional status had effectively diminished her interest in and application to schoolroom ritual. Now she was actually fretting to be in the movies. To her closest friends she confided her mother's agreement that she could drop out of school as soon as she had a tangible start in pictures. Almost immediately, she appeared to have accomplished that. She stopped attending classes with her junior term having barely begun, just before her sixteenth birthday (after which she could not be listed as truant). Her birthday became the occasion of an almost-surprise party at home, attended mainly by school friends. Bess reckoned it would be a last opportunity for Jane/Carol to enjoy group socializing with her own school crowd, but the event became a more earnest celebration because of the sudden fact of a contract with Fox.

First there had been another false alarm, and then one thing led to another. Bess had a tip on a casting call at United Artists for *Little Annie Rooney,* a Mary Pickford vehicle. The picture required several children as satellites for the star, and Carol Peters reported in pigtails and was cast on the spot, or so it seemed. She was told she was hired, possibly by Al Lichtman. She was very quickly unhired when Mary Pickford herself arrived to assess the new novices and found Carol Peters overly mature and competitively too pretty, pigtails or no pigtails. Whatever his involvement to that point, it was Al Lichtman—the longtime all-purpose executive and gadfly of the studios—who put Bess Peters in touch with Louella Parsons.

Bess ingratiated herself with Louella, who had ready sympathy for anyone who had come so close to working first with Charlie Chaplin, then with Mary Pickford—the two biggest stars in the firmament. Louella kept her power by exploiting it, and she put in a call to Winfield Sheehan, the production chief of Fox Films. Sheehan was in a position of owing Miss Parsons a favor. Carol and Bess received a personal appointment.

The veteran Sheehan was wise to every kind of hustle, but when he met the dewy-fresh Miss Peters he was beguiled beyond critical logic. During Hollywood's most blatant spasm of nepotism, he was accustomed to sweet-talking and even signing to contract many a feebly endowed girl who was related to someone important, or had other formidable connections. But this girl gave his office a glitter. Easy as that, he said he'd like to sign her for pictures. Not even a screen test would be necessary. (Sheehan conceivably had seen her test for Chaplin, or knew of it.)

An agreement was easily reached: Fox Films would pay Carol Peters $65 per week for a one-year period, with allowance for a bonus if her performance exceeded their modest expectation during the year of indenture. There was no renewal clause; the term contract with options had not yet become the almost prohibitive practice of the movie companies. Carol understood that if she did well, the contract could be extended to five years.

Having previously earned almost no money on her own, Carol thought it was a fine salary, although some of her friendly elders thought she should get more. The newly merged M-G-M organization, for instance, was known to be starting even its inexperienced contract players at very nearly a hundred a week. But Bess did not want to derail Carol's opportunity by haggling. She counted on her daughter's ability, the proof of which would logically translate into better money soon enough.

Now her new employers didn't like the girl's name. The Carol part was all right. The Peters surname, they thought, lacked intimation of glamour, but was mainly to be avoided for its connotations. A Fox actor of the day was House Peters, whose very name was said to perpetuate closet jokes and some comically misinterpreted headlines.

Candidate names were tossed about. It was a custom to consider other family surnames, and the new contractee almost became Carol Knight. But Winfield Sheehan had the idea that moviegoers were subconsciously lured to actresses whose two-syllable surnames had strong opening stress, as in Pickford, Talmadge, and Swanson. Bess came up with Lombard—reminded of her longtime banker friend Harry Lombard and his wife Etta, both of whom were almost "family" to Carol. Sheehan liked the name Carol Lombard; and Carol thought the very idea of a completely new professional label was exciting. At home she sat at a writing table practicing a Carol Lombard signature in every conceivable slant, settling on an autograph dominated by a great flourishing *L* in the surname.

The contract was signed in mid-October, 1924, just after her birthday. It was no ceremonial thing and it went unacknowledged by the press, even by the Louella Parsons column—although in the future Miss Parsons would sometimes identify herself as Carole Lombard's actual "discoverer." It was clear enough that she was starting at the approximate rock bottom: she was immediately assigned a one-scene part in a quickie western that held her fellow Indianan, Buck Jones, in its primary focus.

Most of the western features were shot in the vagrant hilly ranchlands north of Hollywood, but there were minimal attentions to studio interiors. Carol's brief stint was for one of those back-at-the-ranchhouse episodes, and she was friend to the leading lady. She was occupied with preparation for half a day, getting made-up and into costume; and in the same afternoon she started and completed her assignment before the cameras. But it was all very exciting, and at Fox Films' almost-new studio on Western Avenue, a lighthearted atmosphere prevailed.

Carol was not uncommonly young in the studio environment. The movie business was young. The old-timers, who perhaps only a decade earlier had been the Hollywood pioneers, were in their thirties. Most of the craftsmen and supernumeraries of the studio apparatus were in their twenties or even younger. Informality reigned. Carol was assigned a corner in a large dressing room shared by girls doing walk-ons in several pictures that were in production simultaneously.

Most of the girls were only slightly older than she despite a prevalent shopworn demeanor, and some were even younger, although all were "mature" as shadow images. Carol thought it was like the best part of school, without the spelling and the math.

She was not given billing in the Buck Jones picture called *Gold and the Girl,* and her brief footage was deleted entirely from her second picture, a more formidable endeavor entitled *Dick Turpin.* This time the star was that erstwhile monarch of the sagebrush, Tom Mix, who on this rare occasion was to impersonate the storied highwayman of eighteenth century England. Even if she would not be visible in the final print, Carol could preen herself in petticoats and ruffles and aristocratic coiffure. Her awareness of the dramatic ineptitude of Kathleen Myers, the leading lady, also gave her confidence and a sharpening of competitive instinct.

She would be summoned regularly to the Fox studio for publicity photos or test photography, or for some experimentation by the cosmeticians. But she had an abundance of idle time; and with studio procedure already geared to an early-morning start and a more leisurely afternoon, she usually managed to leave the studio, by bus or some other means, and arrive at Fairfax High as classes were letting out. She would give rousing accounts of the picture-making activity, and particularly of the traipsing by the stars themselves. This would spark the envy of Sally Eilers and other coeds nurturing earnest movie ambitions.

Status as a movie contract player enhanced Carol's standing with her former school friends who wouldn't let her go. They were moths to her flame, and her immediate prospect was more dates and parties than she could handle. George Rosenberg was her most aggressive pursuer now, but other boys sought to pay court. Carol encouraged their attentions, enjoyed their company, and then fretted that she didn't really care *enough* about any of them.

The brash fervor of the Jazz Age got to southern California and the kids were wild with the new kind of dancing. So there was plenty to *do.* The Charleston was everywhere, and Carol gave herself giddily to the step. She practiced in the Peters living room with Stuart, who sometimes would condescend to join Carol's younger crowd for evenings of dancing all over town. But if Stuart was along, Carol would not roll her stockings as the other girls did. And she was fickle: the best male dancer in sight was her boyfriend of that moment.

The filmland offered many opportunities for ballroom exercise, but the new Ambassador Hotel with its exotic Cocoanut Grove was paradise for the more privileged teen-agers. Usually with Dixie Pantages in a double or group date arrangement, Carol became a regular at the Grove on Friday nights when the younger element gained dominance and, by indulging their own amusement, provided entertainment for the older clubbers. The ballroom was a clearing in a palm jungle inhabited by real monkeys. Some of the more enterprising monkeys hurled cocoanuts onto the dance floor. The Grove challenged the adventurer: once an airborne cocoanut skulled the illustrious Maurice, the headliner specialty dancer. (Maurice Mouvet was his name, and his partner was Lenore Hughes; some years later George Raft and Carole Lombard would impersonate them in a thinly disguised film biography.)

Inevitably, there was the Charleston contest. For a while it was just as inevitable that Carol Lombard, customarily introduced as a new starlet with Fox, would win the competition, especially if she had Tommy Lee's service as partner. Tommy was the twinkly handsome son of radio tycoon Don Lee, and his gregariousness and casual wealth made him the most coveted young bachelor in town. Tommy was not interested in a serious liaison. He only wanted to dance, and he was a sensational dancer. So he and Carol conspired to pair off on the dance floor, even when their consorts were rather awkwardly abandoned.

Carol's and Tommy's reign at the Grove was then seriously imperiled by the arrival of "the M-G-M- group," marshaled by a breezy dress extra named Shirley Dorman. One night Shirley's entourage included a new Metro contract player named Lucille LeSueur, ready and able to meet all competition in a Charleston. The LeSueur girl, very soon to be rechristened Joan Crawford by her employers, was Carol's own age but moved with a faster crowd that spiked the Grove's famous fruit punch. On Friday nights kids could buy a huge pitcher of tropical elixir for a dollar and a half, and Carol's friends swilled it without tapping the hip flask of Prohibition-era celebrity. Joan Crawford became the physical centerpiece of her own set of mostly transient youths, as surely as Carol Lombard was queen bee to the celebrants who had never left home.

The two groups retained their separate identities but merged socially; and one of Tommy Lee's even-richer pals, meat-packing heir Mike Cudahy, became Joan Crawford's longtime steady fella and dancemate. Eventually Carol's crowd followed Joan's to the more abandoned atmosphere of the Montmartre on Wednesday nights, when contest winners received trophies and loving cups. When the Montmartre got in trouble for having spoken too easily, the favored place became the Pavilion at Catalina Island, with dancing to Jan Garber's orchestra. But always the flaming youth returned to the Cocoanut Grove where Carol, as the entrenched local favorite, usually had a fifty-fifty chance of winning—although the general opinion was that Joan Crawford did the best Charleston in town.

Much later Carol would recall that "Joan had great body tension. She was better than I but she seemed to be working at it, and for me it was all play. It was a thrill to beat her, and she liked to beat me, too. But that wasn't the big thing with her. She didn't just want to get a start in pictures, she kept talking about reaching the very top. She wouldn't be satisfied until she was a real star, and that didn't worry me. I never thought about it."

Dancing at the Grove was Carol's joyful ritual—good counterpoint to her movie-making odyssey—until the stock market crash abruptly scuttled the Jazz Age. She said she even got to like the smell of the monkey shit, even though it was a hazard on the dance floor. She romanced and danced with Tommy Lee, Dick Olson, Danny Dowling, Heinie Cooper, Johnny Westwood; and her chattery girl friends followed her into films—Doris Dawson, Helen Twelvetrees, Jean Wood, Audrey Ferris, Dorothy Sebastian, and Loretta Young's older sisters. Dixie Pantages, who shunned every overture from the studios, insisted from a later perspective that Carol and her companions were remarkably chaste when neither the time nor the place made that particular demand.

Anticipating an obscure beginning in pictures, Carol counted on her memory of the acting fundamentals from Miriam Nolkes's school, to grease an upward ladder to larger roles. Such a course might have been more beneficial to her, but Fox soon had a more meaningful exposure immediately in mind—or Winfield Sheehan did. Tipped by Charles Clarke, a studio cameraman, that the Lombard girl had photographed beautifully in the footage excised from Tom Mix's *Dick Turpin,* Sheehan impulsively decided to push the untrained girl into lead roles.

Winnie Sheehan had kinship with a fellow Irish-American who was earning regard as the most reliable of Fox's younger directors.

Sheehan delivered Carol Lombard to Jack Ford—as he was still identified on the credits—with the thought that she would serve nicely as the ingenue for the *Lightnin'* picture Ford was preparing. Based on a bucolic comedy that had enjoyed a famous long run on the Broadway stage, it figured to be one of the studio's more important pictures of the season.

John Ford got acquainted with the pretty novice, and in a much later recollection of their first meeting he characterized her as "a remarkably unaffected girl, very bright, and rather obviously virginal. All of these qualities were appropriate to the needs of my picture, but I saw that the poor child was frightened by the other actors. Now *Lightnin'* was basically a piece for character actors, and my principal players had been in pictures as long as there had *been* pictures, and with stage experience before that—people like Jay Hunt and Otis Harlan and Edith Chapin.

"Well, Carol was afraid she couldn't hold her own in their company, and when I saw that it really bothered her, I told Sheehan it might be a better idea to put her in with less experienced people, perhaps more nearly her own age. But then Winnie did her a bad turn by having her take a part she wasn't ready for."

She didn't do *Lightnin'* and would wish she had. So would John Ford, who never had another opportunity to direct her. Carol was assigned instead to *Marriage in Transit* to impersonate a mature married woman. The director was Roy William Neill and the leading man was Edmund Lowe, past thirty and plenty handsome. Sheehan's thought was that since *Marriage in Transit* had no design on prestige, there would be less pressure on Carol.

It was a minor item in the Fox routine of producing fifty-two pictures a year, of which only a dozen had the "special" treatment that a *Lightnin'* would receive. *Marriage in Transit* was a modern domestic comedy-drama, a formula piece designed mainly to test up-and-coming Edmund Lowe in a leading role. He had joined Fox two years earlier after local stage experience and the studio was optimistic about his future. In *Marriage in Transit* he was the only player given feature billing, yet he was not a star: *What Price Glory* would accomplish that in time to come.

But Lowe had already measured and mastered every trick of acting for the camera, especially for one so static as Bill Neill's. He effectively upstaged Carol Lombard in their every scene together, so that her debut performance—it was essentially that, and the first public awareness of her name—went entirely unnoticed. The picture accomplished its primary objective. Lowe's popularity increased, and from that time he would play only leading roles, in pictures of graduating importance. But the picture created no particular impression, and did not obtain a first-run booking in a well-known Broadway movie house. Review attention was slight; Carol Lombard's beauty drew comment but not her ability. The studio folk did not detect a national reaction to her, so Sheehan decided that she had been assigned to leading roles prematurely.

It wasn't that they thought her too young. In the silent movie progress, most of the girls had started out playing mature roles while in their mid-teens, from Mary Pickford and the Gish girls to Gloria Swanson and Colleen Moore. Both Bessie Love and Bebe Daniels were essentially doing "leading lady" stints at age fourteen. But what had worked only a decade earlier was ever riskier as movie audiences became more sophisticated and therefore more exacting in their demands.

Carol Lombard was in the unbosomy tradition of the tender silent heroines, and her admirable facial bone structure did convey an older appearance. But she needed more experience; and one way her governors could provide it, without jeopardizing the dramatic content of a film, was to employ her in the quickie westerns that were a lively item of the Fox commerce. So it was back to Buck Jones country for Carol.

In that expeditious era, the *Gold and the Girl* picture in which Carol had appeared briefly with Buck Jones was shot in November and released in January, 1925. Shooting for *Marriage in Transit* began in February and was completed in March. The edited print was ready in April and the picture was released nationally in May. And by June, Carol was again working before the movie cameras, playing the second female lead in *Hearts and Spurs*—as the wealthy girl who loses Buck Jones to Marian Nixon.

She was hardly discouraged. During the shooting schedule of *Marriage in Transit* her salary had been raised to $75 a week. Through the studio's gossip network she knew she was well-liked personally, by Sheehan and others, and this was certified by the extension of her contract to a five-year term. She went on a clothes-buying rampage and alternately spent her income whimsically or practically—but spend it she did. Bess Peters wanted Carol to enjoy her youth as she had her own; money, she said, was for spending, if you've got it.

Apparently there was satisfaction with Carol's work in *Hearts and Spurs.* She was ticketed for another Buck Jones outing, but in *Durand of the Badlands* she would have leading-lady status—in fact, would be the only female in the picture. It was a more versatile assignment, with opportunity to show how well she could ride.

Ride a horse? She couldn't, at all. On an early Fox questionnaire she said she could ride, because it was smart to be affirmative about everything. She wasn't about to admit otherwise if it meant losing a lead role. So there they were, shooting *Durand of the Badlands* on location in the badlands of San Fernando, and she was ordered to mount her pony and ride away from the cameras. Carol mounted, and moments later she sprawled in the dust while her steed jerkily danced a criticism of her horsemanship. It was obvious that Carol had not ridden before, but nothing was said when she laughed off her spill with "How did that happen? Oh well, let's do it again!" The camera was positioned for a retake, and Carol gripped the reigns and pressed her booted feet hard to the stirrup cup, and let the horse do his work. She held on, and the director got his shot without a hitch. After that Carol never doubted she could ride, but cultivated a new ambition to ride well. She took lessons, learned in a hurry, and decided there was nothing more enjoyable.

Durand of the Badlands, her last quickie western, was filmed entirely away from the studio in just one week's time in the fall of 1925. It was released before the year was over. Today no print is known to exist of the feature film containing Lombard's first screen kiss. Unlike most stalwarts of the movieland sagebrush, Buck Jones enjoyed a clinch with his leading lady and customarily paid lip service to her in the final fadeout. In a 1942 interview shortly after the plane crash that deprived Hollywood of its favorite screwball comedienne, the Hoosier Buck Jones said yes, she was the prettiest girl he had kissed or even seen, ever. Later that same year, Jones would be one of the victims of another famous disaster—the burning of Boston's Cocoanut Grove, unrelated to the Los Angeles Grove where Carol had danced.

Sheehan apparently decided that Carol was ready for another level of exposure. Although she was not immediately assigned to another project, she reported daily to the studio to be photographed in diverse guises, and stories about the new screen hopeful were fabricated and dispatched to news services around the country. The studio arranged a date with Leslie Fenton, one of its young actors, and had them photographed around town. Carol did advertising layouts for manufacturers of bathing suits and soft drinks, and never knew if they were used. She did know she wasn't paid for her modeling services.

Her picture began to appear in the fan magazines, with nominal identification in the captions. She cut the ceremonial ribbon that opened a new Safeway store on Santa Monica Boulevard. She presented the game ball to the winning captain of the USC-Stanford football game. And she heard betimes that she was going to make another picture with Edmund Lowe, or one with George O'Brien. She was tested for the lead in one of Fox's more ambitious efforts, the spectacular *The Johnstown Flood,* only to lose the part to one of her new studio friends, the winsome Janet Gaynor who had joined Fox at about the same time, a graduate of Hal Roach's two-reel comedies.

To the collective mind of Fox Films, Carol Lombard was merely a face. Despite the dramatic renown a Lillian Gish or Norma Talmadge might accrue, and despite the singular charm of a Mary Pickford and the distinctly giddy tradition of film comediennes from Mabel Normand to Colleen Moore, the picture makers seldom thought of their silent ladies as actresses in any professional way. Sometimes the men were required to emulate an acting storm but the women were an adornment to be photographed. Carol didn't especially mind. She had no illusions about herself; she supposed real actors were a special breed, not of her kind. She loved the gamelike ritual of movie making and fretted over her continued inactivity, but had assurance that her name and face were becoming a topic around town.

They were. Harry Rapf at M-G-M inquired of her availability for a Tim McCoy western. First National wanted to know the duration of Carol Lombard's obligation to Fox. Finally, the great John Barrymore saw some of her publicity stills and decided she was a girl he'd like to meet and perhaps play around with.

Winfield Sheehan wouldn't say no to a John Barrymore. Although the Great Profile had never amounted to much at the movie box office, his prestige was undisputed. He brought skill and elegance to his film roles, and his vehicles for the struggling young

Warner Brothers company always were accorded the maximum promotion. Barrymore now planned to take a holiday from his home studio and make independently a spectacle film with a rich romantic quotient. This would be *The Tempest,* in no way related to Will Shakespeare's last great play. Barrymore was beginning to "test" unknown actresses for the role of his paramour (his testing method seldom involved photography) and he wanted to test Carol Lombard. Sheehan was delighted. Exposure in a Barrymore picture could return Carol Lombard to Fox as an important screen personality, something they might not otherwise accomplish in perhaps two years of careful grooming.

Carol was appointed to meet the great man in his new suite at the United Artists studio. She was properly warned: there was a bed right there, in a room adjacent to his "office." Some of the girls envied Carol's likely experience; others were apprehensive about the fate worse than death. Carol was fortified by the confidence Bess had given her.

"My mother believed that in any civilized meeting between a man and woman, there was no such thing as seduction. The woman, she said, was the one who controlled the events."

Carol met with John Barrymore and controlled the events. "I wore a smart, ladylike suit and tried to be friendly but reserved. I was awed by him but didn't want it to show. I tried to act as if I met people of his magnitude on a daily basis. Perhaps I overdid it. I just kept my legs crossed and he never so much as put a hand on my shoulder. Later I wondered if I just hadn't been attractive enough."

She didn't worry long. One of Barrymore's emissaries notified Fox that they'd like to have Carol make a screen test after all, and that was accomplished. Barrymore probably was wary of her youth. She was now a fully contoured seventeen, but he was a seedily grand forty-four, not yet subdued by dissipation but well on his way. It was three years after his great stage Hamlet, and he was living up a long separation from his second wife, the poet Michael Strange. Now the gossip was that he had fallen emphatically in love with his most recent leading lady, Dolores Costello, and wanted a divorce so he could marry her. At least temporarily, his devotion may have immunized him against other feminine graces. Barrymore personally made the screen test with Carol, giving vigorous mouth-to-mouth resuscitation while the camera spooled;

but he was otherwise respectful, even gallant, toward the pretty ingenue.

Carol never saw the test print but Barrymore must have been assured that the discrepancy of their ages was not worrisomely visible. She received the formally given word at the Fox studio: Barrymore had chosen her from a large roster of candidates, and she would be loaned to him for *The Tempest.* It was a news item in the papers.

But there were problems concerning the financing of an obviously expensive picture that also had some complicated logistics —there was a need for a considerable amount of real snow, and the location they had chosen was having to wait for it. So *The Tempest* was delayed and Barrymore consented to do *Don Juan* for the brothers Warner: it was the picture that would ultimately be accommodated with a synchronized musical score—the first step in the incremental transition to talking pictures. Rather than have her continue to be idle, Fox decided to put Carol Lombard to work in a romantic comedy called *Early to Wed,* speculating that director Frank Borzage might turn her into an actress before John Barrymore could.

As a preliminary, studio beauticians bobbed her hair to fashion, and lightened it beyond its natural ash blond shading. (The initial suggestion was Barrymore's.) Then she met the gregarious Frank Borzage in a way that was most agreeable to her: on the tennis court. They talked about the picture they were going to make, and Carol became infected with inspiration.

But she never made *Early to Wed* and she never made *The Tempest.* Her special world went to pieces like the windshield of Heinie Cooper's Bugatti roadster.

Heinie was Harry Cooper, scion of a Los Angeles banking family. He was in the Cocoanut Grove gang—an amiable playboy who was not so much a suitor to Carol as a smooching buddy. On a foggy night in the Hollywood winter, they were returning from a basketball game and were stopped on a hill by one of the brand new traffic signals, the second car in line. The brakes of the car ahead suddenly failed, and it skidded backwards into Harry Cooper's swell little auto. It was not a major collision, and Heinie was merely shaken without injury. But somehow the impact shattered the windshield, and a knifelike sliver of glass sliced a deep long gash in Carol's face, from the corner of her nose to her right cheekbone.

Even as she drank her own blood, she did not lose consciousness or common sense. Heinie gave heroic assistance, and Carol was hustled into the nearest hospital. Briefly there was a fear that she might bleed to death, but after the emergency attentions to her facial wound it was apparent that she was in good condition, and remarkably calm. She was mother-trained to stay calm.

Bess Peters, summoned immediately to the hospital, also kept her wits while others were chorusing the horrible injustice of it all, and doing nothing about it. Carol's life was not imperiled, but the prospect was a brutal permanent scar that would destroy any claim to beauty. At that moment concern for a career was not with Carol or her mother, but there were plenty of reasons for saving a seventeen-year-old-girl's face. Bess conferred forthrightly with the physicians and introduced her own ideas. She had heard of the new plastic surgery: was such a thing possible? It was possible, although risky, if it could be accomplished while the wound was fresh. But no one on the staff was capable of performing the operation, nor was the necessary equipment available.

Bess made a series of phone calls, and within a matter of minutes assured her daughter that a specialist was on his way and would soon have her face as good as new. And to the emergency crew she relayed the surgeon's important instruction to perform the necessary stitching without the anesthetics they were just then preparing. The muscles could not be allowed to relax; the danger would be an altered face, with or without successful plastic surgery. Carol gripped her mother's hand while she endured the pain.

The operation was a four-hour ordeal. Through all of it, Carol's eyes were taped down. The plastic surgery followed eighteen stitches. When his labors were over, the surgeon said he had salvaged Carol's personal appearance but doubted that she would ever regain normal muscular action in her face. He did not discount the possibility of additional surgery later on. The most important thing, he stressed, was that Carol should keep her head as motionless as possible for at least a week. For ten days she didn't move a muscle in her face, and accepted liquid food through a straw. In constant attendance, Bess reaffirmed her conviction that Carol would suffer no permanent impairment.

Bess was substantially correct. For months after the accident Carol had the annoyance of a stiff upper lip, but its effect was diminishing and her talking was not jeopardized. From any reasonable distance she appeared no less beautiful; but seen up close, the facial scar was not to be denied. Aside from an area of pinched skin tissue that could be cosmetically obscured, the scar was basically one of coloration. By adroit use of makeup, Carol soon was able to hide any suggestion of disfigurement. But at the time it did not seem likely to Carol or her mother that resumption of her film career was possible. Nor did it occur to anyone else. Frank Borzage made *Early to Wed* without her; and soon it was announced that Dorothy Sebastian, one of Carol's own good companions, would play opposite John Barrymore in *The Tempest*. (She didn't. The project encountered still another delay, and a foreign beauty, Camilla Horn, eventually took the role originally intended for Carol.)

Carol thought—and almost everyone agreed—that she was dealt with very rudely by Fox Films in the aftermath of the accident. The studio paid the basic hospital expenses but not the surgery, which was covered by Bess and by Carol's own earnings. Then Fox abruptly canceled its contract with Carol, without severance pay or other compensation, because there was small print concerning a player's own responsibility for his physical being. They were sympathetic: she was a nice girl after all; but they were business-minded people, and for all practical purposes the girl was through.

Filmland chroniclers have reflected on how the accident checked the progress and then radically altered the direction of her career. More significantly, it restructured her personality, bringing the essential Carol Lombard into freer play. Dixie Pantages Karlson, who knew her perhaps better than anyone immediately prior to the accident and just afterward, would recall that the young Carol had not given evidence of a big, dominant personality. She had been an irrepressibly merry girl, but one responsive to humor rather than an inciter of it.

"Carol during her recovery became very self-critical, ashamed of herself for having been so shallow. And while she became even more jovial later on, you were aware of her depth. To her there was nothing frivolous about having a good time. She went at it in dead earnest."

By her own recollection, Carol Lombard during her days of silent stillness in the hospital had repeatedly thought, "I might have been killed." She heard the inevitable murmurings that she was lucky to be alive, and she reasoned that even when you think you know all your options, the real possibility of death to anybody at any time is seldom acknowledged. She came to appreciate that her mother's devotion was entirely selfless; more than anything, Bess wanted Carol to enjoy in the fullest measure her own life, whatever she chose to do with it. Carol became a fatalist. Any day of living might be her last, and she had no great confidence that there would be enjoyment in an afterlife. Her mute contemplation resulted in a dedication to enjoyment—not for herself alone, but for everyone about her. Bess, quoting Emerson, maintained that to have a friend you must be one. Carol's governing determination was to be a friend, most especially to her mother.

When Dixie visited the Peters home after the homecoming from the hospital, Carol answered her gift of sympathy with "Isn't it better to have a scar on your face than on your soul?" Dixie said the people who sought to cheer Carol were themselves the gloomy ones who would lament the shattered career, and it would be Carol's function to restore *their* morale.

Soon she was back on the dance floor at the Cocoanut Grove, learning the new steps. But if the scene was the same, the personnel weren't. High-school graduation had splintered the unity of girls who had been her durable pals, and their wealthy young escorts of yesterday had become collegians of the respectable East. Carol's former rival Joan Crawford, having advanced to leading-lady status at M-G-M, was making pictures with such ranking players as Lon Chaney and John Gilbert, and she no longer required the exposure that Charleston contests could give.

Carol went searching for a new direction. She joined The Potboilers, an amateur theater group in Hollywood, taking small parts in *The First Year* and another comedy whose title she would not remember a few years later. She enjoyed the activity but knew she was only marking time with self-serving amusement, purposeless and therefore silly. And the plays were too talky, having little real kinship with what she wanted to do.

She had turned eighteen, and during all of 1926 she had not faced the movie cameras, nor was it openly discussed as a possibility. But oh, she thought about it!

❊ III ❊

Bathing Beauty

FROM THE moment she adopted it as her professional calling card, she considered Carol Lombard an exceptional and marvelous name. There was no reverting to Jane Peters during her extended layoff from picture making. It was a hint that she considered her career derailed but not wrecked. She began to make subtle inquiries around the studios. Whatever the condition of her face, it was no longer "new." So interest was a difficult thing to arouse.

She was not lacking for encouragement. John Bowers in particular coaxed her to continue and increase her assault on the studio doors. Bowers, who had waged his own campaign for more than a decade and had finally attained the rank of an unstarred leading player, was a member of the movieland's Indiana colony. He met Bess and the Peters children through Monte Blue, and had watched Jane's progress since she played Blue's kid sister in *The Perfect Crime*. Bowers had a contract with Warner Brothers but at one time he had worked for just about every extant company, and at all of them he "put in a good word" for Carol Lombard.

Bowers obtained an interview for her with Samuel Goldwyn who, if he remembered her name in any way, played possum. Noting her indication of some experience as an actress in pictures, he asked why Fox had not continued her contract. Carol said she may not have been what they wanted, but she'd welcome an opportunity to *test* for Mr. Goldwyn. A few days later she was invited back to his office, and she encountered Sam at his most indelicate. He pointedly examined her face and said, "Did you think I wouldn't find out?" Later John Bowers told Carol what he had learned: that Goldwyn had telephoned William Fox, curious to know how his company could have allowed so gorgeous a girl to slip away. Goldwyn then had berated Bowers for causing him to waste time on an "imposter."

But the point was brought home: Goldwyn hadn't been aware of the scar during their first meeting. It had almost disappeared. Bowers now had the notion that Carol should merely take an entirely new name and start afresh, without credits or other credentials. But Sam Goldwyn was not typical, and Carol could not expect to prove anonymity. Merely as a girl about town, she was already too well known, who might be glimpsed at a formal occasion squired by Pasadena's rich young Ward Fleury, or more leisurely dating a lanky young movie player named Gary Cooper. So she would sink or swim as Carol Lombard.

Indeed, she would swim. An unexpected call from Sally Eilers concerned a vacancy in Mack Sennett's "chorus": the assembly of bathing beauties who, with the latter-day descendants of the original Keystone Kops, inhabited the two-reel slapstickery that Sennett filmed mainly at the southern California beaches.

Carol had met Mack Sennett at—where else?—the Cocoanut Grove. He knew about her accident but didn't suppose it would matter in his comedies, since he seldom indulged in close-up shots of the girls. His situation farces were mainly improvised, and his attention to the bathing beauties was almost entirely in medium shots of the entire group. The only thing that counted with Mack Sennett was whether a girl could do comedy, and he would leave that to Eddie Cline.

Carol knew Eddie Cline, too; but then, Cline knew everybody. He was one of the most congenial men in the whirl of the movies, and he had no enemies. One of the original Keystone Kops, Cline was an industrious deviser of visual gags and he became Sennett's most reliable assistant director. When Sennett hit upon the previously unexploited bathing beauty as a comedy gimmick, he chose Cline to get the series going. Gloria Swanson, soon to become one of the dramatic mainstays of silent entertainment, was a charter member of the Sennett sisterhood. A brunette Marie Prevost and a blond Phyllis Haver were other graduated bathing beauties who had attained fair measures of movie fame; but the bathing-beauty farces were no longer regarded as stepping stones to glory. Still, Sennett was loyal to his charges, the work was regular, and it was a living. It was also great fun.

In truth, Mack Sennett had had his day. He was only in his early forties although quite gray, but his legend was spun in the days before the First World War, when laughter was the leitmotif of moviegoing, and when feature-length films had not reduced his specialty-line slapstick shorts to a subordinate function on the varied movie program. That was when the enchanting Mabel Normand was the soul of mirth in his haphazardly wrought comedy, and his paramour in a private life that was anything but conventional. In those days inspiration struck Mack Sennett most often while he relaxed naked in a bathtub that was stationary in the middle of his office. The water was boiling hot, and he said that every bead of sweat emerging from his pores was accompanied by a new gag, or an unused idea for two reels of gaiety.

Eventually he ran out of ideas but retreaded the old ones. He kept making pictures but didn't grow with the medium, certainly not as Chaplin and Keaton grew, or even as Hal Roach did with his Laurel and Hardy sequence. But his most routine comedies remained serviceable as filler, and Mack Sennett was still a deity. It was also said that he provided the most agreeable atmosphere for spending the day making pictures.

Eddie Cline, a feisty bantam who had left Sennett earlier to direct feature films and would do so again, had returned briefly to help the old master in what seemed to be a time of need. Cline understood the basic grammar of visual comedy—the deliberate build from the chuckle to the belly laugh, the boffo. He orchestrated little touches into a unified comical idea, continuing to embellish that idea until he had the boffo—then he dropped it and started afresh. Most importantly, he understood pace in terms of rhythm rather than mere speed. Pictures, he said, did not have to be fast to *seem* fast; the main thing was just to keep them moving.

Carol asked Eddie Cline for the job. She knew he would give it to her if empowered to do so. He was wary, reasoning that small-potatoes slapstick might be anything other than what Carol really wanted. The Sennett habit was to break in any number of inexperienced girls, retaining those who learned the ropes of comedy. They were not accustomed to hiring girls on the way *down;* having played feature leads, even in quickie westerns, was prestigious by comparison. Carol reminded Eddie in a friendly way that at eighteen, she was anything but a broken-down broad. She thought she could play comedy; she *knew* she would enjoy it. To emphasize her willingness, she said, "I'd work for fifty dollars a week if you were to ask me." Eddie studied her with a glint of sympathy and said, "Honey, for a girl just starting out, fifty dollars is our *top*." Carol said, "Then we'll agree I'm just starting out."

Who would she be replacing? Eddie Cline told her one of the newer girls was getting a break in features—Sally Eilers would be leaving them. Carol's longtime friend was now her benefactress as well, but she was still on the scene when Carol joined the Sennett gang at the Santa Monica beach to watch them shoot *The Goodbye Kiss*.

Carol met the girls who, as matters would have it, were to be her giddy soulmates romping in sand and surf for all of a year and a half. The primary comediennes were anything but ingenues: both Dot Farley and Daphne Pollard were well into their thirties, and their continuity testified to Mack Sennett's uncommon loyalty as much as to his belief in their skills. Dot Farley had been in pictures even longer than Sennett himself; still a charmer if somewhat stocky, she knew every trick of visual comedy. The secret lay in the timing, and the wisdom was shared by Daphne Pollard, a fireplug of a girl just four feet eight—the younger sister of Snub Pollard, one of the best and funniest of the old Kops. The other members were kewpie dolls in their teens or early twenties: Ruth Hiatt, Kathryn Stanley, Anita Burns, Laska Winter. Also employed regularly was a precocious moppet, Mary Ann Jackson.

Sennett made irregular use of his more famous alumni—Ford Sterling, Snub Pollard, Mack Swain, Chester Conklin, Hank Mann —as rotating male leads, as well as newer comics such as Billy Gilbert, Irving Bacon, and a corpulent Vernon Dent. There was a trained dog named Omar. If the director was not Eddie Cline it was Harry Edwards, another veteran; or it was Sennett himself, whose interference was inevitable in any event, and was easily tolerated.

Mack Sennett liked his girls plump. Greeting his new recruit, he said, "Ain't you a scrawny thing, though! We gotta get some meat on you. Carol honey, you go right home and eat some bananas. A lot of bananas—just keep on eatin' 'em. That'll fatten you up, especially in the tits." By the criteria of the time, Carol Lombard's figure was approximately perfect: the Jane Russell mammary revolution was still many years in the distance.

Rather apart from the pleasingly plump bathing chorines, Madalynne Fields was comically fat. From the beginning, the Sennett ensemble had included a vibrantly obese young lady. Mack said, "There's only one thing visually funnier than a fat girl, and that's a fat girl in a bathing suit." Aloud to himself, Mack Sennett said, "Maybe I have my own Laurel and Hardy in drag." He told Carol Lombard that she and Miss Fields should get acquainted.

Get acquainted they did. Madalynne Fields was a bright, knowing girl only slightly older than Carol, and they immediately became great chums. Carol started calling her "Fieldsie" and soon she was Fieldsie to everyone else. Both girls thrived on the atmosphere of a group, but they also coveted a private association. They achieved it with permanence.

On Carol's first day as a Sennett chattel in a bathing suit, she sunburned badly and could not work on the following day. While Fieldsie and another girl rubbed her neck with mineral oil, Carol explained to Eddie Cline that she had unusually delicate skin tissue and always tended to burn quickly and sorely. Eddie told her to keep the vulnerable spots covered when she wasn't actually performing for the camera. But perhaps some of the sharper-eyed patrons who viewed her first two-reeler could wonder what happened to the pretty blonde who frolicked with the gang only in the opening scenes, then disappeared without explanation.

Eddie Cline decided against using Carol in one of the beach romps until she had acquired a tan that was in no danger of peeling away, so she was cast in a domestic two-reeler, an all-interiors job shot in Sennett's old studio on Santa Monica Boulevard. It was called *Smith's Pony* and Eddie Cline was the director. Raymond McKee, who began his long career in slapstick, then moved into romantic and tragic roles and now had come full circle, was Smith. Ruth Hiatt played his wife and Mary Ann Jackson was their little girl. (As a rule, Sennett would not depict marriage *without* children, which to him meant an unconsummated union.) Omar was their dog, Billy Gilbert their neighbor, and Carol was Gilbert's wife —in later years the pixie-plump Gilbert liked to confound people with the revelation that he had once been teamed romantically with Carole Lombard.

The picture was a conventional two-reeler to be part of a standard program including a feature film, a serial, an animated cartoon, and perhaps a one-reel comedy as well. At the studio or at the beach, Sennett's custom was to begin shooting a picture on Monday—a new picture every week—and to stay at it until photography was completed and the spools could be handed over to the editors. It meant that Carol Lombard now was working for fifty dollars a picture, for no two-reeler rated the luxury of shooting into a second week. This was great incentive for the players to hurry and do their best. They didn't want to work into Sunday; and they didn't have to report on Saturday or even on Friday if they could wind it up before then. They were never technically behind schedule because, technically, Sennett had no schedule. But everyone learned to work with an urgency, and usually there was an excess of idle time during the latter stages of the week.

Before she had been put to work in another comedy, Carol met with Mack Sennett at his request—their only session that was frank and entirely private. The *Smith's Pony* picture had been put together and he had run it off and didn't like it. Oh, the picture was all right; it played. But he didn't like *her*. She wasn't playing comedy, and didn't she know the difference?

Carol said yes, she knew: comedy was supposed to be funny; and if it wasn't supposed to be funny, then it was drama. Mack Sennett cackled and told her she was wrong. Everything in life, he said, can be viewed as something funny or something sad, depending on what you make of it. The elements are the same but the playing has to be different. Sennett said that in *Smith's Pony* Carol had responded to a basically serious domestic situation as if she believed every bit of it. But comedy, he said, was merely the desired alternative to truth. She could be a comedienne only by playing the *Smith's Pony* charade as if she didn't believe it for a minute. He may have told Carol what a wearily old, long inactive Mack Sennett told a filmland reporter in 1952: "As soon as the actors appear in a play or a movie, the audience needs to know if it's watching comedy or drama. It doesn't matter how the script is written—the audience must learn from the attitude of the players."

Carol had given a realistic, proper little performance, one that would have done nicely enough for Buck Jones or even Edmund Lowe. But she came to understand what Eddie Cline had meant when he said she needed to play with more abandon. "Just act

everything the same way you behave normally," he told her, adding
that in her everyday chatter she never seemed really serious.

Attired once more for the beach, she followed *Smith's Pony* with
The Girl from Everywhere and was funny with a vengeance, cutting
up with Fieldsie in the corners of the frame while Dot Farley and
Daphne Pollard occupied the comical center. Being both observant
and responsive, Carol studied the Misses Farley and Pollard and
mastered the antic art of timing for an effective gag. She had often
heard that comedy was more difficult to play than serious stuff but
now she had her doubts. After reshaping her basic attitude along
the lines of Sennett's suggestion, doing comedy seemed easy enough
and was also larkish fun. She found herself becoming wise in the
ways of comedy, but moviegoers who continued to embrace the
Sennett two-reelers wouldn't give her the credit. She was distinctive
mainly in appearance. If they thought of Madalynne Fields as "that
fat one" and Daphne Pollard as the tiny imp, Carol Lombard was
simply "the pretty one."

Carol's first escapades for Mack Sennett could be glimpsed in the
theaters toward the end of 1927. Her appearance in the shorts
caused no stir; but then, the Sennett efforts could not grab the
limelight in the season of *The Jazz Singer*. The first feature film
that was at least partly a talkie came and went, but it caused a lot
of talk and the talk didn't subside. Rival moviemakers were annoyed by the Warner Brothers who showed every intention of continuing to make talking pictures—indeed, to intensify that effort.

But few of the princes of industry were truly worried. Talkies,
they said, would have novelty value for a while and then go away.
Mack Sennett was not alarmed, so confident he was that the people
out there didn't really want talking pictures even if they thought
they did. "Did you ever see anything so dead as any one of those
Vitaphone musical shorts?" he asked. "Talking pictures would destroy everything we've been building over the years—our own art.
Talk is what nobody needs. It'll never work."

Bess Peters once told Hedda Hopper that she had stopped thinking of her daughter as a child when she was, indeed, still a child—
because she had the full measure of common sense found only in
adults (and in too few of those), and because she gave every evidence
of emotional maturity. Mother and daughter regarded one another

as equals, and collaborated on making their house charming while leaving its business management in the hands of Fred. Carol's older brother, still unmarried, progressed securely with the Bullock's firm and put Stuart through business college. In contrast to Bess's permissiveness, Fred remained authoritarian toward Carol, adamant that she would always look respectable and also act the part.

Carol customarily addressed her mother simply as that—Mother—and never as Bess, but in the company of friends she adopted their pet nickname of Totsie. Sunday dinner at Totsie's became a custom for a large, informal guest list—not only Carol's friends, but also Stuart's and Fred's. Their mother was a catering wonder, with waffles her famous specialty. She could usually conjure a monumental fruit salad for the Sunday buffets, with sliced cold ham, chicken breasts, and all the trimmings worthy of the finest picnic spread. Dixie Pantages said Totsie was everyone's favorite hostess "because she had class." Her home became the unofficial headquarters for her middle-aged contemporaries. They played cards and talked religion or politics—1928 would be an exciting election year in California—without forgetting about the movies, the factory product of their hometown. Totsie *always* talked about the movies when she entertained Carol's friends.

Bess Peters was an intermediary between two quite different groups, both of which provided an abundance of gossip for her to digest and pass on. She learned who was sleeping with whom. She savored and digested every tidbit and used it as social contraband. Only to a point would Carol tolerate her mother's passion for petty scandal. "You're wicked, Mrs. Peters," she'd scold. "Now cut it out!"

Their house on Wilton Place became the vortex of the most innocent merriment, and sometimes it took on the character of an oasis. Bill Rockwell of Fort Wayne and Carol's own generation related a youthful, adventuring trip to California that was made beautiful by Bess's graciousness. Lonely in Los Angeles and almost broke, he was taken in by Bess, who gave him a royal dinner and a diplomat's orientation to the wonders of the southland. They were barely acquainted: Bill was a son of former friends, but Bess delighted in being ambassadorial. If anyone from the hometown planned a visit to southern California (whose primary lure had become Holywood itself), the senior Fred Peters told him to look up Bess and expect a wonderful time. To the Fort Wayne folk, dropping in on Bess was the most gratifying obligation of western travel.

When Carol started work for Mack Sennett, the Peters home became a magnet for the other cavorters in Mack's mad little photoplays. Bess got to know everyone on a first-name basis, not just the bathing girls but the drones of movie making as well. "Carol's place," with strategic access both to the heart of Hollywood and downtown Los Angeles, was like a latter-day wayside inn.

Its appeal was especially pronounced for the Sennett girls, most of whom yearned for the conventional home life they never had, or remembered only dimly. If Hollywood was the city of dreams, broken or otherwise, the dreamers often sought compensation for shabby lives. The girls who streamed into movieland in still larger numbers were usually running away from bleak, unsatisfying existences. Loneliness was not a matter of having no one to talk to but was a condition that dwelled inside; and Hollywood was an anthology of loneliness, a crowded house that still wasn't home.

Carole Lombard at her cresting celebrity once told an interviewer that most of the girls that came to Hollywood hated their mothers—hated them for their neglect on the one hand, or for their strangling attention (the movie mamas) on the other. "It's always a wonder to them how well I get along with my mother, but it's such a simple thing. The word is respect. We respect one another and always have. Other than that, my mother is the most interesting lady I know, and the most generous and considerate. Sometimes when I forget that I'm not still a little girl, I find myself saying I want to be just like her when I grow up."

So they were best friends, and the anchor of a home made Carol less susceptible to the traps that snared the wildlife of Hollywood. She did not resist temptation, because she wasn't tempted. At nineteen she could describe herself as "the most chased chaste girl in town, and vice versa." She enjoyed the attention and the company of men (all men were "boys" to her) but insisted she had never experienced a truly deep feeling toward any one. With no expression of arrogance toward men, her attitude bewildered her girl friends, who usually were obsessed by nothing so much as men. Carol said she fully expected to fall in love "when I meet some man who has the best qualities of both of my brothers . . . and none of their flaws."

Carol's friendship with Madalynne Fields flourished because, among other reasons, Fieldsie shared her friendly detachment toward men. To be their good buddy rather than a romantic objective was her well-fleshed legacy: she had few dates. But Fieldsie also shared with Carol the worldly interests that were alien to most of the Sennett girls. Fieldsie was well-read, attentive to intellectual themes, and a sophisticate at heart. She may have had the inner makings of a versatile actress, but her visible broadness relegated her to a comic prop. Fieldsie, too, developed a special relationship with Bess, and became a favorite to Carol's brothers.

On Carol herself, Fieldsie was a definite influence. Carol was easily pleased by the activity of making movies. Her objectives were modest—foolishly, so, Fieldsie thought—and she was satisfied by any meager proof of progress, as when Mack Sennett raised her weekly salary to eighty-five dollars. Fieldsie lectured Carol on the kind of income a girl could expect making *real* movies, and badgered Carol to try again. Fieldsie became her champion, convinced that she was star material with looks and talent in equal measure. Carol did get back into the rhythm of "asking around," and now and then John Bowers or another friend would tip her on a casting opportunity. No jobs came of it, however. Carol suspected that in some quarters identity as a Sennett comedienne reduced her to a commodity and counted more as a liability than an asset.

Her facial scar, lingering almost undetectably, had ceased to be a logical barrier. In the rapidly evolving Hollywood history of that day, two years ago was ancient history; few people of consequence to the industry would remember the accident, or would connect Carol Lombard with a brief Fox starlet apprenticeship. But in 1928 there was a slowdown in the taking-on of new talent—an unofficial moratorium while the industry argued a wholesale conversion to sound, and braced itself for the possibility. The timing was wrong for renewed speculation on feature films, but Fieldsie kept the idea in Carol's head.

Meanwhile, they had a ball. Being a Sennett girl perhaps wasn't the greatest job in Hollywood, but it was hardly work either. Carol caught on: she got the feel of slapstick, its tempo and spirit; and she knew Mack Sennett was aware of her responsiveness because her exposure increased steadily from one two-reeler to the next. In *Run, Girl, Run* she was the girl of the title—her first Sennett lead. In the first four months of 1928 she worked every other week and completed eight two-reelers, in bathing suits and other attire. The titles tell the story: *The Beach Club, Hold That Pose,* and *The Swim Princess; The Best Man* and *His Unlucky Night.* Carol got another pay raise—to $500 a month—and was *The Bicycle Flirt.* Sennett also inaugurated a series of collegiate farces—*The Campus Carmen, The Campus Vamp,* and so on.

She had to run a lot. She learned pratfalls and the rest of the antic slapstick ritual, and she heaved a few pies while catching her fair share in the face. It was director Harry Edwards's notion that picturegoers, especially bleakly endowed women, got a thrill out of seeing a really pretty girl variably smeared; so besides the heritage of custard pies, Carol was often dipped in the California mud.

During her Sennett phase she met her modest competition but by no means was at her prettiest. Her glossily blonded hair was cropped marginally too short and often frizz-curled, unattractively so from the hindsight of later fashion. But in the judgment of Sennett's archrival Hal Roach, the Lombard girl was flawless for glamour, and he spoke of trying to hire her away from Mack. Carol was never approached by a Roach emissary, but when Roach took on a new girl the grapevine identified her as his Lombard counterpart. Her name was Harlean Carpenter and she was totally bereft of Carol's natural beauty, but she was blond like nobody else. They changed her name to Jean Harlow.

Even when he had a player under an "exclusive" contract, Mack Sennett didn't mind the player picking up occasional work else-where if it did not interfere with his own schedule. So in the spring of 1928 Carol sandwiched a minor feature-film appearance between two Sennett shorts, sadder but wiser for the experience. She accepted a call from Rayart, one of the distinctly marginal Hollywood companies that collectively were labeled Poverty Row, to take a second lead in something called *The Divine Sinner.* (It bore no relationship to either of two contemporary films, Garbo's *The Divine Woman* and Corinne Griffith's *The Divine Lady,* but may have been deliberately titled to capture a confused audience.)

When she spoke of it at all, Carole Lombard put down *The Divine Sinner* as a ridiculous picture but an illuminating experience for her. The production was a slipshod sausage-grind, as if the only objective were to expose five thousand feet of film. She received no guidance or other instruction from one Scott Pembroke, who nominally directed most of the pictures Rayart made in California. It was unfortunate enough that the picture was a predestined misery; what was worse, Carol thought, was that no one cared. Such exercises usually realized a small profit because they were made so cheaply. (Not even the coming of the talkies could snuff out such enterprise, but the Great Depression would.)

The most painful thing for Carol was to observe Vera Reynolds and sense her humiliation. That she had been a fan of Miss Reynolds only a few years earlier led to Carol's capricious acceptance of the part. Vera Reynolds had been a promising young leading lady, brought along by Paramount in the DeMille pictures; but at the first sign that her popularity was slipping she was cut adrift. The rest was sad but typical. Such players could hang on idefinitely in the more humdrum reaches of picture making, and it often seemed that half the gainfully employed people of Hollywood were some kind of has-been. Vera Reynolds was two years older than Carol Lombard.

Carol urged her friends not to see *The Divine Sinner* but there was little opportunity anyway: the picture managed only a few Los Angeles bookings. She said she never saw the picture or received full payment for her services, but it made her want to work in features again under more favorable circumstances. She stepped up her effort to know all the studio casting directors on a personal basis. The new man at Fox, Jack Gardner, was a friend of Stuart's. Carol paid a visit to Gardner, and shortly afterward was called in for a minor role in *Me, Gangster,* an unpretentious melodrama Raoul Walsh was directing. Don Terry and June Collyer took the leads and Carol had one good scene, convincingly trampish as Blonde Rosie, with hideous dark eye shadow and heavily rouged cheeks. She was convinced that Winfield Sheehan had not recognized her when their paths crossed at the studio.

In the summer of 1928 Carol had a heart-to-heart with Eddie Cline, no longer with Sennett but still Mack's most confidential ally. Eddie said Mack was worried about losing Carol—he was always worried when one of his players began sniffing after other jobs. Now Mack had a notion of building a new character especially for Carol; she would be starred in a continuing series. She would get a raise, of course; but first he had to determine her loyalty.

Carol felt trapped. She had no prospects for steady work other than with Sennett, nor did the most remote possibilities have lucrative potential. Carol asked Eddie Cline what *he* thought she should do. His answer, coming after a long pause, surprised her.

"Sooner or later you'll have to leave Mack," he said, "because Mack's about through. This whole business is changing and he can't get the rhythm. He'll take care of you as long as he can, but how long is that? You're really very employable, once you decide what you want."

Carol learned from Eddie Cline that Pathé would not be renewing its agreement with Sennett. The Pathé company, whose history dated to the very roots of the movie business, distributed all of Sennett's projects. There was little chance of Mack's getting an arrangement with one of the major distributors, so he was on the downslide and knew it. In effect, Carol was being warned to leave a sinking ship. If she needed further motivation, Eddie Cline revealed that Pathé had made repeated inquiries about Carol's availability and Sennett had ignored every overture, despite a gentleman's agreement that he would share his resources to accommodate Pathé's occasional needs.

But the raffish, vain Sennett was a heroic figure to arouse Carol's considerable capacity for sympathy. She wouldn't desert. If something came along, well, she'd have to decide what to do; meanwhile, she was entirely willing to talk salary and the future with Mack himself.

Nothing more was said about a new series possibility, but she did get another raise. Under conditions of her revised contract she would also be "loaned" periodically to Pathé to satisfy its temporary needs. She drew a walk-on in a Pathé entry called *Power* featuring William Boyd, whose later silver-haired destiny was Hopalong Cassidy. In *Power* Carol had a fanny-shaking sequence as one of the two girls identified merely as "dames." The other dame, a true blonde, was the eighteen-year-old Joan Bennett, playing to the cameras for the first time. Having married at sixteen, she was already a divorced mother, but without the assurance one would expect of Richard Bennett's daughter. Soon she would begin to acquire assurance by joining her famous father in *Jarnegan* on the Broadway stage, and Carol never expected to see her again.

The *Power* interlude was a preliminary step toward transferring Carol's Sennett contract to Pathé. Paul Stein, a Viennese and one of the directors imported by Hollywood from Germany's great Ufa organization—and something of a connoisseur of blondes—liked what he saw of Carol in Sennett's *The Bicycle Flirt* and thought she would do nicely as the second female lead in *Show Folks*. It was a colorful part but not a sympathetic one—the "heavy." Carol would be a physical contrast to the Latin heroine, Lina Basquette.

What most appealed to Carol was that *Show Folks* was a comedy with serious overtones and afforded a nice display of her Sennett style, but in a more civilized framework. Also, *Show Folks* was about as important a picture as the middle-rank Pathé company turned out. The male lead was Eddie Quillan, then being touted as the Pathé answer to M-G-M's brash William Haines. On the basis of his European credits, Paul Stein as director gave a picture some intimation of prestige.

Carol liked making *Show Folks*. To enact a believable character was rather a new challenge for her, and she made a concentrated effort to combat a major distraction: Paul Stein couldn't keep his hands off parts of Carol's body where hands were not casually welcome. She didn't mind returning to the Sennett harness to work with people she knew, but she was riding a Sennett-Pathé yo-yo without knowing where she stood.

With the coming of the autumn of 1928, she was in the unusual position of having appeared in three feature films—two for Pathé, one for Fox—that were slated for release almost simultaneously. That was not even counting the obscurity she'd done for Rayart, or a Paramount effort called *Half a Bride* from which her one brief scene (with Gary Cooper) had been excised. All of the pictures were silent, but around Hollywood—not only at Warners but also at Paramount and now, suddenly, at Fox—the emphasis was shifting toward the talkies. The public was showing a clear preference for pictures with speech and sound; but would it be only a passing fad? The likelihood was that Mack Sennett and other veterans whose product was rooted in pantomime would be in real trouble.

It was Bess's idea: to get the lowdown on anything, go to the top —to the head man who knows, or can decide. At Pathé the head man was Joseph P. Kennedy, an Irishman whose Midas touch had been validated in every business line he'd entered—except, perhaps, motion pictures. As a business wheelhorse for United Artists, Kennedy had been the catalyst for Gloria Swanson's independent career after her defection from Paramount. The word was that Kennedy,

a family man with important Eastern connections, had fallen hopelessly in love with Miss Swanson, and their professional association
had ended. But now he was chief executive at Pathé, possibly flog-
ging a dead horse. The company was in trouble.

Part of the difficulty, though, was its deficiency of potent star
personnel, and Joseph Kennedy had been brought in to put things
right. He was popularly known to be looking for "new faces." The
astonishing success of the recently merged company of M-G-M
under Louis B. Mayer and Irving Thalberg had turned the industry
around, so the thinking was that stars—always an important thing
—really were the *only* thing. On that premise Carol Lombard
bought a new, tasteful dress, artfully powdered her scar, and called
on Joseph P. Kennedy.

They got along. He knew who she was, and was complimentary
about her work in *Show Folks,* which he'd seen in a rough cut and
which Carol hadn't seen at all. She was forthright in confronting
him, not at all coy, and he seemed to like that. He also said he was
sick to death of dealing with talent agents, and welcomed the idea
of direct negotiation with a player . . . so what did she want?
Carol wanted a contract and ample opportunity to prove herself.
She'd done a lot of picture work but with little chance to act, and
her objective was to play leading roles.

"What about talking pictures? Can you talk?"

Carol made a show of annoyance, but in moderation.

"What do *you* think? Am I talking to you now?"

Kennedy said he meant talk like an actress, which isn't like
normal people-talk. Carol said maybe it should be, and sensed that
she'd said the right thing. Joseph Kennedy suspected that Carol
Lombard was already eligible for leading roles and told her so.
He thought they could agree on a contract. But he was not ready
to accept Mack Sennett's definition of a good female figure.

"I'd say you can stand to lose maybe twenty pounds," he told her,
and offered her a contract on that condition. Whether Carol had
obeyed Sennett's advice about bananas was not known, but indeed
she was overweight for the first time since her adolescence. She
enjoyed Kennedy's needling game and wouldn't be intimidated.

"You're not so slim yourself," she countered. "You could lose
at least twenty pounds!"

Kennedy's idea was that a studio masseuse could slap the residue
off Carol quicker and more healthfully than it could be dieted

away. She said, "I'll let her work me over if you'll let her give you the works, too."

He said it was a deal. Later one of Carol's best blue-word stories described Kennedy's earthy yelling while the studio masseuse pummeled him—the same masseuse who had worked ever so gently on the Lombard anatomy, but went after Kennedy with a vengeance, on the basis of Carol's precise instructions.

In the beginning of their association, she liked Joe Kennedy very much. But she was critical of his business management even when it endeared him to her. There was no bargaining, but Pathé could have had her happily and cheaply. Joe Kennedy had been apologetic that with times as uncertain as they were, he wouldn't be able to give her much money at the start. Perhaps he was still under the spell of the Gloria Swanson economics.

Four hundred dollars a week.

She fulfilled her obligation to Sennett, consenting to appear in one additional two-reeler at a future time of their mutual convenience. And on October 6, 1928—her twentieth birthday—she became officially a featured player under contract to Pathé.

By that time she was already at work in a new picture. It wasn't a leading role but the project was one of primary importance— the film of Sidney Howard's very successful play, *Ned McCobb's Daughter*. Carol took the part of Jenny, the saucy waitress at Carrie's Spa in Down East Maine; and in a company of extraordinarily professional actors she became miserably aware of her limitations.

Carrie, the daughter, was Irene Rich, veteran leading lady of generally discerning silent pictures; and old Ned McCobb was Theodore Roberts, grand veteran of both stage and screen. Robert Armstrong, the male lead opposite Miss Rich, also had broad experience, and the other actors went about their chores with admirable sincerity. As a comedy of character rather than a farce or synthetic drama, *Ned McCobb's Daughter* was Carol's first brush with realism. She suspected that the director—William Cowen, a new man—was not pleased with her work. Mainly she feared a poor showing that might taint a picture of general excellence and overstate her deficiencies, thus preventing her getting solid footing in the Pathé assembly.

She needn't have worried. *Ned McCobb's Daughter*, like every other silent picture good or bad that was filmed in late 1928 and released the following year, would be one of the foundlings of film history, consigned to oblivion by the industry-wide panic that convoluted Hollywood.

The talk around Paramount and M-G-M, and at Fox and First National and Universal (as well as at Pathé and lesser studios) was that the Warner boys had spoiled everything. As Mack Sennett had said, talking pictures were what nobody needed—except, it would seem, the Warner brothers, whose oversubscribed indebtedness made them desperate for survival. They had nothing to lose by experimenting with talking pictures. They had everything to lose by *not* doing so. Finally they defied the wishes of their more powerful competitors, even denying compensation for laying off the talking apparatus, and got to work making talking pictures. Slowly. Gradually, a step at a time. A synchronized musical score for John Barrymore's *Don Juan* (the music was nice, but didn't lure customers); talking (mostly singing) Vitaphone short subjects featuring notable musical artists (once the technical achievement was acknowledged, the public just didn't care); and finally *The Jazz Singer,* only partly a talkie but with mesmerist Al Jolson singing like a cyclone (a sensation, all right, but not necessarily an oracle of revolution).

The Warners could have stopped right there and bliss might have prevailed. But more increments: sound effects added to completed silent pictures (for a spectacle such as *Noah's Ark* the public was impressed); talking sequences, usually the climactic reels, appended to dramatic pictures otherwise shot as silents (even if crudely done, the commercial response was not to be denied); and in July, 1928, the first completely talking (and singing) picture, *Lights of New York* (as inept as any picture made, but the public clearly wanted this, and the hell with silent art).

The other studios capitulated. Fox and then Paramount, and it became a horserace. Universal, First National, RKO; even distinctly minor operations such as Columbia and Tiffany started experimenting with talk or sound or both. Pathé was almost the last major firm to enter the sweepstakes. M-G-M was the holdout, but its motives were misread. Irving Thalberg wisely delayed the studio's conversion to sound until a fair degree of technical refinement could be achieved; and from the time of its belated entry in the talking picture competition in mid-1929, M-G-M easily outclassed the field, including the pioneering Warners.

Significantly, M-G-M had Hollywood's most illustrious lineup of stars: John Gilbert, Ramon Novarro, Lon Chaney, Buster Keaton, William Haines; and Greta Garbo, Norma Shearer, Marion Davies, and Joan Crawford. Their faces, even such as those of Chaney and Keaton, were their fortunes. What would the talking requirement do, particularly in the case of a tantalizing Swede only vaguely acquainted with English? Some Metro careers could not be saved—John Gilbert's identity as the foremost casualty of the talkies would eventually outstrip even his great silent fame. Yet Garbo, Shearer, and Crawford all became "bigger" stars as talking actresses.

The panic was not focused especially on the stars and what to do about them; conversion to talking pictures affected every aspect of planning and production. Who would "write" the pictures? Title cards were one thing, spoken dialogue quite another. Enormous investment in the technology of sound was unavoidable. But the public was joyously immersed in its own movie-star mythology, and that above all had to be protected. The studio rulers could not immediately predict the brutish fickleness of the moviegoing public. Players who had retained popularity for year after silent year were anathema if they failed to come up to snuff in their first talking opportunity. Perhaps the public would have been more tolerant, more willing to forgive; but the studios became enamored of silken-voiced stage stars. The ultimate jettisoning of established players was the studios' doing, not the public's. It was a nightmare of parallel ladders—equally crowded with people—one going up and the other down.

Joseph P. Kennedy's manifold challenge at Pathé involved the upgrading of picture-story content, refinement of production as a discipline, and the development of attractive and distinctive players who could be marketed as stars. The Kennedy regime had a promising beginning. The purchase of *Ned McCobb's Daughter* typified the effort to close the sophistication gap. The character of Pathé production values also improved; but there was no appreciable increase in the popularity of Pathé feature films, primarily because of the continuing failure to discover and promote exploitable players. Kennedy mistakenly tried to restore some basically attractive people he supposed still had a foundation of popularity —William Boyd and Lina Basquette, DeMille castoffs both. He adopted the agreeable but fading Phyllis Haver, who recalled an earlier cycle of Mack Sennett bathing beauties. Pathé speculated on the development of Robert Armstrong as a virile leading man, and Eddie Quillan as a college-man comedian. Early results were negligible but the public as jury had not returned a clear verdict. Nor would it: the talkie upheaval shattered Kennedy's star-building campaign in midpassage.

Carol Lombard had signed a three-year contract with Pathé but the company was obligated only for the first year, the remaining time being renewable by options. To cancel the Lombard contract therefore would not mean the loss of a considerable Pathé investment. Or it would cost them nothing at all: in a possibly unique arrangement, her contract could be reassigned to Mack Sennett without her consent—something she learned only when that became a distinct possibility.

In the month of September, 1928, Carol Lombard was visible in several new feature films of variable merit, in large or tiny roles. *The Divine Sinner, Power,* and *Me, Gangster* sank without a trace and Carol remained a nonentity to the paying public. In *Show Folks* she gave a performance that caused favorable comment at the Pathé studio, but again audiences gave no reaction. (But the picture created some discord because some people thought they were paying to see *Show People,* a similar but much better concurrent picture of King Vidor's.)

Then there was discussion, amid the explosion of hurriedly made, frantically marketed all-talking pictures, of scrapping *Ned McCobb's Daughter* and shooting it over as a talkie, following Sidney Howard's original dialogue. In that event, Carol's role probably would have been taken by one of the new girls riding Broadway's first wave; for the Napoleonic code of the moment presumed that a movie player who had not talked for the movie sound recorder *could not talk.* But wisdom shifted against a remake; even with the original sets intact, it would be foolishly costly. Better to simply add some noise and sell it as a "sound" picture; so *Ned McCobb's Daughter* belatedly acquired a sound track with sloshing waves, cawing gulls and other distractions, but no voices. Released in early 1929, it earned a respectful press. Contrary to her fear, Carol was not a weak link in the cast. Her work was favorably reviewed, but it was meaningless because silent pictures were a dead issue.

At about that time, Pathé spirited away from Columbia an able young director named Edward H. Griffith because his background included work on the stage. The medium would temporarily abandon its birthright for motion and become a static emulation of the stage, so the immediate requirement was stage-trained writers, directors, and above all actors. The crucial decision was made: members of the small Pathé list of contract players would walk the plank if they were without stage experience. That would not affect William Boyd, Phyllis Haver, or Eddie Quillan, who, however shakily, all held official star rating. Nor would it apply to Bob Armstrong, say, whose credentials included Broadway. The casualties would be a dozen novice boys and girls signed in the preceding year. But then Ted Griffith introduced a logical and humane idea of a talkie screen test for each of the imperiled youngsters. At least they would have a token of chance. Ted Griffith—no relation to the founding father of American film art—would direct test scenes using dialogue from *Paris Bound*. Pathé had purchased Philip Barry's play for Griffith to direct.

Carol memorized a dramatic scene and read opposite a scared young man whose hillbilly inflection was excruciating in its effort toward Eastern society talk. Later she would mercifully forget his name, but hoped he'd found the way back home. She was certain her test was a disaster on every count; nor was she encouraged that Joe Kennedy, not Griffith, would make the final decision on which players—if any—would remain under contract.

While awaiting the verdict, she checked in at Mack Sennett's studio, recently relocated in North Hollywood and gloomy in its telltale austerity. She rejoined some of the old gang for her valedictory two-reeler, a domestic charade called *Matchmaking Mamas*. It was a sentimental occasion, not just for Carol but for the loyalists of Mack's company, because silent two-reelers were near to being an extinct species.

The art of silent screen comedy, with its rich endowment of pantomime, had reached its apogee many years earlier. It declined throughout the twenties, becoming mere commodity support for feature films with conventional story lines. The isolated high achievement of Chaplin and Keaton, of Harold Lloyd to a lesser degree and of Harry Langdon in his Frank Capra pictures, gave the genre a false appearance of continued vigor. But the tradition was dying hard and slowly. Mack Sennett in particular had stretched his early reputation to its latter-day limit. If the advent of talking pictures had been denied, his eclipse would have been no less inevitable. Even his best comedy shorts were echoes.

The talkies would come, and Mack Sennett would roll with the punch. Tying in with Paramount, he would briefly reinhale the scent of glory with a succession of two-reelers that would deliver Bing Crosby and W. C. Fields to Paramount features as established performers of the talkie screen. But two-reelers were living on borrowed time even as talkies, and his attempt at directing a feature-length talkie farce (Moran and Mack in *Hypnotized*) would be a rank embarrassment, probably because his heart wasn't in it.

He was a man of the silents. And as the ogre of sound hovered over his motley kingdom, Mack Sennett was a tragic figure. His legacy would illuminate the ongoing careers of talents he'd nourished—Carol Lombard's among them. In 1929 she could not have fathomed the extent of her fame to come, or understood that in no small part it would be due to having once been one of Mack's girls.

Just for the talking present, the training had a positive result for Carol. Confronted with speaking responsibilities, most of the starlets had been immobilized by fear during their Pathé tests. Carol, at least, had kept moving. A Joseph Kennedy memo indicated that two young actresses had shown to particular advantage in screen tests conducted with sound. They were Diane Ellis, a honey-blond ingenue whose only picture had been a silent *Leatherneck* with William Boyd, and Carol Lombard. The prognosis was that the Lombard girl, with an ordinary but pleasant speaking voice, seemed equipped for leading roles without additional grooming.

Mr. and Mrs. William Powell oblige the cameramen, moments after June wedding in 1931.

Visiting Powell at Warner Brothers shortly after her divorce from him in 1933, Carole incites rumors of reconciliation; but don't say the picture isn't posed.

Carole and Russ Columbo as their romance moves into the serious stage, five months before the crooner's tragic, accidental death in September of 1934.

In 1935 she was an agreeable visual adornment for anybody's tennis court, and Carole was one of the filmland's best competitors.

Paramount's master couturier Travis Banton admires Carole in one of the gowns he has fashioned for her 1936 comedy, The Princess Comes Across. The studio fitter is Mary O'Brien.

The great romance begins: Carole and Clark Gable at the Romeo and Juliet premiere at the Carthay Circle (Beverly Hills) in 1936.

✳ IV ✳

Talkie Starlet

IT WAS a problem that would seldom confront a plain girl. It dated to her premature "development" as a student at Virgil Junior High. It caused her annoyance at Fox before the auto accident turned her first career into a false start, and it caused her friendly but awkward embarrassment amid the camaraderie of the Sennett scene. At Pathé it was getting entirely out of hand.

It was Carol Lombard's running battle with those fabled warriors, Roman Hands and Itchy Fingers. She was a mauled virgin—a fanny pinched raw, and bosoms squeezed in crass overtures. Still without a serious romantic involvement, she was coming into her most luminous beauty, still in control of the situation. But she regretted that there was, in any event, a situation. Boys and old men were on the make and she wanted to discourage them at the quarter turn, not in the homestretch.

She got an idea.

Carol had heard the familiar Mae Murray stories. At the peak of her fame in silent pictures, Mae Murray was notorious for getting her way by cussing her antagonists. Men do not like to be cussed at, Carol reasoned, or to hear a woman indulge in blasphemy and profanity. It put them off. But putting them off was precisely what she sought to accomplish.

She was not above being friendly with the boys. She had been a good girl without being a prude. The chums of her school days who were still knit together loosely as a "set" had not thought her in-hibited. Betimes she'd smooch amiably, and participate in the rather innocent petting parties that were a ritual of coming of age. But generosity was a thing to be bestowed upon people you liked or, at the very least, upon the people you knew. And now, as she groped for a professional footing in the movie-making arena, strangers were accosting, assaulting, and propositioning her—not always in that very order.

She decided to do something about it. First she sought the guidance of her brothers.

Fred Peters, many years later, would remember the way it got started:

"We were at home, both Stuart and I, and Carole came in all up-set—from the studio where she was working, I suppose. Without beating around the bush, she said she wanted us to teach her all the dirty words we knew—when to say them, and what they meant. Now that certainly wasn't anything either Stuart or I wanted to do. We weren't angels, of course. We *knew* all the vile words and I'm sure we used them ourselves often enough, maybe too often—but in our own way, and I hope discreetly. We didn't use dirty talk around Carole. For one thing, Mother wouldn't tolerate it.

"But Sis wouldn't let us off the hook. She'd hit on the idea of discouraging her would-be seducers by swearing at them, and the amazing thing was that she really didn't know very many dirty words—anyway, she didn't know what they meant. So we more or less said all right, you asked for it, and started at the beginning. Just getting started was the only embarrassing part. Soon it became a little game, and we all relaxed and enjoyed it. I remember that Stuart especially couldn't stop laughing.

"Well, Mother didn't like the idea at first, but then she also began to see the humor in it. And I suppose we gave Carole as good a concentrated lesson in sex education as a girl could have. She memorized all the terms and our definitions like she was studying for a test. And from then on, if some guy made a pass at her or tried to, he'd hear such talk as he just wouldn't expect to come from such a beautiful girl, who was also a nice girl in every way.

"Carole picked out the words and phrases she wanted to use as her weapons. I know she didn't use all of the information we gave her. Her language never became as blue as some people said, and she was always proper—she never forgot herself. Some words women throw around today—well, Carole would simply never use them. But everything was different then, and a girl could get herself into a lot of trouble just by talking dirty. But she had the style to carry it off."

The way she talked was destined to enhance Carole Lombard's personality, not restrict it. For immediate purposes, the orientation from her brothers accomplished its mission. She learned every vulgarism for the copulative equipment of both sexes, the intricately obscene terminology of the act itself, all the catchwords that were spinoffs of the perversions. She gave free rein to her newfound knowledge and stopped her would-be attackers cold. Word of her brazen verbal accomplishments got around the Pathé studio and gave her the aura of personality. Then the word spread around town generally, and that didn't hurt either.

The legendary blue talk of Carole Lombard began as self-defense, but in time it became anything but a shield. She refined it as a technique to advance herself professionally and to attain personal objectives, particularly the grail of friendship. She soon discovered that after the first shock had penetrated a man not accustomed to a woman's swearing, the man was likely to become relaxed and more accessible. By adroit use of language, she could accomplish an informal atmosphere that protocol might never yield.

Her real language was honesty, and men as a rule would reply to her in kind. So cussing was a strategic breakthrough: she found that she enjoyed talking to men at their own level, and *on* the level. Over the years she spread her sailor's talk with calculation, by degrees for contrasting audiences. The catchphrases she employed with the men she knew well were not the same ones bestowed upon comparative strangers. It was no different in her dealings with women. An uninhibited gabber among the girls who were her intimates, she altered the texture of her conversation with women she knew less well, or whose own reticence she respected. Only in the early stages was this a studied effort; with the security of her fame, it became instinctive. And as Fred Peters said, she never forgot herself.

Her flair for the raunchy squelch would work into the folklore of Hollywood. If she detected someone's devious pressuring or otherwise rejected a suggestion or idea that galled her, "Kiss my ass" was her most customary putdown—a sarcastic invitation to do something that doubtless played on men's minds, but was clearly forbidden by the ironic terms of her special style.

* * *

She marked time, awaiting assignment to her first talking picture by reporting to the studio regularly for publicity photo sessions, elocution lessons (in 1929 a movie company could not do without a vocal coach), and other devices and ruses of a starlet's promotion. She had a pragmatic approach to personal exploitation, and if the publicity department didn't find her background sufficiently colorful, she'd say, "Well, let's dream something up that'll sound good." Don McElwaine, the young publicity director at Pathé, became perhaps her best friend there, but she was critical of his work and thought she could tell him a thing or two about building someone into a star. She'd already known McElwaine for years: he was one of the Indiana natives in a closely knit colony within the colony, and had been at Fox in the Buck Jones entourage when Carol made the early westerns. McElwaine was himself a facile writer but too pedantic, she thought. She provided his department with a handwritten autobiography and he complained of her wholesale misspelling—for spelling was not among the Lombard faculties—and she told him his press releases were well spelled and dull. If people were going to spend their time reading about movie stars, she said, they should be entertained. Whether or not the facts were right, she said it wasn't all shit if it was interesting.

McElwaine's official studio biography of Carol Lombard was interesting enough and it stayed close to truth. The only dubious reference was to a weak heart that had been chronic during the Jane Peters childhood. For the most part, the campaign worked. Tidbit items about Carol Lombard began working into the newspapers as filler. A publicity photo flashing her open laughter convincingly turned up as a toothpaste ad in which Carol Lombard was identified as a Pathé player soon to be seen in *The Flying Fool.* That had been her own idea. There was no thought of her being put into *The Flying Fool,* a William Boyd picture nearing completion as an all-talkie. But she had reasoned that it would be a way of getting one of the studio's upcoming titles before the public, as well as one of its players, with no real harm done. Such innocuous deceit would become customary in promoting a starlet who was without assignment after all. When asked if such a commercial display could really help in selling a picture, Carol countered with "Well, does it sell Ipana?"

Her photographs circulated with effect. M-G-M's Irving Thalberg asked about the status of her Pathé contract. Winfield Sheehan, meeting Carol at a party, intimated that he wouldn't mind having her at Fox again. She became an entity in the minds of people who counted in movie congress, and such a person was Cecil B. DeMille: he notified Joseph Kennedy that he was interested in possibly making good use of her in a future picture.

Finally they put her to work again. *High Voltage* was what the title suggested: studio pulp (a "programmer") with emphasis on the action. The ubiquitous William Boyd was the star, but Carol would have featured billing and was, in fact, the leading lady. Diane Ellis, the other silent ingenue who survived the studio's talkie purge, had an equally large part, but Carol would share the ultimate clinch with Bill Boyd. Also in the cast was the aging Owen Moore, a long-time reliable leading man of the silents. One of three Irish immigrant brothers who enjoyed remarkably durable popularity in the filmland society, Owen Moore was probably best known as Mary Pickford's first husband—the one she had scandalously divorced to marry Douglas Fairbanks. In the time frame of Hollywood that was ancient history, but Owen Moore was not so far gone that he could not appreciate the endowments of the Lombard girl not half his age; and he was one of the optimistic seducers cut short by her purple invective.

Another properly squelched roué was Howard Higgin, the director, whose reputation was as anonymous as the films he made. *High Voltage* was one of those pictures that merely came and went, causing neither joy nor consternation. Its positive claim was the certification of Carol Lombard for talking pictures. It was a hundred-percent talkie, the only kind being made in mid-1929 Hollywood other than the Garbo vehicles, although most pictures—and all of the Pathé product—were still being concurrently shot in silent versions to appease exhibitors who could not afford to wire their theaters for sound.

During the five-week production schedule of *High Voltage*, Joseph Kennedy agreed to subcontract Carol Lombard to Cecil B. DeMille. His reputation then in decline, DeMille had quit Paramount for a one-shot autonomous producing deal with Pathé. After an extended deliberation, the king of spectacle was ready to venture into the troubled mystery of the talkies, which already claimed so many of his illustrious contemporaries as casualties.

Carol reported to DeMille on location. His first talkie was an action adventure shot mostly in the Hollywood hills. ("A tree is a tree: shoot it in Griffith Park.") If it would be remembered as anything other than a flop, it certainly wasn't dynamite, although that was its title. In casting *Dynamite* DeMille obeyed the current practice of bringing in new players from the stage—the brawny Charles Bickford, who would succeed in films, and blond Kay Johnson, who wouldn't. They carried the leads, but two veterans from DeMille's own contract list were also assigned—Conrad Nagel and Julia Faye—and there was an obligatory juvenile romantic interest as well. Carol's function was to supply half of it, and opposite her was a statuesque youth she'd been seeing around town for years—Joel McCrea from Hollywood High, rampant-haired and handsome, but still very green.

Carol worked in *Dynamite* for several days, then was fired. DeMille was vexed that she didn't know her lines. But he was nowhere in sight when Carol was given the word by Mitchell Leisen, DeMille's assistant director, costumer, and sometime troubleshooter. Carol was devastated. John Cromwell who, like Leisen, would be a Lombard director during her later "big" period, would recall that the first time he saw her, she was gushing tears for having lost the part in *Dynamite*. (Cromwell was then married to Kay Johnson, the leading lady, and was a visitor on the set.) The firing was never publicized. The only scene she had shot was scrapped, and she was replaced by a girl named Muriel McCormack, who has not been heard from since.

Years later Mitchell Leisen would say that Carol was dismissed not because she was thought inadequate, but for not taking her part seriously, which rankled DeMille. He had told her, "This isn't a Keystone comedy," but Carol had found the dialogue pretty silly nonetheless.

Leisen said there had been a detectable vagueness about her that seemed contrary to the forthright, eagerly working Carole Lombard he would later know and direct. It is the only case of her having been remiss in application, but there may have been a logical reason. At about the same time, Carol's private life was a serialized, clandestine drama that might have been called Her First Affair. She had fallen in love, but it wasn't something she could talk about because, for reasons of his own, her paramour wanted secrecy in most if not all of his dealings.

It was not a triangular situation: the man was not married. But while he was normally visible in his own office, he seldom appeared in public socially and was known to prefer company at home—and home was one of those mystery-draped Hollywood castles, compartmentalized for business, recreation, and private rendezvous. When he entered into his brief liaison with Carol Lombard, he was still linked romantically (for the popular consumption) with a reigning beauty of the late silent period named Billie Dove.

The affair obeyed a strict regimentation. The lovers were never seen together. Carol was driven to the trysting place in a chauffeured limousine that received her at appointed times and places. Only her most intimate friends were taken into confidence. Even the nature of their initial acquaintance was shadowy; he had seen her photograph and, being interested, had requested her presence in his chambers.

Carol's knowing friends held the guilt of betrayal at bay by never mentioning the man's name; but they could put together a formidable dossier from descriptions. He was tall, dark, spectacularly handsome, and still very young. And rich—no, he was very rich indeed, the heir to an enormous industrial fortune. Yet he did not conform to the prototype of a playboy. He was not the tuxedoed bon vivant but rather the vigorous outdoorsman in a lumberjack shirt . . . or a pilot's uniform. He loved to fly, was famous already for his aviation exploits, but with greater fame still in his future; and for a number of years he had been making "the flying picture to end all flying pictures." Yes, movies were his passionate hobby. He had produced an immensely successful silent comedy and had begun his flying picture before the coming of sound caused him to scrap everything he'd shot except the aerial footage. The pretty blonde who was the spectacle's erotic diversion would have to be replaced because she was Swedish and less accomplished with the English language even than Garbo. He reportedly "interviewed" scores of predominantly unknown actresses in the search for a very sexy baby to replace the unfortunate Greta Nissen, and perhaps Carol Lombard was given consideration. Anyway, the girl he'd eventually choose would become maximally famous and would initiate one kind of beauty revolution, as one of his later "discoveries" would spearhead another. Rarely in the public eye, he was often in the public mind, but secrecy was his art. Once, years later, it would fail him: surprised in bed by the sudden appearance of his lover's cuckolded husband, he would absorb a brutal physical beating that would be followed by slow and difficult recovery in the hospital. His assailant, formerly a collegiate athlete of national celebrity, would never be apprehended because another explanation would be fabricated for our man's physical status. Carol's first big crush dwelled in the vastness between legend and myth, largely shaping his own fable.

The affair consumed a period of a few months; and was terminated, apparently, because the man had lost interest, and Carol admitted privately that she hoped to get him back. But disappointment dazed her only temporarily. Long before the involvement, she had resolved never to lose her equilibrium over a man; and even as she confessed to being in love, she was not despondent. It was not evident that she carried a torch for any appreciable period. Her resilient good humor was always her salvation.

If Carol hadn't been able to take a DeMille project seriously, she could hardly be expected to develop an abiding interest in the assignment that awaited her upon the return to Pathé. *Big News* was no big news—another sleazy program picture originally planned as a silent. Still, it marked another increment of progress in the Lombard buildup. No one was starred, but she would be co-featured with Robert Armstrong, and they would lead off the billing below the title. The director was Gregory LaCava, a sophisticated fellow of engaging disposition, not yet in possession of the considerable reputation he would later enjoy, when among other good credits would be found one of the great Lombard vehicles, *My Man Godfrey*.

Carol had a wisecracking friendship with Gregory LaCava from the start, and they reached an early point of agreement on the hopelessness of *Big News*. Seven years later, during the *Godfrey* production, there was more than a mild hint of her admiration for LaCava when she recalled the first conference over their Pathé picture.

"Greg said, 'Well, I've read the script and I'll tell you what I think. I think it stinks. And when something stinks you try to do anything that will distract people from the smell. So let's be very distracting about this. If we rattle the dialogue real fast people won't be able to reflect on how rotten it is. And even if it isn't very exciting, you can pitch your voices a little higher and they'll *think* it's exciting. I guess the main thing is to be busy all the time, just keep moving. Stand still and the picture might die.' And you know what? It turned into a game, and I think we won it . . . because Bob Armstrong had a good knack for fast talk, and I rose to the bait to keep up with him. I don't think anyone said it was a shitty picture."

But it came and went. *Big News* was small sausage, acknowledged only by a few reviewers who were mostly noncommittal. The players and the direction were praised but only in perfunctory terms. The box office was neutralized. There was nothing to indicate that Carol Lombard had made a public impression or acquired the beginning of a personal following. No longer a new face, she was an accepted piece of the Pathé furniture. In any event, the studio officials were sufficiently pleased with the Armstrong-Lombard teaming to give it another go.

Carol's next assignment was her first of many molls, and Armstrong was *The Racketeer*. It held more initial promise than *Big News,* but the equivalent to zany inspiration such as a Gregory LaCava might provide did not come from Howard Higgin. But as usual, there was fun to be had, and Carol enjoyed the company of a supporting veteran player who had some community fame as an acerbic wit. She was Hedda Hopper, not yet a columnist herself, but ironically then a very good friend to Louella Parsons; and she coaxed Louella to say some nice things in her column about Carol Lombard.

Again recalling her Pathé days, Carole would have only two things to remember about *The Racketeer,* other than its not being very good. One, the stock market crashed while it was in production, and not yet having an understanding of economics, she couldn't understand why so many people had become so easily upset.

The other thing she remembered was that *The Racketeer* was her last picture for Pathé. Her career had started to move right along, without reason for herself or her employers to be discouraged over her prospects. She had complained, but nicely, about the humdrum level of her pictures and her parts, and there had even been a nice promise for the future. She had been told she could play Ann Harding's sister in *Holiday* when they got around to filming it. Ann Harding, one of the better young actresses snatched from Broadway, was rated the best of the Pathé stars (almost by default) on the strength of an excellent break-in. She had sparkled in Philip Barry's *Paris Bound* with Ted Griffith directing—the vehicle for Carol's Pathé test; and *Holiday* was considered an even better Barry play. Carol agreed to darken her hair, for contrast to Ann Harding's blond bun. Then very suddenly, she was notified that the first year of her contract had been completed, and her option was not being renewed.

She was included in a wholesale lopping—Diane Ellis and two distinctly minor starlets were also cut adrift. But something was fishy and she had no idea what. Asking around and getting no fair explanation, she stormed into Joseph P. Kennedy's office, shouting down a protesting secretary.

Kennedy was gracious enough, and made a great show of sympathy. He explained that the company was really in awful trouble financially, and that if the stock market had held steady, her contract could surely have been renewed. They had no choice other than to cut back personnel in all departments, not just the performing end. They were going to make fewer pictures, but possibly it was simply the end of the line for Pathé. (Indeed, a capitulative merger with RKO was already under way, and the Pathé rooster soon would vanish as a logo for feature films.)

Everything Joe Kennedy said seemed to make sense, but one thing puzzled Carol. "Why *me?*" She asked the question and Kennedy had no ready answer. Or why Diane Ellis, an actress of real promise? They had trimmed the roster without getting rid of the deadwood, and it didn't figure.

But Diane Ellis had heard another story entirely, and hers came to be accepted as gospel. Shortly after Ann Harding's arrival, Pathé began negotiations with another young stage actress, also a blonde and quite alluring, although very different. She was Constance Bennett—Richard's willful daughter, Joan's older sister, and a girl who brought her lawyers when she wanted to talk contract. Possibly she also had a great press agent. The word was that this girl couldn't possibly miss. To get her name on a contract was going to be an expensive proposition because every studio was after her, but it would be worth it: she could be the big box-office miracle that could save the company. Well and good, until Constance Bennett or someone in her entourage screened the inventory of Pathé players and found a couple of girls whose resemblance to Connie was emphatic enough to be inadmissible. The contract terms offered by Pathé were satisfactory . . . but those two girls would have to go.

So Carol and Diane, who had become best friends at the studio, went. The two other girls were throw-ins to camouflage the motive. Carol did not deal in euphemisms, so when an unbelieving co-worker said, "Carol, say it isn't true that your option's not being picked up," she replied, "Okay, it isn't true. But it's goddamned true that I've been fired."

To commemorate their severance, Carol and Diane opted for a steak dinner at the Brown Derby and invited the entire Pathé wardrobe crew to be their guests. They chased disappointment with loud laughter, and were asked to leave as soon as the check was paid. Outside the restaurant Carol shouted "Why, that bloody son of a bitch!" and someone asked if she meant the Brown Derby manager or Constance Bennett.

"No, I mean Joe Kennedy. He didn't even have the balls to tell me the truth."

It was as Eddie Cline said more than a year earlier, Carol had become very employable. She didn't have to knock on Mack Sennett's door, although he was making talkie shorts and certainly would have taken her in. She could get work. The studios wouldn't rush her with contract offers, but they would consider her for a specific role here and there. She was no longer an unknown commodity, but an "established" player who could free-lance around, and not expect a contract offer until a studio decided it wanted to "build" her; then she became an investment, and exclusively was more or less mandatory. There was no real security in free lancing unless you were a really powerful star, but she welcomed a chance to shop around the studios.

She counted on M-G-M still being interested, but she was unsuccessful in obtaining an interview with Irving Thalberg, and was advised to steer clear of Louis B. Mayer. She had an amiable meeting with Harry Rapf, whose job was to oversee the lower-grade M-G-M pictures, and he said he would have something for her in a little while. He did get back in touch, but Carol had gone to work at Fox.

Winnie Sheehan still was on the job as chief of Fox production and a few of the young faces from Carol's earlier tenure there were still aboard—George O'Brien, Edmund Lowe, Victor McLaglen, and Janet Gaynor, now a very big star. But she barely recognized the interior of the Western Avenue studio, now a waffle of sound stages.

She was in a western once more, but not at the Buck Jones level. *The Arizona Kid* was Grade A all the way, with the distinction of having as its star the player only recently honored as the year's best actor. Warner Baxter was only the second actor to obtain the Academy Award. Its emblematic statuette was years away from being Oscar, and the award itself had not acquired world fame, although it held importance in the community. Baxter had been cited for having created for the screen the character of the Cisco Kid, from the O. Henry legacy, in the first talking superwestern, *In Old Arizona*. It was the prodigious hit that prompted Fox to abandon silent movie making altogether, and within fifteen months every major company had followed suit. After a decade in pictures but with no real distinction other than having been *The Great Gatsby* in its excellent silent version, Warner Baxter was a late-blooming important star. Now the thing to do was a Cisco Kid sequel, and that's what *The Arizona Kid* was.

In the hierarchy of Hollywood, a few leading roles for Pathé did not necessarily qualify a girl for leading roles at Fox. Baxter's leading lady was Mona Maris. Carol's was the main supporting role, a beautiful villain, but she accepted the part with undiluted zeal: the girl was just plain mean, inside and out.

True to the fate of most sequels, *The Arizona Kid* did not emulate the fame or commercial success of the first picture, although it was a superior effort on all counts because of the rapid refinement of sound recording technique. Of particular gratification to Carol was the opportunity to show off her horsemanship. She tried without success to get Buck Jones to watch the filming.

Alfred Santell, her director at Fox, came to adore Carol Lombard. He also suspected that her dramatic potential had not been investigated. No less charmed was S. N. Behrman, the sociable playwright who was then doing a stretch as a Fox screenwriter. Later Behrman would say Carole Lombard was the most refreshing girl he encountered during his years in the film colony. Since Behrman in 1930 was preparing a film script from Jack London's *The Sea Wolf* for Santell to direct, Santell and Behrman lobbied with Sheehan to have Carol cast in the only female role, a grim and unglamorous one. Sheehan preferred to delay a decision on Carol—on both *The Sea Wolf* and a term contract that had been lightly discussed—until *The Arizona Kid* was in the can. But by that time Carol had accepted an assignment at Paramount, where an eventual contract was also a possibility; and her "second" Fox career turned out a one-shot adventure.

At Paramount she joined the cast of *Safety in Numbers,* a juvenile romance with echoes of the Jazz Age, catering primarily to the teen-aged trade. She was one of several pretty faces clustered in support of Charles (Buddy) Rogers, billed at the crest of his brief popularity as "America's boyfriend." The nominal female lead was Josephine Dunn, and one of the other girls was a blond Lombard look-alike, Virginia Bruce. But it would be Carol's distinction to "steal" the inane but decidedly popular picture, not by any great show of skill but because the dialogue was in her favor. She also could still be regarded as a newcomer by patrons addicted to Paramount's run of mindless but breezy romps.

It was the first occasion of her appearance in a picture arousing the attention of the general moviegoing audience. Some of Buddy Rogers's fans even wrote letters protesting that he didn't "get" the likable Lombard girl. Victor Schertzinger, the *Safety in Numbers* director, would remark some years later that he had not detected evidence of talent but had been impressed by Carol's good-sport personality, which came through on film. Schertzinger said he may have thrown the picture out of balance by giving her too many close-ups, but then, she was such a pretty girl. Schertzinger, a movie director with an unlikely past (a concert violinist and sometime composer of operettas), also noted Carol's dancing ability and recommended her employment in the studio's musical exercises.

B. P. Schulberg, who pulled most of the strings at Paramount's opulent studio on Marathon Avenue in Hollywood, had more ingenues on his payroll than could be accommodated, and resisted Carol's own pitch for a contract. But she found the support she needed. Something of the pragmatist was taking hold within her. She had instinct for winning and wooing people of influence, particularly the men she addressed on their own terms. Very quickly her good buddies included Sam Jaffe, Schulberg's general manager, and department heads Fred Datig (casting) and Arch Reeve (publicity), as well as Schulberg's young new assistant, David Selznick—still something of an unknown quantity. Each descended upon Schulberg in turn, warning that if the studio didn't lay exclusive claim to her services, another company would.

She got the contract. Seven years with options, starting at $375 weekly, with substantial increases upon option renewals. By gambling on Paramount, she made what would have been just about any bright girl's choice in the spring of 1930.

As the pulsating twenties ended, Paramount Pictures—for want of better description—was indeed paramount, and the centerpiece exhibit of movie history. In the time frame of that history it was an ancient company, all of eighteen years old and proud of its origins.

In 1912 a moderately prosperous furrier named Adolph Zukor imported four reels of Sarah Bernhardt impersonating Queen Elizabeth, and marketed the film successfully. Later in that same year, he formed the Famous Players company for production of story films, and placed under contract a score of variably famous stage performers. In their number was the ringleted Mary Pickford—not the first "star" of the movies, but the prototype Great Star.

Movies were a game for a horde of speculators to play, and one such was a small-time showman and ex-bandleader, Jesse Lasky— perhaps the most idealistic and visionary among all the true pioneers. Lasky had important help: his brother-in-law Samuel Goldfish (later Goldwyn) had great business acumen; and their director, Cecil DeMille, had theatrical background and notions of innovative movie making. Pictures had been shot in southern California as early as 1908, but in 1913 the Lasky Feature Film Company built the first studio in Hollywood, on a site now represented by the fabled intersection of Hollywood and Vine. There DeMille shot *The Squaw Man* as Hollywood's first feature-length film and its success enabled Lasky to challenge Zukor's solidarity. Soon Hollywood flourished as a factory town whose sustenance was the new motion picture industry. Zukor came, too.

In 1916 Zukor and Lasky settled the supremacy issue by merging into an enormous operation that outstripped any other. Famous Players-Lasky's distribution subsidiary was Paramount, with its imposing logo of a cloud-adorned peak; and according to the advertising legend, you could trust a Paramount picture. Because the public trusted, antecedent competitors withered and died—Biograph, Mutual, Select, Kalem, Triangle, and finally Vitagraph. Then Fox and First National emerged mighty, and United Artists gave independent producers a distribution outlet. While Universal grew strong on a smaller scale, Warner Brothers started modestly, then overextended themselves, and finally talked their way into the hierarchy. Pathé, Metro, and Goldwyn became substantial operations. But through every shifting of industrial sands, there was that mountain, towering above the rest. Even after Louis B. Mayer orchestrated the M-G-M merger, Paramount's sovereignty was only mildly challenged. M-G-M acquired an aristocratic demeanor, courting every connotation of prestige. But Paramount, while characteristically less pretentious, had the durable compensation of power itself. Its advantage was familiarity based on tradition; and tradition itself was an intangible asset. Certain super-scale M-G-M pictures might captivate the public fancy above any other, and that studio's genius for marketing its stars was a drastic refinement of an old practice. But *every* Paramount picture rated as some kind of event for the workaday people who simply went to the picture show.

When Carol Lombard made her first picture for Paramount, the company was committed to producing sixty-four features annually, more than any competitor. And Paramount did not have a second-line product akin to the programmers that were a primary issue of other studios. No quickie westerns were milled by Paramount, no serials either, and short subjects were de-emphasized. It was first class all the way. Most companies maintained small, limited-purpose studios in New York where the corporate offices were, but production of features had become strictly a Hollywood activity—except with Paramount, which operated a vast, full-service studio on Long Island, equipped with new sound stages, and responsible for exactly half of the annual production quotient.

The roster of Paramount stars and featured players underscored a rapid drastic overhauling for the talkies. The company had been the vortex of the silent firmament, the longtime home base for Gloria Swanson and then Pola Negri. It had been the heroic scene of Thomas Meighan, Rod La Rocque, and Richard Dix, and memories lingered there of titans taken by early death—Wallace Reid and Rudolph Valentino. But now the assembly included only one player who had been a silent star of consequence—Clara Bow, the naughty-baby It Girl, adequate of voice and still a box-office bell ringer although challenged in her own specialty line by the upstart Joan Crawford of M-G-M.

The talkie transition had raised the prospects of three actors from the late silent period who profited from their earlier stage experience: Clive Brook, a dour English leading man; William Powell, an urbane villain come to talkie fame as the detective Philo Vance; and burly, mature George Bancroft. The youthful trio of Gary Cooper, Richard Arlen, and Buddy Rogers also survived the switch to sound with promise fortified, as had ingenues Fay Wray and Jean Arthur.

But most of the Paramount players in whom the stuff of real stardom was acknowledged came from the New York stage or the international music halls. The man of the moment was Maurice Chevalier. Everyone's notion of the perfect Frenchman, he was modestly advertised as the most charming man in the world. The new high priestess of drama was Ruth Chatterton, who had made the first vivid impression among luminaries defecting from the stage. Younger players with good legitimate experience but less renown were starting smartly: Claudette Colbert, Nancy Carroll, and Kay Francis; Fredric March, the screen's best new all-purpose leading man; the comically engaging Jack Oakie; and musical comediennes styled high (Jeanette MacDonald of the champagne soprano) and low (the pudgy boop-a-dooper, Helen Kane). As surrealistic adornment for a crazy-quilt personality montage, there were four zany brothers named Marx.

Paramount also was the first company to assemble a stock company of supporting character players, who would become the atmospheric common denominator for all the studio's output. Imparting a comforting familiarity, they were the grassroots soul of Paramount —Charlie Ruggles, Zasu Pitts, Eugene Pallette, Skeets Gallagher, Leon Errol, Emma Dunn, Stuart Erwin, Paul Lukas, and a breezy child actress named Mitzi Green.

Picture making at Paramount was seldom constrained by the dogma that afflicted competitor products. B. P. Schulberg supervised Hollywood's least regimented production style. In contrast to M-G-M, where pictures had a sameness that reflected producer dominance and the reduction of director to functionary status, Paramount gave a director autonomy for the essential shaping of his film. If the director had the extraordinary faculties of a Josef von Sternberg or an Ernst Lubitsch, extraordinary results could be expected.

Paramount actors worked for salaries no higher than those of other strong studios, but they were accorded considerably more respect. A shooting schedule measured into months rather than weeks. Most players came to expect a few days of liberty during the production cycle, and a modest vacation between picture assignments. But even the workaday picture-making atmosphere was airy and exuberant. There was a level of camaraderie among artists and artisans that Carol had not experienced elsewhere. Paramount among all entrenched companies was the fun studio—the result, some said, of Jesse Lasky's congeniality.

Such an atmosphere was most conducive to facets of the Lombard personality that had been aching for expression. She had literally grown up in the movie business without having really been a part of it, except fitfully and only as a pawn; but during that time she had come to understand movies both as entertainment and commerce. She was intrigued. The fascination gave illumination to her intelligence and common sense: she could articulate her often refreshing views on the medium. Others at Paramount could appreciate her brightness—which was not so unusual—but her keenness for the inner workings of movie making was indeed extraordinary. At that time Paramount was very much a man's studio, and her strong new friendships were with men very unlike those of her previous experience. They were sophisticated, intellectually alert, worldly, and decidedly continental—the kind of men whose awareness of a girl's braininess would not obscure her beauty. They were attracted to her.

Almost from the time of her arrival at the studio, to the end of her Paramount service and beyond, Ernst Lubitsch was perhaps Carol's best friend among all the Hollywood males. He already had some small acquaintance with her mother because he was into the numerology fad and shared Mrs. Thomas Platt with Bess Peters. Lubitsch was the German cinema's foremost gift to Hollywood, and was also a great ladies' man. Lubitsch considered physical lovemaking the supreme human experience—a belief that Carol was just beginning to come around to. Lubitsch rather typified the continental influence on Carol's personality and career; but there were others, too.

The enigmatic Harry D'Arrast, once Chaplin's most valued assistant and then one of the more stylish directors of silent pictures, came to Paramount to try his hand with a talkie. The Argentina-born, Paris-trained, London-groomed D'Arrast was captivated by Carol; and she, briefly, by him. Another of her new studio acquaintances was the Armenian Rouben Mamoulian, a much-heralded new movie director after well-advertised innovative work on New York's dramatic and operatic stages. Carol did not become immediately chummy with Dietrich's Svengali; but Josef von Sternberg, too, was made aware of her.

To become better acquainted with a girl of good looks and agreeability, the custom of the sophisticated middle-European male was to take her to bed. The experienced continental knows when a girl says no and means yes, but they adored Carol because she wasn't a tease. Carol responded to the gentlemanly and quite European art of seduction. She thought then (and would say later, when her big-star autonomy afforded an easier frankness) that the sex act could be the most glorifying or degrading thing a girl could experience, depending on its *aura*—before, during, and after. (The *Collier's* editors fearfully deleted some great Lombard observations in a Kyle Crichton interview story that was published after she had reached her peak.) She loathed sexual hypocrisy and mock virginity, both of which were in glaring evidence at Paramount when she joined it; and she rejected totally the notion that sex was a "need" of men more than of women. She did not consider herself promiscuous, because her affairs were always restricted to men she genuinely *liked,* and never involved conventionally married men.

Not all of Carol's new table-talk conquests were directors. Two instant chums were writers as glib and disarming as their scripts— Preston Sturges and Donald Ogden Stewart. Both were well-born Americans who had acquired polish through European education and travel. Sturges, then a bachelor fresh in from Broadway, gave Carol a romantic rush, only to have their brief affair terminated abruptly when she learned that he was making studio table-talk of his conquest. Sturges said she taught him a lesson, and soon they were good friends again but nothing more than that. Donald Ogden Stewart was a candidate for ardor but he was married, ostensibly happily (Bea Stewart became a good friend in the Lombard "set"), and Carol set him straight. But Stewart may have been the first of many writers to put trust in the Lombard instincts about a script. He was concocting an original screenplay, by definition a dialogue comedy, for Harry D'Arrast to direct. If Carol responded favorably to a line of dialogue, that line stayed in the script.

Carol was now dating and "being seen" with a number of young men, all of whom were discouraged from serious designs. Some of her more public romances were hardly that at all, but were

fabrications of the studio publicity department, usually for the purpose of promoting not one but two Paramount chattels for the
public awareness. Gossip columns linked her with a briefly promising Paramount juvenile lead named Stanley Smith before, in fact,
they had even met. But she did not object to such canny misrep-
resentation, seeing it as an essential part of a game she was learning
to enjoy. She would give Arch Reeve and then Tom Baily—Reeve's
successor as chief studio publicist—plenty of phosphate fodder. The
revelation that Carol Lombard preferred sleeping naked created a
mild sensation and appeared to enhance her popularity with coworkers. She also provided the studio with the very true information that she did not wear a brassiere ("Maybe I would, if I had
anything worth covering up."), but the publicity department rejected that tidbit because of the studio's advertising arrangements
with manufacturers of ladies' undergarments.

The shadowy liaison with the very rich young producer was not
so far in the past that Carol was not wary of again losing her
balance; but during her early enrollment at Paramount she may
have had a love affair which never became general knowledge
within the community. Not even those few Lombard intimates who
had known of her earlier clandestine romance seemed even to
suspect the intrigue with Horace Liveright. He was a man twice
her age, a brilliant publisher during the twenties, but a victim of
the Crash. In Hollywood he was an almost penniless refugee, briefly
on the Paramount payroll as a story researcher—mainly exploring
the movie possibilities of books published by his own bankrupted
firm.

Liveright's dalliance with Carole came to light only many years
later when his papers were examined, and Ben Hecht identified
Liveright's unspecified filmland paramour as Carole Lombard.
Hecht also said it was Horace Liveright who introduced Lombard
to Florenz Ziegfeld during one of Flo's visits to Hollywood. It was
reported that Ziegfeld was regaled by Carol's beauty and show-girl
formfulness and petitioned to build her to stardom in a new edition
of his stage Follies. But apparently Hollywood was all she wanted
and not even Horace Liveright could lure her to New York.

His one-year "contract" not renewed by Paramount, Liveright
returned to New York and failed in a comeback try at publishing.
They would have a last meeting when subsequent events sent Carol
to New York, but apparently they never corresponded. Horace

Liveright died at forty-six a few years afterward, and then became the prototype of *The Scoundrel* as portrayed by Noel Coward in a film both written and directed by Ben Hecht and Charles Mac-Arthur—and produced, ironically, for Paramount. (Carole Lombard declined an opportunity to appear with Coward in the film, although they became great friends. She once admitted to having had a serious crush on Noel Coward who could not, however, respond to her physically.)

While Carol was accruing popularity on an intramural basis, there was no certainty on what was to be done with her in the way of subsequent picture assignments. *Safety in Numbers* had been edited and previewed before she was given another job, although she was "announced" for a number of pictures in the routine of perpetual publicity. She was not announced for *Laughter,* although it almost became her next assignment. Instead she joined the cast of *Fast and Loose*—originally called *The Best People,* the name of the Avery Hopwood play on which it was based. Her two writing pals got into a friendly fight over her services, and Preston Sturges won.

Laughter was the Donald Ogden Stewart script she had applauded while it was being written. The leading role—a young woman in love with a free-spirit artist but married to an older man—was one Carol itched to play for all the right reasons, one being that the director would be the engaging Harry D'Arrast. But *Laughter* was envisioned as a major picture and fashioned especially for Nancy Carroll and Fredric March, with Frank Morgan to make his talkie debut as the husband. But Stewart had conceived a secondary female role, brief but amusingly tart, and D'Arrast thought that Carol Lombard would be an inspirational bit of casting. No one seemed to object, and Carol endorsed the idea; but about that same time Preston Sturges was writing a screenplay for *The Best People* and developing a role especially for the girl who so entranced them all in the studio commissary.

Although *Laughter* went into production first, B. P. Schulberg elected to assign Carol to *The Best People* because the part was considerably larger, and because it was being cast without stars; she would be the member with the nearest approximation of establishment as a screen personality. Because *The Best People* experienced delays in getting started, it would have been a simple thing for Carol to have appeared in both pictures, as Frank Morgan ultimately did. Yet she took an active part in getting the second lead in *Laughter* assigned to her friend Diane Ellis, who hadn't worked since they both were shown the exit at Pathé.

Laughter finally emerged a brilliant, witty film, possibly the best early talkie conceived especially for the screen. It was the pinnacle for Nancy Carroll, the often acknowledged first "star" developed by the talkies, but whose subsequent career foundered on a string of bad pictures. It advanced Fredric March, gave Frank Morgan an anchor in films, and offered quite a captivating performance by Diane Ellis, who, according to Harry D'Arrast and others, had a most hopeful future once again. The irony was that *Laughter* was her last picture. Diane Ellis married upon completing it, and while on honeymoon in India she fell victim to an exotic disease and died suddenly. This was one of the events that would later cause Carole Lombard to condemn herself as a jinx because "good people get to know me and then they die." (Her friend John Bowers, unable to keep his footing in talking pictures, was a suicide and a theoretical model for the Norman Main character in the original *A Star Is Born;* and Robert Williams, another Lombard pal, died tragically young after scoring a solid hit for Frank Capra in *Platinum Blonde* opposite Jean Harlow.)

Although *Laughter* would seem to have fallen unjustly into historical neglect, it became a reference point whenever Carole, as the later reigning queen of "screwball" comedy, would trace the origins of the genre. When she was filming *Nothing Sacred* with Fredric March, a reporter remarked that Carole had started the screwball business with *My Man Godfrey* and March intervened with the opinion that Carole's earlier *Twentieth Century* was properly the first such comedy. Carole countered with "Freddie, you idiot: you and Nancy Carroll had the first good screwball comedy with *Laughter* and I had the second one, but it wasn't *Twentieth Century.* Just ask Preston Sturges, who wrote it."

There was some lingering curiosity about *Laughter* that tied in with the legend of Harry D'Arrast, an artist of superb faculties who nevertheless directed only one later film (the excellent *Topaze*). But few would remember *Fast and Loose,* retitled from *The Best People* to catch the spirit of what was the first of many nimble Preston Sturges screenplays. It contained most of the traditional elements of screwball farce. The spoiled rich girl played by Miriam Hopkins would become infected with social consciousness and marry a truck driver, poor but handsome—but not until the foibles of her own class had been thoroughly and delightfully exposed. Not much of Avery Hopwood's original was retained, and Sturges stocked his script with great chunks of pure Lombard as if he possessed secret information about the great comic presence that would only be acknowledged several years later.

Sturges, doomed to disappointment that he could not get Lombard into one of his pictures after he became his own director, denied that he was her prophet. "I liked her, that's all. Everybody did. I wrote a part for her because I always liked to have someone in mind. When she almost walked away with the picture I was taken quite by surprise. I had no idea she could dispense smart-ass remarks with such authority for the screen, although the part was very much *like* her, you understand. But then, I only wrote it. I wasn't around when the picture was being shot. But if *Fast and Loose* had been any kind of hit, she would have gone right to the top a lot earlier than she did."

In point of fact, *Fast and Loose* was one kind of hit. The critics did not conceal their enjoyment. But of all the Paramount pictures produced in 1930 (all of which made money), it returned the smallest profit on its investment and therefore acquired the dubious distinction, not entirely deserved, of a box-office flop. Miriam Hopkins played the lead and she was an accomplished young stage actress but totally unknown to movie audiences, making her first film. The handsome young leading man, from Dartmouth and the stage and also making his screen debut, was Charles Starrett, whose destiny would be pulp westerns—eventually and for a long time as the Durango Kid. Lombard, playing Miriam's playboy brother's mistress, was actually the filmland veteran of the company, although Frank Morgan had been in early silents. *Fast and Loose* was released in the waning days of 1930, when box-office receipts were beginning to show the encroachments of the Depression. The public was also weary of photographed staged plays, and no longer enamored of new faces and voices. So *Fast and Loose* faded, although it had a breezy visualness that matched its dialogue, as directed by the same Fred Newmeyer who had guided Harold Lloyd's best comedy efforts.

Her first scenes for *Fast and Loose* had been shot in Hollywood, but after a delay the production resumed in New York at Paramount's Astoria studio—a fortuitous bit of logistics that enabled both Carol and her mother to attend to personal business in Fort Wayne while en route to New York by train. Alice Knight, Carol's grandmother and Bess's mother, had died leaving a will that was open to interpretation, although a bequeathment of ten thousand dollars to Carol was not disputed, albeit viewed curiously. Carol returned to the city of her birth and early childhood for the first time since leaving it, and stayed four days. Subsequent visits were promised but never made, although Bess traveled to Fort Wayne during her affluent later years.

Carol was reunited with her father—who no longer made periodic visits to southern California—and with a multitude of relatives she no longer remembered. In the prejudiced view of Fort Wayne folk, she was now one of the important stars of the screen, so it was only appropriate to honor a hometown girl who had made good. Margaret Ann Keegan, the vivacious daughter of an attorney friend of Fred Peters, was hostess for a "brilliant tea" that became the social event of the season. It was attended by every Fort Wayne woman having money or position or both, and forty years later it was still talked about as an occasion for which every woman in attendance auditioned a new and expensive gown. Carol minded her tongue and created the best possible impression. While she toured the countryside with her cousins and retraced the familiar steps of her childhood, Bess and Fred Peters closeted themselves with Hugh Keegan and worked out a divorce agreement, because Fred wanted Bess to have the freedom to remarry if she should ever consider it.

In New York, Carol held her first "press conference" (arranged by the Paramount home office) which yielded no major interview stories but only a few innocuous items for the chatter columns. But the good impression she made on the Manhattan press would continue to pay dividends in years to come. She also passed muster with the New York executives; and Adolph Zukor, still the president, was properly impressed. At the Long Island studio she met some of Paramount's more illustrious players for the first time, Chevalier among them. Before *Fast and Loose* finished shooting, Lubitsch checked into the studio to direct Jeanette MacDonald and Jack Buchanan in *Monte Carlo;* and the gregarious Lubitsch, who Knew Everybody in the society of Broadway as well as Hollywood, became an effective catalyst for Carol's initial fling at partygoing on a grand scale. Then Bess Peters joined her daughter and they made the rounds of the hit plays. Carol saw Horace Liveright for the last time. She also turned down a stage offer proffered by playwright Rachel Crothers, saying she was sure she wasn't ready for that kind of challenge. But she returned to Hollywood with a new measure of assurance.

Although *Fast and Loose* was the only picture she would make with Miriam Hopkins, they would be involved in a succession of casting intrigues, with most cases having the result of Lombard acquiring a role because it didn't suit the Hopkins fancy. In the long view, this was decidedly beneficial to Carol and injurious to Miss Hopkins, whose career was far from inconsequential nonetheless. Another fringe benefit of *Fast and Loose* was the acquisition, entirely by accident, of a final, silent "e" on the Lombard girl's given name.

She had bounced around from studio to studio as Carol and came to Paramount as that, so billed in the featured roster of *Safety in Numbers*. But when the large display posters were printed for *The Best People*, the spelling was Carole for her fourth-billed status. It was inexplicable, apparently unintentional; but, as they explained to her, it was too late to do anything about it. The title cards had not been prepared for the release print so she could be Carol inside the theaters; but to recall the "wafers" simply because a supporting player's name was misspelled would be a foolish expenditure, particularly since *The Best People* had already gone over budget.

Ever the creature of whim, Carol Lombard became Carole Lombard in an instant. She said, "What the hell, let's keep it with the *e*. I don't think I've ever seen it spelled that way, and I sort of like it." So it became Carole Lombard for the main titles as well, and then for all time. But Carole prodded the publicity department to issue stories about her name change, and to think of a better story than its having been an accident.

Ernst Lubitsch came up with the idea of attributing the new spelling to numerology. The publicists fabricated a story about thirteen letters producing the right vibrations for Carole's favorable destiny—and some practicing numerologists endorsed the idea anyway. It turned out to be a master stroke of press-agentry: Carole received a windfall of publicity as a girl ruled by superstition, with a mother who was some kind of medium. The numerology idea became widely accepted as the reason for her modified spelling; but then, so did a variation on the same theme—that she altered her name upon advice from a ten-cent astrology booklet.

In typical Hollywood irony, new advertising posters were issued anyway when Paramount abandoned *The Best People* in favor of its flashier title, but Carole retained the new spelling that was so widely publicized. She also was moved up in the billing from fourth to second, just below Miriam Hopkins, a move probably based on preview reaction. Now the studio was encouraged to try her in leading roles.

Upon arriving at the Paramount studio on October 6 to begin work on *It Pays to Advertise,* she was treated to a surprise party in honor of her twenty-first birthday. When asked if she was *really* surprised, Carole said, "I'll tell you how surprised I am: I thought I was twenty-two!" Arch Reeve grinned and said the studio had decided to knock off a year. Her first claim to popularity seemed to be with the teen-aged moviegoers, so they would emphasize her youthfulness. Every studio biography was amended to make 1909 the year of her birth rather than 1908. She thought it was a foolish caper, but in years to come she regularly recorded 1909 as her birth year. Later on she got to thinking that maybe it was 1910, after all.

Her first leading part for Paramount was in a distinctly minor but nonetheless bright comedy. *It Pays to Advertise* was possibly the first picture to make fun at the expense of the advertising industry, coming all of nine years before Preston Sturges's *Christmas in July.* That it was limited to a three-week production schedule was strong indication of an economic retrenchment program. Paramount was in trouble, no longer concerned about retaining its "number one" status but in just keeping its balance. Hard times were more than a mere rumor. Budgets were trimmed, and new emphasis was placed on such pictures as *It Pays to Advertise,* which could be made expeditiously and without ostentation. Paramount suddenly canceled all musical pictures other than the Chevalier vehicles; and that meant a fare-thee-well not only for the Helen Kanes and Stanley Smiths, but for a girl named Ethel Merman, who had made only one Paramount picture.

Schulberg had Frank Tuttle direct *It Pays to Advertise* as a test case for possible semi-permanent teaming of Carole with Norman Foster. Fox's Gaynor-Farrell duo was still going strong, and on a lesser scale Paramount had achieved some success by selling Gary Cooper and Fay Wray in tandem as the screen's "glorious young lovers." The reasoning was that two could be sold as easily and more cheaply than one, and Foster and Lombard ought to look good

together. With dark wavy hair and softly intense eyes to complement a readily acknowledged ability, Norman Foster seemingly had
all the requisite credentials of a young leading man. He was also
then married to Claudette Colbert, whose own Paramount career
had shifted into high gear, and had played opposite her in his first
picture, as the *Young Man of Manhattan*. Still, he had not caught
on, while M-G-M's similarly constituted Robert Montgomery
zoomed right to the top. The wisdom of the industrial grapevine
was that Paramount no longer knew how to develop star material,
as M-G-M surely did. If the theory needed proof, perhaps the
studio's continuing disposition toward Carole Lombard would provide it.

Shooting commenced for *It Pays to Advertise* after Thanksgiving
and finished before Christmas, enabling Carole to enjoy the holidays leisurely at home with her mother and her still unmarried
brothers, in the simple but elegant house on Beverly Hill's Rexford
Drive, rented for Bess Peters by her children. Fred was as steady as
ever, while Stuart, doing fitful battle with a drinking problem,
bounced from one brokerage firm to another, but always managed
to be smartly employed. With the security of Carole's Paramount
contract, the advantages of inheritance, and the resolution of personal business that had been long unfinished, Bess chortled about
being rich and justifiably proud of her children's independent accomplishment, but not yet satisfied: she said she wanted to see them
all happily married, so she could get them out of her hair, and they
could be rid of her.

Their New Year's Day celebration was a party at home, a traditional Bess Peters affair, given for Carole and with invitations to
her older friends and also some of the newer ones. The latest
numerological evidence, Bess said, indicated that marriage was
probably right for Carole in 1931, and that in any event it was
bound to happen.

A Perfect Crime *(1921). Even in an obscure screen debut, the adolescent Jane Peters (with Monte Blue) could accommodate a lovely still.*

The Swim Princess *(1927). Although Daphne Pollard is the comical center, a well-dressed Carol Lombard (in the hat, top right) had the title role in this Mack Sennett two-reeler.*

High Voltage (*1929*). *Diane Ellis is the slumbering nice girl and Carol Lombard and William Boyd are the fugitive lovers. It was her first talkie, made for Pathé.*

Fast and Loose (*1930*). *An authentic ancestor of the screwball comedy, with Miriam Hopkins making her film debut and the newly spelled Carole Lombard (far right) getting good laughs. The men are Charles Starrett, Herschel Mayall and Frank Morgan.*

I Take This Woman *(1931)*. *Gary Cooper seems to be doing the taking, over Lester Vail's protest—although Carole seems indifferent.*

No Man of Her Own *(1932)*. *Clark Gable's and Carole's expressions establish her small-town-girl dilemma. With Walter Walker, Elizabeth Patterson and J. Farrell MacDonald.*

Brief Moment (1933). On loan to Columbia for an S. N. Behr-man "serious comedy" she rather liked, Carole's the center of attention for Florence Britton, Monroe Owsley, Arthur Hohl and Gene Raymond.

White Woman (1933). Carole is gorgeous, Charles Laughton somewhat less so, in a Paramount tropical jungle.

Bolero *(1934). Carole and George Raft liked each other and this film. Wesley Ruggles, beneath the camera (with the pocket handkerchief), is the director.*

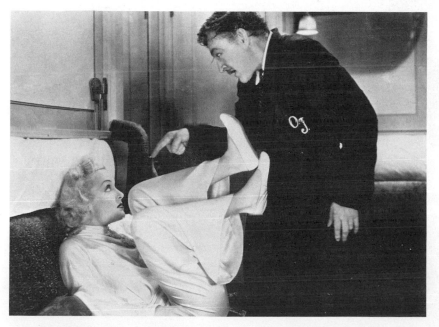

Twentieth Century *(1934). The Hecht-MacArthur shenanigans with John Barrymore are Carole's glorious turning point.*

Now and Forever (1934). Neither Carole nor her unseen leading man, Gary Cooper, was likely to steal a scene from Shirley Temple, but the picture was likely to make money.

Hands Across the Table (1935). The prototype Lombard "vehicle" and the first of Carole's four pictures with young and rising Fred MacMurray.

My Man Godfrey *(1936). Carole and ex-husband William Powell
in Gregory LaCava's screwball classic, about the daffy rich girl
who finds a "forgotten man" in the city dump and turns him
into a butler.*

Nothing Sacred *(1937). Satire comes in Technicolor, and Fredric March and Walter Connolly are fine straight men for Carole Lombard's clowning.*

True Confession *(1937). Carole and John Barrymore score a farcical bull's-eye in the last of 22 pictures she made for Paramount.*

Fools for Scandal *(1938). The silver service had more glitter than the dialogue in a picture that killed Fernand Gravet's American career and certainly was no help to Carole's.*

Made for Each Other *(1939). Carole and James Stewart in the stirring final scene of John Cromwell's underrated comedy-drama.*

In Name Only *(1939). Carole's and Cary Grant's love was true. The problem was that he was married to Kay Francis.*

Vigil in the Night *(1940). George Stevens directed Carole and Anne Shirley in an impressive tragic film, but the paying customers weren't pleased.*

They Knew What They Wanted *(1940). A light moment in a mostly serious picture with Charles Laughton. Carole decided that what she wanted was another comedy.*

Mr. and Mrs. Smith *(1941). Alfred Hitchcock's admirers couldn't understand why he was directing a marital farce, but Carole and Robert Montgomery were a team well-matched for laughter.*

To Be or Not to Be (1942). Both mistimed and ahead of its time, Carole's last film (released posthumously) is a still-glistening Lubitsch classic—with Lombard and Jack Benny as Polish ham actors outwitting the Nazis.

❋ V ❋

The Orchid Lady

SHE WAS going to be The Orchid Lady. The designation wasn't even original, but it had worked before. "Orchidaceous" was a description invented for Corinne Griffith, whose silent stardom was successfully exploited in an atmosphere of aristocratic flora. It was a gimmick, and it indicated that Paramount had weighed the Lombard attributes and determined that elegance was her long suit. Carole was caught up by the screen's new emphasis on high glamour, which related directly to the crystallizing agony of the Depression.

The drab shopgirls didn't want to see their own kind on film. They wanted to fantasize in the overdressed photoplays of Constance Bennett and Lilyan Tashman. Paramount already had successfully marketed Kay Francis in that tradition; and the accent on elegance was further justified by the exotic appeal of that sensational import Marlene Dietrich, whose presence at the studio diminished every other charmer—especially after Clara Bow abruptly quit the movies. Carole's new image would be a calculated hybrid of the Dietrich and Francis attributes. She would be photographed with orchids all around her for the sake of publicity, and they would become adornments for her pictures.

They weren't *her* pictures just yet. But the evidence of *Safety in Numbers*, *Fast and Loose*, and *It Pays to Advertise* prodded a studio consensus that if she were something less than solid star material, she could still be marketed as a glamorous feline. This least successful phase of her career would be initiated with *Man of the World,* and the man in question was William Powell. He was the star, the only player whose name would go above the title. But then, Carole had never experienced star billing, and it was a sign of progress that for the first time she would be leading lady to a male star of primary importance in the regimented order of picture personalities. In fact, Carole fancied herself in love with Bill Powell before they met.

Stardom had not been Hollywood's expectation for Powell. He came into pictures almost a decade earlier for minor service in John Barrymore's *Sherlock Holmes,* then supported Marion Davies when Mr. Hearst produced *When Knighthood Was in Flower* for her. Not considered handsome, Powell was a young character actor capable of blending comedy with melodrama in such important Paramount pictures as *Beau Geste* and *The Great Gatsby.* Film players took the star system seriously enough to socialize mainly with others of their own professional status, but there were exceptions and Powell was one. His easy sophistication enabled him to move into the elite of filmland society, and he became famous within the community as a "third musketeer" for two undisputed male stars, than whom few were "bigger." During the filming of *The Bright Shawl* he became an intimate friend to Richard Barthelmess, its hero. Powell possessed ample stage experience and had good knowledge of literature and the arts, and of fine wine. Barthelmess was well born and moved gracefully in the upper reaches of the filmland society which, nevertheless, always suffered a collective inferiority complex for its paucity of true "class."

Arriving in Hollywood not long after Powell, the British charmer Ronald Colman had class, all right, and other qualities that won him silent stardom almost immediately. Colman played Beau Geste, and at about that time formed the inseparable social trio with Powell and Barthelmess. Each had endured an unhappy marriage (Powell had also fathered a son), but in the last hurrah of the silent film, all were bachelors once more. They were regulars of the Hollywood nightclub set, squiring a succession of filmland coeds and occasional fair ladies from southern California's organized society. Fan magazines traced every movement of the musketeers, who were photographed at the races and the polo matches, at concerts and art exhibitions, on yachts and at the beach, in the clubs, and sometimes at San Simeon as party guests of Mr. Hearst and Marion Davies.

In 1928 William Powell gave a much-praised performance in support of Emil Jannings in Josef von Sternberg's *The Last Command,* and this had an effect of moving him into the ranks of the leading Paramount players. He scored a dramatic hit in the studio's first all-talking picture, *Interference,* and his own major stardom was assured. Melodrama was his forte. He gave thinly disguised portrayals of Arnold Rothstein (*Street of Chance*) and lawyer Frank Fallon (*For the Defense*); and as Philo Vance, he mixed glibness with his detective work.

Carole Lombard had been a Barthelmess fan since childhood, and had experienced adolescent tingling when Ronald Colman romanced Lillian Gish in *Romola* and *The White Sister.* Her appreciation of Powell's screen work came with her maturity, but she had followed the affairs of Hollywood's three most popular bachelors for years on end. When she was assigned to a Powell picture, she felt very like Cinderella mistakenly invited to the royal ball. She could affect nonchalance in the midst of celebrities even at the Lubitsch level, but was belatedly smitten by an accumulation of dormant school-girl fantasies.

She had seen Bill Powell around the studio, where he was one of the busiest star players. (In 1930 alone, he made seven films.) He gave her friendly acknowledgment but their aquaintance did not graduate to private conversation. Yet she heard nice things. Harry D'Arrast rated Powell as one of the more subtle actors in silent films and had tried without success to borrow him for *Dry Martini,* a well-known Fox picture directed by D'Arrast.

Powell's costar in *Man of the World* was to have been Miriam Hopkins, until Miriam landed a part Carole had earnestly coveted —opposite Chevalier in *The Smiling Lieutenant.* Director Richard Wallace selected Carole from among several candidates for Miriam's replacement. The conception of The Orchid Lady followed Carole's confirmation for the Powell picture.

Man of the World was designed as a change of pace for Powell, to bring his screen image nearer to a likeness of his sociable self. He was tiring of Philo Vance and so, it seemed, were the moviegoers. *Man of the World* would fade from memory very soon after its mid-1931 release, but it was a "major" production with a long shooting schedule. If reviewers gave the picture serious attention, they tended to find Carole's work disappointing; a lazy performance was implied. Carole later said it was true, and that she hadn't been concentrating on her part. She was concentrating on Powell instead, and fancied herself in love with him.

Her interest didn't end with the shooting schedule. The talk was that she had become Powell's mistress, even though the studio's demands on her did not encourage such a liaison. The "orchid" angle was yielding positive results, and there was sudden studio anxiety to get Carole Lombard into as many pictures as possible. This was the Explosion principle of starlet promotion. Before she had completed work on *Man of the World,* she was shooting *Up Pops the Devil,* a reteaming with Norman Foster; and before it was finished, she was beginning her second picture with Powell and, almost simultaneously, yet another assignment—this one opposite Gary Cooper.

Carole didn't complain. Unlike so many screen actresses who relished every aspect of Hollywood life except the actual shooting of pictures, she loved nothing so much as the production grind, which was an adventurous thing to her. But it taxed her stamina. For several months she obeyed a six-days-a-week schedule without a day off, with a 6:00 A.M. start. Later she would admit that the ordeal began to wear her down, so it was little wonder that her performances in these pictures evidenced none of her characteristic vitality.

The romance with Bill Powell flamed in earnest when they got to work on their second picture, *Ladies' Man,* whose title was the closet possible echo of the first one. She began to agitate for a vacation, and by the time she was assured of a substantial one, she was ready to plan her wedding.

Carole played only featured support in *Ladies' Man.* The lispy, serene Kay Francis was Powell's costar, but Carole gained dominance of the publicity issue for having obviously conquered one of screenland's most eligible and elusive bachelors. The *Ladies' Man* set became a swarm of gossip purveyors, arousing the jealousy of Kay Francis, whose recent marriage to Kenneth MacKenna had passed almost unnoticed.

Powell said he'd never known a girl like Carole and doubted that another existed. Winning his heart was easy enough for Carole; winning his friends was rather more difficult. They tolerated her with an unmistakable note of condescension, regarding her as a typical social-climbing starlet. Not to be intimidated, Carole told

Powell his friends were awfully stuffy, and did he have to see so *much* of them?

She would believe throughout her marriage to Bill Powell that she had not gained acceptance by Ronald Colman; that indeed, he would not acknowledge her equality until she had actually surpassed him in popularity if not in prestige. She had better success with Barthelmess, whose wife Jessica became one of her close friends. (The Barthelmess marriage in 1928 had splintered the musketeers' bachelor solidarity and, some thought, had incited Powell's urge to marry.) But Carole also experienced a lingering chill from Ralph Forbes, another Briton who was also a Powell intimate since *Beau Geste* days. Forbes's own marriage to the esteemed Ruth Chatterton was nearing a dismal end, but Carole sensed that Miss Chatterton also regarded her patronizingly.

Whatever the initial objections of his friends, Bill Powell's interest could not be dissuaded. His courtship of Carole was straightforward and brisk—"whirlwind" was an appropriate cliché—and each considered himself the pursuer. It was a limousined, tuxedoed romance, and Powell was a true ladies' man of the world, who had smart connections and acquired the best Scotch whisky by the caseful for formal delivery to Carole. She acquired his liking for good Scotch; otherwise they could hardly have been less alike in tastes.

Their interests were as different as their temperaments, but each recognized in the other a complement of the qualities lacking in his or her own self. Powell was moody, intellectual, inward and sardonic, motivated primarily by propriety and the social graces. Carole had never been anything other than an athletic girl, most comfortable in the outdoors. To get from one place to another she would run, not walk, because she liked to run. She was informal, spontaneous—as casual in manner as in dress. She hurriedly scanned the newspapers but would rarely become involved with a book. The popular rhythms still captivated her, while she reacted only neutrally to classical music and formal ballet. Powell was an accomplished ballroom dancer, but Carole was a flapper —still throbbingly agile for the latest jazz steps.

Their engagement was announced informally while Carole was filming both *Ladies' Man* and the Gary Cooper picture called *I Take This Woman*. The big story, long anticipated, was Powell's romantic capitulation. Although Carole rated as a promising comer in pictures, some reports of their engagement were underscored by cynicism. If Powell's friends feared that he was about to marry beneath himself, the press all but painted Carole as a gold-digger. Powell was quietly divorced from his long-estranged first wife, an accommodation given specifically to enable him to marry Carole. Otherwise their only personal problem was resolving a disagreement over Carole's professional future.

Powell was quoted to the effect that Carole would give up her career for full-time wifehood, with motherhood an eventual possibility. But Carole drew the line for Powell: she wouldn't object to becoming a mother, but even then she would not abandon the career that represented half a dozen years of struggle, and most of the fun she had known. And she reasoned: suppose the marriage didn't work out? Could she then pick up broken pieces of a career and reassemble the picture? She believed herself neither jaded nor cynical; she was merely respecting the doubts that many people were expressing openly, and that others were conveying as clearly in silence. People generally doubted that a Powell-Lombard union had a fair chance of endurance. In addition to their other differences, there was a possibly crucial age gap. Even if she was a year older than the not-yet-twenty-two the studio said she was, Powell was on the threshold of his fortieth year.

Then the logistics of their intended nuptials were complicated by the continued sagging fortunes of Paramount Pictures. The home office demanded a drastic reduction of overhead expenses. A priority order of business was the renegotiation of certain star contracts, William Powell's among them. The affected players stood to lose a great deal of money, against the promise of salvaged prestige. But Powell wanted no part of the arrangement; that is, Myron Selznick wanted no part of it. Powell was a client of David Selznick's older brother, who had become the most powerful talent agent in Hollywood. By exploiting the familial tie-in with Paramount, Myron had negotiated lucrative deals for several of his more valuable clients. He would exploit *any* advantage to accomplish the objective that possessed him, which was one not in the best interests of the entrenched motion picture companies.

By a typical Myron Selznick ruse, Carole became one of his clients in the spring of 1931, when the first year of her Paramount contract was nearing completion. Her impending marriage to one of the studio's important stars was leverage for Myron to obtain a more financially favorable arrangement for the balance of Carole's term. The revised contract was *without* options, binding Carole and Paramount to one another until 1936. Soon her employers would cry foul, blackmail, and other chicanery; for while they believed a generous deal with Carole would pacify Powell and prevent the possibility of his bolting the company, Myron Selznick already had schemed the immediate delivery of Powell to Warner Brothers at a salary higher than he was drawing at Paramount. *Ladies' Man* was his last Paramount vehicle; and while Carole was still occupied with her Gary Cooper picture, Powell checked in at Warners and began shooting *The Road to Singapore,* bearing no relation to the pilot film of the subsequent Crosby-Hope farcical series.

The idea of Carole affiliating with Myron Selznick was Powell's, not her own. But it occurred when she had begun to feel insecure without strong representation, since the studio in its uneasiness became increasingly callous toward its players, particularly the ingenues. In the spring Paramount jettisoned without warning three girls who previously had been held in high regard. They were the attractive Mary Brian and the magical, lovely Louise Brooks; and a less pretty ingenue but one whose talent would enable her to share with Carole Lombard the very throne during the talking screen's impending golden age of comedy: Jean Arthur. Mary, Jean, and Louise were unceremoniously dumped in a move interpreted as a warning to bring dissident contractees into line.

Paramount was contractually stuck with Carole Lombard, but the possibly fraudulent way in which her security was obtained did not enhance her popularity with the front office. It probably discouraged her continued rise during a succession of studio upheavals that was only beginning. She did not immediately understand this, nor could she be greatly concerned. The wedding plans were not altered, and marriage loomed as the adventure that would subordinate every material consideration. As soon as Powell completed his Warner picture, they were married—on June 26, 1931.

Glamour with the edge of novelty was their mutual attraction. Powell succumbed to Carole's sheer loveliness, and spoke admiringly of her frankness and honesty. Briefly rejecting her old values, she was smitten by his aristocracy—symbolized by sartorial elegance, sleek motorcars, luxuriously appointed quarters, and an abundance of servants. Each professed a desire to become more like the other;

yet as soon as they were married, each seemed determined to remake the other in his or her own image.

A Congregationalist minister performed the wedding ceremony in Bess Peters's Rexford Drive home. For a kingdom of opulence, it was a remarkably austere occasion. Bess designed an altar and wreathed it with seasonal flowers. Other than Carole's mother and brothers, only Bill Powell's elderly parents attended. In a switch suggested by Carole, Fred Peters served Powell as best man while Horatio Powell gave the bride in marriage to his own son. After the brief service the families sat down to an early-evening catered dinner, engaging only in subdued small talk. Later in the evening there was a very small reception attended only by intimate friends —Jessica and Dick Barthelmess, the Clive Brooks, veteran actor Ernest Torrence and his wife; and only Dixie Pantages from Carole's own circle.

Louella Parsons and her errant physician husband Watson (Docky) Martin, were uninvited drop-ins—a two-pronged pain in the neck who nevertheless required discreet cordiality. While Docky was holding court with one of the tales that grew inevitably out of his inebriation, the newlyweds slipped away unnoticed, to spend the night at Powell's house on Havenhurst Drive. The next day they sailed for Honolulu on the Matson-Lassco liner *Malolo*, and Carole was a seasick bride.

Hawaii's promised idyll was enjoyed only briefly. First Carole was felled by toxic poisoning, then she contracted a mild case of malaria. After her recovery there was little time for enjoying the islands, as Carole had to report to Paramount for a new chore, tentatively *The Beachcombers* opposite Phillips Holmes. She suffered a relapse and was unable to work, so the picture went on the shelf. Later it became *Sinners in the Sun,* without Holmes.

For all the evidence of exuberant good health that Carole usually presented, she had chronic low resistance to the common cold and the larger perils of pneumonia and influenza. She was progressively susceptible to illness throughout her career, but most markedly during the two years of her marriage to Powell. Psychosomatic influence may have been at work. She also had painful menstrual cramps. When Paramount executive Sam Jaffe questioned her excessive sick time, she explained that "God switched the formula on me; there are just three days a month I *don't* bleed."

She had a bout with the flu in the fall of 1931; it would become an annual event. Not long afterward she submitted to an attack of pleurisy. She was plagued by chronic anemia. Each time an ailment kept her at home, there was a new round of rumor concerning her possible pregnancy. Then she would return to the cameras, revived and eager for the studio's busy pace.

Carole became mistress of Powell's modified Tudor mansion, done to the most exacting taste inside and out. For long years after their divorce, a "Homes of the Movie Stars" picture postcard album circulated commercially, showing Carole Lombard in full color, standing before the Havenhurst Drive edifice. The same album offered Powell in similar pose, with no further explanation. It was a splendid house but Carole couldn't overcome a misery in just being there when Powell was away—at his new studio or in the company of old friends. He could not wholly abandon the kind of life a part of him still craved.

Bill Powell was the essential agent of Carole's flowering sophistication. At the same time other influences were taking hold, different from Powell's and also from each other. First there was Fieldsie —Madalynne Fields, Carole's blithe stablemate from the Sennett pie-throwing days. Even before the liaison with Powell—indeed, right after Carole acquired the security of her Paramount contract —Fieldsie joined her at Paramount as a sort of personal secretary, handling all the red tape that is the peculiar heritage of the movie player. Theirs was not an employer-employee relationship; rather, it extended Fieldsie's already acquired role as Carole's confidante, adviser, and above all her good buddy. Fieldsie shared Carole's consuming interest in the picture business, without a real performing ambition of her own. She had quit the Sennett gang when it started making talkie shorts, and pursued a deeper friendship with Carole. Fieldsie's early encouragement would never go unacknowledged. With no evidence of deviousness, Fieldsie nevertheless was a match for Carole in shrewdness. As much as anyone and perhaps more, she gained awareness of how much (and in what way) Carole was catching on with the movie public. Carole once told Hedda Hopper that most stars investigate fan mail only to the point of knowing how many letters they received, but that Fieldsie was interested in what the letters *said* . . . and so was she.

A more complex relationship was evolving between Carole and the mercurial Myron Selznick. He was in that army that rushed

Carole with ardor but settled for friendship which, nevertheless, acquired extraordinary dimension. If Carole initially was merely a pretty appendage to Myron's business with Powell, she soon became more than that—in fact, his favorite client.

Myron's personality was considerably more outgoing than that of his brother David, who left Paramount late in 1931. Named production chief for the newly merged RKO Radio company (whose components included the old Pathé enterprise), David was succeeding where Myron had failed. Their colorful father, Lewis J. Selznick, despite lasting industrial accomplishment in his own name, had also played the movie game and lost. Myron's obsession was that his father, not having failed on his own, had been betrayed and ruined by the calculated strategy of hated and jealous rivals. When Lewis was effectively eased out of the business, Myron protected the family name as a producing entity, becoming at one time the youngest person ever to hold the presidency of a picture-making company. But Selznick Pictures came to bankruptcy, and a demon got possession of Myron. He vowed revenge against the motion picture industry that had humiliated his father and then himself.

During Hollywood's most frantic hour of transition from silence to sound, Myron organized his own talent agency and brought many of moviedom's premier artists into his clientele. He flourished immediately as a ten-percenter, but getting rich was not his objective. Nor was it the well-being of his clients. Myron was simply committed to making life miserable for the moguls, and his success toward that end was not questioned. More than any other person, Myron Selznick was responsible for raising star salaries into the stratosphere beyond reason. He fortified his position by trafficking almost exclusively in "indispensable" stars. Carole was an exception, but briefly so.

"I'll bring them to their knees and watch them crawl," he said. *They* were the studio heads and executive producers, and Myron dealt with them mercilessly. "When I've finished, the producers will be the slaves and the stars will have all the power."

For all his vindictiveness, Myron was an often ingratiating personality—to Carole, at least, who admired his vibrancy, his positivism, and the way he burned up every day with a full-throttle exhibition. Being Jekyll and Hyde simultaneously may not have been easy for Myron, for he began to drink to excess, usually becoming ugly drunk rather than lovably so. Myron intimidated almost everyone, especially his own clients; but Carole would be openly critical of his attitude and behavior, and he listened to her. She did not reduce his mania for revenge, but she earned his respect and a pledge to make her "the best-paid dame in town."

Myron was in a small coterie that suspected Carole of harboring a major talent. She was never without her own cheerleaders, but they proved either fickle or ineffectual. Even Ernst Lubitsch, who gave early encouragement, may have begun to doubt her comedienne substance on the basis of some lackluster performances she delivered, mostly in 1931. Lubitsch was a near-deity at the studio and customarily was granted the players he requested. He could have obtained Carole's services without a battle but he obviously preferred Miriam Hopkins. He employed Miriam repeatedly and not without charming effect, in roles that seemingly could have been written especially for Carole. In *Trouble in Paradise* Miriam played a merry jewel thief; Carole got into a regular rhythm of speed-reading the scripts of upcoming productions and particularly liked that one. But she didn't put in a bid. Myron Selznick told her to get tough, to start turning things down and demanding better pictures, just as a matter of policy. "Keep 'em off balance," he said. "Pictures are a bluffing business, that's all."

Josef von Sternberg had wanted Carole to play the rich girl in his version of Dreiser's *An American Tragedy*. She begged off, and most people believed it was because she then wanted to work with Powell in *anything*. Actually it was Powell who turned Carole against the idea of working for Sternberg, whom he loathed inexplicably, despite having progressed smartly under Sternbergian direction. Perhaps Carole would have been more assertive at that time if she had possessed a personal conviction of her talent. She didn't. She thought herself lucky to be in pictures, and she especially enjoyed being The Orchid Lady and wearing the clothes that went with it.

Ladies' Man was the first time she was "dressed" by the brilliant Travis Banton, who had been taken on by Paramount as its chief costume designer. Banton's young assistant was Edith Head, just beginning a phenomenal career. Miss Head would remember that Travis Banton was interested in Carole Lombard even before they had met, on the basis of some striking photographs John Angstead had taken; and that from the time he began dressing her for Paramount elegance, Banton rated Carole his favorite both as person and as a model.

"Throw a bolt of material at Carole, and any way it hits her she'll look great," Banton said. During the next few years he threw many a bolt, draping every Lombard angle with gorgeous emphasis. Banton described Carole as a greyhound or an Arabian horse—possessing the long, slim lines that gave a gown its best showcasing. For *Ladies' Man* he created a beaded shirtmaker dress for Carole to wear as a full-length gown and it caused a sensation and then a designing vogue. In each film she would parade at least one dazzling new Banton creation and usually more. Myron Selznick remarked that if Paramount's scriptwriters paid as much attention to Carole's attributes as the costumers did, she would have the screen's wittiest dialogue.

Edith Head said Carole's secret lay in her not being "actressy": she did not seem to be modeling the gowns. "Her clothes always looked as if they belonged to her. Nine out of ten actresses thought in terms of costumes, but to Carole they were just clothes. Some girls never learn to wear elegance naturally, but it seemed that Carole had always known how."

The movie studios employed a legion of couturiers but Travis Banton was an artist and a perfectionist. Demanding their time and taxing their patience, he could bring drudgery into the life of a movie queen. But Carole was a good sport who, according to Miss Head, set an example for girls who came after her.

"Most people have no idea what goes into making a picture. They think a girl just walks in and gets photographed by the movie camera, and then walks out. That was never the case, but particularly when the thirties pictures were being made, an actress spent more time getting ready to make a picture than she would spend in front of the cameras. We were really selling glamour to the country then, and most folks were starved for it. So great care went into clothes, and a fitting was sure to be a tedious thing for an actress. It required four or five hours at a time, sometimes eight or ten hours of getting weary just sitting around, being measured and fitted and refitted. Most stars hated their fittings, I think, more than any part of the business. Marlene Dietrich was one of the more cooperative ones because she recognized the necessity, but it was still *work* to her. Carole, though, was patience itself. She could turn just about anything, even a dress fitting, into some kind of a party."

Carole was one of the few players who gave presents to Travis Banton and his crew to show appreciation of their own labors on her behalf. She got into the habit of giving presents to just about everyone with some responsibility toward her pictures, even to the workaday technicians to whom she became a pal—the antithesis of the haughty, preening star actress. When she filmed the silent *Ned McCobb's Daughter* for Pathé, she was impressed that Irene Rich, its star, distributed gifts to crewmen as well as to her supporting players, and she began the practice herself at Paramount—conventional gifts for persons she knew less well, humorous ones for intimates whose quirkiness she understood.

The Lombard gowns that were a sheeny effect for the Paramount silver screen were consigned to wardrobe, but sometimes Banton would reward Carole's cooperativeness by giving them to her on permanent loan. The gesture did not go unappreciated: Carole said she was just nutty about Travis's dresses, and she had always been taken by clothes in a play-actressy way. She was no stranger to sartorial elegance, even if the gowns she wore socially had not always been her very own. Carole and Dixie Pantages had identical height at five feet, four and one-half inches, and their other measurements were comparable. They "exchanged," which meant that Carole was the giddy beneficiary of Dixie's privileged wardrobe.

She was a clotheshorse in all of her 1931 pictures following *It Pays to Advertise:* the two sophisticated pieces with Powell; *Up Pops the Devil,* in which she held Lilyan Tashman to a couturial standoff; and *I Take This Woman,* wherein her high glamour dazzled the young Gary Cooper at his most countrified. Elegance notwithstanding, the pictures were not good and she was uninspired. *Up Pops the Devil* passed muster as entertainment; it was marital comedy, deriving from a successful Frances Goodrich-Albert Hackett play. It gave Carole first billing for the first time. The Powell pictures at least were acceptable as commodities, but *I Take This Woman* was a joyless klunker. It bore no relationship to a later M-G-M picture, other than to suggest a jinxed title— for the Spencer Tracy-Hedy Lamarr picture was a famous flop. Although their roles were of equal size, Cooper was solo-starred and Carole led the supporting list.

She retrieved top billing in the first picture she completed after her honeymoon, but *No One Man* was no man's candidate for the Ten Best list: it was soapy melodrama, and Carole displayed less conviction than either of her leading men, Ricardo Cortez and Paul Lukas. But she displayed great clothes.

Indication that her employers were displeased by her recent work was given by a studio decision to farm her out to Warners. Carole was alarmed. She had never been put on loan, and Paramount players were dispatched elsewhere only when they were considered excess baggage. The Warner picture was *Taxi* and its star, James Cagney, was riding a trajectory to real popularity. But Bill Powell reckoned that *Taxi* wouldn't be much of a picture, and Myron Selznick advised Carole to refuse the assignment, just to see what Schulberg would do about it. Carole announced that she simply would not go to Warners to make a picture she didn't feel was "right" for her; and rather surprisingly, Schulberg acceded to her wishes. Eventually she would regret having scorned her only opportunity to work with Cagney. And *Taxi* was a hit.

The Paramount picture she did in its stead was a mild little thing called *Sinners in the Sun*. It had little of sin, and not so much sun, but plenty of fashions and misunderstanding between Carole Lombard and Chester Morris, before they kissed and made up for the final fadeout. Of historical interest, it also had a new supporting player just in from New York by name of Cary Grant.

It was not illogical that the front office was disenchanted with Carole. The suspicion of her real ability seemed to have evaporated. And while a cluster of pictures had combined with a publicized marriage to promote her on a national scale, her box-office receipts followed a declining curve. But that was a story typical of 1932, a crisis year for the movies. If the economics of the Depression were not problem enough, some of the people who could afford to attend the picture show regularly had decided to stay home with their new toy, the radio.

The bloom was off the Paramount rose, and the bombshell hit *Sinners in the Sun* in midfilming: the old company was bankrupt. Paramount went into receivership and arbitrators were assigned to reorganize the corporation. Famous Players-Lasky was liquidated as a producing arm, and Jesse Lasky was a casualty. Soon he would join Fox as an independent producer. Adolph Zukor kept all of his titles but lost much of his power. B. P. Schulberg was dumped as

Hollywood production chief and installed as one of the company's nominal producers. Emanuel Cohen was the new man in charge of the studio . . . the *only* studio. Paramount's Long Island studio was shuttered in the most obvious economy move, and all studio photography was concentrated in Hollywood.

The company's uncertain destiny caused a festering anxiety among the players, and Carole endured another stretch of inactivity after *Sinners in the Sun* completed shooting. It was of no benefit to her position that *No One Man,* her first release of 1932, was a topic of some derision when the arbitration began. Under the circumstances of the reorganization, the stars and featured players were at the mercy of the Fates, because of an industry-wide retrenchment. Carole suspected that only Myron Selznick's maneuvering enabled her to ride out the storm.

An upheaval of the studio star roster had begun earlier, when Kay Francis and Ruth Chatterton followed Bill Powell's lead and defected to Warner Brothers for generous terms arranged by Myron Selznick. That left Marlene Dietrich the undisputed queen of the mountain, but her activity was limited to one Sternberg production annually. Despite waning popularity, Maurice Chevalier retained an aura of prestige that made him king among the studio men. But he was ticketed for less opulent productions, because the confections that teamed him with Jeanette MacDonald no longer made money. So Jeanette was given her walking papers, and the erroneous supposition was that Hollywood had seen the last of her.

George Bancroft, who had kept his gaudy billing while obviously fading, decided to quit the movies rather than accept a lower salary specified by the arbitrators. The moment of Buddy Rogers had also passed but he was playing out his option, while Jack Oakie and Richard Arlen held on somewhat more securely. Clearly the most valuable male stars were Fredric March and Gary Cooper, while a young British character player named Charles Laughton very quickly made a practice of dominating all of his Paramount pictures. The most promising new boys appeared to be Cary Grant and Randolph Scott.

As satellites to Marlene, only four Paramount actresses were accredited stars—Miriam Hopkins, Claudette Colbert, Sylvia Sidney, and Nancy Carroll . . . and Nancy's footing was precarious. Carole Lombard was the only studio girl who was a leading lady without her own stardom; clearly she was ahead of Wynne Gibson, Adrienne Ames, Rose Hobart, Sari Maritza, and Frances Dee, who now were the inevitable hoped-for future stars.

But the prognosis was that the studio's recovery would require players of more magnetism than those presently on board. So George Raft, who had been a steel-eyed hit in the *Scarface* crowd around Paul Muni, was taken on and immediately put into leading roles as a gangster hero. More significantly, a couple of specialists were graduated from the talking two-reelers Mack Sennett had taken to making for Paramount—the bulbous comic W. C. Fields and the crooner of the age, Bing Crosby. Then Manny Cohen played the trump that would strengthen his regime and the studio's box-office ledger, besides inciting the Legion of Decency to action: he decided that the Paramount screen was safe for Mae West.

Manny Cohen would try to beat radio by joining it. The first big production under his auspices would be *The Big Broadcast,* with the brothers Mills and the sisters Boswell; with Burns and Allen, Kate Smith, and street singer Arthur Tracy; but designed primarily as the vehicle that would showcase Bing Crosby for Paramount stardom. They would throw in a thin plot for Carole Lombard and Stuart Erwin to handle, and everybody would be happy.

Everybody except Carole. She had been plotting to get into a Lubitsch picture, and didn't want to be shuttled into a musical picture if they wouldn't let her dance. She counted her lines in the script they gave her and let out a holler. She had nothing to do, except maybe wear a smashing number to the big broadcast. She said she wouldn't do the picture, and this time it didn't work. It was a new regime. It was also rumored about that Manny Cohen decided Carole Lombard was of no tangible value to Paramount only when he despaired of his unsuccessful efforts to get her in the sack. She didn't make *The Big Broadcast* after all, and it was her mistake: the picture was the solid hit her career needed. Instead, she was put out on loan: not to Warners, not to M-G-M or Fox or any sovereign company—but to little Columbia, where broken-down starlets went when they were put out to pasture.

When the smoke of battle cleared after Hollywood's conversion to talking pictures, the American movie industry was concentrated in seven gigantic corporations. The reorganized Paramount remained one of the Big Four, on a level with Fox but now surpassed by both M-G-M and Warners-First National. Solid on a lower rung were RKO and Universal, while United Artists was a powerful distributor and exhibitor for independent producers. Otherwise the Hollywood periphery contained dozens of small feature-film producers such as Capitol, Mascot, Liberty, Beacon, Mayfair, Imperial, Superior, Steiner, Golden State, Principal, Chesterfield . . . a list going on and on, with every season claiming a few victims, but other shoestring enterprises following in their wake. The Depression began the methodical elimination of these companies that were collectively labeled Poverty Row within the industry. Several of the lightweights salvaged their destiny by merging into the Monogram firm, but all were grimly undistinguished, except as a cushion for bygone stars on the skid to oblivion. Well, there were a couple of exceptions: but the promising Tiffany company could not survive the 1932 purge; and that left Columbia in an uncertain class by itself.

In 1919 the brothers Jack and Harry Cohn, then minor functionaries with Universal, lured Universal studio manager Joe Brandt away from Carl Laemmle and established CBC Pictures with Brandt as president. They made comedy shorts, but moved into the features game in 1924 and reorganized as Columbia Pictures. Harry Cohn, who gloried in his status as a self-made man and relished the wheeler-dealing of picture making, strengthened his hand from year to year. By 1932 he had nudged himself into a company presidency that amounted to virtual dictatorship. He was crude and uneducated but feisty, and had both flair and instinct for the movies. He also said he knew high-class tail when he saw it, and he appreciated some of the Carole Lombard attributes that her Paramount bosses had come to take for granted.

In 1932 he offered to "help out" Manny Cohen by buying up Carole Lombard's Paramount contract. He reneged when it developed that she was already in what to him was the big-money class, and was represented by Myron Selznick of whom he wanted no part. But Manny Cohen said he'd be willing to loan Carole to Columbia just about any time.

Exhibitors liked Columbia features because they were crisp, to the point, and addressed to the average moviegoer. They had a professional gloss that belied their modest budgets. Only Harry Cohn's hard line on economics brought Columbia through the talkie transition and the brutal early years of the Depression. Paramount's 1932 collapse was followed immediately by an industry-wide economy wave in which most of the gainfully employed (including actors) agreed to temporarily reduced salaries; but Columbia personnel were less seriously affected because Harry Cohn said his people were already working at rock-bottom wages. The industrial retrenchment gave Columbia employees parity for perhaps the first time. And the exhibitors' 1932 discovery of double features as an antidote to the Depression put Columbia in an especially favorable position.

Double features were a consumer's bargain—two pictures for the price of one. But in the new Hollywood economics, the combined production cost of the pictures exhibited in tandem would only equal the previous cash investment in a single feature. Columbia assumed a strategic importance to the industry for its ability to provide cheaply made but respectable features for the bills' lower halves. An annual Columbia formula of three dozen features (plus serials, comedy shorts, and even an animated cartoon line) began to suggest a major operation. Yet the company had no theater holdings; and other than a San Fernando ranch used for shooting westerns, it had only a small but thoroughly departmentalized studio on Hollywood's Gower Street. Its product was typified by small but elegant interiors, which in turn were populated by middle-rank, small-salaried actors that Cohn most often had to borrow.

Columbia lacked stars of its own, although Jack Holt had a fair following as a hero of masculine programmers. Barbara Stanwyck had been effectively groomed in early Columbia talkies under Frank Capra's guidance, but had moved on to Warners as a star under an arrangement that was, however, financially favorable to Columbia. Capra himself was recognized as Columbia's most precious asset, although his most famous achievement lay ahead, as did Columbia's. The ambitious bantamweight company was destined to write a new chapter in the history of screen comedy, while helping to shape some of the more illustrious careers . . . of which few were as bright or brighter than Carole Lombard's.

Harry Cohn borrowed players from all the larger companies. They could realize long-range benefits from the level of exposure a Columbia picture offered. A second-lead ingenue at M-G-M, say, would only be ticketed to Columbia to play a lead. Even then the players weren't happy about it. Columbia remained an inside joke to screen actors, even after it erased the stigma of Poverty Row and was operating securely in the black. A typical jesting threat among screen actors was "If you don't shape up, they'll send you to Columbia."

Carole did not welcome her consignment, but she did not fight it. The alternative would be salary suspension—something not imposed during the Schulberg regime but entirely likely under the new economic order at Paramount. Having kicked up a fuss or two, she was tentatively viewed as uncooperative by the front office, and it was time for her to show a more amenable side. Powell advised her to make the trek to Columbia dutifully, and Myron Selznick told her to "give Cohn more than the little bastard would bargain for." She did.

Part of Harry Cohn's legend was possession of the vilest tongue in moviedom, among other indelicacies. The language he employed in the presence of women was hardly modified; he was an impulsive, spontaneous rapid talker who used the words he *knew*. When Carole Lombard reported to his office for the first time, there were no polite preliminaries. He said, "Your hair's too white . . . you look like a whore." Carole shot back, "I'm sure you know what a whore looks like if anyone does." He was startled and captivated by her. He tried to soften his approach, but if the purple verbiage slipped out beyond his control, Carole replied in kind, and they waged a sort of card-stacking profanity contest. Harry Cohn decided that this here was one tough dame, but a looker, and he made a sensuous overture. Carole said, "Look, Mr. Cohn, I've agreed to be in your shitty little picture, but fucking you is no part of the deal." According to fable, Harry Cohn straightened his trousers, cleared his throat, and said, "That don't mean you can't call me Harry." To his surprise and delight, he and Carole Lombard would always get along.

She cackled uninhibitedly when Cohn said the name of her picture was *Virtue*. Because virtue was what a brassy dame named Mae was after. Now Mae was a fashionable girl trying to forget her streetwalker past and keep the knowledge from her upright boyfriend. Carole played opposite Pat O'Brien, before he had hit his best stride as a movie hero. The picture was shot in four weeks and Carole had fun. She convinced Harry Cohn that the script needed a lot of hot water to dissolve some of the soap grains, so Robert Riskin was called in and rewrote it, scene by scene, while it was being shot.

Her month at Columbia did not suggest slumming. Carole reveled in the royal treatment accorded her, which included the largest dressing room at the studio. She refashioned it from a truckload of decorative ornaments brought from her home, added a festival of flowers, and gave Harry Cohn's little factory an uncommon touch of class. Bess Peters, who almost never visited Carole at Paramount, was a frequent presence on the *Virtue* set, along with Fieldsie, who now was a fixture. Bill Powell, vacationing between his own assignments, often dropped in to kibitz, and Carole started giving little dressing-room parties on a *daily* basis, inviting studio crewmen along with her old friends. Dixie Pantages was aboard during much of the shooting, serving as Carole's stand-in—as would become her custom whenever Carole filmed away from her home studio.

One of the minor virtues of *Virtue* was its introduction of a new Lombard hairstyle, of her own creation. Topically called the Olympic bob in homage to the international games then under way in Los Angeles, it featured a cloud formation of loose curls covering most of her forehead. Previously her blond tresses had been distinctly parted and combed back and upward to reveal a high hairline and a shiny large forehead that conveyed icy glamour. Whether or not she was responding to Harry Cohn's advice for an unwhorelike appearance, the hair shading was darkened slightly for an ashen rather than platinum effect. Altogether she acquired a softer physiognomy, more nearly realizing her own personality.

She kept her new look upon returning to Paramount. Her new chore was supposed to be *Hot Saturday,* a minor romantic comedy in which Cary Grant and Randolph Scott would compete for her affection. The reason for making the picture was to test Cary Grant —fresh from promising exposure in Dietrich's *Blonde Venus*—in a leading role for the first time. Carole reckoned that another paper-doll role would neither aid nor harm the shape of her career. Rather than risk suspension and ill feeling, she resolved to do as she was told. Then the studio began having difficulty with Miriam Hopkins, and Wesley Ruggles conspired to have Carole replace her in a picture he was preparing.

The picture was *No Man of Her Own* and it was not a project of particular importance. But the leading man was to be Clark Gable, and it would be his first picture away from M-G-M since the sex-bomb detonation that had made him an important star. Because William Randolph Hearst very much wanted Paramount's Bing Crosby to play opposite Marion Davies in the *Going Hollywood* picture M-G-M would make, Louis B. Mayer offered irresistible bait to pry Crosby away from Paramount, if only briefly. Clark Gable for one picture was the bribe, and Paramount took it. *No Man of Her Own* was being shaped for George Raft but fitted Gable to form, so it was upgraded by the addition of Wesley Ruggles as director and Miriam Hopkins as Gable's costar. Miriam did not object to making a picture with the still decidedly "hot" Gable, but she objected to being billed below him—which M-G-M demanded—so she became conveniently ill, unable to work. The studio's other star actresses were all unavailable. Wesley Ruggles said Carole Lombard should fill the vacancy nicely, but Manny Cohen said they would need a stronger name to team with Gable and might have to borrow one; besides, Carole Lombard was going into *Hot Saturday*.

Ruggles already appreciated the offscreen Lombard personality. She had taken his measure on the tennis court, and she was responsive to his own acerbic wit. They connived. He told her not to mention *No Man of Her Own* but to tell Manny Cohen that she absolutely would not appear in *Hot Saturday*—that she wanted stronger opportunity than Paramount was giving her. It worked. Actually Carole didn't see Cohen at all: she called Louella Parsons, who agreed in print that Carole had earned better treatment. Manny Cohen got in touch with Carole and told her she would be Clark Gable's leading lady. Subsequent announcement to that effect was said to arouse consternation in Miriam Hopkins.

Apparently it aroused no disapproval from Clark Gable, who wasn't keen on being farmed out to Paramount, but whose favorable disposition toward Carole Lombard was probably something Ruggles knew in advance. Ruggles and Gable had gone on a hunting trip together, and the fact that they were already friends resulted in the assignment of Ruggles as Gable's director.

Paramount was giving every accommodation to Wesley Ruggles, a respected veteran new to the studio and prominently associated with *Cimarron*, which had taken the Academy Award as best picture although it was not typical of his work. Wes Ruggles, older brother to Charlie (a popular character actor on the Paramount roster), also had a performing background. He started with Mack Sennett and briefly was one of the original Keystone Kops, and it was Sennett who had promoted him as a director of comedies.

No Man of Her Own was not intended as a comedy but it would become one, at least in its first half. The picture divided oddly into two distinct parts, the first occurring in a small town where Carole was a librarian dying on the vine. Gable was a big-city sharpie pretending interest in the bucolic surroundings, while fronting a bootleg operation. In the second half he has married Carole as an extension of his charade and has taken her to New York where she remains ignorant of the actual nature of Gable's activities—with a formulated working out of the complications from that point. The second half enabled The Orchid Lady to dwell among her customary trappings but the first half was much more interesting. The small-town myth was rudely jostled by Carole's personification of boredom and frustration, periscoping Katharine Hepburn's *Alice Adams* of only a few years later.

A staple of the trivia games as the only picture in which Gable and Lombard appeared together, *No Man of Her Own* is deserving of better recognition, as Wesley Ruggles attested:

"When we ran it off for the first time I was damned impressed, though nobody else seemed to be. I loved the first part of the picture —it had a lot of realistic comedy crammed in, and this was what we had decided to work for. Carole and Clark both knew exactly what they were doing. Clark was a damn sight better light comedian than he ever got credit for being. Yet I thought Carole was the revelation. Somebody complained that she didn't seem to be acting, which was one hell of a complaint. Because it didn't *look* like acting, it was so damn natural. Look at the picture today. It's dated, but her work hasn't. She's very fresh. She's playing straight, but using comedy technique, too. Those idiots who'd taken over the studio—they couldn't even see that. Well, the critics didn't see it either. She was wonderful, but it just passed by."

Clark Gable did not miss the evidence of Carole's varied wonderfulness. They had great rapport making the picture, but Wes Ruggles saw nothing unusual in that.

"Carole was married to Bill Powell, which wouldn't have mattered to Clark, but it mattered to her. I think he was given to understand that other than kissing her for the camera, she was off limits. But yes, they got along, and it was a delight, just working with them together. I don't think they knew each other before we started shooting, but Carole got to be anybody's pal pretty quickly."

They had not been personally acquainted earlier, but Carole had seen Clark Gable intermittently in the traffic of filmland. Gable had done an early tour of Hollywood beginning in 1924, and had picked up work as an extra at several studios. He had been at Fox

for crowd scenes in Tom Mix's *Dick Turpin* film in which Carole
also appeared until her footage was left in the cutting room. Bess
Peters had also met with a woman named Josephine Dillon on a
possibility of acting lessons for her daughter; and Miss Dillon,
mistaken by Bess as the mother of the young man sharing her
residence, was in reality the wife of the young man—Clark Gable
indeed. Years later Carole had seen Gable play the lead role of
Killer Meers—Spencer Tracy's Broadway part—in a Los Angeles
stage production of *The Last Mile*. She also had responded to him
in his early, clarion success at M-G-M, shoving around the likes of
Norma Shearer, Jean Harlow, and Joan Crawford.

Still, she knew very little about him before shooting began for
No Man of Her Own. Nancy Carroll, who had acted with Gable
in Chicago before she came to Hollywood, warned Carole to keep
her legs tightly closed. Hints of Gable's roguishness struck no fear
in Carole, but may have rendered even more intriguing the picture
of the man who once again was married to a woman much older
than himself—this time to a wealthy socialite named Rhea Langham.

Throughout the filming they got along swimmingly. At the inevitable studio party marking the completion of shooting, Carole
presented Gable with a large ham, over which was pasted his photograph. The gag served a purpose: it appeared in almost every fan
magazine of consequence before the picture's release. But the Gable-
Lombard friendship appeared to terminate with the actor's return
to M-G-M.

While most bona fide film stars fraternized at their own level,
Bill Powell and Clark Gable were not at all friendly until later on
when Powell also became an M-G-M actor. The Powells and Gables
would meet only remotely at some of the filmland dress-up affairs.
Late in 1932 the rumors started in earnest, to the effect that the
Powell-Lombard marriage was less blissful than the magazine accounts made it. But the shakiness of the union was not attributed
to either party having a divided heart.

For both Carole and Bill, 1932 was a hectic year, complicated by
their careers at different studios where, however, each worked very
hard. Powell starred in a succession of high-budget Warner films
but only one of them—the memorable *One Way Passage* with Kay
Francis—made much of a dent. His popularity was waning, and
while this never resulted in a show of irritability, it may have contributed to his withdrawal from the Hollywood high life in which

he had been a primary figure. With Powell, getting married really meant settling down. After a day's shooting, he wanted nothing so much as to relax at home and retire early. Even while Carole worked through most of the year without a break, she was ready for the kind of night life she had enjoyed when Powell paid her court. Powell's appetite for partying had been satisfied, but Carole was bored by idleness at home. Twice during the year she was excused from work for conditions described as nervous breakdowns, implying overwork; but she confided that her home life had put her nerves on edge. She had no quarrel with Powell. Their relations were entirely friendly, but the difference in their ages began to assert itself.

After completing the picture with Gable, Carole was drafted into the large and generally rollicking ensemble of *If I Had a Million*—a classic of its rare kind, and a studio curiosity venture as an entirely major production shot in just nine days. In a sleight of hand of studio logistics, it was put before the cameras all over the lot, eight directors filming separate segments of an episode movie on eight sound stages. It was a fanciful idea. Lubitsch was directing one of the vignettes, and Wes Ruggles another. Charlie Ruggles and Mary Boland teamed in one installment; W. C. Fields and Alison Skipworth in another; Charles Laughton solo in a single-take sequence without dialogue; George Raft punctuating the comedy with stark melodramatics, and so on. But Carole complained once more. She liked everything about *If I Had a Million* except the sequence of her scheduled appearance—with Gary Cooper and Jack Oakie. She had lobbied unsuccessfully for the streetwalker yarn which cast Wynne Gibson in her stead, and now the front office was plainly irked that Carole was protesting assignment to one of their pet projects, in which even an insignificant appearance was to be taken as some kind of honor. Apparently she had not learned her lesson the first time, so it was reinforced: she was put on loan, again to Columbia and Harry Cohn.

She checked in at a fortuitous time. The *Virtue* film was just going into national release and Columbia officials were pleased with audience reaction to one of their assembly-line program pictures. This time Harry Cohn would give her fair reward: solo star billing, above the title for the first time in her career. She was put into a mild little comedy drama still without a title, but it was Columbia formula 4-B: girl has money, girl finds love, girl must choose between love and money . . . and love wins. Carole's leading man was young

Lyle Talbot of presumed promise, and the company included such experienced actors as Walter Connolly and C. Aubrey Smith.

"Got any ideas what we can call this picture?" Harry Cohn asked. "How about *Roses for Annie?* I've always liked flowers in titles, especially roses." Carole, who was already determined to play the role of Annie Holt without her customary surface of sophistication, said "Roses, snapdragons, lilies, call it any flower except orchids—I'm ready for some other angle. No more orchids for me." And the story went that her new Columbia assignment was dubbed *No More Orchids* because Harry liked the sound of it when she said it: it also became dialogue in the film. The title approximated a slap in the face to her home studio, but the orchid gimmick hadn't really caught on—and wouldn't be revived later at Paramount.

No More Orchids was only a trifle, but it had a healthy resource of witty dialogue. Carole's winning way with a bright line made a believer of Walter Lang, the director. The picture had not been conceived as a comedy, but Lang saw the possibilities of broad comic vistas in the Carole Lombard personality. As shooting progressed, he increased the emphasis on humor; and since it was shot entirely in sequence, the effect was of a fairly serious but overly familiar story line becoming increasingly merry. Walter Lang, then barely known but destined for an illustrious series of popular entertainments, was perhaps the first director to encourage Carole's all-out assault as a comedienne. She always credited him. Lang became a permanent friend and adviser, as well as the squire and eventual husband of Carole's Girl Friday, the reliable Fieldsie.

No Man of Her Own and *No More Orchids* were put into release simultaneously at the end of the year and were in competition with one another around the country during the early months of 1933. In second-run situations the two features sometimes shared a double bill. While neither provided more than temporal entertainment or offered exceptional accomplishment on Carole's own part, the coupling of a costarring stint in a "major" picture opposite a popular male star, with a minor entry in which *she* was the attraction indicated that she had survived a difficult year for the movies and their players. In 1933 she was professionally secure. Matrimonially she was not. Her brief tenure as Mrs. William Powell was about to be committed to the oversized ledger of romantic mistakes made in Hollywood.

❁ VI ❁

The Ex-Mrs. Powell

"I'M LAZY," Carole protested when an interviewer sounded the familiar theme of her boundless vitality. "You'd never believe how lazy I really am. And dammit, so is Bill. My being lazy doesn't bother him, but the fact that he's that way makes me restless and angry at myself. Bill never *drives* me, and someone has to."

Carole's energy and enthusiasm already were the stuff of legend, but she said if she always gave in to herself she'd never accomplish a thing. She said her mother created an environment of activity—that it jabbed a needle in Carole's behind to get her busy, so her laziness didn't show. Her energy was the residue of nervousness and guilt, and she felt most guilty about the time she wasted.

When she separated from Powell, she described their marriage as "a waste of time—his and mine." She said she loved him as much as she ever had, and probably more, and that she did not believe she had been a disappointment to him. She believed that to some extent a husband and wife should maintain an adversary relationship, and she felt that was something she and Powell missed. They were terribly nice to one another, and their mutual lethargy became a constraint on each.

Certainly their prospects for successful marriage had not been enhanced by professional demands on their time. During most of the period of their marriage, both Carole and Bill Powell were working steadily, a few miles apart, and their home was a place to unwind. By

1933 a change in their relative professional status, subtle at first, became more apparent. Powell was still the solvent star, with the prestige of a proven veteran. But his career seemed to lose its momentum not long after he joined Warners. His popularity dipped only slightly, but his employers were vexed that they had been "taken" by Myron Selznick—they considered Powell grossly overpaid for what he meant to them at the box office. Other than *One Way Passage,* none of Powell's Warner pictures was esteemed, and the studio even got him to reprise his Philo Vance charade without encouraging results.

Carole, on the other hand, was still technically on the rise, although her pictures issued in the first half of 1933 did not suggest that her career had an ongoing promise. After her return from Columbia, Paramount put her in *From Hell to Heaven,* an unabashed parody of *Grand Hotel* with a racetrack setting—an agreeable low comedy, but with Carole wasted in support of Jack Oakie. She played the daughter of a bookie. *From Hell to Heaven* was leagues above *Supernatural,* the ridiculous spook yarn she and Randolph Scott suffered through. And yet, without having made a dent on the popularity chart, she was in demand. Other studios made regular inquiry as to her availability, and Fox's persistent Winfield Sheehan made a serious overture to purchase Carole's expensive contract outright from Paramount. Almost no one had occasion to describe her as a "good" actress, but she was a reliably adequate one for what was asked of her. Clearly she had become something more than Mrs. William Powell to the movie-making establishment. She was "good copy"—a screen personality in her own right, whose publicity now regularly surpassed her husband's.

This may have produced an added tension. When Warners loaned Powell to RKO for an Ann Harding picture, the grapevine interpretation was that Bill was through; and his separation from Carole was confirmed soon afterward, in the late spring of 1933. Carole resumed residence with her mother. Her decision to vacate Powell's home was admittedly sudden, and probably impulsive. Yet she immediately disclosed her intention to terminate the marital contract and saw no reason to delay it. She and Powell engaged George Thatcher as counsel for an uncontested divorce action, and Carole established residence on the Nevada side of Lake Tahoe in June.

On August 16, 1933, her case required just six minutes. Extreme cruelty was the formal charge, and Carole's testimony seemed almost

comical to her intimates. She told the judge that Powell used foul
language, of which she did not approve. She said he was "very emotional, cruel, and cross, and had repeatedly given temper displays
almost from the day they were married." She sought no alimony,
and the judge granted the divorce before Carole had completed her
presentation.

Her return to Los Angeles marked the first occasion of her travel
by air. Bess Peters did not want her daughter to fly, but Carole said
it was the coming thing—soon everybody would be riding in planes.
Besides, it was something she wanted to experience. Jessica Barthelmess drove Bess to the tiny Los Angeles commercial airport to receive the newly unmarried Carole. Reporters and photographers
were also on the scene, and Carole was gracious without being entirely cooperative. The photographers wanted her to smile and wave
but she wouldn't. "I'm not at all happy about this, you know, so I'm
not going to give you a smile I don't mean. After all, a divorce is a
divorce."

She told the press she would resume residence with her mother.
But both Bess and Carole were agreed that such an arrangement
could only be temporary. Bess particularly was sensitive still about
the stereotypical notion of a movie mama, and she prodded Carole
to start looking for a house of her own. Together they scouted for
a residence that could accommodate a bachelor girl with live-in
servants. Then the search ended abruptly when Carole started
dating Bill Powell once more.

Married, they had become stay-at-homes. Now they were doing
the Hollywood scene once more, becoming regulars at Ciro's on
the Sunset Strip. There were reflexive rumors of a pending reconciliation, and Carole's denials were thought to lack real conviction.
The "rambler" column in *The Hollywood Reporter* hinted that the
divorce had been Powell's idea all along and now he had changed
his mind. But Carole told Louella Parsons that she had taken the
initial action toward both separation and divorce. She said she
wasn't opposed to marrying again, and wouldn't entirely discount
the posibility of another term as Mrs. William Powell; but she did
not expect to marry as long as she was a working movie actress. The
pressures, she said, were too great and also unfair. "Right now,
having a career still means so much to me. If I think enough of a
man that the career becomes meaningless, then I'm sure I'd want

to marry him. But I doubt that will happen, at least for a long time."

The Parsons journalese had a way of imparting a deadly seriousness to even the most frivolously given statements, yet Carole's friends had noted her becoming increasingly serious and uncharacteristically subdued during her marriage to Powell. Yet the divorce released her from melancholy. Her extroverted self was reasserted; and while Powell remained the dominant man in her life, she was rushed by a new cadre of male admirers. Although they were ardent, her own disposition was summed up in the lyric of a popular song of the day: "Can't we be just friends?" When she changed her own mind, it was over the very singer of the song—an Italian-American crooner, Russ Columbo.

Carole and Paramount had contradictory feelings toward one another. The studio was home to her, and its workers at every level were her family. In the period immediately following her divorce, the outgoing personality became magnified and she was unchallenged as the most popular person on the lot—male or female, artist or artisan, novice or veteran. Merriment took its cues from her every movement, and people schemed to be in her proximity at lunchtime and in other idle moments. She drove a little motorized kiddie car around the studio: it had been given as a birthday present from her coworkers. Or she roller-skated, and touched off a fad.

She said she could not get her fill of making pictures. Even when she knew she was working in a turkey, the whole business was fun to her. Yet she found herself giving more of her time to complaining that the studio was misusing her, or not using her at all when perhaps it should. Her attitude changed as she began to suspect that first-rate screen performance might not be beyond her capability after all.

A few years later she would say she became a better actress when she became less of one. She had thought of acting as an artificial craft for which she had not been properly trained and that kind of thinking had inhibited her confidence. She casually shared Hollywood's general awe of stage diplomas, and did not question Paramount's consistent distribution of its more coveted star roles to the Misses Colbert, Hopkins, and Sidney, all of whom had experienced success on Broadway, as had most of the ladies who had flourished earlier in Paramount talkies—Ruth Chatterton, Kay Francis, and Nancy Carroll. Even Marlene Dietrich had flashed her famous legs live, in German music halls during the twenties. Carole suffered Hollywood's built-in prejudice against its hometown girls.

Ernst Lubitsch had been telling her for a matter of years that she undervalued her own talent. He scolded first B. P. Schulberg and then Emanuel Cohen for not putting Carole to a challenging test. Yet when Carole was available to him he would usually choose Miriam Hopkins, as he did again in *Design for Living*. But when Wesley Ruggles and then Walter Lang at Columbia began to lecture Carole on her untapped potential, she was in a mood to listen, and ready to believe. She was agitated that Paramount was again treating her so shabbily, and the first assignment after her divorce was so small it gave her pause.

The Eagle and the Hawk was a World War I flying picture, grimly dramatic and certainly more than a programmer, with Fredric March, Cary Grant, and Jack Oakie in the star parts. It was favorably received, but Carole's participation amounted to one brief sequence. She meets gloomy pilot March at a party and takes him to bed to cheer him up, only to leave him depressed once more as they say good-bye in a horse-drawn taxi. Her character didn't even rate a name: she was "Beautiful Lady" in the cast and credits.

When Fox petitioned to buy her contract, it was with the aim of having her replace a dissident Sally Eilers. Carole's friend from school days had become an instant star in Frank Borzage's highly regarded *Bad Girl,* but the subsequent series of vehicles teaming her with James Dunn had not made her happy. She staged a walkout, refusing to appear in a picture actually called *Jimmy and Sally.* Carole was not averse to the assignment on a loan basis, but Fox wanted her exclusive services; and while Paramount might have agreed to a transfer, Myron Selznick would not, and small print in Carole's contract favored Myron's position. As a consequence, being Jimmy's Sally gave Claire Trevor her first movie lead.

The best Paramount could offer was *The Girl Without a Room,* and its hopelessness amounted to an inside joke at the studio. Wesley Ruggles had been asked to take over the direction, but his brother Charlie, who was in the cast, advised against it. And one of Carole's screenwriter pals, Claude Binyon, was brought in to work on the script but despaired of reviving a stiff, and warned

Carole against accepting the role. Carole wanted no part of *The Girl Without a Room* but she also did not want to tangle with the Paramount front office, which had a way of penalizing her unco-operativeness. Nor did she want to hurt Charles Farrell's feelings: he was an old friend but his career was faltering—Fox had sent him packing, and he was at Paramount to play the male lead in *The Girl Without a Room*. So Carole thought of something. She got dolled up in a smart new sports suit with a matching hat that left most of her blond locks exposed, and paid an impromptu call on Harry Cohn.

Didn't Harry have *something* she could do? He was taken entirely by surprise. Cohn spent a good part of his working day begging other studios to loan their pampered players to him; and he grew weary of trying to persuade transient actors that appearing in a Columbia picture wasn't necessarily their ruin. And here was this beautiful girl asking him to help her out of a spot. Okay, he said, let's figure out what we're going to do.

He told her about a picture called *Master of Men* that was ready to go into production but was still without a leading lady for Jack Holt. Hell, he could pour a little extra money into that one if she wanted to do it . . . whereupon she called him a shithead.

"Harry, I want you to help my career, not kill it. I want something that's better than what my own studio is giving me, not worse. Besides, they'll only let me go if they think it's a good investment for them."

Frank Capra's *Lady for a Day* was already in the works at Columbia, with Glenda Farrell doing a part that Carole might have liked. But every upcoming Columbia picture was strictly potboiler stuff; Cohn didn't have anything up to the level of *No More Orchids,* which hadn't been all that sensational, anyway. But Cohn showed Carole a list of properties the studio owned, and said, "Anything here that'll wet your pants?" Carole scanned the list and said, "What about *Brief Moment*?"

She recognized the title of a respectable play by S. N. Behrman. Cohn had bought the movie rights hoping to get England's Gertrude Lawrence to play the role of Abby Fane, then had dropped the idea. The project was still scheduled for the vague future, but he told Carole there were no big problems with sets or costumes. In short, if she wanted to do *Brief Moment* he could whip up a production in a hurry. How about right now, she suggested. And

Harry Cohn called in his secretary and dictated instructions to all his department heads. He grinned at Carole and said, "You gotta have balls to be in this business, and I got 'em."

"Harry, do me a real favor," Carole connived. "When you call Paramount, don't ask for me. Ask for Miriam. You won't be able to get her anyway, so ask. It won't seem fishy if I'm second choice."

When Carole reported to Columbia for *Brief Moment* just two weeks later, Cohn said, "They thought I was a lunatic, asking for Hopkins, and after they stopped laughing they said could they send me Lombard instead. So it was Manny's idea, not mine. Except I gave him a hard time. I asked who else was available. They said Frances Drake and I said who the fuck is Frances Drake and never mind, I'll take Lombard."

After so much intrigue, *Brief Moment* on film would disappoint admirers of the play, including Behrman himself, who regretted that he had not been available to do his own adaptation. Nor did Carole benefit from David Burton's static direction, although she liked the Abby Fane role that Francine Larrimore had played on the stage. Carole had been given too few opportunities for clever dialogue and *Brief Moment* had a lot of that. She played a night-club singer who marries a drunken playboy and is scorned by his family; but sure enough, she'll be his salvation. Gene Raymond of the wavy blond locks played the errant youth, and Monroe Owsley and Donald Cook also counted as leading men. Even if the picture failed to arouse a special following, it presented a Carole Lombard who was somehow more beautiful than one encountered previously. Significantly, *Brief Moment* was her first picture to enlist Teddy Tetzlaff as cinematographer. He had an unmistakable flair for framing her in a lighting that purged the slightest hint of "hardness" that was a taint during her early career. Carole's own instincts were strong: she saw what Tetzlaff had accomplished, and she expected Paramount to be more appreciative of her.

They weren't. She was asked to dispense the necessary girl stuff for a Chevalier picture, *The Way to Love*. The Frenchman's frothy vehicles had collapsed into a maudlin formula, and on any basis were not charming Depression audiences. Carole refused the assignment, even when Lubitsch advised her to accept. Again she was in the studio's bad graces, but this time her rescuer was Charles Laughton.

Just back from England and his famous romp as Henry VIII,

Laughton agreed to film a tropical melodrama called *White Woman* as a means of freeing himself from a Paramount contract that had not given him satisfaction. Elissa Landi was his assigned leading lady, but Laughton and Miss Landi had not gotten on well when they made *The Sign of the Cross* for DeMille. Laughton surprised the studio chiefs by requesting Carole Lombard. The actor had enjoyed some of Ken Murray's "home movie" footage shot on the Paramount lot, showing Lombard and Laughton cavorting together, and that incited his whim that they should make a picture. They figured to be an incongruous twosome, but Paramount granted Laughton's wish.

The picture was trash, but emerged as high-class trash on the strength of the Laughton and Lombard performances. The Motion Picture Academy gave Laughton its Best Actor award (for *The Private Life of Henry VIII*) while *White Woman* was being filmed, which had an effect of unleashing a hamminess Laughton had struggled to subdue in the early shooting. But even when his *White Woman* portrayal worked entirely out of control, his juiciest playing bespoke a powerful talent and Carole's underplaying provided an effective contrast. She was an alluring incongruity in the jungle setting. Although she got little help from the direction (Stuart Walker's) she got plenty from Laughton. Not overtly: just playing a scene with him, she said, was an exciting thing. It made her body tingle and her earlobes burn, and it gave her dramatic work a fine edge of tension.

Unlike the old days at rich and leisurely Paramount, nothing was wasted any more, including time. Carole went from her *Brief Moment* loanout right into *White Woman* and then into *Bolero* without getting a day off. Thanks mainly to Miriam Hopkins, she had a high level of job security. *Bolero* was another picture Miriam was supposed to do, but didn't especially like. Carole confronted her personally and urged her to turn it down, because *she* wanted it for herself.

Miriam Hopkins was not really the difficult creature that Hollywood legend has painted her. She simply disliked making movies, about as much as Carole delighted in it. Miriam would later recall her early Paramount years with anything but affection, saying that only the three pictures she made for Lubitsch had given her pleasure. Cooperation on her part surely would have resulted in her emergence as a major box-office attraction, but she remained primarily a critics' actress, one who thought herself slumming in Hollywood. She was always eager to get back to the stage. At the end of 1933 Miriam also wanted to be freed from her obligation to Paramount, while Carole only shared the general discontentment with the front office. Besides Charles Laughton, Fredric March also sought a release from contract. Nor did the studio put forth a great effort to retain its high-salaried dissidents. As with Laughton, Paramount agreed to cancel the Hopkins and March contracts after one more picture from each. Miriam grudgingly consented to *Bolero* as a means of extricating herself, then became suddenly "ill" as an accommodation to Carole. Carole wanted *Bolero* because it was the thinly disguised story of Maurice Mouvet, the ballroom dancer who had regaled her some years earlier when she was in the Cocoanut Grove's young Friday night crowd, and Maurice was the headliner there. In *Bolero* he would be impersonated by George Raft, still being marketed by Paramount as a second Valentino. But Raft was a reformed hoofer, eager to do his own dancing. Carole, too, wanted to surprise her studio and Hollywood generally by displaying her own dancing ability—something she could do more comfortably than Miriam Hopkins.

Another of Harry Cohn's intrigues now involved Miriam directly and Carole remotely. Since Frank Capra's *Lady for a Day* had scored a surprise smash hit that gave Columbia its first real intimation of respectability, Cohn had Capra's blessing to make an earnest pitch for Miriam to play in *It Happened One Night,* hopefully opposite M-G-M's Robert Montgomery for Capra's direction. Miriam read the script and decided she wasn't interested—it was "just another silly little comedy." Paramount gave her permission to take the assignment but made it clear that she would still owe them a picture, so Miriam backed away from *It Happened One Night.* Other ranking movie actresses expressed interest as long as Montgomery was the leading man; but when Montgomery refused assignment to Columbia, they all echoed his veto: Margaret Sullavan; Myrna Loy; and Constance Bennett. Harry Cohn suggested Carole Lombard but was startled by Capra's reaction: Frank Capra couldn't seem to place her. He thought he had *heard* of Carole Lombard, but who was she? What had she done? Harry Cohn decided to drop the matter of Carole Lombard and concentrate on getting Loretta Young assigned—she and Spencer Tracy had both been successfully

borrowed for *Man's Castle,* which another "name" director, Frank
Borzage, was then filming for Columbia.

The next development was that Clark Gable, against his will, was
ordered by Louis B. Mayer to report to Columbia for *It Happened
One Night.* In a familiar, incredible story with possibly apocryphal
trimming, Mayer was said to have exiled Gable to an approximate
Siberia because he didn't like him personally, and thought Gable
was through as a box-office attraction; while Cohn was said to accept
Gable reluctantly, convinced that Montgomery was the bigger star.
Certainly Montgomery was the likelier choice, as the screen's unchallenged master of light comedy prior to the emergence of Cary
Grant. But Capra was delighted to have Gable's services, and was
confident it would enable him to obtain a leading lady from the top
shelf.

Gable and Capra could get along amiably, but with Harry Cohn
and Clark Gable it was loathe at first sight. On only one matter
would they find themselves in agreement: they both liked Carole
Lombard, and Cohn hoped to pacify Gable by getting Carole to
play opposite him. Capra wanted a bigger name, but Gable and
Cohn in their strained alliance had a secret weapon named Bob
Riskin who, besides being a sometime Lombard boyfriend, was
Frank Capra's regular screenwriter. Riskin brought the message to
Carole: if she wanted to make another picture with Gable, it could
probably be worked out with Capra, and it could surely be arranged
with Paramount. Carole thought it over, and intercepted a rumor
that Gable expected to bed her down now that Willam Powell was
no longer an obstacle. She told Riskin to scratch her from the running for *It Happened One Night,* but apprehensiveness about Gable
was not the factor. She liked Riskin's script, she knew Capra was a
top director, she enjoyed her "vacations" at Columbia, and she
really adored the Harry Cohn that everyone else hated . . . and
yes, she was attracted to Clark Gable. But Wesley Ruggles assured
her that she couldn't do both *It Happened One Night* and *Bolero*
because the production schedules would coincide. Ruggles was the
Bolero director, and with Miriam Hopkins out of the picture,
Carole's assignment was guaranteed. She chose *Bolero* and later
would not regret the decision, despite the fantastic success and historical importance of *It Happened One Night.*

Very soon afterward, Capra obtained a "bigger" star than he had bargained for to play opposite Gable—Paramount's own Claudette Colbert. Both she and Gable would be compensated for their "slumming" by Academy Awards—the only time both the male and female stars of a picture snared top honors. Capra would also be cited as Best Director, and *It Happened One Night*—duly recognized as Best Picture—became an early model for "screwball" film comedy. It rehabilitated Gable's career, which may not have been in jeopardy anyway—but now everyone knew he was adept at romantic comedy. Claudette Colbert moved into her best career phase, while Miriam Hopkins counted her rejection of *It Happened One Night* as the worst among many errors of judgment she made in Hollywood.

On its own terms, *Bolero* was an agreeable picture, stylishly produced, and it was quite popular. Carole indeed was a revelation, not only in the presentational dance numbers—in which she and George Raft approached flawlessness—but in the story line, where her straight dramatic work was dominant. *Bolero* was a serious romantic film without being heavy, and Carole exhibited an authority that she attributed to Wes Ruggles's confidence in her.

George Raft in later years would say that he had always fancied himself somewhat in love with Carole Lombard, and that among his many films *Bolero* had pleased him especially. If Raft did not come near to approximating Valentino on film, he was, however, one of Hollywood's more reliable offscreen Casanovas, and perhaps he was merely a victim of mistiming where Carole was concerned. They made the picture at a time when she was very much under the spell of Russ Columbo who, by physical appearance at least, could easily pass as George Raft's younger brother.

Also in *Bolero,* with a moustache to give him a less youthful demeanor, was the Welsh-born Ray Milland, in whom Carole detected more talent than confidence. He had failed to catch on in an earlier Hollywood tenure. *Bolero* was his first assignment under contract to Paramount. Carole took him under her wing in a way that was becoming typical of her; she tried to make young and upcoming players feel at home in the studio jungle.

Miriam Hopkins, meanwhile, was up to her old tricks. She had agreed to take the female lead in *We're Not Dressing* opposite Bing Crosby, because Sir James M. Barrie's *The Admirable Crichton* was its presumed source. Many years earlier DeMille had filmed the Barrie tale as *Male and Female,* and Gloria Swanson became a household word. But Miriam changed her mind when the writers brought Barrie down to a low-comedy level, with the addition of George Burns and Gracie Allen to the cast. Leon Errol was also tossed into the salad; and then, from Broadway, Ethel Merman. Substituting Carole for Miriam had become a reflex action by the studio, and form followed, although she was still at work on *Bolero* when *We're Not Dressing* went into production. Since the transmogrified Barrie comedy was scheduled for shooting almost entirely on Catalina Island, Carole had two weeks of commuting by air from set to set until *Bolero* was completed.

With Burns and Allen as ringmasters, the shooting schedule of *We're Not Dressing* was entirely chaotic; all they needed was the Marx Brothers, and even that possibility had been considered. Carole noted that Gracie Allen, her instant pal, was a fairly straight young woman very unlike her radio personality, if George Burns was briefly removed from her vicinity. But George was a catalyst for such merriment as others would concoct, especially Gracie. Carole said she never had so much fun making a movie, and since the company as a whole shared her enjoyment, director Norman Taurog elected not to intervene. Predictably, *We're Not Dressing* would be an utterly forgettable charade, but entertaining for its moment. It was about shipwrecked castaways, and Carole played the rich girl—spoiled at first—who comes to depend on manservant Bing for everything, finally including love. There was a pleasant Mack Gordon-Harry Revel score for Bing and Ethel Merman. Bing sang "Good Night, Lovely Little Lady" to Carole, and she dueted with him, not at all badly, on "Once in a Blue Moon."

Because she was in obvious fast company, Carole's most wacky comedy effort to date escaped meaningful notice. So, for that matter, did Crosby's very able showing as a farceur. It was their only picture together, but their employers could hardly have missed the evidence of their compatibility as a team. Crosby, too, encouraged an atmosphere of relaxation on the set.

During their Catalina exile, Carole decided that the old folks at the resort hotel where the company stayed were entirely *too* relaxed. So she shook them up a bit. Crosby recalled that one morning at breakfast Carole froze the resident guests but delighted the film crew by shouting across the dining room at him: "Hey, Bing, did I leave my nightgown in your bedroom? I can't find it anywhere!"

Ray Milland was also in *We're Not Dressing*, showing nicely in a part that Carole obtained for him when it became vacant. She advised Fred Datig, the casting director, that Milland would be perfect, and to please assign him. Perfect he was, and then Bing Crosby wanted Milland for his next picture, too . . . and Ray was on his way.

We're Not Dressing finished shooting before the Christmas holidays. It was the seventh picture Carole had made during a hectic and strenuous 1933 that had been punctuated by her divorce— although both *Bolero* and *We're Not Dressing* would be among her 1934 releases. The work had not been without a tonic effect, and from the nadir of *Supernatural* she felt she had attained her apogee with *Bolero.* But she was tired and wanted a vacation, and was sure she deserved one. She wanted to take her mother to Fort Wayne, then on to New York to see the new season's plays, as they'd done before. A reconciliation with Powell was a recurring rumor, with likelihood of a second honeymoon in Hawaii. But Paramount said no. If she would agree to a salary suspension, fine, she could take as long a vacation as she liked. But they were paying her by the week, not by the picture, and if she was going to carry home two thousand dollars a week, she'd work for it. Carole ranked ninety-fourth on the *Motion Picture Herald's* rating of movie box-office personalities for 1933, and apparently Paramount accepted that as evidence of her being overpaid: they refused to concede her value to them. They were also miffed that Carole, taking a cue from Miriam Hopkins, had contracted her annual influenza when they had tried to loan her to Fox for *Worst Woman in Paris,* and they had lost out on a one-picture trade for Warner Baxter.

Her ordeal resembled nothing so much as musical chairs. She started throwing things when they asked her to do something called *Eight Girls in a Boat.* The alternative to a salary suspension was another detour to Columbia, and she said she'd take it. At least Harry Cohn appreciated her. She reported for *Sonata,* title later changed to *Sisters Under the Skin,* and liked the script and also her costars, who were Frank Morgan and Joseph Schildkraut. She rehearsed with them before shooting commenced; then Paramount reneged, sent Elissa Landi to Columbia in her stead, and reclaimed Carole for *Wharf Angel,* with Victor McLaglen and Preston Foster. She wasn't happy about being tossed around like so much luggage, but she minimized her grumbling because *Wharf Angel* looked like an interesting change of pace for her. It was one of the infrequent sallies into straight direction by one of the screen's great production designers—William Cameron Menzies, a man Carole liked. Getting her had been his own idea when Fay Wray, the intended girl on the wharf, was detained by M·G·M's distended *Viva Villa* production. The next twist was that Carole didn't even get into makeup for *Wharf Angel*. She was right back at Columbia, but not for *Sisters Under the Skin*. What *Wharf Angel* accomplished was to render her available for *Twentieth Century*.

In the annals of Hollywood, 1934 was Columbia's coming-out year. Capra's *Lady for a Day* and Borzage's *Man's Castle* had been only a prologue in 1933. Besides *It Happened One Night*, Harry Cohn was putting together a new season schedule that included *The Captain Hates the Sea* for Lewis Milestone to direct, and a pretentious opera film in which the Met's Grace Moore would score a much-fussed-over success—*One Night of Love*. Then there was the screen version of a popular Ben Hecht-Charles MacArthur play, *Twentieth Century*, which Howard Hawks had negotiated to produce and direct for Cohn's company. For the role of the egomaniacal theatrical producer Oscar Jaffe, Hawks had the great John Barrymore—soon to be toppled, or rather tippled, from the ranks of the screen elite, but for the moment still as illustrious as any. The role of sophisticated actress Lily Garland (low-born as Mildred Plotka but remade Pygmalion-style by Jaffe) could match Oscar's every exaggeration of color. Cohn and Hawks hoped to corral an Ina Claire or a Tallulah Bankhead, although both of those estimable women had washed out as movie attractions. But they wanted no part of a Barrymore picture because suffering through his inebriation had become too much of a trial. Eugenie Leontovich had played the stage role to some acclaim but was judged too old for the picture, and was no movie name besides.

Cohn's attempt to sign Gloria Swanson was rebuffed, although many years later Miss Swanson and José Ferrer would successfully revive the Hecht-MacArthur play on Broadway. The faltering Ruth Chatterton said no. Constance Bennett, Ann Harding, Kay Francis—all were mentioned, even Joan Crawford. Howard Hawks said he'd prefer Miriam Hopkins to any of them, and that may have prompted Cohn's tentative suggestion of Carole Lombard. To Cohn's surprise, Hawks was quite receptive. He knew of Carole's work and suspected an unrealized promise. So Harry Cohn got on the phone to Paramount's Emanuel Cohen.

"Manny? Have you put her to work in that angel picture yet?

You know who I mean—your longshoreman girl, the truck driver, what's-her-name Lombard. Yeah, I want her. Howard Hawks wants her. And Jack Barrymore wants her, but he don't know it yet. Trouble is, *you've* got her. Manny? Why ain't you saying something? Hell yes, I'm talking *Twentieth Century*, I won't shitcha. So can you spring her for me?"

Carole was sprung, although she registered the disbelief that prevailed at Paramount, and around Hollywood generally. The term *superstar* had not yet come into vogue, but to Hollywood's way of thinking, John of the Barrymores was an authentic superstar, even though he had never become a guaranteed box-office draw. His pictures were prestige events for he was a prestige star—the personified touch of "class" the nouveau riche of filmland customarily lusted after. So it hardly figured that Carole Lombard, a middle-rank fixture in commodity pictures, would be in the running for the Lily Garland role that logically should accommodate another superstar of Barrymore's equivalent aura. Yet the role was being delivered to her on a silver platter, without Carole having declared her own candidacy.

Of course Paramount yanked her immediately from *Wharf Angel*, considering the likelihood that *Twentieth Century* could make her a major star as they had failed to do. A saucy Mississippi girl named Dorothy Dell, with a Ziegfeld Follies background but new to pictures, replaced Carole in the McLaglen film. Carole reported immediately to Columbia, the Cinderella company of upstart ambition that now was purging the stimga of its Poverty Row heritage. It was February, 1934, and *It Happened One Night* had just been released around the country.

If Carole Lombard's assignment was regarded dubiously, the uncertainty surrounding Barrymore's participation was a fair match. For irony's sake, his career was periled when it was most deserving of its prestige, by the measure of his recent achievement. John Barrymore had experienced a run of glittery films either critically successful *(Reunion in Vienna, Night Flight, Counsellor-at-Law)* or immensely popular *(Dinner at Eight, Rasputin and the Empress)* or both *(Grand Hotel, A Bill of Divorcement)*. It was a slate unmatched in the corresponding two-year period by any other star, yet a supposition prevailed that the Great Profile was finished, washed up. Dolores Costello, his third wife and perhaps the great love of his brilliant but turbulent life, had left him. Now he was drinking more heavily and yielding to the more lurid excesses of his personality. His latest performances revealed a tendency toward ham, but producers were most wary of his instability. A dissipated actor, however eloquent during his best behavior, was always a risk.

Howard Hawks wanted John Barrymore for the Oscar Jaffe role because he *was* Jaffe—histrionic, preening, ego-driven almost to clownishness, outrageous and yet persuasive. Ben Hecht, who with Charles MacArthur adapted their own play for the screen, confirmed that the Jaffe character was conceived for the stage in the Barrymore image; and that Moffat Johnston, who originated the role, was essentially impersonating Barrymore. Hecht, who also endorsed the casting of Carole Lombard, said the real problem lay in finding an actress who wouldn't be grievously upstaged by Barrymore. So the primary consideration was not ability, but personality. The offscreen Carole Lombard was accruing a reputation as a good-time girl—generous, uninhibited, delightful in all her excesses. Hecht said they counted on that quality coming through on film as it hadn't before. He had not conceived Lily Garland as a great actress (although Jaffe made her think she was one) but as a personality functioning with the benefit of high glamour.

Carole was not so much miscast as overcast. In the regimented Hollywood order of that era there was no official apprenticeship, but a player working regularly on a studio contract was expected to find his level within two years, perhaps three. A player's signing was publicized; the dropped option was not. Once a player became classified, it was very unlikely that he would rise to a higher echelon. The challenge was to retain one's own plateau.

A discipline for star-rating was apparent to the trained eye. Among the women, Norma Shearer, Greta Garbo and very few others inhabited the topmost rung. Claudette Colbert, Barbara Stanwyck, and Irene Dunne typified the next level—solidly established and assured of permanent stardom. Next, the Elissa Landis and Dolores Del Rios, without commercial pedigree, had a tentative hold on stardom but were less secure, say, than a chronic near-star such as Maureen O'Sullivan or a perennial lower-case star like Joan Blondell. All of these girls had "made good" in the movies. So had Joan Bennett and Loretta Young, choice morsels in the ingenue salad, climbing at a slower pace but climbing steadily. Such players might be leads in one picture and give support in the next, depending upon the makeup of the cast and the stature of the picture. A Madge Evans might be Robert Montgomery's leading lady, but not his costar. Enduring at that level was Carole Lombard's accepted destiny prior to *Twentieth Century*. She had been leading lady to Clark Gable, William Powell, and Gary Cooper, but only in their distinctly minor vehicles. More often she would be found in the company of a Chester Morris or Gene Raymond or their (and her) equivalents. To become John Barrymore's leading lady in a famous property was the most extraordinary development in her career.

Carole had observed John Barrymore on occasion since her emergence as a movie regular, but usually at a distance. They had hardly spoken since her audition for him eight years earlier, when she lost the opportunity to appear with him in *The Tempest* because her automobile accident intervened. She expected him to remember her, but he didn't. When reminded of the early screen test in which he'd made love to her, Barrymore became sympathetic, denying his rumored hostility over her casting. (His own choice was said to have been the English actress, Diana Wynyard.) Soon they became affectionate toward one another, without prospect of passion. Barrymore, a fabled roué, confessed that he was all burned out; but he was no less impressed by Carole's beauty, luminous in its maturity.

Early on they discovered that acting together had a mutual tonic effect. They were largely on their own, with important assistance from Walter Connolly, an excellent character actor particularly adept at farce. Howard Hawks, not primarily identified with comedy films but responsible for a surprising percentage of Hollywood's great ones, determined the shape and rhythm of a picture—its *style*—without resorting to coaching his actors. Hawks exhibited an extraordinary respect for professionalism. He relied on Barrymore and Lombard without imposing external ideas that would inhibit their own creativity. Only rarely would he caution Barrymore about bloating his ripe characterization out of proportion. Barrymore's Jaffe had its own poetry of theatrical duplicity. The entire play is a seduction: Jaffe playing on Lily's ego, desperately persuading her to star in the next play he will produce. His performance was wild but entirely right in its lunacy, and Carole rose to the bait with her own neglected resourcefulness.

Years later, when she could discuss her work frankly from the perspective of major stardom, Carole said, "I'm really not a leader but a follower. If I'm chatting with someone who talks slowly, I talk slowly. If they speak fast, so do I. I respond to any pace but I don't set one. If I do a scene with someone who underplays, you can expect it of me, too. There are different kinds of good actors but I sort of connect with all kinds. My best work—this is my opinion, but I believe it isn't argued—always comes from playing with terrific actors."

In *Twentieth Century* John Barrymore established a tempo and dimension to challenge any reasonable performer, but Carole caught his stride. Acclaimed only a decade earlier as America's greatest Hamlet, Barrymore said his real skill was in comedy and that the only remarkable thing about his Hamlet was his appreciation of the Prince's humor. He said he played comedy and tragedy the same way, only slightly varying the shading. Carole wasn't sure she knew what he meant, but when Barrymore went into histrionic orbit, she tapped the legacy Mack Sennett had given. *Twentieth Century* was a farce both verbal and visual, and Carole knew how to build both kinds of gags for the climactic belly laugh, the boffo. It was all in the timing, and if you had it instinctively, it wasn't a thing easily lost. John Barrymore surprised the film colony by proclaiming Carole Lombard as "probably the greatest actress I have ever worked with." It sounded like press-agent stuff and fell on cynical ears; but Barrymore restated the opinion in later years, generously dropping the "probably."

Twentieth Century went lickety-split, a long screenplay text dispensed in just ninety minutes. Released in the early summer of 1934, it prodded the critical superlatives. Every notice conveyed some astonishment over Carole's spirited performance, as in this anonymous but incisive example:

"The selection of Miss Lombard caused some misgivings when the casting was announced. In the succession of films in which she has appeared, Miss Lombard, who is attractive to the eye although too much addicted to 'the Hollywood makeup,' never seemed to be more than a passably fair performer. There was a lethargy that dulled the edge of her characterizations, a cold, aloof attitude; and although she continued to play featured roles, many moviegoers were beginning to ask 'why?' But she has now given a more than ordinarily good performance in which she holds attention even though she is opposite one of the finest actors in the films, in one of his best roles. She is alive, vivid, colorful, filled with the fire one would expect from a temperamental and spoiled beauty of the stage and screen such as Lily Garland is sketched. She has learned from Barrymore and there is a frequent use of gestures and tricks of the stage which are mannerisms of his."

The huge commercial success that was anticipated simply did not transpire. Harry Cohn would often refer to *Twentieth Century* as a flop, for it did only ordinary business, realizing a tidy operating profit. Ben Hecht reckoned the comedy was too sophisticated for the broad movie audience, as an inside joke on the theatre. For all its zaniness, it was not the seminal "screwball" comedy as is often said, although some of the customary screwball elements undoubtedly were there. But screwball comedies were morality plays of the Depression, with the vested rich always functioning as the butt of the jesting, finally gaining redemption from the struggling poor. No social consciousness was concealed within the *Twentieth Century* humors, no hint of poverty blighting a nation. Its hilarity was confined to an encapsulated world of affluent theatrical folk, who for most of the distance were riding the rails on the Twentieth Century Limited. On the other hand, *It Happened One Night,* still playing extended second runs in the hinterlands because people simply wouldn't let it go, painted the rich as a contrast. Its runaway heiress was tamed by a workaday reporter of consummate integrity, whose example wins even the favor of the tycoon father (Walter Connolly again, abetting the Gable and Colbert accounts). The two pictures, each remarkable in its own way, contained between themselves the screwball elements that would fashion the brightest movie genre of the second half of the thirties decade. *Twentieth Century,* despite its financial disappointment, validated Carole Lombard's credential as a zany—one capable of dominating a new movie vogue.

So how did Paramount react to her belated and hard-won emergence? Her homecoming present was the script of *Kiss and Make Up,* a mélange of banalities whose only possible compensation was its enlistment of Cary Grant. Carole hollered bloody murder. Here was the clotheshorse stuff all over again, and where were the *lines?* In a meeting with Emanuel Cohen and his satellites, Al Kaufman and A. M. Botsford, she sprayed a blue invective that was authentic Lombard, but with a flourish that suggested a hangover of Lily Garland. Since *Twentieth Century* had not then been released or previewed, the caliber of her performance was not yet suspected by the men who paid her keep. They still regarded her as a gamble for a role requiring maximum authority, and they supposed the Barrymore experience had merely endowed Carole with a big-star complex she did not merit. Flatly refusing *Kiss and Make Up,* she said if they still thought her grossly overpaid, she'd take her freedom and release Paramount from obligation to *her.*

They were startled, all right, and not at all willing to let her go. Claudette Colbert's hiatus to Columbia had transported her into the elite, and it might conceivably happen with Carole Lombard. Besides, Miriam Hopkins was winding up her Paramount contract in *She Loves Me Not* opposite Bing Crosby, and the studio faced a shortage of female stars.

They were at an impasse when *Twentieth Century* went into national release. And on June 8, 1934, while the executives were digesting Carole's glowing notices, Dorothy Dell was killed instantly in a Los Angeles automobile accident.

The throaty-voiced, blond Dorothy Dell who had stepped in for Carole as Paramount's *Wharf Angel* elicited no public reaction when that picture sank without a trace; but she glowed in her follow-up exposure, as Adolphe Menjou's hearty companion in *Little Miss Marker*—the picture that ignited the Shirley Temple explosion heard around the world. Paramount decided to groom Dorothy Dell as Miriam Hopkins's replacement on the star roster, and rushed her into an ambitious musical—*Shoot the Works,* with Jack Oakie and Ben Bernie. Not all of her scenes had been shot at the time of her death, although one Paramount official was heard to remark, "But we can still release the picture with what we've got, that's the main thing."

The studio had scheduled Dorothy Dell to costar with Gary Cooper in the humdrum, arbitrarily titled *Now and Forever.* But the project's obvious asset again was the six-year-old Shirley Temple (and if you believed the publicists, she was only five). Fox, holding Shirley's contract, had lost out to Paramount in the bidding for *Little Miss Marker* when all the Damon Runyon stories went on the market in the wake of Capra's *Lady for a Day* smash. But Fox officials, calculating that the Marker role would sell its moppet charmer to America, coaxed Paramount to borrow Shirley—and then Paramount settled for a two-picture deal. Now that Shirley was the sensation of the age, Fox wanted her in a hurry to get her stardom formulated, but Paramount wouldn't miss out on a sure thing. Nor would Carole Lombard. Asked to replace Dorothy Dell in *Now and Forever,* Carole agreed with Myron Selznick's hunch that Shirley Temple would ride another winner. They were right, of course. The picture wasn't very good except as formula stuff— a young couple have their problems and split, until this cute little waif reunites them—but it did great business. And Carole reckoned that sharing the billing with Gary Cooper kept her headed in the right direction.

She had known Gary for years—almost a decade, or about as long as he had been in Hollywood. Briefly she had an early crush on him but found him unreceptive. Gary Cooper had a well-publicized romance with the Countess Dorothy Di Frasso; and when Carole appeared with him in *I Take This Woman,* he was absorbed in a marathon romance with the Mexican bombshell, Lupe Velez. Many people theorized that they were secretly wed. Gary's every maneuver was noted by the fan magazines whose darling he was, but a magazine story claiming he *was* married to Lupe Velez was scrapped just before press time: Gary stunned them all in 1932 by marrying a socialite with whom romance was barely suspected.

Carole remained friendly with Gary Cooper, who was always amiable amid the Paramount trappings. They collaborated agreeably for the publicists on the *Now and Forever* set. Working nicely for director Henry Hathaway—newly graduated from Zane Grey westerns—they also obscured some of the failings in the script. But Carole confided to her intimates that Gary Cooper was the one man she'd worked with whose personality remained impenetrable to her. Off the screen he was the quiet presence suggested by his performances, but the similarity ended there. Carole regarded him as a dilettante—markedly effeminate especially in his mannerisms, and not at all the stalwart he impersonated so effectively on film.

Carole said, too, that she adored Shirley Temple against her better judgment. She did not conceal her prejudice against mothers who pushed their tiny tots into the movie circus, and she avoided Mrs. Temple. But Shirley was not a reluctant actress, nor was she knowingly a scene-stealer. Carole sensed that the little girl merely shared her own attitude, by regarding movie making as an enjoyable game to play.

Conceding at last that they had underestimated Carole all along, the Paramount chieftains sought the best possible use of her talent in pictures that could return a nice profit. The catch was that even in combination with a John Barrymore, she was not really a draw. Her most commercial outing at the home studio probably had been *Bolero,* and it certainly had been the best recent exposure for a faltering George Raft; so *Rumba* was conceived as a facsimile encore for the two of them. Needing time to prepare the project, the studio granted Carole a five-week vacation. But she didn't rest. She spent her vacation working at her home away from home—the Columbia studio on Gower Street.

Harry Cohn asked for her once again. He said he needed help, and Carole probably thought she owed him a favor. If it was a mistake it was her own, not Paramount's; her bosses were opposed to another loan but she extracted their grudging consent, and also overrode Myron Selznick's objection.

Although Carole led the billing, she was not the *Lady by Choice.* That was May Robson, all of seventy and a stage star for half a century, but a latecomer to the movies. It was an unacknowledged sequel of *Lady for a Day,* with Damon Runyon's name not found among the credits. May Robson reprised her Apple Annie characterization, and Carole's role was Texas Guinan twice removed. The queen of the nightclubs had been transparently disguised as Missouri Martin when Glenda Farrell played her in *Lady for a Day.* Carole's version was named Georgia Lee but nicknamed Alabam, a supposed joke on two states, embodied in Carole's unfortunate stab at a Southern accent.

Lady by Choice went the way of most sequels. Mainly it missed the attentions of a Frank Capra. This time the man was David Burton, Carole's *Brief Moment* director. The script could also have benefited from some Robert Riskin dialogue, although Riskin had merely adapted the Runyon argot for *Lady for a Day,* while Jo Swerling was simulating Runyonese from scratch. (In a later era, Jo Swerling would conceive the Broadway musical *Guys and Dolls* from the Runyon legacy, rather more successfully.)

Carole said she did not regret what would stand as her final visit to Columbia. She doubted that *Lady by Choice* had damaged her career. ("Nobody saw it. If they had, I might have been ruined.") She always enjoyed working on Harry Cohn's cozy lot, and appreciated her experience with May Robson. Carole said May knew more about comedy acting than anybody except Walter Connolly, who was also in the picture. "People are always knocking the little pictures that get made out here," she told a reporter, "but they're a great training ground. Now take Walter Connolly. He taught me how to cover a laugh. That was something we didn't worry about in silent comedies when everything was visual, and you just kept on moving. But in a dialogue comedy you have to sort of mark time after someone gets off a good line, because the people in the theater will need time to laugh, but you don't want them to miss anything. So what do you do? You don't want to compete with your own script. Walter Connolly taught me to sort of freeze except for the eyes and eyebrows, and to start acting like hell with *them*."

The pudgy, squeaky-voiced Connolly, who also was a steadying influence on John Barrymore in *Twentieth Century,* became both tutor and pal to Carole. On his advice she visited the set of Capra's *Broadway Bill* in which Connolly was also a participant, and observed the filming of a family dinner scene in which formal monotony was conveyed by the synchronized movement of soup spoons. Watching Capra work gave Carole a notion that she'd like to direct pictures herself—something very few women had done, and almost none successfully. She said she'd hire Connolly, for whom there was a good part in every script ever written. Certainly Columbia thought so. Capra brought Walter Connolly into pictures in *The Bitter Tea of General Yen,* and thereafter he was in virtually every major Columbia picture for several years. Often the studio's shooting schedules were arranged to his own convenience to enable him to work in several pictures simultaneously, and Carole also visited the set of *The Captain Hates the Sea* in which Connolly played the title role. It was a sort of shipboard *Grand Hotel* mixing farce and melodrama, and in the cast was the tragic figure of John Gilbert.

Hollywood's fabulous has-been at age thirty-seven, John Gilbert had been the most popular male star in films just before the coming of the talkies. He was also arrogant, rather typifying the professional snobbery that always had a foothold on the film scene. Some people counted it a satisfaction when talking pictures sent the Gilbert star plummeting. The primitive equipment recorded his voice badly, giving it a distorted high pitch and a suggestion of unmanliness. Gilbert's voice was entirely satisfactory as later pictures would prove, but the damage had been done. The public lost interest in him; and although M-G-M continued to star him in accordance with his expensive contract, they did their part to prevent his recovery, by exposing him in vehicles of utter hopelessness.

Gilbert was certified as "finished" when L. B. Mayer counter-manded Irving Thalberg's casting of the actor in *Grand Hotel* and hired John Barrymore; and Gilbert began drowning his sorrows in alcohol.

Carole had met him before but he had remained haughty and distant, even when they were thrown together for one of Mr. Hearst's parties at San Simeon. But while they were at work on adjacent sets at Columbia, Carole and John Gilbert became very close. Carole was nurse: it was a relationship urged by Walter Connolly, who told her that Gilbert was in danger of being replaced because of instability induced by his drinking. Gilbert and Harry Cohn could not abide one another, and Gilbert was cast in the picture's romantic lead only because director Lewis Milestone insisted.

Walter Connolly had promised to "watch over" Gilbert as a favor to Ina Claire, his good friend and one of Gilbert's discarded wives. Now Virginia Bruce was divorcing Gilbert and he was being drunk-ugly, and Connolly pressed Carole into service because he sensed her ability as psychologist. Carole told of going to Gilbert's dressing room and finding its air stale with fumes of Scotch. Gilbert was most resentful of people telling him not to drink, so Carole scorned a temperance approach and poured drinks for both of them. She tried to bring Gilbert back to a state of sobriety, by playing at vamping him although he had his own design of seducing her. When he was sufficiently distracted, Carole would swill his Scotch as well as her own. She held to the charade, pouring for him but not letting him drink; and she delivered him fit for the cameras, her virtue sacrificed, but heroically.

She won and restored his confidence. Part of John Gilbert's enormous vanity was sheer pride, and he had worked diligently to become an able actor for talking pictures. A comeback had almost seemed assured when Greta Garbo, rejecting the young Laurence Olivier assigned by M-G-M, insisted that Gilbert be teamed with her once more in *Queen Christina*. A once-torrid Garbo-Gilbert love affair was buried in the past and Gilbert's ledger showed four broken marriages, all with actresses. But Garbo, like Ina Claire, was compassionate. In *Queen Christina* they again were an effective romantic team. But M-G-M, no longer bound to Gilbert by con-tract, reduced his billing and marketed *Queen Christina* as a vehicle for a solo-starred Garbo, as a further humiliation to Gilbert.

The picture's disappointing commercial result tolled the oblivion of his career; then came the last, desperate opportunity of *The Captain Hates the Sea.*

By the time Carole departed Columbia, she had John Gilbert on an even keel. He had stopped drinking, and she had got him to thinking it was his own idea. She coached him on his lines, and with Walter Connolly got him to believing in the offbeat goodness of the picture itself: it could be the surprise hit that would give him a professional future as well as a past. John Gilbert hinted that he'd be willing to have Carole share his future, and she said thanks, but she said she already had more romance than she could manage. Yet she was attracted by both the charm and pathos about the man. Not long afterward, she was able to get him an appointment with Thalberg who had remained sympathetic, and there was talk of an austere but encouraging new contract for Gilbert at M-G-M. But then *The Captain Hates the Sea* flopped at the box office despite its emergence as an excellent comedy, and Gilbert went into a well-drenched tailspin from which he did not recover. Less than two years after their hand-holding sessions at Columbia, John Gilbert was dead of excesses popularly attributed to a broken heart. An irony of the Hollywood history is that his adverse fame as the foremost failure of the talkies would far outstrip even his celebrity as the last male superstar of the silents.

Carole returned to Paramount expecting to film *Rumba* with George Raft, but encountered a chain reaction of failed logistics. A picture called *Behold My Wife*—another item that Carole had talked her way out of—had gone to Sylvia Sidney, and complications had delayed Sylvia's reporting to *Limehouse Blues,* a picture about San Francisco's Chinatown in which both Miss Sidney and George Raft were to appear as pasty-eyed Orientals. To replace Sylvia Sidney in *Limehouse Blues,* Paramount borrowed Jean Parker from M-G-M, and the picture started late. Thus occupied, George Raft could not start *Rumba* and Carole was again at liberty. M-G-M had been promised Randolph Scott for a picture in trade for Jean Parker, but now that studio indicated a preference for Carole Lombard if she were available. Carole decided in a minute that she was.

In the first half-dozen years of talking pictures Metro-Goldwyn-Mayer had edged upward into a class by itself, in terms of widely acknowledged prestige. Some of this was due to canny promotion, but there was no doubting that M-G-M had the most illustrious and popular stars in filmdom, particularly its women. Even with Marie Dressler gone to glory, the company had a fabulous and quite varied foursome in Greto Garbo, Norma Shearer, Jean Harlow, and Joan Crawford. Myrna Loy, who had been in films as long as Carole, was on a belated but spectacular rise, and M-G-M also had taken on Jeanette MacDonald, a Paramount castoff, as its *Merry Widow*. Helen Hayes was still on board to pacify adherents of Great Acting. After you got past Clark Gable and Robert Montgomery, the male roster was not nearly so provocative, although M-G-M had exploitable character stars in Wallace Beery and Lionel Barrymore. A faded Ramon Novarro still inhabited the scene from which John Gilbert and William Haines had been purged, but an effort was being made to replenish the masculine complement. Thalberg was lobbying for the acquisition of Spencer Tracy, a dissident at Fox; and in an action more significant than originally seen, M-G-M had picked up William Powell, discarded by Warners. The rejuvenated Powell touted M-G-M in a way that could only encourage Carole's speculation on Culver City as her preferred professional address.

On the other hand, Ernst Lubitsch had incited M-G-M's interest in Carole. Brought in by Thalberg with Paramount's permission to direct *The Merry Widow*, Lubitsch testified to Carole's unique charm. No doubt he was convinced that Paramount was never going to show Carole to her best advantage, and he reckoned that M-G-M might. Irving Thalberg was not hostile to Carole, but L. B. Mayer had divested Thalberg of much of his power, and the two men waged subtle but perpetual war in which Mayer rejected most of Thalberg's enthusiasms. But they agreed to an experiment with Carole Lombard. M-G-M actually conducted the most elaborate screen tests on record and submitted them to the reaction of the national audience: they borrowed players from other companies for one-picture auditions, usually in leading roles of M-G-M's second-line product. They had watched Spencer Tracy closely when he was borrowed for *The Show-Off;* and Jeanette MacDonald was put into *The Cat and the Fiddle* specifically to find out if she rated an M-G-M contract and assignment as *The Merry Widow*. After Carole Lombard's showy account in *Twentieth Century,* interest by M-G-M was easily understood.

Carole didn't bother to inquire if *The Gay Bride* had a promising script. She accepted the odds that always favored M-G-M, and was also made to feel secure by having Metro's tried-and-true Jack Conway as her director. Conway most recently had been represented by *Viva Villa,* a smash hit produced by David Selznick's M-G-M unit. Carole was determined to create a good impression, and vowed to mind her language even if Mayer himself wanted to get familiar and hold her in his lap.

She saw Mayer only briefly at a small tea welcoming her to M-G-M, and she didn't see Thalberg at all. They already had a social friendship for which Marion Davies was intermediary, until W. R. Hearst scorned Thalberg for wanting Norma Shearer—Thalberg's wife—to play *Marie Antoinette,* which Hearst had a notion Marion should do instead.

Carole had hoped for some of the queen-bee treatment such as Columbia gave during her visits there, but she was only a supernumerary at M-G-M; and *The Gay Bride* obviously was not one of the studio's pretentious endeavors. Being somewhat in awe of the studio's well-oiled production regimentation, she did not immediately sense its banality. But her costar Chester Morris did. He spoke grudgingly about going through the motions of another turkey, and Carole said, "Well, you never can tell."

Chester Morris said he *could* tell. He was an able young actor whose dedication was as firm as his jaw, and his career was not faring well. In an earlier, more promising phase he had been Shearer's leading man, and Harlow's, and the hero of a fine prison film, *The Big House.* But touring the studios, he had been mainly identified with dross, of the level of the *Sinners in the Sun* picture he and Carole had made at Paramount two years earlier. Morris said it was easy to tell how an M-G-M picture was doing while it was being shot. The telltale indication was if the primary concern was getting the work started on time each day, and staying on schedule all week. Otherwise no attention was being paid. The executive producer wasn't a Thalberg or a David Selznick but was Harry Rapf, an affable fellow but not a spectacularly discerning one. Jack Conway's proficiency lay in his attentions to paraphernalia, not actors; and the awfulness of the script seemed only to bother Chester Morris, until Carole also realized his assessment was correct.

The most distinctive thing about *The Gay Bride* was that the name of the character Chester Morris played was Office Boy. He was a minor functionary in Nat Pendleton's bootlegging operation, and Carole played Nat's lady friend, a near-moll. Zasu Pitts and

Leo Carrillo were engaged to induce smiles if not chuckles, but *The Gay Bride* was a complicated mess and soon they all sensed this. Carole began to fret over her role, which she concluded contained nothing likable other than what she might give it by the imprint of her own personality.

Apparently that was very little. *The Gay Bride* was shot in seven weeks; then it was processed, canned, and put into release without fanfare. In double-feature situations it took the lower half. And it gave Carole a ready answer whenever someone asked her to name the worst picture she ever made.

The engagement in New York's Capitol Theater was limited to just one week, and the Manhattan reviews were lethal. Richard Watts, Jr., then the regular critic for the *Herald Tribune,* said, "Miss Lombard achieves the feat of being almost as bad as her picture, and plays her part without humor or conviction."

But the ball bounced in a strange way, and it bounced often and quickly. By the time Carole had proof of a flunked audition at M-G-M, she was happier at Paramount than she had ever expected to be. Unexpected events conspired for an upward turn in her career, at a time when that career suddenly meant everything to her. Secretly she had given serious thought to abandoning it completely. She had even reckoned that *The Gay Bride,* which obviously was going to be no great shakes, might be her last picture. She could give up the movies for love, marriage, and babies.

Her life then was jolted, and its future turned around, by an awful event of September 4, 1934. The likelihood of her ever being anybody's gay bride was reduced by the sudden death of Russ Columbo.

VII

Prisoner of Love

SHE CALLED him the great love of her life. Fielding that reference several years later, an interviewer from *Life* said, "Of course you mean other than Clark Gable, don't you, Miss Lombard?" Carole, having attained fame's pinnacle as Mrs. Gable, fixed the reporter in a level stare and said almost grimly, "Russ Columbo was *the* great love of my life . . . and that very definitely is off the record."

That exchange may have occurred during one of Carole's fits of anger toward Gable. Even so, it suggests that many historians of Hollywood amours may have erred in downgrading the Lombard-Columbo affair to a brief involvement of no serious consequence. Serious it was, and fate determined its brevity.

They were the same age. He was born in San Francisco in 1908 —Ruggerio Eugenio di Rudolpho Colombo, the pampered youngest in a family numbering brothers and sisters enough for a full Puccini chorus. He was a musical prodigy, exploited by his family during his childhood and youth. His gift was real, however, and his passion for music was sincere. To every appearance, he was totally without artistic neuroses.

He grew up in Philadelphia, in the predominately Italian southern section that would send so many of its sons warbling into the arteries of music both popular and classical. Ruggerio was a violin prodigy, and as a teen-ager making his first exploration of the Hollywood scene, he earned money as a fiddler, providing mood inspiration for actors of the silent screen. The talkies arrived, and as Russell Columbo he played a small part in the Gary Cooper-Lupe Velez *Wolf Song* in 1929. He also sang its theme song.

The Columbo voice matured into a silken high baritone, and in 1930 he was a meteor. Latin types were in public favor during a continuing posthumous Valentino craze, and his good looks enhanced his hotel stints as band singer. The inevitable big break came when Gus Arnheim needed a replacement for his defecting male vocalist—a chap named Bing Crosby. As baritone for Arnheim's extremely popular dance band, Russ scored a considerable personal hit at the Cocoanut Grove. From there he went to New York, had a sensational engagement at the Brooklyn Paramount, and radio stardom followed. His first recordings were issued, and it was still 1930. In the following year he formed his own band for an extended booking at the Waldorf-Astoria.

While a Crosby-Columbo rivalry was a press agent's dream, no competition could have been friendlier. When Russ returned to California he and Bing became companionable in the same social set, and each was envious of the keener ability he believed the other possessed. They recorded many of the same ballads—"Paradise," "Auf Wiedersehn, My Dear," Crosby's "Where the Blue of the Night Meets the Gold of the Day," and Columbo's own "Prisoner of Love." At the time Columbo was conceded a clear edge in looks, and there was little to choose between them as recording artists. Bing was jauntier, Russ more broodingly emotional in song. Crosby was the senior by four years but Columbo's voice had the velvety finish more suggestive of maturity. But in the personality sweepstakes Crosby moved smartly ahead—a likable, relaxed ordinary Joe. Paramount, bent on developing one or the other as a movie star, rightly picked Crosby over Columbo. Given impetus by his instant screen success, Crosby began pulling away in both record sales and radio popularity. Yet Russ was not quite eclipsed, and some of the hunch players were still betting on him to prevail in the stretch drive. Darryl Zanuck hired him as a specialty singer in a better-than-average 1933 musical film, *Broadway Thru a Keyhole;* and Russ made a nice showing, particulrly in introducing "You're My Past, Present and Future." Then Universal announced the signing of Russ Columbo to an expensive star contract.

Carole had become casually acquainted with Columbo, who

had not married but had a budding reputation as a stallion. There was no indication of romance between them immediately upon her divorce from Powell, yet it might have seemed curious that she should engage Columbo as a vocal coach at exactly that time. She had to sing two songs to underscore her characterization as a stranded singer in the *White Woman* film she made with Charles Laughton, and the curiosity was in her choosing Columbo over Crosby, since the latter was resident at her home studio.

It was said in Hollywood that Russ was everything most folks *thought* Valentino was, and his attentions were encouraged by a quorum of screen beauties. But he loved and left them without serious involvement, until Carole Lombard showed up for one of his return engagements at the Cocoanut Grove, and he was smitten. She sensed conquest, and her heart started jumping.

It was near the end of 1933. She had taken up with Robert Riskin, having first met the screenwriter at Columbia when he wrote *Virtue*—the first of the five pictures she made there. Riskin was giving Carole a romantic rush and also endeavoring to get her cast in *It Happened One Night,* the picture he was scripting for Frank Capra. Perhaps he would try less hard upon realizing that his desired blonde was being swept away from him by an Italian-American crooner. Carole, appropriately stunning in a gown Travis Banton had created for one of her Paramount pictures, was seated with Riskin near the dance floor while Columbo warbled softly into an upright microphone. She knew his gaze was fixed on her throughout his rendition of "You Call It Madness, But I Call It Love." Riskin told Carole she could expect to be hearing from Columbo, and Carole said she wouldn't mind if she did. The next morning a dozen yellow roses from Russ Columbo were delivered to Carole at Rexford Drive, whereupon both Bob Riskin and Carole's former husband were relegated to also-ran status as contenders for her favor.

Russ may have had an easy way with girls generally, but he was uncertain about Carole and boyishly awkward in his caution. She became a goddess to him. His song, "Save the Last Dance for Me," was dedicated to her. She may have been all the more desirable because he thought her unattainable. His romantic pattern revealed a predilection for blond maidens, Carole being last in a long line. (Lupe Velez had been an exception—briefly Russ's steady girl before she discarded him for Gary Cooper.) A determined purge of

Italian phrases and mannerisms suggested Russ's social inferiority complex. He was devoted to his Old World family but embarrassed by their overt ethnic stripe. It was easily noted that his chosen friends, the men included, were Anglo-Saxon types. Because he expected eventually to marry one of his own kind, perhaps of his parents' choosing, he enjoyed a youthful fling he knew wouldn't last, loving the fair-haired girls and leaving them . . . until he met Carole Lombard and she changed his thinking.

He simply adored her. Their romance started slowly, then simmered and worked finally into a boil. It was tracked by the gossip columns, and early in 1934 they were rumored "engaged" without the formal evidence of a ring. Then it was off, and on again. Intermittently Carole was seen in the company of other men, particularly ex-husband Bill Powell; and more often Columbo was escorting Sally Blane in public. She was his girl friend of longer standing—Loretta Young's older sister and a good friend of Carole's since the dramatic-school days of their adolescence.

The fling with Sally Blane was no kind of blind. Carole encouraged Russ to date other girls. She doubted that their love could overcome the formidable barriers of family and religion— meaning *his* family, *his* religion. Carole accepted the tenets of her mother's Bahai faith that appealed to her, and discarded the others. She was not given to religious preoccupation. Russ was a hereditary Roman Catholic but embraced the dogma with a zeal entirely his own. His domestic goals sounded quaint: he wanted a large family, and hopefully one of his sons would enter the priesthood.

Carole met members of his family and got on well with them but sensed that she was an outsider and would always be that. They could tolerate her, perhaps even "love" her, and stop short of acceptance. She suspected that Russ's own effort to break free of his family culture would be a losing struggle. He proposed marriage, saying he didn't care what his family thought about him marrying a divorced woman; yet he would not reveal his intention to his mother, and Carole refused to sanctify their engagement until he did.

The mother had a notoriously weak heart. The family's fear was that any shock would dispatch her. All of ten years later, when the elder Signora Colombo finally succumbed to her condition, she had not been told of her favorite son's tragic death. The family had kept the news from her, constructing a mythology of Ruggerio's continued fabulous success singing all around the world, which naturally prevented him from visiting his mama as he always wanted to do.

Russ acknowledged the devotion to his mother, and Carole often urged him to break off their relationship and reaffirm his heritage. On those occasions Louella Parsons and her lesser counterparts would report that Carole and Russ were no longer "that way," but were an echo of one of his most popular song hits, being "Just Friends." Then they would come together again, because between themselves they had no quarrel.

Carole said, "His love for me was the kind that rarely comes to any woman." He enshrined her as a deity, and was her flowers-and-jewelry courtier, a knight in shining dinner jacket. He pampered and indulged Carole and she reveled in his favors. Often she derided chivalry but his display of it appealed to her, because Russ Columbo was a sort who needed someone to worship and he worshiped her.

The Columbo romance flamed while Carole was in the flush of confidence as an actress after *Twentieth Century*. She had a new sense of commitment to her career, but doubted that marriage with Russ could succeed in concert with her continued activity as a movie player. She began to consider marriage as feasible, but only if she were mistress to *his* career. Much as she enjoyed making pictures, she reckoned she could endure without the pastime. But she was not ready to sacrifice the filmland community life that incited her very personality. Yet Russ seemed to fit nicely into the young Hollywood set to which Carole's own heartbeat was attuned, so she reasoned that even if she withdrew from acting, she could continue having a sociable good time as Mrs. Russ Columbo. She confided to her most intimate friends that the resolution of Russ's own movie career probably held the answer for their future.

The test case would be *Wake Up and Dream,* his first star vehicle for Universal. It started filming while Carole was at Columbia for *Lady by Choice,* and she was into her unfortunate detour at M-G-M when *Wake Up and Dream* was completed. She was working at M-G-M there when his picture had its first and only sneak preview.

After a dreary day of shooting, she accompanied Russ to a movie house in Inglewood. They went in disguise, and were unrecognized even by others connected with the picture. Russ did not want to risk a public commotion over the two of them, so Carole rigged him up in the makeup and costume of Sam Hardy, an actor in her movie. She got herself into a wig and a plaster of uncharacteristic makeup, and wore one of Zasu Pitts's character dresses. Even after a hard day's work or *especially* then, she could still enjoy a charade.

Wake Up and Dream was a very ordinary picture, although Russ was relieved—even pleased—by his own performance. It was apparent that the preview audience reacted positively to his likable screen personality, and the people at Universal were encouraged.

Russ was no actor but Carole suspected he was programmed for pictures. He was most winning in the musical turns, and was himself the composer of some of the songs—including "Too Beautiful for Words," written especially for Carole. She supposed he would become a better actor with continued exposure, and in any event she thought he would become a potent box-office draw —something she was not.

Soon after his death she confided all of the feelings she had experienced to Mitchell Leisen, and possibly to very few others. Her mother, perhaps, had known that Carole had decided on taking instruction in the Roman Catholic faith. Had the possibility of a union with Columbo been more generally suspected, many would have given Carole an argument against it. She knew she had lost her heart, and allowed that she might have misplaced her head as well.

Only a few days after he and Carole had caught the preview of his picture, Russ was in the company of Lansing Brown, a commercial photographer who had become one of his closest friends. Carole had introduced them. They were in Brown's studio, examining Brown's collection of antique handguns. Russ had thought of adopting his friend's hobby as his own. Brown was relating his acquisition of twin pistols of the Civil War era. They did not suspect an ancient charge housed in one of the pistols. Brown struck a match on the cap and the pistol discharged. The bullet struck a piece of furniture and ricocheted into Russ's right eye, lodging in his brain. And that was that. He was twenty-six years old.

In 1954 the body of Russ Columbo's older brother Albert was found bruised and mud-spattered, reviving talk of Mafia connections and speculation that Russ's own altogether extraordinary death may have been part of a sinister design. Carole Lombard would have hooted at such a notion in likely rage. In her own grief she found herself giving consolation to Lansing Brown. For many years after the accident, Brown was a gloomy, tragic figure around Hollywood, overcome by despair and a sense of guilt that continued to haunt him. Carole said she would not let that happen to her.

She had been given a few days off as her M-G-M film neared completion ahead of schedule, and had gone to Lake Arrowhead with her mother. That was where she had been notified of Russ's accident, when they finally located her. She was given none of the details, and quickly chartered a private plane from San Bernardino, hopeful of finding Russ alive at Good Samaritan Hospital, where he had been taken. She had steeled herself, though, for a lost cause. Sally Blane was there before her, and the pronouncement of Russ's technical death was reportedly given while Russ was in Sally's arms. Carole kept her composure while meeting the press. No, she said, they had not planned to be married; she and Russ had been very dear friends.

She abhorred every display of professional mourning. Once she told Mitchell Leisen that if death should snatch her early as it did Jean Harlow, she hoped there would be no great carrying-on. If she mourned all her filmland pals who'd been taken young, Carole said she'd need an all-black wardrobe. She echoed Bess's platitude that life is for the living, vowing to enjoy it again and soon.

Carole decided not to attend the funeral. She said, "Russ liked to hear me laugh and that's something I can still do for him"; but she couldn't laugh at a funeral. Changing her mind at Bess's urging, for sake of decorum, Carole went to the ceremony and then wished she hadn't. Despite having sworn off crying, she found herself sobbing out of control, and was comforted by Bing Crosby, one of Columbo's pallbearers.

After the funeral she returned to M-G-M for some retakes as *The Gay Bride*, then went home to Paramount. She decided to concentrate on her career more intensely than she had in the past, for she doubted very seriously that she would ever fall in love again.

Watching the tennis matches, late in 1936. Clark has just started to grow sideburns for his ill-fated Parnell *film.*

A somber study of Clark Gable and Carole Lombard at Jean Harlow's funeral in June of 1937.

Watching the Pastor-Nestell fight at Wrigley Field in Los Angeles early in 1937, Gable and Lombard are accompanied by Sally Eilers, Carole's friend since school days.

A carefree Carole gets ready to canter the trails of Hollywood with her steady fella in the fall of 1937.

And here's a contrasting study of Carole at Warner Brothers in 1938. She may be having second thoughts about Fools for Scandal.

Married at last! The Clark Gables posed for scores of photographs on March 30, 1939, but this one's a candid shot.

The honeymooners pose again upon occupying their Encino ranch in the summer of 1939.

Rhett Butler conquers Atlanta: The Gables at the world pre-miere of Gone With the Wind, *shown with Mayor William Hartsfield and his daughter, Mildred.*

Carole saves the "situation" once again, at the Los Angeles opening of GWTW.

❊ VIII ❊

The Good-Time Girl

FOR MANY years a large, full-length photograph of Carole Lombard
—a blowup of a still from *Bolero,* and glamorous to the extreme—
hung over George Raft's bed in his Beverly Hills home. In his later
years, a mellowed Raft spoke often and affectionately of Carole and
admitted having been in love with her throughout the five years
they were together at Paramount. He said she was unlike any woman
he'd known in her frankness and easy friendship, and in her ability
to relax a man into naturalness.

They became friends during the time of her marriage to William
Powell, but Carole was divorced before she filmed *Bolero* with Raft,
and there had been talk of a romance going on, before the affair
with Russ Columbo percolated in earnest. But it became very evident during the filming of *Rumba* that George Raft was providing
plenty of consolation for his bereaved costar, much as he would later
rehabilitate Norma Shearer after Irving Thalberg's premature death
left her a young widow. On celluloid Raft never quite fulfilled Hollywood's expectation of a second Valentino, but off the screen he
was the genuine article where Rudy hadn't been. Fielding an interview question on who was Hollywood's greatest lover, Carole once
answered "George Raft," then seeing that her answer had provoked
disbelief, added "or did you just mean on the screen?"

Robert Riskin refueled his courtship of Carole at about the same
time, but she found Raft's attentions more agreeable because "when

George gives me a smile or a present, I don't hear wedding bells behind the thought." Raft was long estranged from a woman who refused to grant him a divorce, which frustrated his later romantic designs on Norma Shearer and Betty Grable, among others notable and lovely. Carole's romance with Riskin was carried out in public, but the Raft episode was a clandestine affair, thought to be ardent.

However, their rapport could not make *Rumba* a picture to serve memory. Where Wesley Ruggles had given *Bolero* a sparkle, *Rumba* merely plodded along under Marion Gering's limp direction. Previously Gering had directed one of the least applaudable Lombard performances in *I Take This Woman*. Her *Rumba* performance was better than that one, but the primary thanks were to her own dramatic ingenuity. Carole was at her most stunning in a new season of Travis Banton gowns and costumes, and she showed to decided advantage as photographed by Ted Tetzlaff. He had been Carole's lensman at Columbia for *Brief Moment* and *Lady by Choice,* and Paramount contracted him at Carole's urging—suggesting an altogether new relationship between Carole and her studio.

George Raft's passion for Carole did not completely subdue his professional jealousy, however, and after Carole's *Rumba* role had been built to a point of parity with Raft's own, Ted Tetzlaff's attentions to Lombard seemed to take the show away from the first-billed male star. Yet they were such attentions as Carole's career needed at that moment. Both of the pictures she had made away from the home lot went into release while *Rumba* was before the cameras, and they both fizzled.

The schedule called for Carole to accompany George Raft right into his next picture—a musical melodrama called *Stolen Harmony* —to be directed by Alfred Werker, whose recent prestige credit was *The House of Rothschild.* Carole was not pleased with the shape or size of her intended role, and she was rescued from what undoubtedly would have been a misassignment when Paramount was jostled by another major upheaval.

During the two-and-a-half-year regime of Emanuel Cohen, the artistic level of Paramount product had declined without the compensation of a satisfactory financial recovery, and no one was happy. In a general housecleaning, Cohen was reduced to mere producer status as B. P. Schulberg had been earlier, and Adolph Zukor took personal command once more. But in his new reign Zukor delegated many responsibilities, and the appointed "superintendent" of production was a provocative surprise: the great Ernst Lubitsch. The hope was that his inimitable "touch" might affect the whole body of Paramount feature films.

Ernst Lubitsch's opinion of George Raft's abilities did not brighten the actor's future with the company, and when Lubitsch ran off a rough cut of *Rumba* he decided that making better use of Carole Lombard would be a priority consideration of his new position. The quality of her pictures subsequent to *Twentieth Century* had prodded a theory that her joyous capering in that drollery had been some kind of fluke, but Lubitsch was unruffled. He said "Those weren't Lombard pictures, they were just pictures and you merely were in them. So now, my dear Carole, we'll make some Lombard pictures."

This meant that stories would be purchased and shaped especially for Carole, as they were for Marlene Dietrich and Claudette Colbert. No matter that *Rumba* wasn't expected to make a ripple (it didn't, although it made money) or that M-G-M had declined an offer by Paramount during the waning Cohen era to assume the Lombard contract at its across-the-board level of $3,500 per week. The new emphasis at Paramount would be on comedy and that was Carole's acknowledged forte. Signs at the other studios had pointed to a golden era of comedy, for which Frank Capra now was the acknowledged catalyst. The appointment of Lubitsch underscored Paramount's pursuit of mirth. Lubitsch endeavored to get Miriam Hopkins, earlier identified as his favorite actress, back on the studio payroll, causing Miriam to regret that she had just signed an exclusive contract with Samuel Goldwyn. The *Hollywood Reporter,* without quoting Lubitsch directly, said he rated only Claudette Colbert and Carole Lombard as long-range assets among actresses in the studio employ. And now Lubitsch was telling Carole that she could have her own choice of directors, wishing all the while that he could give the assignment to himself.

Besides delivering Carole from *Stolen Harmony,* Lubitsch also scratched her as a possibility for both *My American Wife* and *Wedding Present,* in roles eventually taken by Ann Sothern and Joan Bennett, respectively. She was penciled in as Bing Crosby's costar for *Sailor Beware,* for Richard Wallace to direct. Wallace, who guided Carole in *Man of the World* just before her marriage to Powell, was not enthusiastic about the project that Lubitsch had okayed, so Lubitsch sought Carole's opinion. She was acquiring some intramural celebrity as a keen judge of scripts—other people's pictures as well as her own—and she called *Sailor Beware* formula junk that would do a disservice to Bing Crosby. The story was put back on the shelf. (Later it was resurrected but downgraded as *Lady Be Careful,* with Lew Ayres and Mary Carlisle in the leads.)

Lubitsch concluded that all of the pictures in planning were either unsuitable or unworthy of Carole, and that a "vehicle" would be developed from scratch. She could expect to be at liberty for a while. Carole said that was fine, she was too damned tired to go to work again anyway. She had toiled steadily for years on end, and the recent hard grind and private-life complications had brought her to the brink of a nervous breakdown. Fortunately for her, Lubitsch believed that well-rested actors gave healthy performances, and he agreed that she deserved not just a vacation, but an extended rest.

Her holiday spanned the first half of 1935. It wasn't all that restful, but it stimulated her. She welcomed the opportunity to enjoy her new home, and to glory in her crystallizing identity as filmdom's funmaker. Really, she had herself a ball.

After the divorce from Powell, Carole had resumed residence with her mother but immediately undertook a search for a house of her own. Househunting as a weekend pastime spanned several months, during which she accrued expertise in southland real estate and refined her own system of property evaluation. She was not bargain-motivated but said her Scotch heritage made her both canny and cautious. She wanted a place that would accommodate both her needs and her whims. Fieldsie joined in the search, for the idea was to locate a residence ideal for two bachelor girls, with Fieldsie the co-occupant. In 1934, certain that she had investigated every crease in the Hollywood Hills, Carole settled on a modest-sized, multi-level rambler in the heart of Hollywood. Its charm was mostly in its potential, but Carole obeyed instinct and engaged a decorator who had not previously done a complete house. William Haines was not then thought of as an interior decorator at all.

Billy Haines was a true child of the century—born, he said, right after the stroke of midnight in the very first moment of 1900. He was an M-G-M contemporary of John Gilbert and Ramon Novarro; and while his fame as an actor did not have the continuity of legend, he was quite popular for a time. His abilities were narrowly mea-

sured and the Haines pictures were only trifles, but he was an effectively marketed type: the brash, razzle-dazzle college-man hero of
the Jazz Age, and the screen's most frequent modeler of raccoon
coats. He was only the second player put under contract by the
newly merged Metro-Goldwyn company (Norma Shearer was the
first) and he attained full stardom in the late silent period. By coincidence he and Gilbert began new contracts just before the talking
advent, and retained a hollow stardom until their completion in
1932. For more than a year Haines haunted the studios but was
unable to obtain work other than a quickie assignment for the
threadbare Mascot company. Yet his high spirits never flagged, even
as he courted bankruptcy. He counted on his many friends, and
Carole became a strategic one. Getting Billy Haines back in business became her personal mission.

The antithesis of a John Gilbert—whose obsession was his virility
—William Haines did not acquire enemies or discard lovers along
the Hollywood byways. Admittedly but discreetly homosexual, he
never married but was a surrogate brother to almost every friendly
girl in pictures. Polished, witty, and gregarious, he hobbied with
interior decoration until Carole nudged him to do it for a living.

"She said if I did her place, I could write my own ticket," Haines
reflected during his long tenure as the best-known (and most expensive) interior decorator in the film colony. "She was my first
major commission and I offered to do her house without charging
a fee, knowing that if people liked what I did, I'd have a business
foundation."

Carole tried to pay him, but Haines explained that she wouldn't
have offered unless she was satisfied. "Carole approved of my overall
ideas but wouldn't rubber-stamp a conception of mine if she had her
own thoughts, and often she had them. She had a knack that was
her very own, and she could have been an outstanding professional
decorator . . . or an outstanding anything, once she put her mind
to it. She did her own decorating at the later places, without so much
as a consultant. But she had rather liked my original idea of decorating her home to match her personality."

As executed by Haines, the interior design of Carole's house was
as gay as her laughter, and unmistakably feminine. Never mind the
way she talked: the physical presence of Carole Lombard was the
most distinctly feminine one he ever encountered in Hollywood,

Haines said. He told of having observed that femininity in all its naked loveliness, to his great astonishment, while Carole was waging a breathless filibuster about her ideas on furniture.

"She was late for a tennis date and I'd driven her home, but she wanted to continue our conversation while she changed. At the studios, of course, people were always changing clothes, and being seen in one's underthings was a commonplace. But I was startled when she stripped completely, staring at me all the while, going on about Heppelwhite and Sheraton. She never wore a bra, you know. That was no secret, but oftentimes she didn't wear panties either, and this was one of those times. She was more comfortable without them and it was as simple as that. She was being nonchalant, but then she saw my surprised look, and I remember her saying the cutest thing: 'I wouldn't do this, Billy, if I thought it could arouse *you*.' And she got into tennis shorts, nothing underneath, and I took her to her match. Arousal or not, I've never lost the image of how magnificent her body was in its deliciously raw state. She should have known Phidias, and he her."

As background for a goddess, Haines was opposed to the "Hollywood modern" that had become a prohibitive fashion with its accent on white. He produced a festival of color as an effective contrast to her blond beauty. Within the community the house was a sensation.

Haines immediately obtained several lucrative commitments. "So I went into business for myself and never acted in another picture." When Carole learned how much he was charging for subsequent assignments, she wrote a check for that amount as her own payment. Haines said he never cashed it. For four decades he was a top decorator who told everyone his first commission would always be his favorite.

Carole had wanted a place in which parties could progress comfortably. Haines produced a setting for trailing gowns and evening dresses. The drawing room was hung in velvet, in six shades of blue. He selected furniture of the Empire period as most reflective of Carole's personality—seductive, elegant, sophisticated. They argued about Carole's bedroom, but his final design made it her favorite room. The centerpiece was an oversized bed covered by plum satin, with a threefold mirror screen to either side. The mirror screen soon became a necessary adornment in every new Hollywood boudoir.

In her new residence Carole came to heady fame as a hostess and an ideal people jockey. In bringing people together who would mix well, she consciously followed Marion Davies's lead. In Carole's opinion, Marion took a bum rap in the back-fence gossip of Hollywood, for not being as good an actress or as big a star as the Hearst press insisted she was, year after year. Carole said Marion didn't give a damn about making movies and had gotten all of that out of her system years ago, but indulged Mr. Hearst's whim . . . or was it his obsession? She also believed that Marion's enormous generosity was falsely attributed to Hearst charities; she said Marion "helped more people than the Red Cross."

Carole took instruction from Marion Davies in the art of orchestrating people not according to who was already acquainted with whom, but in their shared interests and complementary personalities. Marion's parties that Carole had particularly liked were not so much the elaborate affairs at the Hearst "ranch" that was San Simeon, as those at Marion's beach house with its hundred bedrooms. They were characteristically lavish, but they also gave Marion a freer expression of herself. Marion said that only people she *liked* got invited to the beach; and when Carole began to entertain at home, she sent out invitations only to people who were her friends.

A few years later, when she had stopped playing hostess altogether, she said she had never given a party for the reasons so many other people did—to pay off an obligation or to incite a new one, or to make points with the people who gave them. Sometimes she even placed a ban on movie shoptalk, saying a party at her house was for having fun, not for doing homework.

To request an R.S.V.P. was not Carole's custom. She said they would always be welcome if they were invited, and she trusted people to notify her if they couldn't come. To plan a party properly consumed a full week's time for both herself and Fieldsie, yet she was likely to ask any number of people at the last minute, on spontaneous impulse.

She guarded against having to ask, "What would you like to drink?" She would make a point of knowing in advance the preferred liquor of each arriving guest, who very quickly found a drink in his hand.

Noel Coward told of a Carole Lombard dinner party at which he was captivated by the only girl not in formal dress. "I took this enchanting hoyden to be some sort of starlet, and the novelty of her having not heard of *me* was rather appealing. She was awed that I had personal acquaintance with Mr. Kipling, whom she rated the world's greatest writer, and she knew *If* by heart and of course had to recite it *all*. When I asked about this strange creature, Carole only knew that she was Toby's wife, and she didn't know Toby's last name. This Toby was a carpenter at her studio, but Carole *liked* him . . . and so she asked him to her party."

Rightly spotted as Toby was an intense young man who engaged publisher Condé Nast in a political debate. When Noel Coward asked about the conversation, Nast said, "Oh, he has some odd economic theories—odd but interesting. The chap's in lumber, you know."

Carole said, "Anyone who can afford to buy the booze can give a party, but it doesn't guarantee fun." As hostess, she reacted to the boredom she experienced at many filmland galas distinguished only by their sameness. She had gone the formal route during her apprenticeship, with cocktail parties for the Barthelmesses, Brooks, Taurogs, Warner Baxters and others of Powell's circle during their marriage. She opened her new home for a series of buffet suppers in the fall of 1934, and thereafter collaborated with Fieldsie in working out the details. Within only a few months a leading fan magazine would identify her as "the foremost hostess in the Hollywood social whirl." Later Carole would say that was exactly what she intended to become, admitting that she became a madcap party-giver with rank calculation, courting the kind of publicity that would identify her, personality-wise, with the roles she wanted to play. No matter: she couldn't help having fun anyway.

A crazy theme or motif would attach to a Lombard party. At a time when many of her friends nursed some well-reported physical ailments, she staged an elaborate "hospital party," changing her living room into a hospital ward, with trappings rented from a surgical supply house. Hospital gowns were issued for guests to don over their dinner clothes, and they were escorted to white iron beds with their names and charts hanging over the footboards. Dinner was rolled in on an operating table.

Once a friend complained of being "too tired to sit up at the dinner table" and Carole got the idea of staging a Roman banquet, depositing guests on mounds of pillows before low-reclining individual dinner tables. That was the occasion of Docky Martin, Louella Parsons's husband, passing out in a drunken stupor, his naked crotch exposed to view beneath his toga. When Carole Lombard, one of the beholders, asked "What is *that?*" the reliable Wilson Mizner said, "Why, that's Louella Parsons's column you hear about."

Carole's parties initiated Hollywood vogues, as did many of her whims. One year she was delinquent in ordering Christmas cards, and from the leftover stock could find none that appealed to her. So she sent telegrams instead, giving a personalized greeting in every message, whether serious or comical. Copycats made an expensive thing of wire-sending, but Carole adhered to her practice, finding that she liked the uniqueness of each communication. She sent telegrams for Valentine's day, Thanksgiving, even April foolery —and very often, impromptu messages when no occasion existed. The telegrams, like the often zany, sometimes ribald gifts Carole presented to her coworkers after completing each picture, tested the imaginations of other stars who sought to emulate her. Eddie Cline, whose kindness to Carole during her Sennett days was not forgotten, could expect a gift of a dozen custard pies every Christmas. After Mitchell Leisen became a favorite Lombard director, she acknowledged both his fondness for horses and for floral decoration with a hobby horse adorned by orchids shaped into horseshoes.

The gift of a ham, such as the one bestowed on Clark Gable after their picture together, was a Lombard standby but with multiple variations on the theme. George Raft told of receiving an enormous box, magnificently gift-wrapped, within which was another box with matching wrapping. A succession of fancy boxes fitted into one another like a canister set, until the smallest one revealed a modest-sized ham with Raft's photograph pasted over it.

W. C. Fields, having once regaled Carole with a messy yarn from his vaudeville days (involving a bicycle act and a diarrhetic pig), was in a Pasadena hospital recovering from a siege of pneumonia and was making life miserable for the nurses. Carole sent a get-well present consisting of a bicycle and a live piglet, around whose middle was tied a gay ribbon. It got Fields well enough to ride the bicycle down the hospital corridors while the leashed pig squealed in flight—until Fields and pig were both evicted.

Committing Carole to an interview "tintype," Sidney Skolsky revealed that she regularly updated a complete file of all her friends' birthdays, wedding anniversaries, and other dates of special meaning to them. (Among the columnist's other gleanings: the lily, not the orchid, was her favorite flower; undiluted Scotch on the rocks was her drink, but she also liked a glass of beer with studio crewmen; she had a mole on her behind; and yes, she slept in the nude . . . or sometimes in oversized men's pajamas.)

Another facet of Carole's triumph as hostess was her menu management. Edgar, her new cook, won local acclaim for his exotic culinary achievements, but some were Carole's own inventions. Cooking was her secret vice. She said she couldn't boil water and she probably *didn't,* because anything ordinary was a drudge. But she liked to get into a kitchen and mix up wild combinations, trusting the trial-and-error method. She often devised original hors d'oeuvres from her imagination, not from cookbooks. Yes, she said she probably could do anything by putting her mind to it. Or *be* anything.

Much was made over the years about Carole's comradeship with furniture movers, trash collectors, newspaper delivery boys, and other denizens of the workaday world—including the carpenters, electricians, and other technicians of the studios. To them she was one of the boys—noisy, kidding, laughing raucously, utterly shockproof. On the other hand, conservative older women—Bess Peters's friends, for example—found her a sweet, quiet, stable girl.

In a remarkably candid interview Carole admitted she was "A fooler . . . I try to be what people want me to be." She suspected that the "real" Carole Lombard would not fascinate. "Perhaps actors reach a point where they're acting all the time and can't do otherwise," she said. "What you hear about how naturally I behave is so much horseshit. I mean, what's natural? Of course there is a real me, but I don't value her so highly that I have to force her on people. I like to be liked, but everyone might not like me as I am, so I bend. It's a kind of acting and psychology and lying all mixed up, trying to be what people want and expect. But I don't apologize. I like people to reveal themselves to me, and not devote all their time and attention to trying to assimilate *me.* You see, most people can't be flexible. I can, so I am. I take on the attitudes and tastes of other people. And they like that."

Carole and her mother again planned a vacation together that would not materialize. They talked of Europe at last—England and the Continent during the spring of 1935, between *Rumba* and whatever else the studio was preparing. Bess had never been abroad and nurtured the dream of it, but plans were deferred in February by the death of the senior Fred Peters, following surgery in Ann Arbor, Michigan.

Carole's father was fifty-nine—still youthfully handsome at the time of his death which, however, relieved an agony that had accompanied his final years. While the nature of his final operation was undisclosed, it was brain surgery—a futile effort to cope with the tragic legacy of the elevator accident that had also rendered him lame as a young man, and had made marriage and family life hazardous.

The recent experience of Russ Columbo's funeral firmed Carole's decision not to attend her father's rites in Fort Wayne. There was disappointment in the hometown, even a measure of resentment that its most famous celebrity did not keep up appearances with the rest of the family. But Carole said, "My father is entitled to some dignity and respect in death, and if I were there it would turn into the worst kind of theatrical event." She holidayed in Florida instead.

She checked back into Paramount expecting to make *The Bride Comes Home* which studio hands were fashioning especially for her, with Wesley Ruggles lined up as director—a personal accommodation. But time was ripe for a call from Harry Cohn. Columbia comedies had gained rating as something special within the film industry, and Cohn said this one was one of the best. Carole read the script and agreed that despite its innocuous-sounding title, she'd be interested in doing *She Married Her Boss* with Melvyn Douglas. Not the least of the enticements was that the director was her chum from Pathé days, Gregory LaCava, who had risen into the front rank of his profession.

Lubitsch was rigidly opposed to letting Carole slip out of his control during what he considered was a strategic phase of her career, although his high regard for LaCava counteracted his abhorrence of Harry Cohn. The matter was resolved to everyone's happiness when Claudette Colbert also expressed interest in *She Married Her Boss*, with ample personal motivation: a comedy assignment she had made on loan to Columbia had given her an Academy Award and a revitalized career; and she was in a euphoric state over an unreleased picture she had made for Gregory LaCava —*Private Worlds* with France's Charles Boyer.

Lubitsch now indicated that the picture that had been foreseen as the next Colbert vehicle at Paramount was available to Carole, and probably held more promise than *The Brides Comes Home*. Carole was experiencing another delay anyway, waiting for Wesley Ruggles to finish directing *Accent on Youth* with Sylvia Sidney. Lubitsch confided that *Hands Across the Table* might be the best comedy script in town, and that he would act as overseer to assure an expertly made film in its every detail. The picture could be put into work almost immediately if they could agree on another director. That enabled Carole to pursue her own campaign on behalf of Mitchell Leisen to a happy conclusion.

One of the more familiar "angles" on Carole Lombard was her easy rapport with men, particularly those who exercised clout in the movie-making arteries. Once Clark Gable, with pique showing only barely, asked of Carole, "Is every friend you have in this world a man . . . I mean, don't you know any women, for Christ's sake?" Carole hummed a reply that "Some of my best friends are women. Why, there's Billy Haines, and there's Mitch Leisen . . ."

Her professional life had been early grazed by Mitchell Leisen when he had been a DeMille assistant, but she had been on friendly terms with him throughout her Paramount chapter. She met him through Travis Banton, and Leisen had also been a costume designer during his early career, before becoming DeMille's art director. When he, too, became a director, he was possibly the only one to follow that particular route with anything approaching smart success. Leisen started with impressive somber fare such as *The Cradle Song* and *Death Takes a Holiday*. But he ached for comic opportunity, echoing the general admiration for the Lubitsch pictures and the frivolities of Capra, LaCava, Ruggles, and Leo McCarey. Leisen had wanted to design and direct *Ruggles of Red Gap* but McCarey got that assignment and managed a prestige success. At the same time Leisen was failing appallingly with a supposed romantic comedy called *Behold My Wife*—in which Sylvia Sidney took a part Carole might have been assigned, but for its coincidence with the *Rumba* schedule. In the eyes of the pre-Lubitsch regime at Paramount, Leisen was ruined, a washout. His next assignment was considered bottom drawer: a melodrama called *Four Hours to Kill*. Carole sensed that Leisen was being mistreated, and conspired to help him. She offered to take the female lead in *Four Hours to Kill*, although it was not a large part. The studio vetoed the idea, but she became a sort of phantom associate producer for the picture.

By persuading Leisen and the studio bosses to use Richard Barthelmess in the lead role, she also furthered another of her personal "causes." Barthelmess as friend was the favorite souvenir of her Powell marriage, but big-star eminence had slipped away from him at last. Warners had dropped Barthelmess in the same economy-minded housecleaning that had swept out Bill Powell, as well as Ruth Chatterton. And then there was the matter of Ray Milland. Carole learned that the studio had decided against picking up his option, but she pushed for his assignment to one of the important roles. *Four Hours to Kill* followed the *Grand Hotel* formula and emerged as that sometime thing, a sleeper. There was false promise of a major comeback by Barthelmess, who rated cheers as a handcuffed man crammed into a phone booth for most of the picture. But there was nothing tentative about Mitchell Leisen's revived reputation, so there was no strong objection when Carole requested him as director of *Hands Across the Table*. Lubitsch, in fact, seemed delighted. Later he used this to illustrate Carole's extraordinary instinct, for she had never actually worked with Leisen previously.

Leisen functioned essentially as his own art director. He committed *Hands Across the Table* to an overall design long before shooting actually commenced. He encouraged Carole's advance preparation, and *Hands Across the Table* was the first picture since *Twentieth Century* that she rehearsed completely before going into production. Even before the picture acquired a leading man, she met Leisen daily at the studio for long discussions of every aspect of the picture. Sometimes Lubitsch joined the huddles, perhaps in the atmosphere of dress fittings for Travis Banton and Edith Head, or for making still photographs to keep the publicists busy.

Carole appreciated their sincere effort to provide the best appointments of a vehicle. She later said that with *Hands Across the Table* she felt in an odd way that her career was just beginning— as in an odd way, it surely was. Ted Tetzlaff again was her cinematographer, and the understanding was that he would shoot *all* of her pictures. Now Carole was also being invited for the first time to select her own leading man, from a list offered by the studio.

She indicated Cary Grant as her first choice: his birthright for romantic comedy was hardly a secret any longer. But Grant was as suddenly scratched when Paramount dispatched him to RKO for *Sylvia Scarlett* at Katharine Hepburn's urging. Others under consideration were Gene Raymond and a new man from the stage, Lloyd Nolan—both of whom were briefly "announced." Carole made a pitch for Ray Milland, but Leisen persuaded the choice of a more obviously American type. There was talk of borrowing Franchot Tone, an able farceur, from the M-G-M middle ranks. But when the smoke had cleared, the role belonged to curly, dimpled Fred MacMurray, who was Carole's own age but had been in pictures less than a year.

Carole certainly knew who Fred MacMurray was. She had danced to music generated by local bands that employed him as a saxophonist, before she had made her first real dent in pictures. Later he played the New York scene with an early swing group called the California Collegians; and there he was, with his saxophone on the periphery of Jerome Kern's *Roberta* with its now-legendary cast—Bob Hope, Lyda Roberti, Tamara, George Murphy, Ray Middleton, Sydney Greenstreet, and the grand old Fay Templeton. From such an abundance of obvious movie material it was a typical curiosity that MacMurray would obtain the most attractive studio contract, but in that day looks were approximately everything and he had them.

Back in Hollywood, MacMurray played a bit role in *Friends of Mr. Sweeney* at Warners. Mr. Sweeney was Charlie Ruggles, who tipped his brother about the young man. Wesley Ruggles was seeking an unknown player to romance Miss Colbert in *The Gilded Lily*. MacMurray was given the part and appeared to catch on in an instant, the way a "new face" often would in a picture that made the grade—and *The Gilded Lily* was one of the brightest comedies in a seasonal explosion of many such.

Yet Paramount did not seem to know what to do with him. He was put into a couple of grade-B melodramas, in one of which he enacted an Irish cop opposite a drawling Texas girl named Clara Lou Sheridan, rechristened Ann. It remained for Katharine Hepburn, of the accurate covetous eye for other companies' property, to convince Paramount that they really had something. Miss Hepburn requested and got him for *Alice Adams,* and his fan mail in the wake of that casting announcement verified that he was *hot*. But *Alice Adams* was straight stuff and Wesley Ruggles persisted in his opinion that farce would prove MacMurray's forte.

The significance of the MacMurray casting could hardly have been foreseen. In the retrospective view he was the ideal Lombard leading man in almost every way; indeed, at Paramount she would never have another one. His dark handsomeness complemented her own physical allure; and he brought to the screen an agreeable presence but not a personality so vivid as to compete for attention in a vehicle calculated for a lady star. It was no accident that he would often be found in the screen company of "strong" women— Colbert, Stanwyck, Rosalind Russell. He proved an adept farceur— not so inventive as Cary Grant or Robert Montgomery, but entirely responsive to such outgoing shenanigans as would be expected of a Carole Lombard at her peak. Perhaps equally vital was the healthy sexuality that gave a subtle dimension to the Lombard-MacMurray teaming in all of their four pictures.

When they made *Hands Across the Table* MacMurray was still a bachelor and the Paramount publicists capitalized on the coincidence of two romantically eligible stars doing the honors on film. The studio encouraged a liaison and kept the fan magazines well supplied with photographs showing Carole and Fred obviously enjoying their simulated candid situations. They did get along swimmingly, and a close personal friendship continued after Carole left Paramount. But actual romance did not develop. MacMurray, a rare type of one-woman man, was married soon afterward to a girl without designs on a career. Carole became especially fond of Lillian, his wife, once calling her "really the most decent person I've met in Hollywood."

Hands Across the Table was Paramount's Thanksgiving release for 1935. If not quite a smash, it was uncontestably a solid hit, commercially robust beyond the studio's optimistic forecast. It was the first major release in which Carole commanded solo star billing, but even that changed outwardly almost as soon as the picture was put into release. There had been early misgivings that MacMurray was not "name" enough, primarily by Lubitsch, who wanted Carole's coming-out party to display class on every flank. But in that day of a captive large "regular" movie audience, a reputation could accrue from only a few choice exposures. With the critically acclaimed *Alice Adams* still playing first-run engagements when *Hands Across the Table* was ready for release, the advertising campaign was altered to give MacMurray costar status, above the title in most of the displays. He proved entirely worthy, and Lubitsch still had the "Lombard picture" that had been his quest.

While *Twentieth Century* would stand as the foundation for her reputation, *Hands Across the Table* was really the first of the great Lombard vehicles. Its fame would not be sustained by legend as some of the later comedies were, but it was generally acknowledged a first-rate job of movie management, and "Lubitschean" was a frequent description. Said Otis Ferguson in *The New Republic:* "In this picture Carole Lombard and Fred MacMurray make an all-time copybook example of how to play a movie for what it is worth—with subtlety, much resource in the matter of visual expression, and the open, sustained kind of charm that can be projected through the shadows of a mile of celluloid. They are, after all, the deciding factor in whether the whole business of dinner for two, with hiccups, the evening with its last lap in the taxi, shall end up as a collection of comedy ideas or as a smooth development of the situation, a successful piece of fancy; and whether the faked call from Bermuda shall be a mere crutch for the plot or straight comedy in itself; and whether roofs, stars, etc., are mere stage properties or what make the world go around."

Carole played Regi Allen, a saucy little manicurist (thus the title, which also echoed a recent popular song). She was that hardiest of Depression-era movie blondes, a gold-digger. MacMurray was her prey, an inversion on the heiress so often employed as a fulcrum for screwball comedy—except that MacMurray is also broke, but that's a secret. His pedigree is authentic, but there have been complications. ("Maybe you heard about the Big Crash? Well, that was, uh, us.") He, too, seeks the security of wealth through marriage, and of course the resolution will be the triumph of love over material concern—just what the folks at the picture show wanted to hear, once they had their eyefill of exotica in the scenic trappings. Even a manicurist might possess a stunning Travis Banton wardrobe as a kind of investment, if she were on the make.

Hands Across the Table also took a cue from *Twentieth Century* by providing what would become the obligatory scene in any Lombard comedy: Carole becoming unglued amid the mounting complications of the situation, and exploding like some volcano of mirthful wrath. Ben Hecht was the catalyst for this caper, although *Hands Across the Table* was not his story, but Viña Delmar's. He told Carole that one explosive scene he had written for Jean Harlow in *Bombshell* had sold the platinum blonde to America as a comedienne. Carole's own explanation was that a movie audience likes to be knocked off balance; and with a bow to her early training, she knew how to set it up.

According to plan, Fred MacMurray did go directly into *The Bride Comes Home* for Wes Ruggles, but the bride was not Carole Lombard. She was Claudette Colbert; and the fact that roles designed for Colbert and Lombard had become interchangeable was a tip on Carole's positive emergence, for Claudette had reached the height of her career.

For reasons entirely her own, Carole wanted to make a picture at Universal. No one at Paramount approved the idea, and Lubitsch was firmly opposed to it. Perhaps if *Hands Across the Table* had already been released and its box-office triumph certified, she wouldn't have been allowed to go slumming in what they considered a second-rate studio. But her first picture with MacMurray had only been screened in an unedited version when the idea of *Love Before Breakfast* came up; and in that era of assembly-line production, a player usually had at least one unreleased picture among his credits while shooting another. She got her way on the loan, and then it was too late to recall her, for *Love Before Breakfast* was under way.

She got around Lubitsch by intimidating him. She said, "Lubesy, don't you know by this time that you can trust me to know a good script when I read one?" He decided he'd have to trust her, but she sensed his lingering uncertainty. "We'll make a deal," Carole glittered. "I do the picture at Universal, and if it turns out a stinker, you can have your way with me in the fancy hotel of your choice." Lubitsch beamed roguishly while the omnipresent cigar twitched in his mouth, until Carole yanked it out and lectured him with it. "On the other hand, if *Love Before Breakfast* is a hit, I'll take over your job and shove this black thing up your ass!"

Despite protestations of her own laziness, Carole committed her 110 pounds to an ordeal of pure energy. This inspired the observational cliché that they just didn't know how she managed all the things she *did*. She remained an outdoor girl, becoming quite an expert horsewoman despite limited opportunity. She became a proficient archer under Jessica Barthelmess's tutelage, and Spencer Tracy taught her polo. Her athletic essence was exemplified by her walk, said to be the quickest stride by man or woman within studio gates. She said if she didn't keep on the move she'd go to fat for all the eating she did, and besides, why waste the time you have?

A swimming pool was obligatory and Carole took her regular dips, along with daily soapy tub baths "because I like to smell good." But tennis was her consuming passion. Perhaps only partly in jest, she said that on any scene and with any partner, she'd prefer tennis to sex every time. Whatever the sport, she appreciated skill in the arena.

Along with an oversized swimming pool, she had two tennis courts built on her property. She got in at least one fast set every day, even if she was on a work schedule. During idle time she could play for hours. Carole said hell no, it wasn't just for exercise; she played to win. Yet if she knew she could win easily, she lost interest. She was a competitor for the sternest challenge, losing more matches than she won only because she took the court against the best available talent. Some other film actresses—Katharine Hepburn, Ginger Rogers—were as accomplished as she; but Carole tackled even bigger game. Eleanor Tennent, her tutor, arranged the matches. Carole said she'd quit the movies in a minute and turn tennis pro if she could take the measure of Alice Marble on the court. She couldn't beat Alice, but she could give her a hard-fought contest. They became special friends, Alice displacing Helen Wills as Carole's court idol when Carole found the older woman too icy on closer acquaintance. Alice Marble might have traded lives with Carole, had she been less adept at tennis. She was pretty enough for the movies. As it was, Carole was the early sponsor of the Marble tennis career until it moved into professional high gear.

Although Carole tried golf and found it too slow for her, she acquired a set of friends who shared her athletic zeal but not her orientation to the movies. She entertained them at parties the film people knew little of, while a Lombard movieland party was sure-fire copy.

Her reign as a Hollywood hostess, while spectacular, was actually quite brief. She phased out that aspect of her life when the attainment of a really significant career became a reasonable prospect.

"You can't have it both ways," she said. "I went through the motions of making pictures for too long, spending most of my energy having a good time. Most people gripe about the elusiveness of stardom but do little to deserve it, and even less to hold on to it. When I saw that I was really getting a fair chance, I decided to work for it."

Significantly, she never gave a large-scale party after *Hands Across the Table* went before the cameras. But during her long 1935 holiday she concocted a couple of social events that would permanently enrich the folklore of Hollywood.

In the spring she topped herself in daring if not in ingenuity, on the occasion of a birthday fete for Bob Riskin. Here was Carole the casual, sending invitations specifying formal dress. Photographers were put on the alert for what promised to be a gala of the season, rivaling the tony affairs given by Basil and Ouida Rathbone. When the guests arrived they were greeted by a Carole Lombard in frazzled straw bonnet, checkered shirt, and rolled-up jeans—also freckled and with one tooth blacked out, and barefoot. Yes, pigtails. The furniture, drapes, rugs—everything had vanished. Instead there were only bales of hay. A few live chickens roamed the house, ducks were skimming the pool, and a pig, a goat, and a cow inhabited a small corral rigged in the backyard. There were no horses, but Carole boasted that some authentic horseshit was included in an educational exhibit of animal manure located adjacent to a portable outhouse complete with its carving of a crescent moon.

The guests were bewildered in their formal attire but ultimately were delighted by the novelty, and were tolerant when a very drunk Mischa Auer peeled down to his birthday suit for a solo roll in the hay. Carole had more fun than any of her guests. She was photographed milking the cow.

That was "the barnyard party," and most of the work came in making the house livable afterward—in any event, that was the thing she always deplored, the big anticlimax. For her valedictory as hostess she solved even that problem.

On a Sunday in June, on the eve of reporting for *Hands Across the Table,* she rented the entire Ocean Park amusement pier and got out an invitation list for several hundred friends, most of the picture people she knew and liked. It cost a fortune, but as Carole said, "It won't break me, and besides, it's my last party." Favored by ideal weather, it was a unique event in the annals of Hollywood, and a party easily crashed; invitations were to complete families.

Actresses shed their glamour and actors their dignity, donning play clothes to ride the roller coaster, descend the diving bell, spin in the barrel (Cesar Romero cracked an ankle), take a tumble in the whirligig (Claudette Colbert was left black and blue), and ogle the sideshow attractions. News photographers could not invade, but Carole's Ocean Park outing gave Jerome Zerbe his first opportunity to take candids of the stars at play.

A new boy in town spent most of his time in the tunnel of love, and girls competed to share the boat with him. His name was Errol Flynn. He couldn't conquer Carole with a tennis racquet, or coax her to come see his etchings. But rumor said he wasn't deprived. The Flynn lad had made only a couple of minor appearances for Warners, but word reached his employers that he was the sensation of Carole's party and quite the perfect specimen in the consensus view. Whether his social triumph actually hastened his inevitable rise, it was right after the outing that he was given the title role (plus Olivia deHavilland) in *Captain Blood,* and was on his way.

Extraordinary in the extreme was a party in which a studio janitress might ride the merry-go-round and notice that the adjacent horse was being jockeyed by Marlene Dietrich in shorts. The party lasted until the wee hours. It concluded with a braying community sing. Carole said, "I've done my bit. Now someone else can do the honors."

Afterward she confined her hostess attentions to small dinners and barbecues. But large-scale affairs sponsored by other persons became "Carole Lombard parties" nonetheless. She was the idea girl, the central funmaker. Her counsel was sought for devising games and activities, and for dreaming up weird door prizes.

They played follow-the-leader at a party staged in a large Beverly Hills mansion, and Carole was the obligatory leader. Her whims dictated the fun, as every guest had to follow suit in whatever she did. It was a casual-dress affair and Carole noted that only Samuel Goldwyn, against whom she held an old grudge, had shown up in formal attire. She requested his placement in line immediately behind her; then she led the guests through the house, doing such inane things as plunking the piano and nibbling petals from a flower arrangement. She had connived to have a bathtub filled with water, and she marched into the bathroom and sloshed right in. Sam Goldwyn halted and then was hooted when Carole vacated the tub and he still hesitated. Trying to be the good sport, he finally splashed in and out of the water but could not disguise his unhappiness.

Universal was an old, established company, still operated by aging, fabled "Uncle Carl" Laemmle who very soon would sell his majority interest and retire. But it was Hollywood's back alley of feature-film production, seldom represented by distinguished or expertly made fare. Nor was there anything especially promising about *Love Before Breakfast* when Charles Rogers, the Universal production chief, engaged Walter Lang to direct it. But Lang was more than just a casual friend to Carole Lombard.

Walter Lang was then gaining recognition as a proficient craftsman, although his considerable fame lay well into the future at
20th Century-Fox with comedy and musical films such as *Sitting
Pretty* and *The King and I.* In the fall of 1935 he saw *Love Before
Breakfast* as a yes-or-no, hit-or-miss venture, but he doubted that
it *could* miss if it had just the right female star.

Rogers dangled Wendy Barrie, Binnie Barnes, and Carole's one-
time schoolmate Sally Eilers—blondes every one, but none of them
especially noted as a comedienne. It was obvious that Carl Laemmle
and Charles Rogers counted *Love Before Breakfast* as only a minor
item, because the estimable Margaret Sullavan—Universal's only
prestige star—was then unassigned yet not considered, although
qualified. Walter Lang stressed the need for an actress with high
glamour and a light touch—someone on the order of Carole Lombard, who of course was out of the question. Except she wasn't.
Carole heard about the project from Lang, read the script and
liked it, and insinuated herself into the scene. She brought her
own "unit" with her: besides Ted Tetzlaff as cameraman, the
Lombard entourage included several Paramount workers who had
become fixtures for her pictures.

Carole chose to disregard the company's track record because
she believed in Walter Lang, who had asserted his belief in *her*
when he directed *No More Orchids* at Columbia almost four years
earlier. Since then he had become one of Carole's favorite ad-
versaries on the tennis court, and in her midst he had also taken
up famously with Madalynne Fields . . . and soon they would
be married. Besides having Lang and Fieldsie for setside kibitzing
on *Love Before Breakfast,* Carole also had Dixie Pantages standing in for her, as she had always done at Columbia. Dixie, in turn,
was being romanced by Lang's assistant director, Phil Karlson;
and they, too, would marry. In those instances when Carole Lombard played Cupid, people also *stayed* married to one another.
Like Lang, Phil Karlson would have a long career as director
(continuing to the present), dispensing melodramatic films with a
forthright, personalized style.

In an environment flavored unmistakably by the vapors of romance, Carole was herself an objective. The picture's second male
lead, Cesar Romero, had a well-reported crush on her. A relative
newcomer to films, Romero then approximated the last of the line
in the Valentino image, and was in the physical pattern of the
recent Lombard involvements with Raft and Columbo. Carole

was fond of Romero who, like Raft, would be said to have her photograph still hanging in his bedroom many long years afterward. But she was on her guard against another serious liaison, and at this time she appeared to fear nothing except marriage. Yet Romero's emergence had an effect of terminating her affair with Robert Riskin, who had been nothing if not patient.

Bob Riskin had been Carole's first persistent suitor after her divorce, other than Bill Powell himself. Then he had yielded lead position to Russ Columbo, but had been the first to console Carole after the crooner's death. Riskin squired Carole during most of 1935, although her date book accommodated other admirers as well. There was no mistaking matrimony as his objective, yet Riskin was not interested in becoming a father, and Carole thought having legitimate children was the only sensible thing to get married for. Otherwise, she said, why risk ruining a perfectly good relationship, and why be contractually bound to something that lacked the permanent investment that children represented to her. She said she also hoped to attain motherhood, but wasn't about to marry in desperation or without love just to achieve it. Meanwhile she enjoyed Bob Riskin's repartee, which had kinship with the dialogue he wrote for Frank Capra's pictures. But she was wary that Riskin may have been more in love with her likely fame than with her self: he launched his most fervent proposal of marriage after *Hands Across the Table* was an established hit. Carole didn't say no.

Indeed, she was thinking it over. She was still considering the prospect at Christmastime in 1935, when Riskin's gift to her was enormous diamond-and-ruby earclips. They never had a spat, but Carole refused to be pushed by an ultimatum; and the romance disintegrated with the old year, and Cesar Romero became her most frequent beau.

Love Before Breakfast finished shooting just before the holiday season. Surrounded by her closest friends, Carole had a delightful time making the picture, and never worried about whether it would succeed or fail. Her confidence would be justified, although she would allow Ernst Lubitsch to retain both his position at Paramount and his cigar. Anyway, she said, Preston Foster had worried enough for all of them. He was the leading man in *Love Before Breakfast,* and while he was an able straight actor, he was not accustomed to romantic comedy and was not at ease with the assignment. He also appeared to be hurt upon learning that he would not have costar status with Carole. She told production boss Charles Rogers that if it really mattered to Foster, she thought he should get second-but-equal billing, especially since he was a Universal player and she wasn't. But she learned that Paramount had agreed to the loan only with the rigid stipulation that Carole have star billing alone above the title, in letters specified at least twice as large as any other player's.

Earl Eby, who had a small role in the picture and was a companion to Foster during production, told of Carole "sneaking into Preston's dressing room, pinning a multitude of various-sized paper stars all over—on the walls, on the ceiling, and on the furniture. I dropped in to see Preston and surprised her there, except that she only winked and went right on with her business. Preston got a big kick out of it. Later when I went to a dressing room that I shared with some of the other actors, there was a huge star taped on the door, with 'Earl Eby' written on it in a big looping handwriting that was Carole's for certain. I kept that star for many years, until finally it just fell apart."

Love Before Breakfast wasn't all parlor-and-boudoir fluff. There was manly stuff along the way, in which Preston Foster was properly in his element. One of the studio scenes simulated a storm at sea, with Carole's small sailboat overturning so she can be rescued by Foster. The company took a yacht out into the Pacific to shoot additional scenes, and Carole underwent an ordeal by water— taking, she said, as much punishment as a Coast Guardsman during a shipwreck. But at her own insistence. Some of the action was too close to the camera to permit the use of a stand-in, and Carole told Dixie there was no good reason for them both getting drenched, so she'd take all the soaking herself. Time after time, after a thorough baptism, she would dry off and get herself regroomed to shoot the same sequence over again, providing alternative shots for the picture's final editing.

Although the budget was increased only to meet Carole's salary, *Love Before Breakfast* was upgraded to major status after having been efficiently filmed in just seven weeks. Production was completed while Carole was dazzling critics and her growing public alike, in the first-run engagements of *Hands Across the Table* all around the country. Consequently Universal found itself temporarily in possession of an even bigger star than had been bargained for, and this translated into a bigger "look" for the picture itself. The advertising campaign for *Love Before Breakfast* was scuttled because it wasn't classy enough, and the new posters suggested one of the important screen events of the season.

It certainly wasn't that. It was a trifle, enjoyable for the moment and easily forgettable, yet very smoothly done. *Love Before Breakfast* kept Carole on a positive and promising trajectory, showing every bit as favorably as the Colbert-MacMurray *The Bride Comes Home,* although not quite matching its box-office return. But it was Universal's most profitable picture released in the spring of 1936, just before a little girl named Deanna Durbin rescued the old company from absolute financial despair.

Carole returned to Paramount and found waiting for her a story she rather liked—*My American Wife,* foreseen as a stylish romantic comedy to team her with Germany's Francis Lederer, who had been unsuccessfully oversold as an American matinee idol after scoring a Broadway hit in *Autumn Crocus* some years earlier. The only difficulty was that Carole could not get any of the directors she wanted, and was determined to hold Lubitsch to the bargain he had made. Mitchell Leisen was directing Fred Mac-Murray again, with *Thirteen Hours by Air* opposite Joan Bennett; and Wesley Ruggles was changing pace for the dramatic *Valiant Is the Word for Carrie* that would give Gladys George an Academy Award nomination in her American film debut. Carole would also have accepted Richard Wallace, but he became ill. And it was the old, old story: something else came up. Something bigger, and better.

The something was *My Man Godfrey* and the studio was again Universal, except this time there was no reluctance to loan Carole because the picture resembled a winner in the advance reckoning. The original story had acquired fame in a minor way as an immensely popular serial in *Liberty* magazine, under the title *1011 Fifth Avenue.* Charles R. Rogers bought the screen rights with a plan of producing it personally, hopefully as a vehicle for Constance Bennett. Rogers wanted the redoubtable free-lancer, Gregory La-Cava, to direct; and LaCava liked the script that Eric Hatch, the original author, had devised with Morrie Ryskind's assistance. The catch was that LaCava had gone through an ordeal directing Constance Bennett in *The Affairs of Cellini* in 1934 and said he wanted no part of a package that included her. Later he softened, saying he would take either Bennett sister—he considered Joan the better actress and the nicer person—if William Powell could be pried away from M-G-M to play the leading male role, a penniless hobo remade into a fashionable butler. Getting Powell did not seem likely. M-G-M did not loan its accomplished stars except in extraordinary circumstances; and in the up-and-down pattern of his career, William Powell was suddenly hotter than he had ever been before.

But the word had trickled into all the studios that Universal had one honey of a script. Ronald Colman, wearying of costume elegance, was only one of several actors known to be interested in the male role. Louis B. Mayer's hunch was that sending William Powell on loan could be a smart idea, even to Universal of all places. Powell had a contract that said he could not be loaned to another company without his consent, and he surprised Charles Rogers by saying that he would take the assignment only on the condition that Carole Lombard play the female lead—inevitably, an heiress. LaCava, of course, was delighted, and Rogers was not displeased. The important thing was that Ernst Lubitsch thought it was a wonderful idea, and so did Carole.

Historians shuffled through the records and could find no precedent of a divorced couple functioning as a romantic star team in a movie, other than Margaret Sullavan and Henry Fonda, who had been briefly married years before either had entered pictures. The new casting might have revived rumors of a second Powell-Lombard romance, except that Powell had fallen in love with Jean Harlow and everyone knew it. His insistence on Carole Lombard as his costar was merely pragmatic: he sensed that she could bring to the picture the quality of personality it needed for hitting the comedy bull's-eye. He expected the picture to accomplish more on her behalf than it would for himself. Actually it would be an historic occasion for both of them.

With Powell assigned, the title became *My Man Godfrey* to emphasize his participation. Paramount raised no objection to M-G-M's stipulation that he have first billing, and it would be the last occasion of Carole yielding the honors. The parts were equal in size, dimension, and color, and everyone agreed that it looked like great casting. It was that.

The role of Godfrey could represent the pinnacle of Powell's long career, which would endure respectfully for another two decades and terminate only because of a retirement that was entirely voluntary on his part—after playing the role of Doc marvelously well in *Mister Roberts* in 1955. Powell was forty-four in 1936, and only two years before Warners had written him off as a hasbeen, which he had also briefly resembled upon departing Paramount in 1931. But he had been remarkably transformed at M-G-M, a talent rescued by that studio's legendary hurry-up director, Woody Van Dyke.

Carrying his Warner pinkslip, Powell checked into M-G-M early in 1934 without a contract and with only one picture guaranteed. But it was a good assignment—a costarring role with Clark Gable in *Manhattan Melodrama* with Van Dyke directing a David Selznick production. Gable and Powell played boyhood friends who retained their mutual respect after one became a hood and the other a district attorney . . . and likely governor material. In the same year that *It Happened One Night* won Gable his Academy Award, *Manhattan Melodrama* was cited as the best original story, even though many moviegoers objected to an ending that found Gable getting the electric chair and Powell getting the girl. Or in this case, the "lady." She was Myrna Loy, the picture's third star, and very much the image of a lady in her own astonishing emergence at M-G-M, after a decade of shopworn existence as a featured player, working regularly but drudgingly at all the studios without distinction. But Woody Van Dyke had a hunch about Powell and Loy functioning smartly as a team, and M-G-M signed Powell to a star contract. Van Dyke rushed Powell and Loy right into *The Thin Man* and filmed it in seventeen days. The result was an historic blend of comedy and melodrama, garnished with a sophistication that owed as much to the stars' talent and rapport as to their lines.

After that there was no stopping Bill or Myrna, individually or collectively. Both astonished their new studio by zooming into the annual reporting of the nation's top ten box-office stars, and Myrna Loy was briefly the most popular leading lady in pictures. Everything touched by either party became gold. Powell made a picture called *Reckless* with Jean Harlow, who was then only twenty-three but newly divorced from her third husband, M-G-M cameraman Hal Rosson. They fell in love immediately and spectacularly—the way observers said Powell had never been in love with Carole Lombard, or Harlow with Rosson or the late Paul Bern. Powell clicked in other pictures with Loy, and with brand-new actresses such as Luise Rainer and Rosalind Russell—both of whom stepped in for Myrna when she staged a well-publicized strike for a better salary. With both Loy (as Billie Burke) and Rainer (as Anna Held) alternating as his leading ladies in a garish three-hour extravaganza that nevertheless would win the 1936 Academy Award as Best Picture, Powell essayed the plum title role of *The Great Ziegfeld.*

Strangely enough, after the Ziegfeld stint and before he was Lombard's man Godfrey, Powell had accepted another loan assignment, this time to RKO. And the hunch—Irving Thalberg's rather than Mayer's—was that Powell would work nicely with another actress who was also on loan. Harry Cohn was in the unaccustomed posture of lender and the girl was Jean Arthur. She was herself a late-blooming wonder whom M-G-M hoped to lure away from Columbia, but never did. The picture she made with Bill Powell was *The Ex-Mrs. Bradford,* a proficient job that mixed murder with merriment and seemed to give final certification to the word *screwball* as an identifiable genre of screen comedy. The word actually had come into play in connection with the two bright Columbia pictures that essentially established Jean Arthur's remarkable talent—John Ford's *The Whole Town's Talking* (in which Edward G. Robinson played a good guy-bad guy dual role) —and Frank Capra's famous *Mr. Deeds Goes to Town.* As counterpoint to Gary Cooper's Longfellow Deeds, Jean Arthur created almost a new and certainly a vivid type of urban heroine—the hardworking professional girl (here a newspaperwoman) caught between her own high principles and the duty to compromise.

While altogether as refreshing a personality as Carole Lombard on the one hand or Myrna Loy on the other, Jean Arthur could not possibly be confused with either. She would share the throne of screwball royalty about equally with Carole without ever becoming her rival, so distinctive was each in temperament, style, and screen personality. Off the screen Carole was the most outgoing girl in pictures, Jean the least accessible. Their only common denominator was their excellence, in the view of Wesley Ruggles who directed them both—Miss Arthur in Columbia's *Too Many Husbands,* a classic of the screwball idiom. Ruggles also thought it remarkable and proper that the two girls were never under consideration for the same role.

There was a departure in their degree of glamour. Jean Arthur managed only an average prettiness, certainly no match for Carole; but her unique violin of a voice was one of the treasures of screwball comedy and would make her beautiful in the country's eyes. Possibly because she became somehow mired at Columbia (which nevertheless would eventually supply her with one smash hit after another), she never became a star of showy, Crawfordesque aura, but her own reclusiveness surely explained that in part. Yet through the changing personality cycles punctuated by temporary star sensations, she was one of the very few whom *everybody* always liked.

The crowning irony was that Jean Arthur, Carole Lombard, and Myrna Loy could all trace their movie experience back half a dozen years before the talkies gained their final dominance. Carole had been a Sennett bathing beauty, Jean was a leading lady in silent quickie westerns (before her Paramount starlet days when her voice was misinterpreted as a liability for the talkies), and Myrna's custom had been the playing of Oriental vamps in some of the sleaziest pictures ever made. Yet amid the glittering assembly of stage-polished mistresses of dialogue brought into Hollywood from Broadway in the first half of the thirties, they were the trio who became the mistresses and the justification of a new movie vogue. Their wit was visual and verbal, in even measure. And in epochal 1936, William Powell had the curious occasion to be their perfect foil, playing opposite all three in successive assignments.

If Lombard and Arthur were clearly the screwball superiors, Myrna Loy was in an honorable satellite company that enlisted several splendid film actresses capable of moving with any trend. An Irene Dunne could sparkle in *Theodora Goes Wild, The Awful Truth, The Joy of Living,* and *My Favorite Wife.* A Barbara Stanwyck could make much out of little in *Breakfast for Two* and *The Mad Miss Manton,* and more out of a lot in *The Lady Eve* and *Ball of Fire,* before the coming of the war curtailed the genre. A screwball flair was transmitted by Ginger Rogers in some of her outings with Fred Astaire, and in Gregory LaCava's *Fifth Avenue Girl* and Garson Kanin's *Bachelor Mother.* To Claudette Colbert's inventory, *I Met Him in Paris* (Ruggles) and *Midnight* (Leisen) were honorable additions.

Jean Harlow was a raffish delight in *Libeled Lady,* top-billed in the exalted company of Powell, Loy, and Spencer Tracy; and again in *Personal Property,* opposite a less able Robert Taylor. Margaret Sullavan was perhaps the screen's most wistfully beguiling comedienne in *The Good Fairy* and *The Shop Around the Corner.* Rosalind Russell, last of the great screwballs, defined latent femininity in manly, executive disguise—hilariously in *His Girl Friday* and *This Thing Called Love,* cued almost accidentally by the remarkable opportunity given her in the Shearer-Crawford *The Women.* Bette Davis and Olivia deHavilland, sandwiching Leslie Howard in *It's Love I'm After,* were not helped by the script; but Katharine Hepburn, in a brilliant *Bringing Up Baby* and a fine but more civilized *Holiday,* proved capable of the most nimble challenge. And finally, there was the eternal glory of Greta Garbo as Herr Lubitsch's *Ninotchka,* before the world stopped laughing.

Not fully appreciated in its own time, it was an incomparable era of movie comedy and the world will not see its like again. It was a glamorous charade, with engaging women of independent spirit calling most of the shots, before postwar film content would again reduce women to sex-object status in male-dominated environments. Yet sociologists will say that the new American woman petitioned for her rights during the Great Depression, and the progression of screwball comedy tracks the phenomenon. But with so many titles to choose from, if any one picture had to sum up a lasting impression of screwball comedy, most people with good memories would probably choose a very cherished *My Man Godfrey.*

As Irene Bullock, Carole in this picture played a girl as monumentally stupid as she was wealthy—and she was plenty wealthy, but prettier still. On a high-society scavenger hunt she retrieves Godfrey—a college-educated victim of the Depression—from the city dump where he lives with other human flotsam: she takes him back to the party as the "forgotten man" she was entrusted to find. The Bullock family has an opening for a butler, and scrubbing up Godfrey for the function is Irene's own idiotic idea which nevertheless works out perfectly, until the cards are stacked with complication. Godfrey, of course, proceeds to change the monstrously funny Bullock family into human beings, finally endowing all of them with consciences, and the commitment to good deeds. In the fabric of the screenplay, Godfrey is a lightning rod for the gloriously zany Irene, predictable only for her lunacy. Powell essentially rendered sublime straight-man service to Carole's newest edition of fireworks.

It was not really her standard characterization, but it pointed the way toward metamorphosis as Hazel Flagg and other subsequent Lombard heroines. The hardness seems gone from her now. She is not ego-driven for theatrical glory, or security-driven for wealthy marriage. Irene is soft, and even the brainlessness is winning because it is sheathed in naïveté and she is therefore vulnerable. The severe articulation of the actress in *Twentieth Century* is yielding to the fast-paced, breathless loud whisper of the rich girl who really doesn't need money.

Logicians could shoot down *My Man Godfrey* as an improbability but for the rich vein of sexuality inherent in the Irene-Godfrey relationship, conveyed entirely by innuendo. That Bill Powell and Carole Lombard still enjoyed working together was instantly apparent on film, and LaCava orchestrated them with a fine collection of drawing-room grotesques: fluttery Alice Brady and tubby, frog-voiced Eugene Pallette as the older Bullocks, Gail Patrick as the jealous sister, and Mischa Auer as Miss Brady's gigolo "protégé." That Carole and the dark but glacial Gail Patrick could be sisters stretched the imagination, but perhaps it was as feasible as any notion of Brady and Pallette having conceived offspring by means of normal intercourse in the first place. Screwball comedy permitted poetic license, and made the most of it. Brady, Pallette, and Auer were all quite wonderful, and Gail Patrick was herself unique: beautiful, but in a way that established her as the antagonist within three-tenths of a second after her first appearance in the frame.

Uncharacteristic certainly of Universal, *My Man Godfrey* was an unqualified smash. It left Carole Lombard sitting on the very top of the movie heap: she could hardly have been more secure. But that is getting ahead of the story.

Carole the casual in 1940: home from a holiday in the mountains . . .

. . . and on location with They Knew What They Wanted.

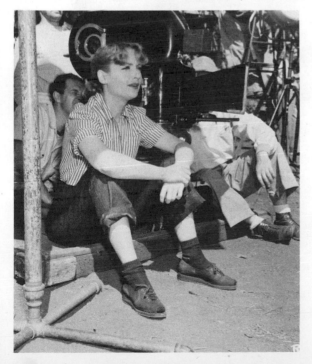

The Gables in their last public appearance together, at Santa Anita racetrack in the first week of 1942.

Indianapolis, January 15, 1942: Carole sells more than two million dollars in "defense" bonds less than seven weeks after the U.S. entry into World War II.

Carole leads the singing of **The Star-Spangled Banner** *at the Cadle Tabernacle. Movie czar Will Hays is pictured at far right.*

Elizabeth Peters and her daughter, just before preparing for homeward flight. This is believed to be the last photograph taken of Carole Lombard.

✤ IX ✤

After the Ball

JUST BEFORE Carole reported for work on *My Man Godfrey,* she answered a summons to assist in the planning of the annual Mayfair Club Ball. When Carole Lombard "assisted" in something, it usually meant that she sort of took charge.

The Mayfair event flourished for a time as Hollywood's answer to the rigid, traditional snobbishness with which the organized southern California society beheld the nouveau riche film community. Not even Mary Pickford and Douglas Fairbanks, wearing the robes of industrial royalty and entertaining international nobility on a stupendous scale during their heyday at Pickfair, were able to construct a filmland social order that would receive a favorable nod from the Los Angeles bluebloods.

The most exclusive clubs—Pasadena's long-entrenched Valley Hunt Club, for example—stipulated "no movie people" for its membership rolls, as clearly as they excluded racial and ethnic minorities. The Mayfair event, originated by the Mayers, Goldwyns, Warners and other industrial fathers at about the same time that they established the Academy of Motion Picture Arts and Sciences, was the film colony's act of emulation. It had its own built-in snobbishness, as *the* event of the year: to be invited for the first time signified that one had "arrived." Some figurehead industry wives were the official hostesses, but they solved most of their administrative problems by giving them to Carole.

She arranged the decor and coordinated the catering services. She hired the musicians and selected their music. She clearly enunciated an "all-white" motif for the gowns. She had no jurisdiction over the invitation list but her consultation was invited because there were unresolvable problems—mainly, the difficulty of knowing the up-to-the-minute status of some of the filmland's shakier marriages.

The Clark Gables posed a particular problem. An engraved invitation was prepared for Mr. and Mrs. Clark Gable, but their long-rumored separation became a fact in December, 1935, just before the invitations went into the mail. Clark Gable moved out of the residence he had shared with Rhea Langham Gable for five years, but a reconciliation try by Rhea had been reported. Carole became arbitrator in the matter and elected to send the joint invitation to the Beverly Wilshire Hotel, where Clark had taken rooms. There was keen speculation on whom the undisputed King of the Movies would bring to the ball, if he chose to show up at all.

Victor Hugo's in Beverly Hills was the scene of the "white" Mayfair, and it glistened with the unique magic of movie folk on the evening of January 23, 1936. Among all the annual formal events, this would command lasting memory as the most successful, thus enhancing the "perfect hostess" description that Carole had sought to abdicate. There were only some minor hitches. Jeanette MacDonald wore a mauve gown, which appeared to be the only discoloration of Carole's all-white edict . . . until the Irving Thalbergs arrived late, and Norma Shearer was wearing a spectacular scarlet gown.

Carole made no attempt to conceal her fury toward Norma for what she considered was a willful act of social treason, but Miss Shearer's blood was about as blue as Hollywood blood could be, so Carole held her tongue. But she seethed throughout the evening, until Clark Gable put in a tardy appearance, slightly drunk.

According to popular legend, Gable arrived alone. But his official "date" was Eadie Adams, a singer who often "dubbed" the voices of M-G-M stars in some of their musical turns. Miss Adams, who was in no way related to the singer-comedienne of the same name in a later era, managed to fade miraculously into the scenery at the Mayfair Ball. To all appearances, Clark Gable was there stag: certainly he did not bring his estranged wife. Indeed, Rhea Gable was in attendance with another escort, and it was apparent that a reconciliation of the Gables was not about to materialize.

Nor was Carole Lombard without an escort of her own. She came with Cesar Romero, but they had difficulty keeping track of one another as Carole busied herself with attentions to the ball. But from the time she worked into a conversation with Clark Gable, she seemed suddenly purged of any responsibility toward the party. After a while it occurred to some of the guests that Carole Lombard was missing. And so, it seemed, was Clark Gable, who had last been seen with her.

Cesar Romero was still in the ballroom, apparently unperturbed. An evening that started late was running even later, but eventually Carole and Clark returned, simultaneously but without appearance of being together. They even denied having ducked out in tandem, although both admitted to it in later accounts. According to Carole's version given shortly afterward, Clark pulled her away from the place to try to persuade her against begrudging Norma Shearer. She agreed to calm down, and they returned to the party, whereupon Carole again saw Norma and obeyed sudden impulse to give her a tongue-lashing.

Toward the wee hours, Gable cursed Carole under his breath, saying you just didn't talk that way to Norma Shearer, of all people. Then he stalked away, shortly before the ball was over. Two days later he came home to his hotel after struggling with M-G-M's notion of the San Francisco ruins, and encountered Carole's peace offering: a bird cage in his room, containing two white doves.

It was the beginning of their historic affair, one of the fabled "great love stories" of the Hollywood firmament.

Only once had Gable attended a party Carole had given, and then he was with Rhea. Since making *No Man of Her Own* with him during her married days, Carole had seen very little of Gable, and had never been alone with him. When she had worked briefly at M-G-M they had lunched together a few times, but always with Chester Morris or William Powell or both. But their mutual attentiveness at the Mayfair Ball had not gone unreported. Every columnist picked up the morsel, and people around the country got a very early suspicion that something was going on between the most popular male of the movies and one of the most promising of the beautiful lady stars.

Carole didn't see Gable again immediately. She had started *My Man Godfrey* and resolved not to be distracted. But he telephoned her, first at home and then at the studio, and then at both places with increasing frequency. Their next meeting was prearranged even though Gable again appeared to be squiring another girl (Louise Woodbury, a Universal starlet). That was on St. Valentine's Day, three weeks after the Mayfair Ball. Gable didn't know what to expect, and he was taken by surprise, along with the rest of the partygoers.

The Donald Ogden Stewarts had taken over Jock Whitney's mansion for a party described as a "nervous breakdown ball" by hostess Bea Stewart, even if the very idea suggested the aroma of the Carole Lombard brain. It was a marathon gala that started at high noon but had its assembly in white tie and tails, as well as full gowns accessoried with tiaras, plumes, and long white gloves. Clark Gable arrived and soon gave the appearance of being uncomfortable in formal duds, and nervously missing someone he'd expected to find there. For this occasion Carole's entrance was late by calculation, and one worthy of a true Star. Supper was already being served when an ambulance arrived, bearing Louella Parsons's Docky Martin and four images of interns in matching white hospital uniforms. They alighted from the ambulance before the main entrance to the house, and removed the prone body of the serenely nervously broken-down Carole Lombard, bearing her into the house on a stretcher. Everything stopped—the band music, the dancing, the eating and Clark Gable's heart.

He was the sensation of the age.

He was a time bomb of seething sex, ticking away in half a dozen pictures all released in the first half of 1931, playing only small or at least secondary roles. His first picture was a Pathé western, then there were a couple for Warners, where he had been considered at least briefly for the *Little Caesar* title role of Edward G. Robinson's eventual historic portrayal. He was immediately typed as a "heavy": certainly he lacked the requisite looks of a leading man. His face was strong but crude, and he was jug-eared.

M-G-M gave him a contract because his looks at least were distinctive, and he was no longer the plug-ugly who had washed out of Hollywood after managing only fitful employment as an extra. In those days he rather resembled one of Lon Chaney's makeup jobs, but he married a much older woman who underwrote an expensive reconstruction of his teeth. She also taught him the rudiments of acting and got him started in his chosen profession, before he cut Josephine Dillon adrift.

He was twenty-four when he married the fortyish Josephine Dillon, and twenty-nine when he took the forty-six-year-old Rhea Langham as his second wife. Rumors that persisted about an intervening marriage to yet another much-older woman were never confirmed and always denied. Yet he privately boasted of sexual exploits that furthered his young stage career in stock and then on Broadway, almost all of them involving actresses in the hunger of their middle years: Laura Hope Crews; Pauline Frederick; and in *Love, Honor and Betray,* his final Broadway appearance, the same Alice Brady who would play Carole Lombard's mother so charmingly in *My Man Godfrey.* One account had William A. Brady, Alice's famous stage-producer father, conniving to have the young stud cast in the road company of *The Last Mile* as a means of getting him out of town. But in 1931 the people at M-G-M didn't know all of these things. Hollywood itself would learn the tawdry details only over a period of years, morsel by morsel; and most of Clark Gable's fans around the world would never know them during his lifetime.

At M-G-M he supported Joan Crawford in one picture, Constance Bennett and Robert Montgomery in another, and with Jean Harlow he shared the background for a Wallace Beery picture, *The Secret Six.* There was no visible picture reaction, but none had been expected; he definitely was not considered star material. Yet he was able enough, and could have expected regular employment at the studio if he kept his nose clean. Lionel Barrymore, doubling in that period as actor and director for M-G-M, took a liking to Gable and sensed a magnetic charm that could break through celluloid. Barrymore tried to get Gable assigned to an important role as a gangster in *A Free Soul.* Barrymore would himself earn an Academy Award for enacting an alcoholic lawyer in the picture. The star part and title role was Norma Shearer's, already in possession of Academy recognition as Best Actress for the recent *The Divorcee.* Her leading man in that picture had been the young and promising Chester Morris, also represented in another M-G-M winner, *The Big House.* The plan was to have Morris play the gangster in *A Free Soul* and Gable was out in the cold. But when Morris could not be freed from another assignment, the part was up for grabs.

Irving Thalberg and Norma Shearer happened then to attend

one of the Hearst weekend outings at San Simeon, and Thalberg became curious when Richard Barthelmess, discussing an unreleased Warner film of his own called *The Finger Points,* said that the new Clark Gable fellow who played the hood would likely steal the show, and could have a good career if he got the right breaks. Back in Hollywood, Thalberg requested and screened a print of the Barthelmess picture, and immediately put Clark Gable in *A Free Soul.* It was third-featured billing but a star-sized part, larger than Leslie Howard's although Howard was nominally the leading man. (Lawyer successfully defends gangster on murder rap; gangster seduces lawyer's daughter; society playboy in love with daughter slays gangster; lawyer successfully defends society playboy on murder rap.)

A Free Soul had everything going for it. Shearer was enormously popular and had made the transition to sound more effectively than any other silent star. The director was Clarence Brown, probably M-G-M's finest pictorial craftsman. The story couldn't miss. Yet Clark Gable, the only dubious entry, became the picture's big story —Barrymore's award and Shearer's Academy nomination notwithstanding. Perhaps the most extraordinary thing was that Clarence Brown and Irving Thalberg sensed what was happening before the picture was completed; the bomb exploded without benefit of public endorsement which, however, was inevitable.

At the end of a day's shooting, Thalberg was summoned by Brown, who thought the studio boss should take a look at the day's rushes—the grainy evidence of the newly exposed film, unedited and without sound. As often as not, such a call meant that an actor might be replaced. This time it meant something else. Thalberg was startled by a scene in which gangster Gable angrily shoved free-spirit society girl Shearer into a chair. A look of astonishment was on Norma's face, and it was better than acting: Thalberg saw that his wife was genuinely surprised by Gable's volatile action, and he sensed that she also *liked* it. If this was a tip on the likely reaction of millions of moviegoing women, Gable could be the biggest thing to hit the studio since Garbo.

On M-G-M's summer shooting schedule was *Susan Lennox: Her Fall and Rise,* a Garbo vehicle. Playing one of the all-time hunches, Thalberg decided on an all-out Clark Gable bombardment, with the certification of stardom to follow his appearance opposite the great Greta Garbo. First he would be put into a programmer that had also been planned for Chester Morris—*Sporting Blood,* with Madge Evans—to see how he would fare in a straight romantic lead. That was finished and Gable was filming the Garbo picture before even *A Free Soul* had gone into release. When it *was* released and the fan reaction exceeded even Thalberg's reckless optimism, Gable was rushed into a Joan Crawford picture (*Possessed*); and when another Crawford picture (*Laughing Sinners*) was released to a disapproving public, Thalberg yanked it from distribution and had John Mack Brown's scenes reshot with Gable. He and Crawford worked on the two pictures almost simultaneously, and before those labors were finished, Gable joined Wallace Beery in the cinema skies for *Hell Divers.* Gable saturated the screen in 1931. *A Free Soul* was released in July, *Sporting Blood* in August. Both the Garbo picture and the revised Crawford vehicle were issued in October, and the Crawford-Gable *Possessed* was M-G-M's Thanksgiving present, with *Hell Divers* for the yuletide.

Without a nominal credit at the beginning of 1931, Clark Gable was the hottest commercial property in Hollywood twelve months and twelve pictures later. He had a new contract that made him a wealthy Star, and he was both a pain and a puzzlement to his studio —particularly to Louis B. Mayer, with whom Gable would maintain loathing.

The Metro-Goldwyn-Mayer company was itself a monument to hypocrisy—the most morally sanctimonious studio in a town thriving on amoral legend and sustained by it. The publicists at M-G-M published the lives of their stars in free translation of the facts, but getting the Gable dossier doctored for public consumption was downright bewildering. Not only was his wife a relative ancient, she wasn't even pretty, and Gable professed no love for her. The conclusion was that he had given the wealthy Texas socialite the favor of marriage for her having financed his apprenticeship on the stage. The studio found out about the earlier marriage to Josephine Dillon but kept quiet about it, and reportedly paid Miss Dillon—who still lived in Hollywood—to maintain her own silence.

If that weren't enough to distress the servicers to the fan magazines, Clark was sleeping around more or less openly, without recrimination from Rhea, who understood his needs and was resigned to them. He tomcatted around the community proper, but also bedded the girls within the studio gates. Billy Grady, a studio flack in 1931 and M-G-M's casting director during most of Gable's tenure as a star there, said, "Clark was the least selective lover in the hemisphere. He'd screw anything—a girl didn't have to be pretty or even clean. The best that could be said for him was that he wouldn't have anything to do with the fairy boys." Grady emphasized, however, that despite everything, most of the people at the studio and around Hollywood—even the self-righteous types—couldn't help *liking* Clark.

"His character wasn't the best, and his ethics were deficient. But you tolerated him the way you would a little boy, if the kid had charm. Whatever he had would be difficult to explain if not impossible, but there was no doubt that he had it. I don't think he was very bright. He certainly lacked wit. He was without grace, but he knew it and it didn't bother him, and we kind of liked him for that. Everyone liked Clark even when they thought they shouldn't, and I suppose you could say the same thing about Clark that was always said of Spencer Tracy. His personality never turned you off. He was a person you liked to have around."

Marion Davies liked having him around, as did Norma Shearer and Jean Harlow. In 1932 releases, he costarred with the Misses Davies, Shearer, and Harlow in succession, and the Gable-Harlow *Red Dust* confirmed a great screen-scorching team. They made six pictures together in as many years during Harlow's young life, and were chummy in diverse ways. After *Red Dust* Gable was loaned out for the first time—to Paramount and Carole Lombard for *No Man of Her Own*. It was his sixteenth picture. After Carole rebuffed his only pass, they became pals.

Gable kept a veritable scoreboard on his leading ladies, and in later years he often infuriated Carole by going into some of the details. She resented even first-person gossip, but at least Clark was honest in both directions and she knew of several or many luminous ladies with whom he *never* scored, and of at least one case where he never even tried: Jeanette MacDonald. His batting average was indeed only ordinary, but as Billy Grady put it, "People who go to bat often enough usually manage their fair share of hits."

The one thing neither Thalberg nor anyone at the studio had foreseen was Gable's staying power at the box office. Because they rated him a limited talent at best, they expected him to establish a level and gradually fade, as the Charles Farrells and George Bancrofts faded. When they thought they detected the beginning of his decline, he was given a role subordinate to John Barrymore's in

Night Flight and it made him testy; and as a disciplinary measure he was exiled to Columbia for *It Happened One Night.* Even by 1936, the rest already was classic history: his Academy Award; the triumph of *Mutiny on the Bounty;* a public more devoted (and forgiving) than ever; and whatever it was that made men admire him and women fall in love with him, both on and off the screen.

Oh, they fell! But the only interest he shared with most of his paramours was Clark Gable himself. His immense ego, which he attempted to cover, was his blind spot. On two occasions was there likely evidence of his having fallen in love with a semblance of feeling for the other party, and each time with a movie actress of undisputed fame. Joan Crawford was the first, and in her autobiography published in 1962 she acknowledged that it was a mutual affair of the heart. She was then between husbands, having shed Douglas Fairbanks, Jr., and not yet involved with Franchot Tone, so she was free to marry and both she and Clark wanted that; but the problem and obstacle was Rhea, and Clark never left home. They put an end to frustration by terminating the liaison, although their friendship continued and they made several pictures together in the years to come.

The other girl was Loretta Young. In 1935 L. B. Mayer made the generous loan of Clark Gable to Darryl Zanuck's independent 20th Century company—just before its merger with Fox—for *The Call of the Wild.* Loretta Young was Gable's leading lady and their affair made chatter over the back fences, even though M-G-M succeeded in keeping it out of the newspapers and fan magazines. Effectively stifled would be a popular community suspicion that Gable had sired Loretta's daughter, but the rumor would gain momentum in later years. In any event, the episode with Loretta was interpreted as the factor that finally severed Gable's umbilical tie to Rhea. But moving out was his idea, not hers; and she vowed never to permit him to be divorced without thorough character assassination.

Historians of Hollywood romance have made Rhea Langham Gable into an archetypical villainess for the eternal triangle, for having frustrated the principals in one of the great love stories. Most of the surviving picture people who remember her claim that she was really a rather lovely person after all, and give her the benefit of many doubts for having "put up with so much for so long." She was an alien who nevertheless found a home in the filmland, and retained some status in its social order after the separation from Gable and even after their divorce. She remained active in Hollywood charities and was never lacking for friends. Clark Gable never disparaged her in his later years.

Because Gable's romance with Carole Lombard ignited almost as a reflex action to his separation from Rhea, it caught the fandom by surprise. People whose primary education in the goings-on of movieland came from *Photoplay* and other monthly magazines had been lulled by the continuing serenade of Gable's steady, placid marriage to that old woman, unfettered by hanky-panky. Now they were finding out about the separation for the first time in the March, 1936, issues, which also carried the first installments of the Gable-Lombard romance that would be a three-year, cliff-hanging serial. Carole had the initial appearance of a homewrecker, but the image endured only briefly. Soon the national pulse was synchronized to the Gable-Lombard heartbeat, and the magazines got behind the romance although M-G-M continued to give it no encouragement. (The Paramount publicists made capital of it.)

When Clark Gable charged into her life in a romantic way, Carole abandoned every other tentative involvement, nor would there be even a rumor of another man in her love life, ever. The combination of manly vigor and innate boyishness captivated her as surely as it swayed others in ignoring his flaws. For two years Gable had displayed the adornment of a moustache that somehow gave accent to the more pleasing aspects of his personality, and in 1936 it was almost inconceivable that he had once been considered unhandsome. Carole did not deny the physical attraction, nor did he, and movie fans breathed a collective sigh of relief that the guy was at last openly in love with someone whose beauty and style could match or complement his own. The hope that they would eventually marry was established early on a national level. It seemed so right; no one wanted to doubt that it would work.

All of the doubts were Carole's. In 1936 she was not at all concerned over whether Rhea might someday submit to a polite divorce action. She didn't think she was ready for marriage, but she knew Clark Gable wasn't. She'd heard all the stories; and very early on, she decided she had her man pretty well pegged. All right, she loved him. He was a great fellow to be with. But he wasn't husband material, not yet: he would have to change. Her mission would be to make him change, without his becoming aware of it.

To accomplish that, she decided that to all outward appearances, she would have to change herself.

In earlier years Paramount executives had thought her overpaid, and anticipated the expiration of her contract with eagerness. While Carole was roughhousing with her ex-husband for Universal, her contract edged toward its completion and Paramount was suddenly desperate to get her signature on a new agreement. A gloating Myron Selznick sensed this. Still obsessed by the idea of avenging wrongs committed long ago by the major companies against his father, he cackled, "Now they'll pay . . . boy, will they pay!"

Paramount offered a seven-year contract, at a reported $5,000 per week. Not enough, Selznick laughed, not nearly enough. He said suppose the Depression ends soon, what would happen? The economy would recover, prices would inflate, and $5,000 would be peanuts—hell, he wasn't going to let Carole sign for as little as *ten* grand a week! What was he trying to do, they asked him, break the Paramount treasury? Myron said that wouldn't bother him a bit.

Anyway, he said, the term kind of deal was no go. Not seven years, not five, not even three. It would be bad business, because Carole was very hot stuff now, and her price would go up God knows how high. Enjoying his own pun, he said he was just going to play it by year. Consulting Carole only on the matter of how many pictures she'd like to make in a single year, he offered her to Paramount for three pictures. The price? One hundred and fifty thousand dollars for each picture, take it or leave it. Everyone at Paramount from Adolph Zukor on down agreed that $150,000 was out of the question. Myron said he could get that kind of money for Carole at any one of three studios, and they weren't sure he was not bluffing. Paramount capitulated.

The news shocked the industry. Carole Lombard was suddenly the highest paid star in films at $450,000 a year, without having ever been in the fussed-over Top Ten at the box office. (In the *Motion Picture Herald*'s rating for 1935 she was No. 67, climbing to No. 28 in 1936 and reaching her high point at No. 12 in 1937.) Industrial leaders wailed that Myron Selznick had sown the seeds of their ruin, and very soon other stars were agitating for comparable salary levels.

Carole rather enjoyed the publicity but said it was like reading a story about someone she didn't know. Later she privately told friends she believed Myron had gone too far. She wished she hadn't signed the new pact—especially when she learned that Sylvia Sidney's contract, having also expired, was not being renegotiated; and that Paramount intended to banish its supposedly washed-up Marlene Dietrich after one more picture. Carole had misgivings about taking money that could have been spread around.

Dietrich's only supporter at the studio now was Ernst Lubitsch, with Sternberg having departed. But Lubitsch, who also had kept the long vigil for Carole, was himself on shaky ground. Before the year was out, he would be relieved of his function as production chief and be returned to the regular roster of directors, for which he was no doubt grateful. He would learn of his demotion not from the studio hierarchy or even from the press, but from his masseur at the Beverly Hills Hotel, who had massaged one of the Paramount chieftains about to do Lubitsch in. When Lubitsch's role as superintendent went to William LeBaron, life at Paramount would seem less satisfying for Carole. But she was still blissful there in mid-1936, and could say she had made the complete climb in half a dozen years at the studio. For having endured every production fad and formula cycle, she looked like a born survivor. As such, she was in exclusive company.

Among the Paramount stars, only Gary Cooper and Claudette Colbert had been there longer. Fredric March and Miriam Hopkins, while both long gone, had never been replaced by players of comparable quality, nor was there likely promise in the youngsters counted on to supplant Sylvia Sidney, who was being pushed toward the exit, or Cary Grant, soon to be departing on his own accord. Discounting W. C. Fields, the only male stars of consequence were Bing Crosby, a faltering George Raft, and the rising Fred MacMurray. On the distaff, only the infrequent Mae West, besides Claudette and Carole, could get her name above the title.

The studio's inevitable "stars of tomorrow" listed the hardy perennials Randolph Scott and Ray Milland, along with such diverse newcomers as Robert Cummings, Lloyd Nolan, and Anthony Quinn; and young but seasoned Frances Dee and Ida Lupino, along with the untried Frances Farmer, Dorothy Lamour, Martha Raye, and Shirley Ross. A failed project would be the marketing of opera star Gladys Swarthout as a rival to Columbia's recent phenomenon, Grace Moore.

Certainly the scene no longer suggested the solvent grandeur of a monarchy, such as had perfumed it when Carole signed on. Despite her financial coup, she had some regret about having renewed her obligation. Particularly after the Gable romance ignited, she found herself hankering to get in the M-G-M fold, and she was wishing she hadn't told off Norma Shearer at the Mayfair Ball.

Some time afterward she had a cyclonic cuss-out with Myron Selznick on the set of *Swing High, Swing Low* when Carole was battling her own uncertainties over enacting a partly dramatic role. Mitchell Leisen, recalling the encounter, said Myron was in a mood for blasphemizing Paramount, and Carole probed him about M-G-M's persent disposition toward her services. Had that been one of the "three studios" that had been prepared to match the salary Paramount was now paying her? Myron said he had sought no other offers, nor had there been any unsolicited ones. So he had been bluffing, after all. Carole glowed crimson.

"You bastard!" she railed. "Do you know what gives so many poor Jews a bad name? Ever-loving pricks like Myron Selznick, that's who! You're why we say words like *kike*. Why, you'd screw your grandmother if doing it caused some producer to suffer!"

Then more subdued, and sensing that her agent had been cut deeply by her outburst, she added, "But Myron, this is the business you were born for. You still haven't gotten over the fact that you flopped as a producer before you had hair between your legs—but Baby, not anybody can play the Hollywood game the way you play it!"

Mitchell Leisen said that in the dozen or so years he knew her, he saw Carole explode in anger only twice and heard of no more than half a dozen other tantrums. "She was really a sweet, even-tempered girl. Strong but sweet—not even her colorful syntax made her less sweet. She had tolerance, and her patience was just incredible, and rare. She didn't fly into rage very often, but she'd let it all come out and then feel cleansed. She was so very fair, and fairness was really all she asked of others. When she became really angry, it was always over someone's dishonesty. She just didn't like to be crossed."

In an autobiography reportedly composed without ghostly assistance, Anthony Quinn told of having been taken under wing by Carole when he was new to the studio and pictures, green and uncertain. She had a material concern for novice screen players in whom sincerity was evident, so she arranged a dinner date with Quinn. When he failed to keep the date for financial and other insecurities, Carole lashed him with an invective of true purple unlike any he'd heard from a woman; but after her eruption, they again became friends.

She had a tantrum scene in *Swing High, Swing Low* which Leisen directed, and it was the last Paramount project overseen by Lubitsch as production chief. But before that, Carole also worked up to a bright explosiveness in *The Princess Comes Across,* the first picture under her expensive new contract and the last of her releases for 1936. It was an all-right picture that might have been a better one—about the pretty working girl who gets passed off as a princess. If a screwball comedy couldn't have a madcap heiress, a bogus princess would usually suffice. As Carole explained the title, the Princess Olga wasn't spreading her legs, she was only sailing the Atlantic.

In what looked like a case of mismanagement, George Raft was engaged as Carole's leading man and William K. Howard as her director. In both cases Carole had notions of rescuing sagging careers. Raft, of course, was a pal of hers; but Bill Howard was a rank curiosity. Carole was barely acquainted with him but liked some pictures he'd made. Howard was young but a veteran director of acknowledged but somehow elusive talent, with a poetic feel for the medium. But neither his work nor his personality suggested a sense of humor, and he had never made a comedy during the talkie period.

For that matter, George Raft was unproved as a light comedian—indeed, prove it he never would—and he may have been looking for an excuse to ankle the assignment. He found one, refusing to make the picture if Ted Tetzlaff was retained as cameraman, as Carole insisted. George said he was on the best of terms with Miss Lombard, but didn't consider himself a good enough actor to trust anyone but the best, and he didn't think Tetzlaff was that. Carole did, and that was George's out. He was briefly put on suspension and was replaced by Fred MacMurray—much the better choice for *The Princess Comes Across.* Carole approved the substitution. Her extraordinary contract stipulated script, director, and costar approval, as well as guaranteed top billing. (Pride may have disguised George Raft's real objection, for in *Bolero* Carole had merely "supported" him, and he still led the billing when they costarred in *Rumba*.)

The Lombard contract actually specified Ted Tetzlaff as her resident cameraman; and the document identified others by name, so that grips, propmen, and other backlot workers including certain dress extras were guaranteed fixtures for her pictures. In the case of electrician Pat Drew, Carole's contract meant job security for one who had been unable to obtain work after surviving a plane crash that maimed him.

Two weeks into production, *The Princess Comes Across* didn't seem to be jelling as comedy and the studio powers considered scrapping it. Carole took charge, with the kind of here's-what-we'll-do authority that always pacifies uncertainty. Bill Howard, uncomfortable in his chore, offered to bow out as director but Carole told him just to worry about his camera angles and she and Fred would establish the pace and style of the comedy. Carole actually rewrote substantial portions of the script to "de-word" the dialogue, and she talked of someday writing and directing a picture all by herself just to get it out of her system.

Princess had required the use of a trained bear. When the turbulent production was complete, Carole purchased a bearcub and had it delivered to Bill Howard as a gift. Inadvertently she proved that Howard lacked a sense of humor, after all. He had the bear carted off to a zoo, explaining how he happened to possess it; and the zoo sent Carole a bill for the cub's upkeep.

She changed her name legally from Jane Peters Powell to Carole Lombard. As a tip-off that she would be less a party girl during the less formal progress of the Gable affair, she sold her star sapphire collection and other jewelry, and instead started taking on pedigreed dogs and cats, soon owning about a dozen. Even more significantly, she sold the house that William Haines had decorated for her and bought another one. This seemed an impulsive maneuver, but Carole sought a residence that would be more conducive to amorous rendezvous. Her Hollywood home had been too much in the public eye, because it was too easily within the public view—and Clark Gable didn't like that. So she acquired a smaller house, in the sequestered reaches of Bel-Air, on St. Cloud Road.

By the fall of 1936, readers could expect a "Will Clark Wed Carole?" article in almost any magazine—not just the movie monthlies, for the romance was also tracked by the general-interest periodicals. Soon the question was not Will, but When . . . and in Clark's own mind, the problem was How. He admitted that he was in love with Carole but made no overtures to Rhea for a divorce. Their lawyers agreed on a separate maintenance formula, but then Clark was recontracted by M-G-M and Rhea made new financial demands. The new Gable contract would net him almost two million dollars in seven years. That was an especially healthy raise since it obligated him for only two films annually, instead of the four he had been making for several years. Any additional pictures, at M-G-M or elsewhere, would mean extra gravy. Rhea wanted her share. Clark argued that there would be no picture making beyond his contractual commitment. During most of his time in Hollywood, he had been frustrated by overwork and not enough time to spend as he chose. Hunting had become his consuming interest but usually it was restricted to weekend activity, with a lot of time eaten up by driving. The new contract guaranteed three months off between pictures, and Clark saw 1937 as his year to relax in the big open country. From his pinnacle as the most popular male star in a world obsessed by movie mythology, he anticipated long hunting trips with his chosen pals, most of whom had little or no concern for the merchandising of motion pictures.

Clark Gable didn't expect a lady friend to tag along when he went off hunting bear or deer. Women had their place and it wasn't in the rugged mountains. While preparing for a hunting expedition to northern Wyoming, Gable was intimidated by Carole's sudden announcement that she was going with him. But when she got herself decked out in boots, jeans, lumberjack shirt, and leather jacket, he knew she meant it. Yet Carole was determined to show true grit. She sought no special consideration, and would refuse it if it was offered. She even purchased a trailer that compressed a bedroom, kitchen, and bath; and if a mountain adventure cast her into otherwise all-male company, she occupied the trailer alone, observing every propriety.

She conspired for time off to coincide with Gable's vacations. When *The Princess Comes Across* did good business despite a lukewarm reception, the studio wanted Carole to make another picture with Fred MacMurray very soon—obviously she was helping him catch on in a hurry. *Swing High, Swing Low* was rushed into shape for Leisen to direct, but Carole hollered that she couldn't be pushed. Since her new assignment would challenge her as both singer and dancer, she said she needed extra time to prepare. She hired Al Siegel to coach her vocally, and LeRoy Prinz to polish her dancing; and she cannily persuaded Paramount that Mac-Murray—who was paid by the week—could squeeze in another picture while she was learning the musical ropes. Once Fred was set in another picture, Carole took off with Gable and continued to "prepare" for her new role . . . in the wilds of the Rockies.

Hunting had been a traditional pastime of the Peters family but Carole never liked the idea of killing for sport. She enjoyed archery, and liked to work with small firearms so long as the target was an inanimate bull's eye. But if Gable hunted live game, so would she. Her mission was to learn to do all the things he enjoyed and did well, and she expected to compete with him in his own proficiencies. While she pursued him, her technique was to appear leading him on, yet not allowing him out of her sight. She reckoned that making him like her and want her, even need her, was not the answer. She would become indispensable to him.

She plotted unsuccessfully to make a picture with Clark, at her studio or his. Despite Clark's vow not to take on outside work, she thought he would capitulate for the right price, particularly if she were part of the deal. Gable could arrange assignments away from M-G-M during his established vacation time, with his home studio taking a cut of his negotiated salary. Now that Carole's employers regularly sought her evaluation of their newly purchased story properties, she scanned the inventory with an eye for a yarn suitable for Gable and herself. *Spawn of the North* was an Alaskan adventure that seemed ideal for Clark and she was able to stir his interest. She got herself assigned to the project, then proposed Gable to the studio. The plan backfired because Paramount considered a Gable-Lombard teaming simply too expensive, although otherwise attractive. With Gable no longer a factor, Carole lost interest in the picture and played sick to get released from her commitment. Her withdrawal automatically freed Ted Tetzlaff from obligation to *Spawn of the North,* whereupon Carole went to bat for George Raft (still her special chum) to play the role she'd wanted Gable to do. Although production was delayed time and again, Raft eventually starred in *Spawn* and it proved his best exposure in years.

Next Carole sought to insinuate herself into Gable's upcoming *Saratoga* picture at M-G-M, and became involved in a musical-chairs game with Jean Harlow, who was becoming less a sex symbol to moviedom and appreciated as a screwball comedienne in her own right. M-G-M had petitioned unsuccessfully to borrow Carole from Paramount to appear in *Personal Property*. The project was designed to polish the fast-rising Robert Taylor as a light comedian, and the thinking was that playing give-and-take with Carole might reveal a latent flair in young Spangler Arlington Brugh. But Paramount put *Swing High, Swing Low* before the cameras and M-G-M, failing Lombard, elected to give Harlow the duty of grooming Bob Taylor. That seemed to create a leading-lady vacancy for Clark Gable's next picture, since *Saratoga* had been planned as a Gable-Harlow event. And Carole went after it. She might have landed the part, except that *Swing High, Swing Low* ran over schedule while *Personal Property* was completed ahead of time, so that by the time Lombard was available, so was Harlow, and M-G-M stayed with its own. Then Jean didn't live to complete the picture.

The death of twenty-six-year-old Jean Harlow in June of 1937 was officially attributed to uremic poisoning. Other causes would be hinted in years of subsequent speculation, even to suggest that the blond bombshell finally succumbed to internal injuries related to beatings rendered by Paul Bern, her husband whose suicide had provoked a sordid scandal five years earlier. The sudden loss of one of its most glittering stars jolted the movie world because it was entirely unexpected. She had worked at the studio until only a few days before her death, showing signs of tiredness that nevertheless often became evident during a production grind. *Saratoga* was roughly half-completed when she died. Carole and Jean were casual friends who appeared to have developed closer kinship during Harlow's long romance with Carole's ex-husband. Hearing of Jean's death on the radio stunned Carole, but her surprise was almost as great when she received telephone calls that same day from M-G-M director Jack Conway and L. B. Mayer himself, matter-of-factly asking Carole to take over the Harlow role in *Saratoga* since Carole's *Swing High, Swing Low* was safely in the can. Carole said, "How can you ask me at a time like this? How can you even think about it?" Mayer remembered to express his great despair over the screen's tragic loss, but said that after all, they did have the *Saratoga* investment to consider, and hadn't she wanted the part in the first place? Besides, Clark Gable was the male lead . . .

Clark Gable accompanied Carole to Jean Harlow's Forest Lawn funeral. On that occasion even the celebrity-watchers were paralyzed in gloom. Harlow's death, following Irving Thalberg's within a matter of months, plunged M-G-M and the rest of Hollywood into a mourning from which it would not emerge soon or easily. Carole's foremost concern at this time was William Powell. He was devastated by his loss, and gossip suggested that he was guilt-ridden for having unofficially walked out on Jean just when she needed him most. (When Powell did not film again for almost two years, the studio version was that he still grieved over Harlow. Actually he was overcoming a serious illness, during which Carole proved his best nurse and morale-builder.)

Carole noted that Clark Gable, beyond uttering grief's proper platitudes, seemed untouched by the passing of either Thalberg, his early sponsor, or Harlow, his supposed favorite costar (and rumored sometime bedmate). Despite Carole's own protestations against showiness in mourning and other allied hypocrisies, she thought it only natural that people should *care*.

Late in 1936 she and Gable had quarreled because Carole canceled a weekend of mountaineering with him when her mother was ill. After it became apparent that Bess Peters was in no grave danger, Gable sulked because Carole still refused to leave her mother's bedside. Carole saw most of her spats with Clark as generating from inconveniences to *him*. He, too, jauntily suggested that she could film *Saratoga,* which only persuaded her anew that she did not want to be a part of it—it was all too morbid.

Gable could make light of other people's monstrous problems but personal difficulties staggered him. Early in 1937 he reacted frantically when a foolish Cockney woman named Violet Norton, whom he claimed never to have met, brought a paternity suit against him. The exhibit was a thirteen-year-old girl supposedly sired in Canada, when Gable was an actor there in stock. The Norton woman was thoroughly discredited in court, but the case stirred up murky headlines and brought to light for the first time some other messy aspects of the Gable past. The fans held their collective breath to see if Carole would stand by Clark. She did, striking a somber and righteously indignant public pose, while kidding him mercilessly about Violet Norton in private, rather enjoying the interlude. Taking their cue from Carole, the Gable worshipers became convinced their roguish boy could do no wrong.

M-G-M kept pressing the *Saratoga* issue and Myron Selznick advised Carole to take the bait, confident the picture would be a large hit. But Carole gave a clearly enunciated rejection and suggested they just use the Jean Harlow scenes they already had, and somehow manage to write her out of the others. The studio people said it would invite too many complications and cut them out of their insurance. But when an announcement was given that newcomer Rita Johnson would assume Harlow's role, there followed a national clamor for release of the picture with the available Harlow scenes, and L. B. Mayer seized upon the commercial wisdom of what had been Carole's initial suggestion. It was tricky, but somehow they managed it. At about the picture's midpoint the blond star seemed to just disappear except as a topic for the other actors to talk about. There was extended use of an obvious double in the long shots, and in closer scenes only the girl's back was in view; while out-takes from earlier passages were adroitly employed—as in the final shot of Harlow on a train with Gable, in which she's wearing the same dress she sported in an earlier train ride. *Saratoga* became a huge box-office hit. While serving as a sentimental farewell to a cherished young star, it also rehabilitated Gable, whose kingly status had been briefly but rudely periled by the flop of *Parnell*.

Carole tried unsuccessfully, she thought, to penetrate the Gable psyche. This man she had fallen in love with, to whom she was helplessly attracted to a point of overlooking his many transgressions, was in her view rather seriously lacking in emotional depth. This seemed to place the demands of a serious biographical film such as *Parnell* beyond his reach; but more importantly to her, it also clouded the prospects of a happy marriage for them, even if the obstacle of Rhea could be cleared away. Too often Gable still showed greater need of a mother than a wife, and spoke of marriage as though it were only an extension of the games they played—the ones that advertised Carole's bountiful sense of humor.

She seemed able to get through to him only by frivolous means. After the Valentine party at Jock Whitney's mansion, she had the ambulance that had delivered her there gift-wrapped in an enormous red ribbon and delivered to Gable, who countered by sending her a toy fire engine. He tried to keep pace with her in the zany gift competition but no one could do that. He came closest when she said she'd like a kitten, and he brought her a cougar cub from a hunting expedition. She teased his mania for fancy cars by buying junk heaps off the used-car lots and having them delivered to him, always done up with the obligatory bright ribbons and sometimes gaudily painted—once with Valentine hearts. Their gift-giving, at least, insured peace. They both had quick tempers and fought often, but making up was their favorite pastime.

They battled over the *Parnell* debacle that was Clark's bitter pill. He took a lot of ribbing about that picture, mainly from Spencer Tracy. (Later when they made *Test Pilot* together, Tracy hatched a daily quip about *Parnell* at the expense of both Gable and Myrna Loy.) The press reaction had cut deeply, for as Charles Stewart Parnell, Clark had made an uncommon effort to really *act*. The Gable naturalness vanished and he became ineffectual. At the preview Carole forgot herself and snickered undiplomatically during Gable's ludicrous death scene. It led to a tiff, which augured the delivery of more doves—this time four of them. The caged doves always represented Carole's bid for forgiveness, or a willingness to bury the hatchet. But she tired of the game. She said the town was running out of doves to buy, and she suspected Gable of eating the ones she'd given him.

Carole caught Clark's funnybone but infuriated the M-G-M custodians when she hired an airplane to fly low over the Culver City studio and drop thousands of printed leaflets bearing the large-type legend, "Fifty Million Chinamen Can't Be Wrong!" In smaller type were excerpts from favorable reviews *Parnell* had somehow received in China.

If there was a chronic sore spot between them, it was money. Clark was irritated by Carole's appearance of just giving it away, sometimes without discretion. Generosity, Carole cajoled him, was the sign of a person with good healthy teeth: issuing cutting quips about Clark's falsies was also irresistible to her. Scolding him as the biggest tightwad in town, Carole said she could afford to be generous because she managed well and saved a lot of money, while he was penny-wise and pound-foolish. Indeed, she had more to show for herself than Clark did, despite his comparable tenure during which he'd made considerably more money than she. Carole was a spendthrift and a gift-splurger, but she regularly invested her money, employing her brother Stuart as broker. She purchased acreage in the San Fernando Valley and talked of building her own "watch-pocket version of San Simeon." Meanwhile Clark complained of being broke, and undertipped waitresses and taxi drivers.

Once Carole lashed out at him for having argued with a salesman about the price of a can of tobacco.

When Clark made a picture with Joan Crawford and her then-husband Franchot Tone called *Love on the Run,* Carole attended the M-G-M party marking its completion, and saw that while set workers displayed presents given them by both Crawford and Tone, there were no gifts from Gable—and to be sure, there never had been. Carole assumed responsibility from that point for getting presents for Clark's coworkers. She picked them out and had them delivered, but sent the bills to Gable.

Nor were they in accord on the matter of the press. Unless Clark knew a reporter personally, he considered one his natural enemy. In any event, he preferred dealing with them on a one-to-one basis. Carole liked reporters and enjoyed holding court for a large group of them. She said they were professionals doing a job, and she had a keen curiosity in their work and how they did it. She often said she would have liked being a reporter, and suspected she'd have been a good one. In time she was able to mellow Clark's attitude. "When you play to the press, you're playing to the fans—and they pay your salary, kiddo, not the studio." She also found Clark injudiciously hostile to the movieland press specialists, and coaxed him into becoming friendlier with Louella Parsons and her satellites.

Newsmen scratched around for new angles on the stars' romance and Carole helped out. She enjoyed publicity as well as she appreciated its value. That she was so accommodating to the reporters was, of course, in no small part responsible for her receiving personally a "great press" year after year. Yet despite the high public profile of the Gable-Lombard affair, it was managed as an essentially private one.

They attended few parties together. Gable hated wearing a tuxedo and said that not having to don one was the first good thing about his having left Rhea. Once, though, when returning from a fishing trip in muddy outdoor garb, Carole and Clark dropped in unannounced at the Basil Rathbones' where a formal party was in progress. It was Carole's own whim: she knew they would create a sensation just by showing up raffishly. But sensation indeed! One of the Rathbone guests was Rhea Gable, no less the social butterfly since her separation from Clark. Carole made the most of the situation, introducing herself to Rhea without pushy-false friendliness but with no trace of awkwardness either. She had seen Rhea only fitfully over the years, and they had the barest personal acquaintance. Rhea initially had effectively painted Carole as a home-wrecker. But now they chatted freely, Rhea proving herself quite gracious. After having disrupted the party, the scruffy uninvited guests departed, but not before Carole was heard to tell Clark, "Don't worry about being able to get a divorce. I've got Rhea pegged, and she'll come through when you want her to. Just expect that it's going to cost you."

The hunting and fishing expeditions increased in number and in their individual durations. Usually they were group outings enlisting various combinations of Clark's rod-and-gun buddies—Harry Fleischmann, Al Menasco, Nat Wolff, Cornwell Jackson; and sometimes their wives or consorts, although not frequently. But unchaperoned excursions became a regular thing for Carole and Clark. When they went off together without an entourage of Gable pals, their sexual union was casually assumed by the film community as well as by the national fandom, without the embroidery of scandal. They behaved discreetly, maintaining separate residences; and in that era, appearance was the main thing if it was not the *only* thing.

In a *Photoplay* article entitled "Hollywood's Unmarried Husbands and Wives," remarkably candid for its day, Kirtley Braskette included Carole and Clark in a roundup with Barbara Stanwyck and Robert Taylor, Paulette Goddard and Charlie Chaplin, Constance Bennett and Gilbert Roland. (Marriage was a result, if not the end result, in all of these cases.) On the other hand, let a naughty French girl such as Simone Simon appear to be living openly in Hollywood with a man who was not her husband, and the studio would drop her even as she was catching on with the movie public as *Josette*. In that sanctimonious time, the studios as well as the social do-gooders—women's clubs primarily—equated and confused the perennial argument of decency in screen content with the offscreen behavior of the well-watched stars.

Not that some of Hollywood's saucier residents failed to provide the copy. The national press was cautious if not ultraconservative, and many stories got killed when they could have sold a lot of papers. Many stars were regularly misquoted because editors would not permit accurate quoting. Carole Lombard was at or near the top of the list of the most edited voices in filmland. The press soaked its saltiest quotes in euphemisms, describing language without illustrating it. Carole enjoyed jawing with reporters, playing frank with them, or merely putting them on, knowing the things she said wouldn't get printed anyway.

Kyle Crichton, a Lombard profiler for *Collier's,* supposedly had editorial autonomy with the magazine but was bitter for a while that higher editors decided to kill the heart of what he said was the best interview story anyone ever gave. Not only did Carole choose to go braless, she also told Crichton she seldom wore panties beneath her dresses or slacks; but the *Collier's* readers would be denied such revelation. Carole rejected the double standard completely. Marital fidelity, she thought, was something men and women could demand in equal measure; and they should forgive strayings accordingly. She didn't begrudge the carnal preoccupations of single men because, frankly, she enjoyed a little playing around herself. She loathed sexual hypocrisy and found sex both pleasurable and therapeutic; and she said most of the unmarried girls she knew were nervous wrecks over their chastity, whether lamenting its loss or trying too hard to get rid of it. She spoke freely of her passing affairs and was seldom reluctant to name names because she knew they wouldn't see print anyway. She told Crichton she'd finally given the aging John Barrymore what he most wanted by invoking the Lysistrata form of blackmail, and that only after she'd come across was she able to pull Barrymore through *Twentieth Century.* And yes, he was a great lover after all.

When she was later reunited with John Barrymore for *True Confession,* the occasion rated a small press conference at which Barrymore said he'd gone on the wagon, prompting a Lombard chortle. Inevitably the newsmen brought up the subject of Clark Gable, and someone asked Carole if she could tell them anything about Gable that they didn't already know. Carole studied for a moment, then twinkled.

"Well, Clark isn't circumcised. Bet you didn't all know *that.*"

Amid the uproar that followed, John Barrymore said he just had to have a drink, and withdrew a miniature bottle from his inner coat pocket.

At other times Carole could be almost defensive about her affair with The King. A fan magazine biographer, harking back to the romantic ignition at the Mayfair Ball, probed Carole about having disappeared from the scene in Clark's company, and of their having stayed out long enough to test one's imagination. Carole said, "I know what you're asking me, but you're giving Clark too much credit, or you aren't giving me enough. It certainly didn't happen *then*, or for a long time afterward . . ."

She teased Clark, who obviously was in ardent pursuit very early on. During his filmland carousings his pattern had been to lose interest in a girl once he'd attained the immediate objective, but there was no discernible point at which his designs on Carole appeared to lose intensity. She knew that if physical beauty prodded his initial interest, other facets would be necessary to inspire his best facsimile of devotion.

On the basis of his marital ledger, Carole could theorize that Clark may have been unknowingly seeking another surrogate mother, but it was clear enough that he had never had a wife who was also a pal. She knew she could be that. She looked at the men who were his closest friends, who might be automobile dealers or attorneys or gun-club professionals. They did not seem to have worked into his chosen circle on the basis of their character or personality, but simply on the matter of sharing his interests. If they liked the outdoors and gunslinging, they were his guys.

So she learned to tie and cast a fly, and how to grease the pan for the newly caught fish. Under Harry Fleischmann's expert instruction, she learned how to fire the different rifles, and practiced the dogma of firearms safety until it was instinctive. The thing she most enjoyed was skeet shooting—firing a rifle at erratically moving clay pigeons. No mortal harm was done. It was a stern test of shooting ability, and Carole provided a sharp eye, a keen aim, and a steadying arm. She liked shooting skeet and soon she excelled at it, becoming easily Gable's superior. She enjoyed getting the better of him, any way it could be.

❋ X ❋

Zany Magic

CAROLE LOMBARD and David Selznick nurtured a friendship dating from her early days at Paramount. He was a promising producer then, before Carole was his older brother's client. When Rudy Behlmer collected the professional memoranda of Selznick's career in book form, one of the earliest representations found Selznick taking credit for sponsorship of Carole at Paramount at a time when no one there seemed interested in her. But later, when David was in charge of production at RKO and Carole's footing at Paramount seemed least certain, Myron Selznick urged his brother to buy up her contract but David resisted. He said he loved Carole for the person she was; and yes, she was a looker. But RKO's penchant was for upper-case Actresses—Irene Dunne, Ann Harding, and the meteoric Katharine Hepburn. David Selznick doubted that Carole could make the weight for the high stakes. But by 1937 he had become the pursuer, and she was the prize.

From RKO, David had gone to work at M-G-M for Louis B. Mayer, his then father-in-law. He stayed there two years, an autonomous producer at the Thalberg level, coexisting uneasily with Irving, who was his close friend and jealous rival. Each coveted total independence. By the time Thalberg's plans for his own company were projected shortly before his premature death, David had already broken free on his own. He went into partnership with Jock

Whitney and Herbert Kalmus to make films employing the newly perfected three-color Technicolor first auditioned successfully in the Miriam Hopkins *Becky Sharp* of 1935.

The way the story went, David was at breakfast with his morning paper when Irene Mayer Selznick remarked offhandedly that Carole Lombard would be a nice study in Technicolor; and at that very moment David was scanning the announcements of the Academy Awards nominations for the 1936 season. There was Carole's name among the five designated Best Actress candidates. Her Irene Bullock in *My Man Godfrey* had been put up against Irene Dunne's wild Theodora, Gladys George's valiant Carrie, Luise Rainer's Anna Held, and Norma Shearer's Juliet. (William Powell was also in nomination—not as Flo Ziegfeld but as Carole's man Godfrey. Alice Brady and Mischa Auer also drew *Godfrey* nominations in the very first year of the supporting awards, and Gregory LaCava was in the running for direction.)

David Selznick put his paper down, went to the telephone and rang his brother: "All right, Myron: let's talk." They talked about Carole's situation at Paramount. Myron said the studio definitely wanted to renew when Carole's first three-picture obligation had been fulfilled. David asked, for the same money? No, the price would go up and they'd pay. Myron insisted he wasn't bluffing. He also hinted that with Lubitsch having been deposed, Carole held no great allegiance to her longtime studio. David wanted Myron to name a price for, say, four pictures in two years. Myron whistled a million dollars, or two-fifty-grand per. David said that was ridiculous; and they were brothers, after all. Yes, but brothers on opposite sides of the business table: Myron said take it or leave it. David had his own way of doing business with his brother. He hung up on him in simulated rage, then waited by the phone for the return call. "All right, David: Let's talk."

Carole's remaining contractual commitment to Paramount was one more film. She had been anticipating a Lubitsch assignment—probably *Bluebeard's Eighth Wife*—as her final obligation, but it could not be worked into the time remaining on her present contract since Lubitsch had gone to work on *Angel,* the Dietrich swan song at Paramount. But Myron hinted that Carole could probably stay in favor at Paramount without signing a contract and could answer Lubitsch's call when it came, meanwhile getting her name on a David Selznick pact. They agreed on a three-year agreement, one picture a year at $200,000 per. Only Garbo, David said, was getting a quarter-million a shot, and not even she was worth it.

Myron said there was a slight hitch. His own contract with Carole was about to expire, and he knew Clark Gable was trying to get her to dump him. The Selznick brothers despised Gable about equally, yet David could not avoid him because Clark was America's idea of Rhett Butler.

Clark Gable, who was not without a mild stain of ethnic prejudice, did not endorse Carole's choice of agents. But Carole had her own reason for wanting to stay in Myron's camp, and it went beyond loyalty and friendship. It was important to her that he was David Selznick's brother.

She wanted to play Scarlett O'Hara.

It was the plum of the age and every star-actress wanted it except perhaps Norma Shearer, who had halfheartedly turned it down when Selznick halfheartedly offered it. Bette Davis wanted Scarlett as zealously as Katharine Hepburn did, and Carole thought their anxiety lessened their chances. She was determined not to let her own eagerness show. Playing against heavy odds, a girl had to be clever. She worked deftly, showing no apparent interest in the part but managing to get her name planted in the general conjecture along with those of Loretta Young, Miriam Hopkins, Jean Arthur, Joan Bennett, even Tallulah Bankhead.

Selznick had owned the property for well over a year, having purchased *Gone With the Wind* almost by chance, before it became the runaway best-selling novel of the decade. When he contracted Carole Lombard in early 1937, he had already rejected a completed Sidney Howard screenplay and had Ben Hecht sketching a new one. There was no way of knowing when the picture could get started; but Carole, who said her own intuition was enormous, suspected that David's seeming need to delay the project was not motivated by script difficulties but by another consideration entirely. He didn't want to be pressured into accepting Clark Gable as Rhett Butler if he could develop an alternative.

Nor was Selznick enamored of a necessary tie-in with his father-in-law on *Gone With the Wind*. Yet Mayer had posed an ultimatum: David could have Clark Gable only if Loew's (M-G-M) could handle distribution of the epic film. The irony was that only Mayer could *force* Gable to play Rhett Butler. Clark earnestly wanted no part of the deal, having sworn off costume period pictures because of the *Parnell* experience. But Carole's own instinct about *Gone With the Wind* told her that no matter who played Scarlett, Clark Gable *had* to be Rhett.

Warners, almost everyone knew, proposed a distribution arrangement similar to Mayer's, but with Errol Flynn as Rhett to Bette Davis's Scarlett. The Warner package also included Olivia deHavilland and Leslie Howard, who would linger in Selznick's mind even after he'd ruled out the Warner possibility because he couldn't swallow the Flynn idea any more than Bette Davis could. But there was also Paramount, trotting out Gary Cooper as a presentable candidate for Rhett, and showing a willingness to augment the financing without interfering with Selznick's personalized production.

Carole was confident that if Paramount could get the distribution gravy for *Gone With the Wind*, she could be Scarlett O'Hara. But according to her intricate plan, Clark Gable, not Gary Cooper, would be Rhett. Her trump was Gary Cooper himself. He had assured her he would never agree to play Rhett Butler because he considered it a supporting part. Carole urged him to stay silent, but to keep his word when the time came. And when the time came, she expected Mayer to unload Clark with no questions asked, even if she had to use Irene Selznick as intermediary . . . or resort to blackmail as Mayer himself often did. She knew where a lot of bodies were buried.

In private huddle with the brothers Selznick, Carole said she wouldn't sign for $200,000—that was simply too much money. David was happily surprised, and Myron flabbergasted. Carole said, "Be honest just once in your life, Myron: you know as well as I that Paramount drew the line at a hundred and seventy-five." Brotherly love withstood a grim test as they all settled on $175,000 per picture, the rate at which Myron had agreed to renew Carole's association with Paramount.

Carole was actually filming for Selznick before she got around to the formal signing in June of the three-year, three-picture contract. Right after Selznick added his own signature, Carole was shattered by David's dry, pointed assurance that there was no way, absolutely none, that Paramount could get distribution of *Gone With the Wind*. It seemed that a new arrangement whereby Gary Cooper's contract would be shared by Paramount with Samuel Goldwyn rendered it impossible that Cooper would be free to take on the

Rhett Butler assignment. Selznick had considered Cooper the only logical alternative to Gable. Shortly afterward the arrangement with M-G-M was consummated and Gable was committed to a role he did not want, but that would stand as the crowning achievement of his career.

Carole's elaborate scheme had effectively collapsed, but she did not abandon hope of being the ultimate designee as Scarlett. That she was officially a Selznick artist should rule in her favor. The Selznick alliance with Mayer merely sealed Carole's determination to terminate her Paramount affiliation with the one picture she still o ed them, whatever it might be. But that would be a secret for a while.

In confidence with Myron she said, "We just won't sign anything. Tell Paramount hell yes, we're still aboard, but let's keep it verbal. I don't want any big noise about cutting the cord, no burned bridges. I don't want the front office fucking things if Lubitsch should want me." The press release reporting Carole's new deal with Selznick International said, "Studio information is to the effect that this will not interfere with Miss Lombard's Paramount contract."

Carole's correct intuition was that David Selznick's capitulation to his father-in-law's whim would cost him a fortune. Now she figured to be a mean filly in the stretch drive for the Scarlett Sweepstakes. According to her own secret timetable, *Gone With the Wind* not only would be the third and last of her pictures for Selznick, it would be the last picture she would ever make. She would quit at the very top, probably with an Oscar to match the one belonging to Clark who would then be her husband.

Then, she would have babies.

At the very time when an ongoing career no longer interested her, she zoomed to the peak of her reputation, inhabiting a then-exclusive circle of authentic superstars. She hadn't planned it that way, but 1937 was her year.

Although the Gable romance had placed her in clear focus for national observation, her continued professional rise seemed a thing apart. Yet speculation that her active career was nearing the finish line appeared to give her work an extra edge of purpose and vitality. Eddie Mannix said she was like a star reporter responding to a hard deadline. Mannix, a one-time café bouncer and later all-purpose M-G-M executive, was one of Gable's few confidential friends at his home studio, and he also became a trusted counselor to Carole, conveying to her the seldom expressed but deeply felt Gable wish of having a son. It was only when Carole began dreaming aloud about motherhood that Gable started to talk in earnest of marriage . . . of finally getting off the pot.

Carole had been correct in theorizing that only money stood between Gable and his freedom. But money was Clark's sore spot. Just ask anyone around town, he was a classic stingy, almost paranoic about people trying to live off him—the haunted reformed gigolo. Carole intimidated him with amiable but persistent kidding about his jealous guardianship of cash. He buckled, he made a fitful show of generosity; but it was difficult for him to be as generous as Rhea Langham Gable demanded. So the waiting game would continue awhile, but Clark's doubts about Carole evaporated. That she was willing to abandon her career to be housewife and mother appealed to his vanity and to his old-fashioned view of how things ought to be.

Sharing Carole's hope that she would play Scarlett reconciled Clark to *Gone With the Wind* and even incited him to enthusiasm. And whatever his personal feelings about the Selznicks, he agreed that staying on Myron's good side was advisable for Carole. Even so, Myron seemed to vanish as soon as he had delivered Carole to his brother, and from that point she called the shots for her own career.

Just before she started to work for Selznick in *Nothing Sacred,* Paramount put *Swing High, Swing Low* into release and found that it was ahead of its time, perhaps not for cinematic achievement but definitely for the public taste. It was tough, hard-boiled, cynical —a slice of life cast in the argot of roughhouse and jazz. Wavering uneasily between comedy and tragedy without attaining pathos, it didn't quite come off; but as late as 1941, Carole Lombard still rated Maggie King as her personal favorite among what she said were her five best roles. The others were Lily Garland, Irene Bullock, Hazel Flagg in *Nothing Sacred,* and Helen Bartlett in *True Confession.* (She never saw the glorious Maria Tura of *To Be or Not to Be* in final cut.)

The role she made much of in *Swing High, Swing Low* was solid to begin with. The girl's name had been Bonnie back in 1927, when it brought the volatile young Barbara Stanwyck to Broadway's attention and made her ripe for movie plucking at the dawn of the talkies. It was the fine old Arthur Hopkins play *Burlesque,* and Paramount bought the movie rights but couldn't use the title because its connotations were objectionable to the Hays Office. But Paramount also owned an unfilmable book about sexuality, Havelock Ellis's *The Dance of Life;* and deeming that a good title, they attached it to the Hopkins play and made an exemplary early talkie that established John Cromwell as a screen director. Most of the Broadway company was imported—it was Hal Skelly's debut in the male lead, also Oscar Levant's—with the notable exception of Barbara Stanwyck, who was already in pictures and contracted to another studio. So Nancy Carroll played the girl with style enough to suggest the major star she almost became. It was a fondly remembered picture, so it was dusted off and remade, becoming the first Lombard release during her greatest movie year.

Actually the remake was conceived as a dramatic test case for Bing Crosby, the crooner having registered nicely as a light comedian. In the play the protagonist is an alcoholic vaudevillian, but for the Crosby film he would become a crooner. Carole Lombard figured to be the girl from the beginning; and when Fred MacMurray was found progressing smartly in Carole's company, the crooner gave way to a saxophonist for the script's second draft, which scrubbed the Crosby idea. Fred MacMurray's musicianly past was then a topic of frequent ribbing, and a yarn about a seedy sax virtuoso could be his likely revenge. But studio ears listened to the instrument, and studio heads decided a saxophone was all right in ensemble work but a dubious thing for enjoyable solos. The script underwent another change and the boy became a whiz with the trumpet. The musical sounds would be dubbed.

Although in outline the plot seemed to favor the male role, the gaudy display and most commanding role had always been the girl's—or would be that until Dan Dailey acted rings around Betty Grable in a still later version, *When My Baby Smiles at Me.* Without question *Swing High, Swing Low* was Carole's picture. It was not a radical departure for her, but she plumbed new dramatic depths in defining Maggie King as a gamy lowlife—smacking her chewing gum and calling everyone dearie, but nourishing a crucial reservoir of integrity and common sense. If the picture was better for its parts than as a whole, it suggested that Fred MacMurray, obviously an able young actor, was being pushed too far and too soon into exacting serious portraiture.

Jean Dixon and Charles Butterworth, both from the stage, brightened the serio-comic fabric; and in Mitchell Leisen's direction one reviewer found "enough concentrated filmcraft to fit out half a dozen of those gentlemen who are always dashing around making just the greatest piece of cinema ever." Some persons harboring the temperament of a later generation would watch *Swing High, Swing Low* and say it had aged only the way good wine will; but even then, they would not likely place it on a par with the Lombard picture that followed—the one that initiated her brief but brilliant Selznick phase.

That picture was *Nothing Sacred.* Mistaken as a great film almost immediately, it never was that. But it was a great screenplay, and one of Hollywood's rare examples of satire achieved within a farce structure. It was a case of the tail wagging the dog: William Wellman's competent journalistic directorial style straining on a leash to keep pace with the splendors of Ben Hecht's script. Not at all a typical Selznick director, Wild Bill Wellman nevertheless became one shortly before that when he brought David his own "original" story that more than casually resembled an early George Cukor subject produced by Selznick for RKO—*What Price Hollywood?*

Wellman's story was *A Star Is Born* and he was engaged to direct it. Filmed impressively in the new Technicolor, it was the first such project that was not a costume spectacle or a predominantly exterior idyll such as *Ramona* or *The Trail of the Lonesome Pine.* Along with Judy Garland's much-later musical version, the first *A Star Is Born* would stand as Hollywood's most mature comment on the substance and mores of its pampered industry. The 1937 film won both acclaim and immense popularity. For Janet Gaynor it was an unofficial comeback, but the really fine work was Fredric March's, so Selznick retained March as leading man for *Nothing Sacred.* In the same kind of reflex action, Wellman inherited the screenplay that Ben Hecht had put together in a hurry. Written expressly for Carole Lombard, it formulated what Hecht declared was her genius.

Shot in color, *Nothing Sacred* was a visual delight without becoming good visual comedy, and it beguiles the imagination to think what a Frank Capra or a Leo McCarey—even a Ruggles or Leisen or an uncontinental Lubitsch—might have made of it. But that would pretty much cover the reservations. It was a smash hit and Carole's Hazel Flagg was a triumphant farcical performance. Fredric March matched her stride for stride; but like Godfrey the butler, he was mainly doing straight-man service in a vehicle set up for a lady. Some would call Hazel Flagg the greatest Lombard creation, and her opening scene was arguably the best she ever played.

March, enacting a reporter, is sent into a small town for a story on a girl dying of radium poisoning. She isn't, really, but the reporter doesn't know that yet, nor does anyone else realize it's just an honest mistake—least of all the bewildered girl. The audience will be first to sense the jest, only seconds after Hazel Flagg comes into the frame—vaguely wistful, dreamily under spell as if dead already and auditioning for heaven: Carole Lombard glorifying color photography as it hasn't been before and saying relax, folks, this is a comedy, and comedies have happy endings.

The satire ignites after Hazel's healthy substance is assured but not revealed to the newspaper-reading public that has adopted her as a national heroine, a symbol of indomitable courage. The charade must continue: the publisher wills it, and the reporter and the girl become knowing participants while they fall in and out of love. Here Carole's great tantrum scene acquires an added fillup: March won't stand for it so he slugs her, and there follows the screen's greatest man-versus-woman bare-knuckles brawl.

There were also two richly endowed character parts. Charles Winninger bumbled right along as the bucolic physician of the original erroneous diagnosis. The publisher role was unassigned until Carole's suggestion of her buddy Walter Connolly, still the breadwinner at Columbia. (Spencer Tracy, having also worked with Connolly at Columbia in *Man's Castle,* similarly had plumped for his assignment to another screwball classic at M-G-M, as Myrna Loy's rich daddy in *Libeled Lady.*)

Selznick had writers doing preliminary sketchwork for another Lombard vehicle even before *Nothing Sacred* had been put on the market. But that figured as her commitment to him for 1938, and she still owed Paramount that last picture, although the studio blissfully expected her to renew their contract. Freedom's aroma seduced her and she was anxious to taste it, but she wanted her last Paramount credit to be a strong one, though nothing to sweat over. She wanted to quit winners, and to have fun making a picture with people she liked. Perhaps the studio suspected her defection, for they seemed intent on getting her into a turkey, an action easily interpreted as a threat. She said the script-approval clause saved her neck.

Indeed, Carole's instinctive good judgment of a script in its raw form probably rescued her more than once. She thought it did, and reasoned that many young players' good early promise had been snuffed out by the dialogue they were required to recite in the often inane traffic of the movies. She was certain she could have acquired a solid stardom much earlier at Paramount if she had been allowed to spend an hour a day in the story department, choosing for herself. The thing that made her most apprehensive about Paramount during William LeBaron's tenure as production chief was the tawdriness of the pictures they *asked* her to make.

She was a proven star at last, a financial asset to her company, and therefore deserving of protection as an investment. But they would ask her to do something called *John Meade's Woman* with Edward Arnold, who did become a valuable businessman-type in many good films, but never the solid, Edward G. Robinson-level character star that had been expected of him. She said she rejected that one without even reading it—she only counted her lines. They dangled *Exclusive*—hokum of newspaper life. She thought it incredible that she should be invited to ride in *The Last Train from Madrid* where she would be entirely out of place, yet they asked her. She also refused something called *The Barrier*. There was her *Spawn of the North* intrigue, and she gave a tentative yes to an ambitious color project, *Men with Wings;* but it was delayed and they told her they'd shoot it the next year as part of her new, richer contract. She gave a coquette's smile and said well, all right.

Then Wesley Ruggles presented a script that Claude Binyon surely had written especially for her. She read every word for the sheer pleasure of it, and the very title smacked of surefire success: *True Confession.* It was shipshape and the studio wanted to start building sets. How soon could she get to work on it? Carole said if they yelled the final "cut!" for *Nothing Sacred* in the morning, she could start *True Confession* that same afternoon—would skip lunch if she had to.

But *Nothing Sacred* wound up on a Friday afternoon in August. She rested a full weekend and was on time for the 6:00 A.M. Monday start for *True Confession.*

It wasn't her smartest comedy but it rivaled *My Man Godfrey* as her wackiest, and was a labor of sheer love. Again she was in a groove of supreme idiocy. You see, this girl Helen Bartlett is sweet and pretty, and what matter that she isn't very bright? Helen has many friends and a keen sense of fair play, and she has a nice husband who loves her—a young attorney with ethics, scruples, and ideals such as young attorneys possess only in certain Hollywood scripts, most especially when they're Fred MacMurray, even with uncharacteristic moustache. They should be happy together and they are, except that, well, Helen has this one hangup. She's a compulsive liar. The girl can't help it. Anyone asks a question, she'll answer anything but the truth. Let a murder happen in the building she works in, and if you ask her who, she done it herself. Not exactly a textbook example of screwball comedy: it's too wild, too much a formula piece for situation farce. But what a piece!

Wesley Ruggles worked with Carole for the last time in *True Confession*. It was only his third picture with her; yet curiously, that was more than any other Lombard director could claim. The credit ledgers of variably talented directors show as many as two Lombard films, but the genial Ruggles almost by default becomes the representative Lombard catalyst. Garbo had her Clarence Brown, Hepburn her Cukor, Dietrich her Sternberg, Arthur her Capra and Stevens, Davis her Wyler and Goulding. The Lombard *oeuvre* suffers from lack of a steadying familiar hand to give it a characteristic shape and balance. Lubitsch could have accomplished that—could have given Carole definition as he did for Miriam Hopkins and Jeanette MacDonald before they slipped away from him. Yet Lubitsch seldom indulged in American subjects, and Carole's essence was irrepressibly American.

Perhaps Wesley Ruggles, also from America's solid middle class, was really Lombard's Man Friday. She considered him that, and they would have worked together more often but for the lunacy of studio logistics. That he was also a close friend to Clark Gable hardly diminished Ruggles in her favor. If Carole could have pondered British critic John Baxter's 1968 observation that the Ruggles comedies ". . . are limp, his style among the most flaccid in the cinema," she would probably have hollered for the man's scalp, after inquiring what the fuck "flaccid" meant, anyway. In a calmer moment perhaps she would ask if Baxter had seen, say, Ruggles's enchanting *I Met Him in Paris* with Colbert, or his exuberant *Sing You Sinners* with Crosby and MacMurray.

Not that Ruggles was her only catalyst. Carole said that LaCava in the first, early picture (at Pathé) convinced her that she had a personality; that Walter Lang made her believe in herself as a comedienne; and that Lubitsch persuaded her that she might be an artist as well. But Ruggles, she said, put it all together for her by bringing out her naturalness. She emerged a personality-comedienne-artist by instinct and didn't have to act at all but could just *be*. From a perspective of later prestige, she cited *No Man of Her Own* as her turning point, with Ruggles endowing her with the confidence that would sustain her through *Twentieth Century*. She said she was most indebted to two men, and *True Confession* reunited her with both of them. Wesley Ruggles was one; the other was John Barrymore.

He was human wreckage, now the most pitiable figure in Hollywood, and the most conspicuously fallen star because he had such a height to fall from. He was a crisis case for stability even before *Twentieth Century* three years earlier, but he got through it because everything was somehow right, and it was his last big one. A fourth and final marriage that friends hoped would resurrect him appeared to have the opposite effect as he became ugly-drunk, desperate for income to the point of parodying himself ludicrously as a ham actor on Rudy Vallee's radio show. After two long and wasting years away from the screen, he was brought back by Thalberg for *Romeo and Juliet* and *Maytime*—prestige credits both, but they were supporting parts in which his work was unsteady despite hints of grandeur. His Mercutio extracted praise enough to become at least controversial, but there was no controversy about his being too old and too flabby for the part.

Thalberg had been determined to rehabilitate the Great Profile, but M-G-M cut him adrift once again when Thalberg died. When the long-projected *Marie Antoinette* finally went before the cameras, restoring Norma Shearer from her widowhood, Mayer somewhat surprisingly honored an ancient Thalberg commitment to Barrymore as the dying Louis XV in the opening scenes. He was brilliant, however brief; and still later intimations of his vanished glory were given in *Midnight* and *The Great Man Votes*. But in August, 1937, he was scraping bottom, having found safe haven in

Paramount's jungle of quickie-B's where sloppiness was tolerated. He was a fixture in the Bulldog Drummond series but didn't even rate the title role; it was John Howard's.

But when Carole read the *True Confession* script she was intrigued by the primary character role of a zany con man—a faded roué every bit as nutty as the girl whose prevarications he encourages. The part was a fringe benefit to the picture rather than part of its spine, but Carole saw in it the color that could nudge comedy out of the commonplace and into the rare. She not only insisted that John Barrymore play the role, she also got Claude Binyon to enlarge its dimensions. She knew that much would be made of his now supporting *her*—the *Twentieth Century* reversal was immediately cited—but she did not want Barrymore to feel that he was stepping down in class. She demanded that the billing order show three stars, not two; and she rode herd on the publicists to see that some ceremonial dignity accompany the announcement of Barrymore's assignment.

Barrymore was seedily magnificent. Almost all of his scenes were with Carole, and they were special treasures. Fred MacMurray played his rather stuffy part with an urgent comic spirit but somehow he got lost in the detours of the script. Lombard's and Barrymore's performances would be the best-remembered things about *True Confession;* and some years later when it was projected as a musical comedy possibility for Broadway, those were the two star parts and the husband role had been eliminated.

True Confession was shot in seven weeks, in contrast to *Nothing Sacred* which had required three months. For its attention to color, the Selznick picture also needed extra time for processing and editing. As a consequence, the two pictures were ready at the same time. By sublime coincidence, they were both released nationally on Thanksgiving Day, 1937, and the nation's thanks were for Carole.

It was her moment. Few players had ventured that high on fame's mountain. The altitude was dangerous and soon she would come down a few paces, keeping a solid hold while retaining a clear-enough view of the very top where her feet briefly had been. She would make no other ascent professionally and her career would be upstaged by a private life which, in the measurement of fame, would scale another peak. But she would cherish the vista from the professional crest, and remember the sweetness of its air.

❊ XI ❊

While Atlanta Burns

HOLLYWOOD's favorite party girl was a social dropout almost over-night. Clark Gable was conveniently cited as the reason, but per-haps wrongly so. There was subtler evidence of Carole's phasing-out as hostess and playmaker even before Gable became her dominant interest. She said she'd enjoyed partying as a hobby but its novelty value finally diminished. Being wth Clark was more fun.

Although Carole and Clark did not house-hop with the social mainstream, their appearances together at Ciro's, the Trocadero, and lesser establishments along the Sunset Strip were frequent if irregular. If a Gable shooting schedule made weekend junkets out of town unfeasible, they were highly visible around town after working hours. In 1938 Hollywood obtained a franchise in base-ball's Pacific Coast League and Clark purchased a season box at Gilmore Field. Bob Cobb, one of the team owners, was one of Gable's boon companions, and the ballpark became an auxiliary headquarters for the Gable inner sanctum, along with the Brown Derby restaurants that Cobb also owned. Carole's vivaciousness thrived in a predominantly masculine environment. If her atten-dance at social events became ever more spotty, her personality was hardly altered.

Her swelling fame instead gave highlight to the most distinctive edges of that personality. The screwball image of the movies became even more overtly the screwball girl of the professional community

—calculatingly, she thought, but for everyone's enjoyment and particularly her own. Yet some of her closest friends doubted that Carole had any notion of how near to her standard screen projection she sometimes came.

At the opposite extreme from those star actresses who preferred a "closed" set, Carole felt encouraged by the presence of friends when she was making a picture. The larger the throng, the better. During the long stretches between camera settings, she took command of an imaginary stage and kept right on entertaining, having a good high time for herself but never missing the fact that she was holding court.

When the basically dramatic *Swing High, Swing Low* also made her a singer, besides adding tap dancing to her inventory of ballroom skills, she staged her own solo-performance mock opera on the set. Parodying the picture and its other players with sly lyrics of her own invention, she garnished her display with a striptease that was more strip than tease, to the rollicking approval of the boys on the crew. She brought an air pistol onto the set of *Nothing Sacred* and shot out electric light bulbs while set workers made wagers on her marksmanship. Director Bill Wellman, coaching her for the great slugging brawl with Fredric March, taught Carole how to tackle and work a straitjacket on an opponent; so Carole and March bought a straitjacket as a present for Wellman, and Carole tackled her director and got him into the jacket for most of the duration of the cast party.

Her shenanigans were not confined to intramural legend. If a Lombard caper was worthy of print, it somehow got printed. She believed that she survived the early uncertain years of her picture making only by her appreciation of publicity and its impact. She always got her share, even by manufacturing it herself. Her canniness was in knowing what captivated readers, and she confessed to a studied effort to become and remain "good copy."

She made a point of putting through a personal telephone call to Louella Parsons at least once a week, and flattered the columnist with occasional impromptu visits to her home, perhaps to present some freshly cut flowers her mother had grown. Later she would do the same for Hedda Hopper when the Los Angeles *Times* posed the veteran actress as a columnist rival to Parsons. Carole kept them supplied with tidbits, and if she lacked news of a personal nature she would say nice things about young people she liked who were new to pictures. In this way she helped such as Robert Stack and Evelyn Keyes to get nice starts in the local press.

The Selznick association brought her into contact with filmland's resident genius of publicity, Russell Birdwell. She became his primary accomplice. Birdwell was a well-seasoned newspaperman when David Selznick made him director of publicity for the newly organized Selznick International Pictures. Later Birdwell went into business for himself but retained Selznick as primary client. Carole's collaboration with Birdwell commenced even before she signed with David Selznick. She met him through Myron and was fascinated by his strategy of employing angles that bred new angles.

The first Birdwell-Lombard stratagem centered around a lovely Texas girl named Margaret Tallichet, of whom Carole had grown quite fond. Like thousands of other girls, Miss Tallichet had come to Hollywood nursing some small hope of acting in pictures; and like so many hundreds, she got another kind of studio employment, writing publicity for Paramount and serving as liaison for visiting newsmen. She accompanied the Louisville *Courier-Journal's* Boyd Martin into Carole Lombard's dressing room for an interview during a lunch break while *Swing High, Swing Low* was being shot. Martin's judgment was that Miss Tallichet was pretty enough to be in pictures herself, and didn't Miss Lombard agree?

Carole more than agreed. Detecting a spark of ambition still thriving within "Tally," as she called her, Carole nudged Myron to get the girl assigned a walk-on role (one scene, one line) in his brother's production of *A Star Is Born*. Then she summoned Birdwell, and Margaret Tallichet got terrific exposure in a Birdwell press release picked up by many papers—because Carole Lombard was identified as the girl's "discoverer." It didn't end there. In a subsequent story Carole became Tally's personal makeup mistress for her movie debut. It became a textbook case for Birdwell's proof to David Selznick of the extent to which publicity can be generated around a rank unknown—continuing right into the Scarlett O'Hara sweepstakes in which Tally joined the dozens of nominal candidates.

Still trying to expel a grainy Southwestern accent, Margaret Tallichet had a brief, lusterless career as an actress, doing only a few minor leads for Republic. But she was a personable girl who might have made her mark with an extended effort. Instead, capitalizing on the social foothold in filmland that Carole's effort had provided, she cultivated a surer charm. Tally became Mrs. William Wyler, and the beguiling satellite of that director's distinguished career.

When she hooked up with Selznick's company, Carole and Russell Birdwell got the Culver City administrators to go along with a gag whereby Carole became the city's Mayor for a Day. It was a capital publicity stunt, especially when Carole's only official action was to give all civic employees the day off. She visited the Selznick publicity office often, hatching one bright idea after another.

When *Nothing Sacred* had its first booking in Fort Wayne, Birdwell plotted to have the city fathers declare a "Carole Lombard Day" for the occasion, with designs on a triumphant homecoming by the star who had become the city's foremost celebrity despite having been there only once in twenty years. Carole said she would go. The people of Fort Wayne, gratified that a member of one of its "best" families had become the hottest thing in the movies, primped for the holiday. They were disappointed and rather obviously piqued when Carole changed her mind and went fishing with Clark Gable instead. But Birdwell salvaged the ceremony. The mayor made a proclamation, and Carole's birthplace and early home on Rockhill Street was rededicated as an historic shrine, complete with an engraved stone tablet that endures to this day—with its Birdwell-worded plug for the new Selznick Technicolor production of *Nothing Sacred*.

When it was revealed to the nation that Carole Lombard, by earning almost half a million dollars, had been its highest-paid film star for 1937, Carole made sassy remarks about 80 percent of her income having been swallowed up by government taxes; but then she added that it was probably worth it after all, for the privilege of being an American. Birdwell leaped on the quote, and extracted a patriotic elaboration from Carole. She felt it was her duty to pay whatever the federal government asked of her, in order to strengthen and maintain the greatest country in the world.

Yes, she'd always had a good press; but now she had a great one. Her patriotic pronouncements were played into major news for national consumption, and President Roosevelt sent her a personal letter of commendation for her stand which, he said, would serve as an example and inspiration for millions of taxpaying Americans.

David Selznick sometimes disapproved the extremes to which Birdwell and Carole would go to obtain unusual promotion, particularly when the Selznick enterprise became only an adjunct benefi-

ciary. But Carole, whose friendship with the droll Birdwell was as
sincere as it was frolicsome, counted on Birdwell as an ally in her
continuing subtle bid to obtain the Scarlett O'Hara role.

She was the ready reserve—Selznick's only contracted major female star other than the unfiery Janet Gaynor. With Carole's
career riding its stunning upward trajectory and critics saying she
could do anything, it was not then illogical that she should get the
assignment. There was speculation that Selznick's waiting game was
merely to allow Carole's star to soar even higher, and that he would
not bypass the promotional opportunity a Lombard-Gable teaming
offered. Actually Gable's presence in the cast lineup was no help to
Carole's quest, but its deterrent.

Many people naïvely supposed that failure to decide on a Scarlett
was what delayed production of *Gone With the Wind* month after
month. Instead, it was Selznick's mounting obsession to make the
greatest movie of all time. When the book entered its third year
of top bestsellerdom, he was still in a muddle over the script. He
had also decided that in any event, he would not identify Scarlett
O'Hara until the project was ready for the cameras. But privately
he had ruled out the Carole Lombard possibility, although not for
reasons suspected. Myron had told Carole that his brother was cautiously fearful of a Gable-Lombard marriage that might be followed
by a separation that would taint an on-screen teaming.

Few understood that Selznick's wariness was not over Carole but
over Gable himself. Certainly Carole did not immediately see this.
When Selznick joined M-G-M as producer he had Gable in three
successive projects—*Night Flight, Dancing Lady,* and *Manhattan
Melodrama*—and they had not gotten along. Gable's later reluctance
to become part of the *Gone With the Wind* package was interpreted as misgiving over the Rhett Butler role, but the actor's real
grievance was Selznick himself.

David was consumed with worry that Clark Gable, whose commercial magnetism alone had made the Selznick interests stepchild
to the Loew's M-G-M monster, jeopardizing his independence,
would in effect be running the picture. In the event of possible
ugly conflict between Selznick and Gable, where would Carole
Lombard's sympathies be? Myron convinced his brother that now
it would be Carole's humor to defer to Gable in all things. That
scratched Carole from consideration. David would not be put in the
position of standing helplessly by while Gable called the shots.

Myron Selznick, who remained a most powerful influence on his brother despite their series of money-based disagreements, may not have been entirely fair to Carole in forecasting her likely allegiance to Gable. In any event, Carole again misread Myron's intentions. She supposed he was doing all he could to strengthen her Scarlett O'Hara profile. Instead Myron was insinuating into David's consciousness the vixen charm of a new client of his, a middle-ranking British actress named Vivien Leigh.

But still another opinion was that all the Myron Selznicks and Russell Birdwells in Hollywood could not have delivered Scarlett O'Hara to Carole after the debacle of *Fools for Scandal*.

As late as 1939, rosters of Paramount contractees still listed Carole Lombard among the star players, although she left the company in the early fall of 1937 after completing *True Confession*. She continued to receive Paramount scripts for consideration, indicating that the studio still honored the "gentleman's agreement" Myron Selznick had obtained. But the quality of the screenplays convinced her that she was fortunate to have no further obligation to her old studio.

The picture she had wanted—*Bluebeard's Eighth Wife* with Gary Cooper—went to Claudette Colbert, for whom Lubitsch may have intended it all along. The properties dangled for Carole's attention usually involved Fred MacMurray. *Invitation to Happiness* finally had him playing opposite Irene Dunne, and starlet Louise Campbell was Fred's leading lady in the Technicolor *Men with Wings*, although both properties had been purchased and developed with Carole in mind. She almost consented to *Invitation to Happiness* because Wesley Ruggles was directing, but Ruggles told her in confidence that the only thing that could make the picture interesting was to shoot it in the nude. Carole also turned down *Stolen Heaven*, a remake of another old Nancy Carroll picture, and the replacement was French ingenue Olympe Bradna. Preston Sturges fashioned a strong comedy-drama script for the Lombard-MacMurray team and Carole's interest revived, but perhaps Paramount began to doubt her sincerity or her worthiness of Myron's expensive price tag. The role Sturges wrote for her just didn't get offered. So Barbara Stanwyck acted it (beautifully) and *Remember the Night* was a strong picture.

No doubt the Paramount chieftains were miffed that as soon as

Myron had their uncontracted word that Carole was a star at $175,000 a picture, he was pushing that figure at every other studio in town. There were likely takers at his exorbitant rate, except that Carole was no help. As marriage with Gable became closer to a reality, she behaved very much as one who wanted only to retire. Myron got her all but assigned to a one-picture deal with M-G-M but Carole reneged because the shooting schedule would not coincide with Gable's *Too Hot to Handle,* and she wanted to be free when he was free. Myron may have felt betrayed; he certainly appeared to lose interest in Carole's career.

Then she capitulated to sudden whim and made a deal on her own. By translating her early Pathé experience into RKO credits, she figured that she had worked for every major studio in Hollywood except Warner Brothers and felt some obligation to complete the circuit. Actually she was quite interested in some of the things going on there, and often entertained wishful notions of making a comedy film with James Cagney. Bette Davis was emerging as the premium Warner tragedienne, and the studio was known to be seeking a female star of comparable stature for comedy. Carole sold her services to Warners for $150,000. Myron Selznick was furious that she would lower his price, but Carole shouted him down, saying Warners just didn't pay his kind of money and in fact were receiving her as they would a *queen.*

It was not a matter of accepting a specific film or even the idea of one. A script would be fashioned especially for Carole. The only certain thing was that Carole's leading man would be Fernand Gravet, a Belgian star of French, German, and English pictures. On the Continent it had been Graavey, but the modified spelling emphasized Frenchiness for a reason. Fernard Gravet rode in on a wave of boudoir diplomats in the wake of Charles Boyer's first big U.S. impact. Dark and agreeably suave, Gravet may have been the ablest of the phosphate Boyers. He was nicely received in reviews of his first Warner picture, *The King and the Chorus Girl,* with Joan Blondell. But the public didn't buy him, and Warners became wary of using him in *Tovarich,* a popular play they had purchased for him at great expense. They got Boyer instead and petitioned Paramount for the loan of either Lombard or Colbert. Paramount sent Claudette, and *Tovarich* was a hit.

But Warners wasn't ready to abandon Gravet. His forte was high comedy, and getting him teamed with Carole Lombard figured to be his commercial salvation. The trouble was that once the casting was settled, no one knew where or how to begin. Julius J. Epstein, one of the first to tackle the chore of producing a serviceable script, remembered Jack Warner's vagueness about what he wanted, other than lots of high fashion and low comedy from Carole, and ardent smouldering from Gravet. Mervyn LeRoy, as director, only echoed Warner's generalizations on what *Fools for Scandal* was supposed to be; and when they didn't warm to his first cut at a script, Epstein asked to be relieved of the writing job. Other hands came into play, and it became one of those projects that entertained a succession of writers until production chief Hal Wallis finally approved a script devised by the brothers Fields—Herbert and Joseph, with clandestine assistance from their sister Dorothy.

Fools for Scandal attempted to encapsulate formula screwball stuff into a glib, sophisticated framework, but the actors were puzzled by its lack of definition. Carole grew suspicious of the script but liked the way she was being treated. Her presence at the old First National studio was regarded as an Event, and she admitted she'd gotten hungry for fashion. *Fools for Scandal* would prove her last outing as a clotheshorse, and her screen dresses had become simpler as her comic powers ripened. Paramount's Edith Head, who finally became Carole's primary designer for *True Confession*, regretted that it wasn't a big-clothes picture, but said Carole's conventional wardrobe properly reflected the background of the girl she played in that picture.

The picture's elegance may have been enough to instill a false optimism in Warner minds, even after *Fools for Scandal* had been previewed for an unlaughing full house. Louella Parsons said, "It looks like Carole Lombard has still another hit." It was no such thing. *Fools for Scandal* was something more than a disappointment or a mere failure. It was one of the horrendous flops of the thirties decade, when almost every picture made an operating profit. Yet not even the presence of a big-name star could salvage the commercial return. Critics blinked in disbelief, and the first audiences circulated the kind of word-of-mouth that made for sparse houses in later engagements. Arriving in the wake of the double salvo of *Nothing Sacred* and *True Confession,* it caused astonishment that any Lombard vehicle could be so scorned by the public. If Carole had been speculating on a rich contract with the economy-minded Warners, that prospect simply vanished. So did Fernand Gravet after one more prodigious failure, as the younger Johann Strauss in *The Great Waltz* for M-G-M.

Graham Greene, who earlier had described *True Confession* as "that rare thing, cinema, and the best comedy of the year," now noted that Carole Lombard's voice had "risen beyond the capacity of the microphone," lamenting that her directors "should have given her so humorless, so hopeless a story (perhaps that's why she has to scream so loud)." The *Herald Tribune*'s Howard Barnes summed up the American attitude: "A witless, wearisome entertainment in which Carole Lombard works overtime to achieve a clowning mood."

Carole usually could be philosophical about a picture's reception, knowing that if critics blistered a *We're Not Dressing* and hoorayed a *Twentieth Century*, the public could reverse both judgments. But in agreeing to make *Fools for Scandal* without having seen a script, she said she made the mistake of trying to do what the public expected of her, when all along you shouldn't second-guess the public's capriciousness.

Some *Fools for Scandal* scenes were filmed in New York, and while Carole was there she was interviewed by William Boehnel of the *World-Telegram,* who wondered if she wasn't tiring of comedy. Carole said, "I don't care what kind of parts I play so long as they are good and the public likes them. Right now I think the public demand is for comedy. It wants to laugh and I don't blame it. I'm not going to do comedy forever."

When *Fools for Scandal* thudded, she decided abruptly that she wouldn't do comedy again soon if *ever,* and reckoned that a long holiday from picture making was in order. She went along with the consensus that made Herbert and Joseph Fields, already bearing the stigma of "New York writers," the convenient fall guys. When asked what went wrong with *Fools for Scandal,* Carole grumbled that it was "those Fields brothers—they couldn't write 'fuck you' on a shithouse wall!"

Carole's attention was to Clark Gable in 1938. *Fools for Scandal* was her only release of that year, and she did not go before the cameras for ten months afterward. She rather liked *The Young in Heart,* a romantic comedy about a family of con artists the Selznick company had been preparing for her. But it was a time of complicated preparation for marriage, so she begged off. Janet Gaynor replaced her.

Rhea might have agreed to a settlement much earlier, but the amount of money she sought was out of the question for such a fiscal conservative as Clark Gable. His public posture was that of a man wanting nothing so much as to marry Carole Lombard; but he had marked time, hoping Rhea's price would come down. Instead, it went up.

Eddie Mannix suggested that Clark might have kept the affair with Carole going on indefinitely if he thought he could hold her. But Carole applied pressure. "She made a show of putting other men completely out of her life, but she had a way of reminding Clark he had no real power over her, no legal rights. Even when they were hitting on all cylinders, she had him off balance, thinking she might break it off any time. Sometimes she *did* break it off and then they'd hustle back together, chummier than ever, but finally he knew that a wedding ring was his only security with Carole. Still, the idea of it costing him half a million clams just made him bleed."

According to terms arranged by their lawyers, Clark would give Rhea approximately $350,000 in cash for a respectable divorce action, but the total property settlement would exceed half a million. It wouldn't put him in hock; but he had to sell a few cars, some stock, and some real estate holdings of potential high value to achieve a clean settlement.

Both Carole and Clark had made speculative real-estate purchases in the San Fernando Valley, and their properties sustained costly damage in the 1938 floods. They had considered building their dream-house on one of their land parcels, but Clark decided that was out of the question under the conditions that had drained him financially, and their decision was to buy an existing house and modify it to their own tastes. The only sure thing was that it would be somewhere in the San Fernando Valley. Clark was living there already, having vacated his suite in the Beverly Wilshire in favor of a house in North Hollywood that he rented from Rex Ingram and his wife Alice Terry; they had been Valentino's director and costar, respectively, in *The Four Horsemen of the Apocalypse*.

Carole and Clark began consolidating their holdings even as the settlement with Rhea was being negotiated. Carole started to sell furniture, rugs, and other trappings in order to have an all-new start as Mrs. Clark Gable. She gave away a multitude of small and large things accumulated over the years. It was her whim to bestow them as gifts to studio laborers, mostly the old Paramount crew that were still her buddies. Disposing of domestic possessions was something she hadn't counted on, for she had expected to turn everything over to Fieldsie. Carole had always expected eventually to marry again, but she had supposed that Fieldsie, the comic-relief fat girl, would remain unmarried. She had expected to turn over their bachelor-girl quarters to Fieldsie entirely, but then Fieldsie preceded Carole into marriage. When she became Mrs. Walter Lang, she also withdrew as Carole's personal secretary and unofficial business manager.

Their friends doubted that Carole and Fieldsie had ever had a serious argument, and Carole had become more and more dependent on her housemate's managerial flair. She credited Fieldsie with pulling off most of the maneuvers that had established Carole Lombard as a good businesswoman. Fieldsie put Carole on caution against making enemies, but said, "It's a wonder people didn't hate both of us—Carole and me. You get so lost in the world of too much to do."

Carole had a tendency to make promises and not kept them because she would forget she had made them. Fieldsie said her generosity was of the moment, that you had to pin Carole down. Fieldsie was herself a good pinner-downer. Being apprised of appointments and other obligations, Carole would likely say, "To-morrow—I'll do them tomorrow." Fieldsie would say, "No, not tomorrow, today!' Carole would sigh and then giggle, "Okay, let's go." Still, Fieldsie said Carole was likelier to forget and neglect the things that would be to some advantage to herself more easily than she would neglect things that advantaged others.

When Fieldsie left, Carole feared the loss of all her discipline. She could not be without a full-time secretary, and to succeed Fieldsie she chose the very different Jean Garceau, who had been employed by David Selznick. The bright, young Jean Garceau already was married, happily and conventionally, to a man who kept his distance from the movie whirl by his own choice. Jean made her own terms and Carole agreed to them because they were terms she really liked. Jean would report only to a workaday job, keeping her domestic affairs entirely apart from her business obligations to

Carole. She did not figure to become a distraction for Clark Gable; and by that reasoning, Carole counted on Jean Garceau as an asset to both of them once the union with Gable was a legal fact.

As she grew restless for marriage, Carole also submitted to uncertainty and fear. Perhaps they had carried on together too long. They were together almost constantly in 1938, but without evidencing tiredness, their relationship had lost some of its romantic hue. Their outdoor junkets brought out their best harmony, but there was a new edge of tension when his movie commitments kept Clark in Hollywood and Carole's continued inactivity kept them shadow-to-shadow. No doubt they were together too often. Carole was in Clark's attendance during most of the M-G-M shooting of *Too Hot to Handle* and it seemed to bother him. She also sensed that her presence annoyed the predatory young studio girls who customarily were the fluttery moths around the Gable flame.

They quarreled more often and less frivolously. Clark's attentions to other girls usually motivated Carole's anger despite her policy of understanding tolerance. In the earlier stages of their romance Clark had boasted of his sexual conquests and she told him to cut it out, she didn't want to hear about it. Now she learned from other sources of his fleeting affairs but he was more likely to deny them, and she resented dishonesty more than his flings. A story got around town that one of her servants had watched Carole rip up her bed-sheets in tearful anger, while screaming into a telephone to Clark that their engagement was off. Then they had put in an appearance at Ciro's, all smiles and affection.

The marriage idea was a risky pendulum, swinging toward optimism and back again. Sometimes Carole gave conflicting attitudes toward marriage, often in interviews back-to-back or almost as close. In an early denial of the "seriousness" of the Gable affair, she sounded ahead of her time: "Marriage no longer holds the conventional values for a woman. Society has not recognized a woman's needs, nor sanctioned her departure from age-old standards, and that's why Hollywood marriages fail. An actress lives a life very different from the majority of women, but must not allow herself to settle into a groove." On another occasion she said she naturally expected to marry again, because despite every pleasure accruing to a movie star, only in marriage could a woman obtain her fair share of life's rewards, "and those include children."

Clark thought he had learned the symptoms of her moods and

could adjust to them. They had an understanding about keeping their distance during her menstrual periods which gave her considerable pain and made her irritable, but were never predictable or regular. But Carole's behavior could mystify him. He did not understand her fury when he gave her as a gift a shrunken human head he'd picked up in South America. She yelled, "You're putting a curse on me!" and stuffed the head into her purse as they were leaving for a party. While their car was spiraling down Coldwater Canyon Drive, she held the shrunken head by its long hair and hurled it into the canyon. Then she insisted on leaving the party to look for the head, suddenly fearful that it would be found with her fingerprints on it. With flashlight and police assistance, they found the head that Carole insisted was hexed; and she put it in a cigar box and buried it in her backyard. She told Clark, "If our marriage doesn't work out, it's all your fault . . . yours, and *its*."

With considerable misgiving, Carole renewed her agreement with Myron Selznick as her exclusive agent in August of 1938. *Gone With the Wind* figured to go before the cameras before the year was over, and the role of Scarlett O'Hara remained unassigned. But that was not the only reason she stayed in Myron's fold, and possibly it was not the main reason. She felt indebted to him, and her natural reservoir of compassion went out to him. Myron was drinking and driving himself into a physical and mental wreck, and she had notions of making him a recovery project, knowing she was challenged.

Although she had been increasingly critical of his tactics, particularly in his merciless and dishonest dealings with producers, he had influenced her thinking probably more than she realized. Affirming her own dislike of producers, she once said, "In the early days of pictures they took all the money and gave the actors nothing. Then came the Guild and the bitter competition among the studios, and performer wages going up to crazy levels like mine did. Most of us are overpaid but there's justice in it after all, because the government comes in and takes most of it in taxes. That's all right with me: I'd rather my money went to feed a hungry man than into the bank account of some picturemaker who doesn't need it."

All the while waging an obsessive war against the producers he would like to see ruined, Myron Selznick ached to become a producer himself once more—to succeed where he had been an inglorious failure. Carole suspected this, and she helped give him at least a nudge in that direction by going into partnership with him as independent producers. The agreement included Gregory LaCava as a third partner and was signed when her agent-client pact with Myron was renewed. The new company was nameless and while it was more than a rumor, it was less than a fact. Presumably the plan was to make pictures with Myron as producer, LaCava as director, and Carole as star. But not necessarily: Carole was talking more forthrightly about retirement after marriage, but still expressing an urge to produce pictures in which she would not appear. In any event, their organization had no staff, no capital, no story properties, and no immediate production plans. Carole hankered to remake the *Laughter* film that had teamed Nancy Carroll and Fredric March years earlier, with Robert Montgomery as her costar; but LaCava was griped at some of the Paramount brass and refused to work there, and the studio would not relinquish the property for filming elsewhere. Nothing came of the Lombard-LaCava union, although they did accomplish some early planning on a director-star collaboration before their partnership with Myron Selznick was dissolved. The property was *Unfinished Business* and LaCava eventually directed it, but with Irene Dunne cast opposite Montgomery.

Meanwhile Carole had some fun at Myron's expense. When he sent the copies of the standard agent contract for her signature, she had a job printer produce a facsimile contract that would not be detected as bogus when Myron received it in his mail, signed by Carole and awaiting his own signature. She suspected correctly that Myron would sign the agreement without rereading it and would not detect her minor editorial revision. Instead of Myron receiving 10 percent of her income, she was to receive 10 percent of *his*. Within a few days her own file copy had Myron's autograph.

Several weeks passed, then Carole had her mystified attorneys seek explanation from Myron of his failure to pay her $20,000. She said that was her cut of the $200,000 he boasted of having made during the period of their new "agreement." The subdued formality of the charade sucked in Myron completely: he was astonished, angry, and downright panicky—all at the same time. Carole was gleeful, and later said she was grateful to learn that Myron could still appreciate her practical jokes. She sent him the authentic contracts, and Myron had the forgery glass-framed before hanging it on his office wall.

Myron may have had his own mixed feelings about continuing his association with Carole, except that she represented a considerable amount of easy income to him. Certainly Myron was no longer her Svengali. His last maneuver on Carole's behalf was to get her assigned as a star-hostess on "The Circle," a dimly remembered but intelligent radio program that was the ancient genesis of the TV talk show. It was a panel discussion punctuated by variety entertainment. Carole was one of the rotating emcees, along with Cary Grant, Madeleine Carroll, and Ronald Colman. She held her own against so glib a lot, until Groucho Marx was worked into the rotation and put them all to shame. Actually Groucho was Carole's replacement: Myron got into a squabble with the J. Walter Thompson agency over payment for her services, and Carole left the air—not without reluctance, and with a fermenting peeve against her agent.

Clark Gable's assignment by M-G-M to *Idiot's Delight* indicated that *Gone With the Wind* was still months away from start of production. Again Carole became a lingerer by a sound stage, yet she failed to show the amusement expected of her as she regarded Gable as Harry Van—a hoofer, no less, accompanied by a sextet of leggy girls in the Robert Sherwood antiwar play that would seem somewhat diluted in screen translation. There was talk of Gable being involved with Virginia Grey, one of the chorines, but perhaps Carole hadn't heard those rumors. She liked Virginia Grey personally—a girl very much like herself in temperament, who had been born in Los Angeles and was a movie brat grown to adult prettiness and talent: Carole thought she had the fiber of a real star. No, it wasn't Virginia Grey but one of the other chorines. The first time Harry Van's girls appeared in their scanty costumes, Carole indicated the girl in question and shouted a general order to director and crew to "Get that whore out of here . . . either she goes, or Gable goes!" Then she stormed off the set and left the studio. But she returned the next day, her instructions having been fully honored.

Such a display was not characteristic of her, nor did she have any authority there. Carole was a visitor to M-G-M, and without power of attorney over Clark's studio obligations or even over his private affairs, since they were not yet married. But Billy Grady, who related the incident, said the studio had arrived at a policy of accommodation to Carole Lombard in all matters and she probably recognized this and seized upon it. From the inception of the Gable-Lombard romance and for a long time afterward, Mayer and his satellites had opposed the liaison and sought to discourage its permanence. They capitulated only when public opinion turned overwhelmingly against the tenacious Rhea, and because Gable's closest studio friends——Eddie Mannix and publicists Howard Strickling and Otto Winkler—had become enamored of Carole. Grady, as casting director, got the call to deliver a substitute chorus girl from the studio's pool of hopeful novices. And shooting continued on *Idiot's Delight*—Gable's last film with Norma Shearer, in which they played roles the Lunts had created on the Broadway stage.

Carole had vowed to be occupied with picture-making only at those times when Clark was, and she was pleased to be in harness again when David Selznick finally had another picture ready for her. This one was *Made for Each Other,* an arbitrary title, and Carole hoped it would be the mouthwash to chase the lingering foul taste of *Fools for Scandal.* Not a screwball thing, it was a romantic comedy-drama, light for the first half and heavy for the balance. The boy she was made for, and he for her, was the fast-rising James Stewart, borrowed by Selznick from M-G-M. It was quality stuff along the lines of a domestic symphony: the young people meet, fall in love, confront employer and mother-in-law problems, have a baby before they have a crucial misunderstanding, and before the happy ending at the New Year's Eve party while the redoubtable "Auld Lang Syne" works its emotional magic.

As the shooting progressed, Carole intercepted the rumors that her performance was virtuoso stuff, perhaps Oscar caliber. It seemed to have gotten her back into the Scarlett speculation, which prodded some urgency to get the picture in the can by Thanksgiving. David Selznick wanted to clear his slate and be occupied only with *Gone With the Wind,* and as late as December the *Hollywood Reporter* would predict Carole's ultimate assignment as Scarlett. And she still had hopes.

She believed that David's preoccupation with *Gone With the Wind* caused him to neglect *Made for Each Other,* but perhaps it was a good thing. She thought they were putting together a fine picture without his intelligent meddling. She had not worked with John Cromwell previously, but they were friends from her earliest days at Paramount when he was a new director there, fresh from the New York stage. Other than George Cukor, only Cromwell among the many directors imported from Broadway had really succeeded in the film craft; and both Cukor and Cromwell had proved themselves in projects supervised by the young David Selznick. The tall, squarely handsome Cromwell, himself a fine actor of the stage, made more pictures for Selznick than any other director—for Paramount, RKO, and David's independent company.

So Cromwell appreciated Carole's setside reminiscence of her first marriage, with particular reference to Powell's monumental primping. "Carole was such a contrast to Bill. She was a woman to delight most men's hearts. She could come in from the day's activities, bathe, do a complete feminine toilette, and dress in half an hour. She could laugh uproariously while recalling the picture of herself as the impatient wife, waiting while Bill painstakingly arranged a handkerchief, adjusted a coat or fiddled for the umpteenth time with an already well-arranged tie, to get the exact effect he demanded before he could face the world. You see, there was a great deal of exactness and precision which only his intimates knew he carried over into his personal life. And Clark Gable? Well, two husbands could hardly have been so different."

Cromwell also said he came to admire Carole Lombard about as much as any woman he ever met, because a large part of her brain worked like a man's. He found her "utterly devoid of those coquetries which almost every woman uses in her relationship with the opposite sex, that in the film business were so much a part of her equipment for success both on screen and off."

Cromwell, meanwhile, was added to Carole's inventory of favorite directors. She was proud of *Made for Each Other* and shared with her director the thought that the only flaw was the one thing David Selznick had brought to it: an interpolated sequence in which the precious serum is delivered by a monoplane pilot to save the baby's life after a dramatic long-distance flight through ice and snow. Yet David was inspired from actual happenstance, for Myron Selznick had experienced a sudden seizure and a rendezvous with death's specter until the arrival of life-saving serum under conditions similar to those depicted in the picture.

Carole also was startled by the range of the James Stewart talent.

He usually came off well on film and he had acquired widespread popularity in three busy Hollywood years, but she had regarded him mainly as an engaging, shy-sly bachelor whose reputation as a lover around town was already as tall as the rest of him. She had worked in pictures with Laughton, March, and others of the premium order, not to exclude John Barrymore; but now she found James Stewart "more sincere than any of them, and just as talented . . . his timing is perfection itself."

She speculated on the perfection of her own timing in abandoning the screwball format that had put her in the top class. The vogue seemed to be passing from the screen, just as the Great Depression that spawned it appeared to be just about over. A popular play of the day announced that it was no time for comedy. Carole hoped that her efforts toward more serious stuff would not go unappreciated.

When *Made for Each Other* was released early in the following year, the critics to a man were encouraging. The film was generously praised, and Carole's work—more natural than dramatic in its basic quality—usually merited such description as "glowing" or "enchanting." Stewart, Charles Coburn, Lucile Watson, Cromwell's direction: it received the highest praise. *The New York Times* selected *Made for Each Other* as one of the year's ten best pictures, even in the year that was indeed the *annum mirabilis* . . . for 1939 was historically the highwater mark of the American film.

Oddly enough, that *Made for Each Other* would have great audience appeal had never been doubted. Although it returned a tidy profit, its failure to win big popular success was an industrial surprise. That it was any kind of box-office disappointment could have only one explanation: the nation's moviegoers, looking for comedy in a Carole Lombard picture, unhappily had found a serious something else.

At Christmastime, 1938, a nation knew that its foremost box-office attraction was about to take a bride. From Cape Hatteras to Puget Sound, they knew that in January Rhea Langham Gable would establish residence in Nevada for the purpose of obtaining a divorce from the King of the Movies.

Clark Gable had instructions to report in January to the Selznick studio—actually the old Pathé lot where Carole once toiled. Principal photography on *Gone With the Wind* would commence in just three weeks. In Hollywood that was cause for celebration, even with the Scarlett O'Hara role still unassigned. But Clark was not happy. He didn't like David Selznick and he didn't like Selznick's choice of director, George Cukor.

As a mock Christmas gift, Clark gave Carole a statue of himself —almost a caricature, slightly less than life-sized but equaling his own weight of 200 pounds. She put it in her front yard, saying it could be a hitching post for such horsemen as may come riding by. But Clark also gave her a Persian lamb coat, and she said she would wear it. Her presents to him were a German camera ("Because I think they're going to be hard to get pretty soon"), a ruby ring, and a motorboat. Clark had never owned a boat, and he could take the present as a hint that Carole was just the least bit tired of the rugged mountains and would like to spend some time at the beach.

January came, and Rhea still hadn't gone to Nevada. She left only after the delivery of Clark's payoff package. He had sold most of his valuable possessions other than his gun collection, but most of the cash went to Rhea. It became apparent that if Clark and Carole found *their* place as a result of their farflung scouting, Carole would have to pay for it. She did. They both fell in love with a forty-five-acre ranch in Encino. Raoul Walsh owned it although he didn't live there, and Walsh wanted fifty thousand dollars in ready cash. Carole wrote a check for the full amount, without wincing.

Over at the Selznick studio there was a great fire in progress, and Clark and Carole joined most of the Hollywood citizenry by going to watch it. The fire was no accident: some ancient sets were being burned away, to clear ground for building the new ones for *Gone With the Wind*. Selznick decided to film the holocaust and to have it represent the burning of Atlanta on the screen. Selznick was on the scene, running the show himself, directing the traffic because sometimes he would not concede that a producer and a director aren't the same thing. But he knew he was getting some great photography for the movie of the ages, and he was pretty excited. Sweating jubilantly, he greeted his older brother who had a gorgeous girl in tow. Myron Selznick said, "David, I want you to meet Scarlett O'Hara." The girl was Vivien Leigh, and in that moment she certainly *looked* like Scarlett O'Hara . . . and David decided that the big question had been answered at last.

In February, 1939, Rhea was in Reno and Carole was at the ranch she had bought, supervising the reconstruction of the main house the way she supervised everything. She engaged Tom Douglas as decorator but she knew what *she* wanted, and what Clark would appreciate. She decided it was all for the best that Clark wasn't around; he hated carpenters and bricklayers' dust and any kind of building noise. Before reporting to *Gone With the Wind,* Clark had done some of his own fixing-up around the place, usually with the help of car salesman Al Menasco, who was probably his closest friend on a one-to-one basis. Carole regretted that the telephone was already installed, because Louella Parsons kept calling. And Carole kept saying, yes, Lollypops, when the knot gets tied it'll be your exclusive . . . you'll know about it before anyone else gets the word. Meanwhile, back at the studio, Clark was miserable and not on good terms with anyone. It was just as well that Carole was not on the set.

In March, 1939, George Cukor was dismissed as director of *Gone With the Wind* after having helped plan its production for more than two years. Selznick was worried about the budget, and had complained that Cukor was too slow; but Clark Gable was thought to be the likely architect of Cukor's downfall. Victor Fleming, well-known to have been Gable's favorite director at M-G-M, now was engaged to direct *Gone With the Wind* although he had not previously worked for Selznick.

And in March, to her own amazement, Carole Lombard was at the RKO Radio film studio in Hollywood, suddenly under contract there. It just sort of happened and there she was, planning her first studio venture, with Cary Grant in tow as costar. She was uncharacteristically nervous, but with good reason—until, on March 8, she heard what she had wanted to hear for three years: "Mrs. Clark Gable was granted a divorce today . . ."

Decree in hand, Rhea was quoted: "He could have had a divorce any time, but didn't seem to want one. In my opinion, a marriage between a movie star and a society woman will be more successful in general than one between two stars."

Carole could scoff, but parts of Rhea's statement worried her.

XII

King and Queen

He was thirty-eight. She had marked her thirtieth birthday in October but the cake had only twenty-nine candles: she was now a party to the antic studio deception, and gave her age as twenty-nine when they were married.

Clark and Carole had enjoyed a long idle stretch together just before Rhea obtained her decree. While the *Gone With the Wind* shooting schedule required Vivien Leigh's presence on the set almost daily, progressively draining the stamina that was hers only in short supply, Clark came to enjoy a filming agenda that had him working sometimes only one or two days a week. But he was recalled to full-time duty before the cameras just prior to getting the news that he was free at last. Carole was left to confront the battery of reporters who wanted only to know when and where the wedding would take place. She honestly didn't know, but she and Clark had already resolved that it would be their secret, an elopement, to prevent their special event from acquiring the character of a circus.

Clark confided only in Victor Fleming, and they devised a four-day holiday for filming without his participation. On the night of March 28 Carole and Clark stayed at the North Hollywood house Clark was renting from Rex Ingram and Alice Terry. Their studious effort to decoy reporters and other would-be oglers was hardly necessary, for most newsmen covering filmland as a regular beat had been deployed to San Francisco for the opening of Don Ameche's

The Story of Alexander Graham Bell. Still, a few reporters congregated outside the Beverly Wilshire Hotel where Clark still kept rooms whenever he was making a picture, while others took up stations within view of Carole's Bel-Air home. Reporters also harassed the Brentwood house that Fred Peters had built for himself and his mother, with a bedroom always reserved for Carole.

Undetected, Carole and Clark left the San Fernando Valley on the morning of the 29th, before dawn, chauffered by Otto Winkler —Gable's friend, neighbor, and studio publicist. Winkler was driving his own car to a wedding site he had selected. Jill Winkler, Otto's wife, packed ample lunches for them so they would stop only for gasoline. The trip still consumed ten hours and they arrived in Kingman scruffy-tired and hot, encountering midsummer weather even in March. They applied for a marriage license at the county clerk's office; and Mrs. Viola Olsen, who issued it, later said, "Yes, I recognized Mr. Gable at once, but of course I certainly was surprised to see *them.*" And flustered: she turned over a bottle of ink on the filled-out document and had to start over again. Meanwhile Otto Winkler had made arrangements for the wedding at the parsonage of Kingman's First Methodist Episcopal Church. The Reverend Kenneth Engle and his wife were briefly startled by the raffish appearance of their guests and then more so by realizing their identity—a little matter Winkler had failed to include in his orientation. Clark and Carole retired to separate rooms to wash and dress for the occasion, after which the wedding ceremony was conducted with efficiency and dispatch, and with considerably more dignity than Carole would have bargained for—she said it was well worth the grimy ride.

Carole's wedding ensemble, designed by Irene, was a simple, conservative suit of powder-gray flannel, with black, white, and gray accessories in polka dot print. Gable wore a conventional business suit of blue serge. When Reverend Engle performed the ceremony, the only witness other than Mrs. Engle and Otto Winkler was Howard Cate, the principal of Kingman High School. The Gable-Lombard ritual would enter into the Kingman folklore with even the minister and his wife issuing contradictory versions, but Carole said that when the minister summoned Mrs. Engle with the news that Clark Gable and Carole Lombard were the ones to be married, Mrs. Engle shrieked, "Oh, my stars!" Carole beamed and said, "Well, that's nice of you, Mrs. Engle, we hope we'll *always* be your stars."

Before they left Kingman, Carole telephoned her mother that she was an honest woman at last, and asked her to be at Carole's own home along with Fritz and Tootie when they arrived there, most likely in the wee hours. Bess Peters agreed to telephone Jill Winkler, as well as Jean Garceau, Dixie Karlson, Fieldsie Lang—the list kept growing. Carole continued to forget her promise to Louella Parsons, even when Otto Winkler stopped at the Western Union office to telegraph the news to M-G-M, whose Howard Strickling would prepare the formal press release.

The newlyweds and Winkler shed their coats but stayed in their wedding clothes during the muggy homeward trip. They were crossing the Colorado River into California, Gable having relieved the fatigued Winkler as driver, when Carole interrupted her own blissful reverie with a sudden, shrieky "Oh, shit!"

Now she remembered the pledge to call Louella Parsons, just before the actual ceremony. Perhaps Louella already had heard: In any event, she was certain to be furious, and had been recently testy with Carole since Hedda Hopper had scooped her with the news of the Lombard tie-in at RKO. Gable was only annoyed; it didn't bother *him* if Parsons got screwed, the old meddler. But Carole's whim prevailed and they stopped in Needles, where Carole tried unsuccessfully to reach Louella by phone. So she called Marion Davies, whose advice was for Carole to telegraph the news both to Louella and her boss, William Randolph Hearst, for what would still resemble a high conscientiousness.

Not so much weary as propelled by nervous energy, the Gables arrived at Carole's house belatedly at 3:00 A.M. Carole's mother and brothers greeted them, along with enormous Jessie—Carole's cook. They had a champagne toast followed by cakes and coffee, then the Peterses scattered and Carole and Clark retired to separate bedrooms. Carole said she wanted the legal consummation to be a strictly private thing when they were both rested, and ribbed Clark about his having enough difficulty performing well even under the most ideal conditions. Otto Winkler took another room, staying on for the morning press conference that had been arranged by M-G-M in advance, with Carole's and Clark's concurrence. They would be getting only a few hours of sleep—except that Carole couldn't sleep at all, such was her extended state of disbelief that it had happened at last. She lay in bed awhile, then turned on the radio and heard the news report of the nuptials. Then, as nude as she was restless, she went into the room where Clark was sound asleep and snuggled up beside him, without disturbing his slumber or disrupting the rhythm of his loud snoring. Later switching her position, she allowed her arm to graze a nightstand and knocked an object to the floor. There on the floor, grinning at her in a beam of moonlight, were Clark's dentures.

Once Carole had given the workmen proper instruction for their remodeling chores on the Encino ranch, there just hadn't been anything for her to do. That was in late February, while she was still awaiting Rhea's divorce resolution. All of the talk around Hollywood, if you believed the trade journal *Hollywood Reporter*, was the multi-faceted discord on the *Gone With the Wind* production sets. Carole had to get busy. She felt a sudden urge—no, a need —to make a picture. That way she could concentrate wholeheartedly on something. She read in the *Reporter* that RKO was readying *In Name Only* for an April start, hopefully for Cary Grant and a comparable female star, for John Cromwell to direct.

Made for Each Other had not been released but was booked into the Radio City Music Hall, and Carole had screened an edited final print. She liked the picture, and found the combination of Grant and Cromwell quite appealing. So she telephoned Cromwell, who said he hadn't agreed to the assignment, and besides, getting Cary Grant was really a doubtful prospect. Carole said, "If I played the girl, would you want to direct?" Cromwell's reply was, "Oh, my, yes . . . then I'm sure we could also get Cary."

The man to see at RKO was Pandro Berman, but Carole was already thinking positively. She was familiar with the property. *In Name Only* was a Bessie Breuer novel she'd read and liked. RKO had bought it for Katharine Hepburn, but Katie had quit the Hollywood scene some months earlier. It was a triangle drama centered around an alcoholic chap who got that way because his bitchy wife wouldn't give him a divorce to marry the nice girl he really loves. My, how ironic! She got on the telephone to Berman and they chatted. Berman said he'd call her back. The return call came instead from George Schaefer, the new RKO president, who said he was interested in talking multipicture contract with Carole if she were. Carole started to refer him to Myron Selznick and then thought, why should I, it's something I can handle myself.

They reached an agreement easily and without haggling. Carole

would make four RKO pictures over a two-year period. She brought
her price down to $150,000—but she would also receive a small per-
centage of the pictures' profits. That part was entirely her own
idea, a novel procedure for that day but standard practice in years
to come. Arrangements were completed within only a matter of
days. Myron Selznick was brought in as Carole's official representative and was resentful of Carole's end-run. She told him to fuck off,
it was the easiest sixty thousand dollars he'd ever made.

In Name Only would initiate the contract. John Cromwell
quickly agreed to direct; and Cary Grant, despite being the hottest
of the current leading men on the basis of *Gunga Din* and *Only
Angels Have Wings,* seemed only too happy just to have been
asked. He signed. So did Charles Coburn, a late starter in films
after a long and prestigious stage career, endorsed by both Carole
and her director after his good work in *Made for Each Other.* Coburn would play Cary Grant's father. *In Name Only* would cast
Carole as a mother for the first and only time (other than as a young
mother of infants born in midpicture), and her little daughter
would be played by a pigtailed charmer named Peggy Ann Garner.
Carole's suggestion that Rhea Gable be auditioned for the role of
the society wife was vetoed, and Cromwell's sentimental choice was
Kay Francis. He had been largely responsible for guiding her to
important stardom at Paramount—Carole had played support to
her there—and Kay had also been a big Warner name until the
studio humiliated her by forcing her to play out her very expensive
contract in a string of B pictures. The gracious agreement was that
Kay Francis would be the third star, Cary Grant billed second in
the balanced triangle. Already the project was being essentially re-
designed as a Carole Lombard vehicle, but not a comedy—this was
soap opera, weepy stuff.

In Name Only would emerge as slick entertainment, a picture no
one could feel ashamed of, or take pride in. It neither advanced
nor damaged the reputation of anyone connected to it. Enough
people would pay to see it, they would applaud, and not carry a
lasting memory of what they had seen. But it certified that Carole
Lombard, the pliable one, was easily adaptable for a "woman's
picture."

Anyway, it kept her occupied, and out of Clark Gable's hair
when the fictional events of Tara and Atlanta provided all the
dandruff he could abide. By concentrating on her first entirely un-

comical role in five years, she also enabled the ranch house remodelers to accomplish their work without her undue interference. *In Name Only* was begun in April, completed in June, edited in July, previewed in August, released in September: RKO was nothing if not expeditious. *Gone With the Wind,* after three years of preparation, commenced shooting in January and finished in July, with Clark Gable summoned for retakes in August. During the spring and early summer the newlywed Gables occupied Carole's Bel-Air home but saw little of one another except for their connubial rendezvous. When their picture-making chores were over, the ranch house was ready and they could begin their real honeymoon.

Less than a month after their occupancy, before all the boxes were unpacked, Carole was felled in August by an attack of acute appendicitis. When she complained of feeling just awful, a doctor who was a nearby resident was called in and immediately diagnosed the symptoms. Clark rushed Carole to Cedars of Lebanon Hospital for an emergency appendectomy and remained at her bedside until she was pronounced out of danger. When she revived from sedation she told him it was really very considerate of God to have planned everything so efficiently. Now she could bone up on hospital procedures: in her next RKO picture she would be playing a nurse.

They were all tense when they saw the private studio screening of the final cut. Four hours later they could relax, confident of having made a picture that would stand apart, in a class by itself. It was September, 1939, and the picture was *Gone With the Wind*. Scheduled for a mid-December world premiere in Atlanta, it would open simultaneously in New York and Los Angeles soon afterward on a single-theater, reserved-seat, advance-sale basis. The turmoil of the picture's production history would graduate from gossip into legend, in a way that could only enhance the mysterious magic of movie making. After all the blood had been spilled, the product was what counted; and if a picture looked like a winner, its combatants were soulmates in triumph. Most of the people involved with *Gone With the Wind* would close ranks and toast one another, saying look what we've done!

But not Clark Gable. He was relieved, he knew it was a good picture, he accepted the consensus that he was a superb Rhett Butler; but that wouldn't change his attitude toward David Selznick, who he said had probably shortened Victor Fleming's life.

Fleming, too, was permanently estranged from Selznick and most of the *GWTW* assembly, although drawn even closer to Gable than before. Fleming had collapsed physically and emotionally under pressure, and Selznick had brought in Sam Wood. Later Fleming returned to complete the picture but Selznick retained Wood and used two directors, shooting separate scenes simultaneously in order to bring the picture in on time within its allotted budget of three and a half million dollars. When the costs were tallied, it was seen that the picture barely had exceeded that figure.

Carole attended the private screening with Gable, and her rave report on *Gone With the Wind* was one of the first received by columnists and passed on to anxious readers. It was a slip of the tongue. She knew David Selznick didn't want it generally known that the picture had been screened at all, and wanted no opinion circulated until there had been an audience preview. The anonymous Associated Press reporter interviewing Carole did not get scent of a scoop. Buried in a chatty duologue was this exchange:

Carole: Clark's doing very well, thank you. I've just seen *Gone with the Wind* and it's terrific.

Reporter: Do you mean Gable is terrific?

Carole: I mean the picture is terrific.

No more than that; but Jimmy Fidler picked it up and devoted most of a column to the "first reports" that Selznick had a smash.

But she did think Clark was terrific and told him so. "After all your pissing and moaning," she said, "this is the part they'll always remember you for." She also joined the legion of passed-over, would-be Scarlett O'Haras who now were chorusing that Selznick's controversial choice of Vivien Leigh was precisely right. But not even the belated knowledge that she wouldn't have been "right" for Scarlett would alter her grudge toward Myron for his failure to support her cause or at least deal honestly with her. What was an agent for?

Carole intended to settle her differences with Myron, but that would have to wait. Her priority mission was as peacemaker between her husband and David Selznick. Gable said he was "rid of that Jew prick once and for all" and glad of it; but the Jew prick was also Carole's own producer and, she knew, one of the best in the business, probably *the* best.

To reconcile Gable with David Selznick became critical to Carole because she recognized the singular importance of *Gone With the*

Wind to Hollywood, even to America and the world, and therefore to Clark Gable's curious status within the mythology of the movies. There was no doubting his popularity, nor was it flukish in any way. But while his magnetism was readily acknowledged, his talent wasn't, and she knew this rankled him. He wanted to be something more than a marketable type. Outwardly he scoffed, saying he was no actor; but perhaps more than anyone, including even himself, she sensed his need for recognition in terms of ability. Yet his policy of self-effacement failed to mask his vanity on the one hand, or his overriding inferiority complex on the other. She deduced this through his avoidance of the Cukors, Thalbergs, and Selznicks, whom he regarded as smarter than himself. She thought there was significance in the fact that none of Gable's close friends were actors.

Spencer Tracy was almost the exception. He was the actor Gable most admired, achieving through his naturalness the conviction that was Clark's own criterion. But to some extent Gable misread Tracy. He thought they mirrored one another in character and personality because there was no pretentiousness, no prissy airs about Spence. At the studio they often lunched together, sharing as friends a salty brotherhood that included Eddie Mannix, Billy Grady, advertising's Frank Whitbeck, the publicists Strickling and Winkler, and such directors as Victor Fleming and Woody Van Dyke. When they made pictures together, Gable joined Tracy in the ribaldry and cutting-up that a certain part of Spence craved. Yet Gable and Tracy seldom met socially away from the studio, although Clark regularly invited Tracy on expeditions. They would meet often at sports events, but usually by chance.

When Carole probed Tracy, he said, "I like The King but not his court. Clark's friends all give me a pain in the butt. They're boobs." Tracy had a circle of gamy, predominantly Irish pals that included James Cagney, Frank Morgan, Lynne Overman, and Pat O'Brien—yet all were serious actors as well; but he also had kinship with the Hollywood intellectual set whose salon master was George Cukor. In contrast, Clark Gable seemed most contented in a fellowship of his intellectual inferiors. Carole liked all of Clark's friends, but together they didn't fulfill all of her social needs, either.

Throughout the fall, while the Selznick and M-G-M organizations devised elaborate celebrations for the *GWTW* launchings, Gable insisted he would not take part—he wouldn't give Selznick that satisfaction. Everyone supposed he was being coy and surely would be in Atlanta for the main event. Gable held firm, and a special plane chartered by Selznick for the Atlanta premiere filled up without him. Carole tried to persuade him, but Gable said he'd do what Victor Fleming did, and Fleming refused to participate in any way. Clark and Carole got into a shouting argument about his professional future, and he yelled that nobody was going to get him into the same plane with David Selznick. Carole suggested he take another plane, although commercial flights from Los Angeles to Atlanta did not exist in 1939. Only days away from the premiere, Atlanta could still not expect Rhett Butler in the flesh, but Carole was assuring Selznick's Russell Birdwell: "Don't worry, he'll be there. I'll make that fat-assed Dutchman the biggest thing in America."

She got hold of Paul Mantz, the famous stunt pilot who was working into Clark's buddy entourage, and asked if he knew some-one who could fly Clark to Atlanta. Mantz knew the president of the new American Airlines and figured he'd fly Gable gratis to Atlanta for the publicity it would give to his company. Carole con-tacted American's C. R. Smith and made all the arrangements, in-cluding accommodations for Howard Strickling and Otto Winkler —and herself.

Clark still said he wouldn't go. He went.

Alighting from their DC-3, they were mobbed even more wildly than the Selznick party had been in its earlier arrival. For a while it resembled a competition. Selznick's group had included officials of his own studio and those of M-G-M, his partner Jock Whitney, the picture's feminine stars Vivien Leigh and Olivia deHavilland, and Laurence Olivier as Miss Leigh's escort. There were two separate celebrity units, Gable's being the pariah, until Carole succeeded in bringing them all together. In later years David Selz-nick would acknowledge that Carole "saved the occasion, first in Georgia, then in California."

The only absentee among the film's four stars was Leslie Howard, but he had gone home to England: his country was going to war against Hitler's Germany and he would assist in its efforts, primarily as a filmmaker. (He would not return to Hollywood: flying over the Bay of Biscay in 1943, he would be shot down by German aircraft.) While Howard's absence was regularly and la-mentedly remarked, Carole thought it ironic that the film version of Margaret Mitchell's "story of the Old South" was presented for an all-white audience. Where, she asked David Selznick, was the glorious Hattie McDaniel, or Butterfly McQueen?

Next the Gables attended the gala California premiere at the Carthay Circle Theater in West Hollywood. Clark again proved difficult but Carole's will prevailed, but only to a point. They left at intermission, although Carole had accepted an invitation to a party David Selznick was hosting after the premiere. She was still trying to coax Clark to the party after their return to the ranch. He had his stubborn streak, all right. Carole telephoned David Selznick with apologies, and he said he understood the situation. She said, "I know you do, but there'll be a lot of talk. David, tell them we were coming but that I got sick. Say that Clark wanted to be there but had to take me home. Is Louella there? Put her on and I'll tell her something. I'll say it's my period and that I also have the runs, and didn't want to stink up your party."

Carole's own professional vanity was generally unsuspected and only her most intimate friends knew its extent. She was as jealous of Clark Gable as he of her. He had an Oscar; she wanted one. She was determined to get one, still nourishing a whim to "quit at the very top, like Mary Garden." She vacillated about retirement, but thought it would be a satisfying thing if she could go out with an Oscar.

When she was nominated for *My Man Godfrey,* she first thought that was honor enough. She supposed she was only along for the ride, like Irene Dunne and Gladys George probably were, and that the winner would be one of the M-G-M standard-bearers, either Norma Shearer or Luise Rainer. The early wagering was on Shearer who, besides having been an admired Juliet, now commanded the sympathy of new and young widowhood. But then a Norma-already-has-one reaction set in, at the same time people started saying that you could rule out Luise Rainer because she was almost certain to win *next* year, for *The Good Earth.* Carole had strong antennae for professional gossip. She intercepted a rumor that the smart money had switched to Carole Lombard. Soon a lot of people were saying they just *knew* she was going to win! She fought against believing it, but on the evening of the awards dinner she fully expected to win.

Since her ex-husband and *Godfrey* costar was also in nomination, Carole attended as part of a dinner foursome that included William

Powell, Jean Harlow, and Clark Gable. When Carole and Jean visited the powder room together, they encountered one of the actress nominees in a deadly drunken state. Gladys George had counted herself a dark horse, the likely winner in case all the M-G-M votes would split down the middle between Shearer and Rainer—because Gladys had the power of Paramount behind her while Lombard and Dunne, representing the more modest Universal and Columbia interests, could be discounted, she thought. But now she'd changed her mind. Gladys George said everything had been decided and Luise Rainer would win. Mark her words. She knew the thing was supposed to be secret, but they already knew. Mayer knew. He brought it about, after Thalberg's death, getting everyone to dump Norma and line up behind Rainer. Thure, Luithe Rainerth gonna win nexthyeer too: Gladys said that for all the reviews, Luise was a box-office dud but perhaps two Academy Awards would brighten her future. Carole believed in the democratic system and the secret ballot. She told Gladys she was full of shit as well as gin, and that any of the five could win.

When Luise Rainer's name was announced as winner, Carole smiled broadly and clapped her hands and burned inside.

It was a foregone conclusion that she would get her second nomination the next year, probably for *Nothing Sacred*. But late in 1937 the talk was that her nomination would be for *True Confession*, since all the Selznick marbles were riding on Janet Gaynor in *A Star Is Born*. That Carole Lombard ultimately was not among the five nominees was the season's big surprise. She concealed her disappointment without a show of bitterness and said, "They don't give awards to comedy performances." Still, she attended that year's awards dinner, again with Gable.

There was no speculation on Carole Lombard's *Fools for Scandal* in 1938, certainly. And her work in *Made for Each Other,* having been on view very early in 1939, was largely forgotten by the time the 1939 bumper crop of great pictures and performances was translated into nominations. But on Leap Year Day, 1940, she attended the ceremony as Mrs. Clark Gable, hopeful of her nominated husband hauling in his second statuette in a likely *Gone With the Wind* sweep. That year's Best Actor category was crowded with quality—the Olivier Heathcliff, James Stewart's Washington-bound Mr. Smith, and Robert Donat's Mr. Chips all commanding some support, while Mickey Rooney's *Babes in Arms* nomination was token homage to his newfound popularity, actually deposing Gable as the top moneymaking attraction. This time secrecy prevailed. So did *Gone With the Wind.* Vivien Leigh won, as expected. The picture romped in. Hattie McDaniel was victor in the supporting category that had also listed Olivia deHavilland's Melanie Hamilton as a nominee. Even Thomas Mitchell, while nominally cited for *Stagecoach,* was believed to have won because his supporting chore in *Gone With the Wind* was equally worthy.

But Clark Gable was turned away. Robert Donat was a quasi-surprise winner for a performance of a brilliance never doubted. But before the evening was over, Carole was hearing that *Goodbye, Mr. Chips* wasn't all that great at the box office and had needed an extra boost.

Driving home from the ceremony, Clark Gable was in a deep gloom. Carole said, "Don't be blue, Pappy, we'll bring one home next year." Clark said, "No we won't. That was it, my last chance. I'll never go to one of those things again."

"Not *you,* you self-centered bastard, I mean myself!" Carole said next year she'd bring home the Oscar.

She really thought she would. She was counting on *Vigil in the Night,* scheduled for release the very next week. It had already been screened for the press, and the word was out to expect only rave reviews. (They were.) The "new" Carole Lombard was not a dramatic comedienne but an Actress of force and skill and Great Tragic Dimension.

Vigil in the Night was RKO's prestige picture of the year, adapted from an admired A. J. Cronin novel and directed by the studio's golden boy, George Stevens. He was certainly eclectic, but everything he touched came out right, whether it was Astaire and Rogers (*Swing Time*), college farce (the Rogers-Stewart *Vivacious Lady*), high adventure (*Gunga Din*) or alluringly different Katharine Hepburns (*Alice Adams* and *Quality Street*). *Vigil in the Night* was his RKO swan song—he was moving over to Columbia on a lucrative producer-director contract—and studio optimists were saying he was bowing out with a masterpiece.

Still persuaded by the misadventure of *Fools for Scandal* that she should veer away from comedy, and not really pleased with her soapflaky RKO initiation in *In Name Only,* Carole had selected *Vigil in the Night* from several vehicle possibilities because it was the heaviest story the studio owned, if not the best. Lewis Milestone, a director she admired, had wanted to get her into *Lucky Partners* with no less a costar than Ronald Colman, but Carole read the script and said it wasn't even a good comedy. Ginger Rogers would film it with Colman and prove her right.

Vigil in the Night was a hospital picture. Carole and young Anne Shirley were sisters, both nurses in work and love with the doctor played by Brian Aherne. After much travail including self-sacrifice (Carole's) and death (Anne's) there was a technically happy ending, but the mood was somber. Carole didn't have a lot of fun making the picture, but she found it an enriching experience. She appreciated George Stevens primarily as a technician, and cited him as a case in point when she said all directors should be photographers first, or at least should learn the craft. Stevens had been a cinematographer, and Carole said he knew lighting better than anyone in Hollywood—knew how to use it for dramatic or comic or purely visual effect. She thought she knew a thing or two about lighting, especially about how it could enhance the image of a star. Stevens regarded photography as a storytelling medium. He preferred leaving his actors alone if they knew their own craft. Carole, at least, considered Anne Lee in *Vigil in the Night* her very own creation.

The reviews were complimentary. (To this day, *Vigil in the Night* is often cited the most authentic hospital film of all time.) Sure enough, there were intimations of Oscar in the critics' response to the Lombard performance, with the likelihood of a supporting nomination for Anne Shirley. The word of mouth turned it all around, however. Audiences simply hated the picture for its unrelieved gloom. The box-office return was never better than sluggish. As a commercial entry, *Vigil in the Night* inhabited the narrow middle-ground between disappointment and disaster. The indigenous Hollywood types who could think of movies only on dollar-and-cent terms would call it a flop. The RKO leadership had not speculated on a box-office champion. Even their jubilation after the first press screening did not delude them into thinking they had a strong "audience picture." But Carole Lombard's star name was interpreted as commercial insurance, all the marquee needed to guarantee a modest profit. What *Vigil in the Night* told them was that Carole Lombard couldn't sell a picture unless it was a comedy —not even as Mrs. Clark Gable. So for the moment, she could forget about an Academy Award or even a nomination.

* * *

Clark Gable had not been in favor of Carole's tie-in with RKO, a second-rate studio in his estimation. He liked the idea of her retiring from pictures and living in his own large shadow, and accused her of saying one thing and doing something else. She said she'd never make another picture if he flatly ordered her not to, and would never complain; but Clark looked at her and saw $150,000 per picture (plus profit-sharing) and would say, well, you don't have to quit for a while, anyway.

He always fretted about money; Carole, never. She said money was only a game she played in Hollywood, that it really had nothing to do with how she felt about the business. "I live well because I can afford to, but I don't think I'm any happier for the money I have. If I were making seventy-five dollars a week I could live on it and be happy. Hell, I *did* . . . and I *was* happy. My mother has never had a lot of money; at least she knows what it means to sacrifice. But I don't know a happier person than my mother, and that's the truth. It's like they say, everything's relative."

She signed up with RKO because she knew she could always quit, any time she wanted to. "Anyone can break a contract. You break it, you only lose what your signature has protected, nothing other than that."

"If I can have a baby, I'll give up acting. At least for several years." She never denied that motherhood was her last unfulfilled goal (on priority terms, it meant more than winning an Oscar), or that she started trying to get pregnant right after becoming Mrs. Gable. She envied Fieldsie, who conceived not long after becoming Mrs. Walter Lang. When Fieldsie had a difficult delivery, Carole kept a bedside vigil and afterward said, "I'd go through it. I'd endure all the pain and all the embarrassment of looking like Oliver Hardy. It would be worth it."

Other than possible amendment to include a nursery, her house was in order. Rather, Clark's was. Her earlier residences had expressed Carole Lombard on her own feminine terms. The ranch was her notion of such a castle as a king should have, since he was The King. She had supervised its every detail with his own taste, comfort and convenience as the guidelines.

The decorative motif was Early American but with more attention to comfort than the pioneers ever bothered with. The furniture in every room was custom-built and oversized. The nine-room house included bedroom suites only for themselves, to discourage the prospect of overnight guests. The large living room was carpeted wall to wall in canary yellow, with quilted wingback chairs, an enormous soft couch, and an imposing brick fireplace. Still, the centerpiece and monument to Clark's ego was the gun room, with its glass-enclosed display of his ever-expanding firearms collection, numbering more than fifty pieces when they took occupancy.

Carole's only whimsical indulgence was her bathroom, mirrored on every wall as well as its ceiling. Clark liked to give his guests a tour of the house and would make her hall of mirrors the final sight-seeing attraction, just after having shown them the two pictures adorning the wall above Carole's bed, in heart-shaped frames: one of a plump but winsome, obviously pretty little girl, and the other of a jug-eared, slick-haired little boy.

The ranch house exterior was white brick with white wood paneling. The 20 acres of cleared ground accommodated more than 400 trees, mainly of citrus varieties. There was a stable of race horses—soon to be sold at Carole's urging because they weren't getting raced; they'd retain a few gentle nags for their own riding pleasure. There was also a cow barn and a pigsty, but no pigs. Chickens numbered into the hundreds. They had the potential of a self-sustaining farm, and for a while Carole hobbied at merchandising "The King's Eggs" until the activity lost its novelty value. She maintained her own flower garden and trimmed her blooms for home decoration—artificial flowers and fruit were both anathema to her. There was a large grape vineyard and an alfalfa field, and Clark played at farming. He operated a large yellow tractor. Carole drove it, too, but it was mainly an adornment. Farming was really something they would "do" for their guests or formally appointed interviewers. If a reporter came exploring, or if M-G-M talked them into being hospitable for some visiting VIPs who wanted to ogle Clark's kingdom, Carole would make a point of gathering the eggs, while Clark did some fancy milking or hay-pitching in the barn It was a charade they both enjoyed, because they never overdid it. And it was guaranteed to enhance the ongoing legend of the "great love story."

But the ranch truly was home and castle to both of them. They had house servants as well as men to work the farm, but they had built servant quarters and could spend their evenings in seclusion. They played gin rummy and backgammon with competitive zeal.

Carole had a wide reading range but a primary interest in biography. Clark was no great reader but devoured murder mysteries. They subscribed to few magazines because he didn't like them cluttering a place, and no newspaper remained in the house beyond its date of issue. Carole read the Los Angeles *Times* more or less completely, and would read aloud to Clark an occasional item from the business page, say, that she thought might interest him. He read only the sport pages, except for an occasional perusal of the Edwin Schallert and Hedda Hopper columns on the drama page, to which Carole was rather more dutiful. They also got the Los Angeles *Examiner* on home delivery, but only because Carole wanted to know what Louella had to say, and because Bill Hearst made a point of knowing which of his star friends did and didn't take his paper.

The magazine rack, other than containing the likes of *Field and Stream* and *Sports Afield,* usually was filled to capacity with movie scripts, including many that would never get filmed. The *Hollywood Reporter* and the *Film Daily* had their own receptacle by Carole's bed, since Clark never read the trade journals anyway.

He really had no interest in the movies as a business game except, of course, as it concerned *him*. They didn't talk shop, although it would have given Carole pleasure; at the studios she debated just about every aspect of the movie art and industry, and felt the old adrenalin flowing. She read all of the monthly fan magazines, keeping track of who was coming up and perhaps sensing who was going down, and finding out who was new. She had real respect for *Photoplay* under editorship of James Quirk and then Ruth Waterbury. She read the trades not only thoroughly but carefully, and remembered what she'd read.

Reading raw filmscripts was her favorite pastime. By her own selective method of reading, she could polish off several scripts in one evening. She brought them home from the studio by the armful. Novice writers sent her their unpurchased screenplays, speculating on her own interest or the likelihood of her recommending a purchase. Producers and directors solicited her evaluation of properties they were considering, or might be *ordered* to film.

Depending on his mood, Carole sometimes was able to stir Clark into reading a script aloud with her. This was often an enjoyable occasion, ripe with revelation, for Clark when least conscious of himself could exhibit an unsuspected resourcefulness. Carole would take the female roles and perhaps some of the male parts as well since they were usually in greater number; and Clark would tackle a wide spectrum of male characterizations, reciting their dialogue half-mockingly but with flair and authority. If Carole paid him a compliment, he might say, "You sometimes forget, honey: I was on the stage for a good many years."

Yet he was hopelessly mired in his own mythology. When he was studying one of his own scripts, whether just for line memory or for sharper portraiture, he submitted himself as if unknowingly to the Gable vocal mannerisms, setting the specifications of his own limitation. He was an expert first reader but improvement was likely to be slight, almost undiscernible; and Carole marveled at his knack for quickly and perfectly memorizing dialogue. She was a dull first reader, sure to improve as she got a better understanding of context; but Carole said she could never catch fire as an actress until the cameras were rolling. Often she wondered aloud if having been on a stage would have made a difference with her.

They were not socially isolated, but they established their own rules. Even their closest friends soon learned that you just didn't "drop in" on the Gables. They entertained on a small scale—usally two or three couples at a time, for dinner or a barbecue. Exercises in exotic cuisine belonged to Carole's past. Clark's pleasure was American fried—steak and potatoes, spareribs and baked beans. Jessie did the cooking except on Sunday, her day off. Then Carole took over the kitchen with an adventurous spirit, and her efforts never met with complaint.

Their guests were Clark's outdoorsmen chums who were inclined to take both stars very much for granted, plus their wives who were much less composed, and always anxious to coax Carole aside for "inside" secrets about other famous stars—topics that never occupied the men. Only on occasion would other film folk make the Encino scene: the Buster Colliers often; the Wesley Ruggleses, Woody Van Dykes, and Tay Garnetts, now and then; Victor Fleming, irregularly; and Spencer Tracy or Walter Pidgeon, rarely. The only filmland lady who might share the masculine environment comfortably with Carole was Gail Patrick, when she was married to Bob Cobb.

Bess Peters was more likely to be a daytime guest when Clark was working at his studio and Carole tending the home. Evenings at the ranch with all of Carole's family had a fixed rhythm and

Clark was an awkward patron; he was never able to warm up to Carole's brothers and was jealous of her devotion to both of them. Carole continued to see much of her family and her devoted long-time friends, but the meetings were usually on their home grounds or neutral restaurant turf, and seldom inside Clark's fortress.

One of Carole's more successful efforts was in bringing two dissimilar male Gables—father William and son Clark—into a kinship they had not known earlier. Clark was a mama's boy whose mama had died too soon. Clark had never understood the gentle, slow-natured man who was his father; and Old Bill could not comprehend the uncontrollable young man who couldn't find his destiny in Cadiz, Ohio.

They had been long estranged, out of touch. Carole nagged Clark into bringing Father Gable and his wife, Pinky, to California; and then into building them a small house on additional property they purchased, adjacent to their own. Carole also built a house for her lifetime nonrelative friends, the Wises—Uncle Claude and Aunt Lottie. The Wises and the elder Gables became a closely knit foursome, and were made to feel at home at the ranch.

Carole grew ever more curious that her husband was inevitably the center of attention, or the distraction from it. It was a unique magnetism she did not fully understand, although she was keener to it than he was. Clark did not seek the spotlight but it gravitated to him. Women were simply aroused—it was not something that happened just on the screen. But the quality also attracted men in a rather different way, a response poised between admiration and envy. Whatever that quality was, it made her love him, although in other ways he fell far short of measuring up to what she expected in a man. But she knew that when she married him.

He would not give money to the Red Cross or the Salvation Army or the March of Dimes, but he bought and discarded automobiles like a boy collecting bubble-gum cards. At any given time the Encino garage might house more than half a dozen automobiles —Lincolns, Chryslers, Packards; a Jaguar, a Mercedes-Benz; the Cadillac he gave Carole at their '39 Christmas at the ranch; and a jalopy or two—hangovers from Carole's practical joking. Clark might buy a used car out of attraction for some spectacular adornment and then decide to sell it, but would feel cheated if he could not sell for a price higher than his own purchase tag. When Carole with Jean Garceau's assistance largely took over the ranch management, some of the underemployed cars started to go.

After their marriage she started calling him Paw—playfully, not as a synonym for Daddy. Paw was what he *did,* she said, when he made love. Nevertheless, his response was to call her Maw, and the nicknames stuck. Even his third-person references to her were as Maw, although "Pappy" was what Carole usually called him for the benefit of other ears, reserving Paw for their private relationship.

The private relationship in its most intimate expression was something else again. From the beginning, she regarded him as boudoir bungler—a bull, all right, but a bull in a china shop. Carole didn't regard sex as life's main course, but rather as its dessert dish.

She prided herself on a healthy sexuality. She said she was not oversexed. "I don't think a person can be oversexed, it's just that some people aren't as dishonest as others." Nor did she think Clark was dishonest; but she would have had him be more romantic.

She said it often, always disarmingly, knowing it wouldn't get printed: "I love the guy, but to tell the truth, he's not a hell of a good lay."

Once when Clark was trying to master bridge under Eddie Mannix's tutelage, he became impatient and said, "Dammit, I don't think I'll ever learn to finesse!" Carole smiled and said, "Well now, Sweetie, every Metro script girl knows *that* . . . isn't that right, Eddie?"

That may have been close to the truth, or right on truth's button. The satisfaction sex had given Clark was a matter of large numbers but small moments. His triumph was akin to a thief's, who'll snatch and run. It was really a statistical thing with him—*his* scoring. It was the difference, Carole told him, between screwing and making love. She liked to make love. She simply believed that part of a man's pleasure should be the satisfaction he could give to his woman.

It was no small problem and it was chronic, but Carole found a way to deal with it, if not to solve it: she joked about it. She teased him for his clumsiness, and she joked about it publicly at his expense. She knew how far to carry the jest, never extending it into the grounds of cruelty or humiliation. His joke became *their* joke, and there were many variations on the theme. According to several witnesses, Carole toyed with him in a routine similar to the following:

    Clark: Tell the truth now, how many men have you known who are better lovers than I am?

    Carole: Do you mean from my personal experience, or do you mean the public domain . . . what one might call common knowledge?

    Clark: Aw, come on, honey, you know I mean personal experience. But not the ones who are just as good as me. Only the ones who're better.

    Carole: You know my memory isn't as good as yours.

    Clark: Just try.

    Carole: I'm sure to forget someone, but I'll try.

    Clark: You could go by studios. You've played 'em all, haven't you?

    Carole: I think alphabetically is the proper way.

    Clark: For Christ's sake . . .

    Carole: I'll start with the A's.

    Clark: Why not go by nationalities? You could start with Dago crooners.

    Carole: Oh, you mean I can count dead people? That'll make it a lot easier.

    Clark: Just stick with the alphabet.

    Carole: All right. There's Richard Arlen, and Nils Asther. There's . . . how about Dorothy Arzner? I know she's a woman, but she's better than you are . . .

    Clark: I'll be goddamned . . .

    Carole: It's going to be harder to remember all the B's.

    Clark: Aren't you forgetting Brian Aherne?

    Carole: Brian? No, I thought of his name.

    Clark: You mean I'm better than he is?

    Carole: Oh, I doubt *that*.

    Clark: Is he better than I am?

    Carole: Well, the odds would seem to favor him, and he's British besides.

    Clark: You mean you haven't—

    Carole: I really can't say about Brian Aherne. I simply don't know.

    Clark: My apologies. I shouldn't have presumed—

Carole: That is, I don't know *yet*.

Clark: Your A's my ass!

Carole: Starting with the B's. Well, there's Wesley Barry . . .

Clark: Wesley Barry!

Carole: That was in silent picture time. He was twelve and I think I was eleven.

Clark: You can't count that.

Carole: Wesley was awfully good.

Clark: You're just making him up.

Carole: Oh, no. He was famous for his freckles.

Clark: Yeah. Now I remember who he was.

Carole: I mean he had freckles *all over!*

Clark: Honey, you're putting me on.

Carole: I just thought of something.

Clark: Yeah?

Carole: We can do this again next week.

Clark: Get on with the B's. Why next week?

Carole: John Barrymore, of course. Better, much better.

Clark: What do you mean about next week?

Carole: And Richard Barthelmess. Now they're getting really *good*.

Clark: They sure ain't getting any younger, Maw.

Carole: Oh, yes they are: Freddie Bartholomew!

Clark: Let's quit this game. You've convinced me.

Carole: Well, I meant that next week you can ask me again about Brian.

Clark: We *will* quit. What'll it be: backgammon?

Carole: Whatever you say. *I'd* rather make love.

❋ XIII ❋

No Time for Comedy

CAROLE got back into the rhythm of working only when Clark did. Although they reported to different studios, they usually drove in together, in her car or his. If Carole had the earlier shooting call, Clark drove over either Coldwater Canyon or Laurel Canyon into Hollywood and deposited Carole at RKO's Hollywood studio before going on to Culver City. If Carole did the driving, she coursed Sepulveda Boulevard out of the San Fernando Valley that was still mostly raw country, through a pass in a Santa Monica mountain range not yet pimpled by houses, and into a Los Angeles basin that hadn't heard of smog. She delivered Gable to M-G-M before angling back to Hollywood; and either way, they drove fifteen miles together.

While Carole kept her *Vigil in the Night,* Clark sailed a boat carrying a *Strange Cargo* named Joan Crawford. It was the last of their eight pictures together. When he was new and hot at M-G-M, Clark had a love affair with Crawford while Rhea looked the other way. Now that Joan was divorcing Franchot Tone, Carole was apprehensive. She was more worried about Gable himself than Crawford. Although Carole sometimes admitted to a lingering ego-based rivalry with Joan that carried over from the Charleston contests of their teens, a deeper personal friendship had developed between them over the years. Carole was rather more concerned about the likely sexual distraction for Gable in his picture assignment to follow *Strange Cargo.*

While Carole and Charles Laughton at least thought *They Knew What They Wanted,* Clark and Spencer Tracy figured that any place having a Hedy Lamarr as well as a Myrna Loy had to be a *Boom Town.* The Viennese import named Hedy was perhaps the most beautiful creature ever to enter American films, beyond which her sexual generosity was already widely rumored. Carole heard talk that Miss Lamarr had already invited the attentions of the responsive King. When Carole completed her picture with Laughton, she hustled off to Texas to join Gable for location filming on *Boom Town* only to find that the location scenes did not require Hedy's presence.

Spencer Tracy attempted to persuade Carole that she didn't have to worry about Clark staying true-blue, but Carole said, "Spence, this is one time you're a less than convincing actor." She despaired when Clark's next picture, *Comrade X,* also listed Miss Lamarr as his costar. And she heard more talk. Without another immediate assignment of her own, she became a not-very-subtle watchdog at her husband's M-G-M set. Clark did not easily accept being spied upon, and the first rumors bubbled that he was tiring of his marital arrangement.

There was no indication that Carole was tiring. In a memoir issued much later, Garson Kanin (Carole's director for *They Knew What They Wanted*) gave his own account of Carole's protestation that she loved Clark despite his clumsiness in the sack. ("I mean I'm nuts about *him,* not about his nuts.") Perhaps the romance was becoming one-sided.

They Knew What They Wanted was fourth in her unbroken succession of dramatic roles, despite indications that a return to comedy was advisable. Disillusioned in the unhappy aftermath of *Vigil in the Night,* she felt a professional need to get back into lighter harness. Jean Arthur was still scoring at her own specialty line with *Too Many Husbands;* and also at Columbia, Rosalind Russell was getting the great laughs as *His Girl Friday.* Harry Cohn had wanted Carole for that one, which would have reunited her with Howard Hawks, her *Twentieth Century* director. But Cohn already had overextended himself financially, and simply couldn't meet Myron Selznick's Lombard price tag. So Carole audited every script in the RKO inventory but found no comedy to her liking. She was not especially beguiled by *They Knew What They Wanted,* although she saw good qualities in the script. As was often the case, she accepted the assignment because some talented people were involved: Garson Kanin, a bright young director putting together a string of hits; and Harry Stradling, one of the great cinematographers.

It was the familiar yarn about the Italian winemaker in California's Napa Valley, and his disillusioned mail-order bride. Sidney Howard's play, a prize-winner in its day, had starred Pauline Lord and Richard Bennett—Joan's and Constance's papa. It had been filmed twice before, most recently as an early talkie at M-G-M. Sweden's great Victor Seastrom directed that version, which was considered a disaster. Edward G. Robinson had played the winemaker, before *Little Caesar* blueprinted his destiny; and the Hungarian beauty of the silents, Vilma Banky, struggled with the English language for the only time on film. On the other hand, the Lombard-Laughton edition marginally was a hit.

Charles Laughton was nobody's Italian, but that didn't diminish his authority. The general agreement was that it was Carole's picture, although William Gargan was outstanding as the stud filling out the eternal triangle. Reliable Harry Carey was in the cast along with Frank Fay, whose comeback failed to materialize; he played the priest. Released in mid-autumn of 1940, *They Knew What They Wanted* did solid but not spectacular business, got all favorable reviews but no raves, and incited no speculation of an Academy Award nomination for Carole. Bill Gargan picked up a supporting nomination, but Charles Laughton and Carole both lost out.

The ultimate disposition of the 1940 Oscars offered a touch of irony. RKO had secured the film rights to *They Knew What They Wanted* because they thought it an appropriate vehicle for displaying the dramatic progress of Ginger Rogers. Since the decline of Ann Harding and the departure of Katharine Hepburn, Ginger had been RKO's only major female star . . . until Carole Lombard signed on. When Carole expressed interest in *They Knew What They Wanted,* the studio deferred to her and assigned Ginger to *Kitty Foyle* instead. And Ginger won the Oscar. It wasn't that most people thought her portrayal superior to Miss Hepburn's Tracy Lord in *The Philadelphia Story.* Ginger won mainly on the departure psychology that Carole had supposed would be in her own favor. *Kitty Foyle* merely proved that she was a dramatic actress as well as a musical comedienne.

Yet Carole considered *They Knew What They Wanted* a worthwhile experience that had introduced her to people whose talents she valued highly. And as usual, the admiration was mutual. Garson Kanin didn't stop at perfunctory acknowledgment of Carole's acting skill and good fellowship; he called her the best producer in the business since Irving Thalberg. "She has great intuition for which writer to get on a script. She knows what kind of story to do and can give pointers in its structure. And she's a great saleswoman. She has one of the best agents in the business but she really doesn't need one. She makes her own deals and does as well as anyone could."

Harry Stradling marveled that Carole knew "as much about the tricks of the trade as I do." He explained that in close-up photography he wanted to cover her scar simply by focusing the lights on her face so it would seem to blend with her cheek. "But she told me a diffusing glass in my lens would do the job better . . . and you know, she was right!"

Charles Laughton's comments about his leading lady were rather more reserved. When she had been his *White Woman* in 1933, she'd said he was so good he made her earlobes tingle, but they didn't tingle during *They Knew What They Wanted*. At Paramount she had been awed by him and hadn't objected to his giving her a hard time, throwing his experience at her as well as his considerable weight. She hadn't forgotten, though, and after seven years she was in a mood to reply in kind. She played a needling game with him, always forgiving *his* lack of experience ("I mean in pictures, Charlie.") compared with her own. And she was delighted by Laughton's dismay when he saw the initial sketches for the advertising campaign and realized he was not to have the lead billing.

"Oh deah me. It hadn't occurred to me . . . I mean, well, I rather assumed . . ."

"I know what you're thinking, Charlie. You remember that when we did *White Woman* it was Laughton and Lombard. Well you see, when Paramount couldn't decide, they just did things alphabetically, so you won."

"Oh. I see. Then tell me, Miss Lombard: how do they *do things* here at RKO when they can't decide?"

"Why, Charlie, that's easy. RKO always bills according to salary. I thought everybody knew *that*. Come to think of it, maybe my letters should be *twice* as big as yours."

Laughton investigated. Yes, lead billing was a stipulation of the Lombard contract; and yes, her salary was exactly double his own. But Carole was unrelenting.

"About that little matter of billing, Charlie, I apologize. The order is correct, but so are the letters. Yours should be every bit as big as mine. Ain't that swell?"

"Why, it's marvelous, Miss Lombard. I wonder if there's a logical explanation?"

"There sure as hell is, kiddo. They're giving you a special allowance on the ego factor."

In later years Charles Laughton would recall Carole with genuine affection, but also suggested that her charm often obscured what he thought was a ruthless ambition.

In earlier years Carole had sounded almost lazy in her self-depreciation and her lack of ambition for a really important stardom. She had been "lucky just to be in the movies, to be working at something she liked to do." She had no pretention of being a genuine actress or any other kind of artist. She just wanted to keep busy at the work she enjoyed. Later, having acquired the major stardom she said she hadn't sought, she talked of quitting the screen just to keep house for Clark—that she didn't need to act. But during the period of *Vigil in the Night* and *They Knew What They Wanted* she gave interviews that reversed all previous judgments of her motivation.

She spoke frankly of her sharp decline in popularity, and admitted that it bothered her plenty. Yes, recovering the ground she had lost was her priority objective.

"Now I know what they mean about wanting water when the well runs dry; and honestly, boys, I need some rain."

And, "They used to call me a clotheshorse. I hated that description, and the pictures that brought it about. But let it be arranged again. I want to wear some gorgeous clothes again, in a smart drawing-room comedy. I haven't had decent clothes on in years, unless that nurse's uniform I wore all through *Vigil* really gets you going."

And then, "All this talk about the mistake I made switching from comedies to heavy stuff—well, it wasn't that much of a studied thing. I just took the best scripts that came my way and they turned out to be serious. I have no real preference. If it's a good part in a good story, that's all that counts."

And finally, "I'm definitely going back into comedy, and I mean *permanently*. Some people will say I've been scared off by drama and that's not true. I know what I can do, and perhaps I'll do an occasional heavy story, but primarily I've got to go the screwball route. I *am* scared by the apparent proof that my name doesn't sell tickets to serious pictures. It's obvious that the public prefers I do comedy, and I think I owe them something. After all, they've made me rich. But the truth is, I regard comedy as more difficult than drama. In a straight part you react as you would react in real life. In comedy you have to do the unexpected."

Carole told the Hollywood *Citizen-News*'s Hazel Flynn that "There's been a lot of talk about me retiring from the screen, and I've thought a lot about it. There have been times when I thought I wanted to, but the only thing that could bring that about would be a baby. Even then, I really couldn't quit. I've said I could, and now I know better. This business is in my blood. I don't mean acting, I mean making movies. God, I love it. I think now I would die without it. Clark, if he had a choice, would rather be on the stage, God knows why. If he never made another movie it wouldn't bother him a bit. But I think your destiny gets shaped as a child, and I was a kid here. I grew up in Hollywood, and this is my culture. I don't necessarily have to act, and I don't want to direct. But produce, maybe, and don't laugh. If I had my choice of being anybody else, I think I'd rather be David Selznick."

Clark Gable choked when he read the last sentence.

In the meantime, Carole and the man she would have liked to have been had committed their producer-star relationship to a secretive amicable divorce. After *Nothing Sacred* and *Made for Each Other* she still owed David Selznick one picture, and the pleasant outcome of both of those ventures disposed her favorably not only to completing the contract, but to extending it—as she expected Myron to request of his brother. But David's experience with Clark Gable on *Gone With the Wind* changed that. The following letter, dated January 22, 1940, and marked PERSONAL explains everything:

Dear Carole:

I have received your messages through Myron and am anxious to get together on the Krasna idea, as soon as possible.

Before we proceed, there is something I would like to discuss with you very frankly. Are you sure, Carole, that we should make another picture together? I know from countless sources how highly you think of me, both as a person and a producer, and this is a source of great gratification to me. And I shall always look back on our past associations as among the most pleasant of my career. Certainly I have always held you up as the shining example of what a joy it can be to work with a star when that star appreciates a producer's problems and cooperates in their solution. But I must face the fact that you are now married to Clark, and that Clark obviously feels quite differently about me.

I had hoped that my dealings with Clark on *Gone With the Wind* would disabuse him of any notions he had about me. I cannot think of any particular in which I would have gone further to make him happy in anything ranging from his costumes to such important factors as the script and direction. I even cost myself a very substantial amount of money through keeping him idle, and paying his salary, in order to accommodate him on the schedule as he desired. All through the picture he was frank in expressing his suspicions that I intended to do him in, and I kept pleading with him to wait until the picture was finished and then tell me his opinion. I was under the impression that he was delighted with the final result, but he apparently disassociates me from this final result, if I am to judge what has been reported back to me, and from items in the press. I regret this more than I can say, because there has been nothing whatsoever on my side against Clark; and because, as I have repeatedly told him, he contributed in my opinion a really great performance to the effort that meant so much to me.

But if I couldn't and didn't satisfy myself, as person or producer, on *Gone With the Wind*, it is not likely that anything I could ever do with him or with his wife would change his opinion. On the contrary, it is much more likely that anything we did together would be regarded by him with suspicion; and that you would be forever in the position of having to defend me and my motives to him; that if everything turned out all right, it would still not obviate any embarrassment you may be under through working with me, any more than *Gone With the Wind* did; and that if things turned out badly, he would have the confirmation of his opinions and suspicions to point to. Neither of us is used to such strained and peculiar situations as that on the night of the local opening of *Gone With the Wind,* when I like to believe we should have been in each other's arms. I certainly recognize the awkward position you are in, and cannot expect to come out on the right side when your loyalties are divided. And perhaps some day in the future, attitudes may change, as they do in this business, and it will again be possible for you to do a picture for me with the wholehearted pleasure we once both knew in our endeavors.

The decision is entirely yours. You would suffer much more from the repercussions in your personal life than I would; and I can stand it if you can. My principal thought in writing this letter is to tell you that freely, and with my blessings and steadfast affection, I will relieve you of your obligation to do a picture for me, provided that I know in sufficient time to avoid making any commitments for it. And believe me, whichever way you decide, Carole Lombard can have no more earnest fan, personally or as an actress, than

> Yours, affectionately and sincerely,
> David

Clark Gable never knew of the letter's content or even of its existence. Carole accepted her release from any obligation to David, but in a later meeting with him she said she hoped they could eventually work together again under conditions more amenable to their collaboration. But the letter may have been a factor in causing further erosion of her faith in Myron Selznick.

In her mind Myron began to emerge as the villain, through his neglect and disinterest, in what she feared was the near-collapse of her career. She said that making her own deals had not been her idea, but was merely her reaction to Myron's inertia. She learned through intermediary sources, after she had signed with RKO, that she could have had her pick of all the studios, at the same price and with other generous terms and conditions. While concentrating on the benefit of his other clients, Myron no longer approached the studios on Carole's behalf. He fielded an overture from 20th Century-Fox with "Get hold of Lombard yourself, she talks her own business." She saw him now as a parasite, and held him responsible for the de facto cancellation of her pact with David, because Myron had made no effort to resolve the problem. She was contracted as Myron's client through 1943, but she wanted to be rid of him and requested a contractual release. Myron refused, so she took him to court.

It was a strange litigation. Carole insisted that she "loved the guy personally, but lately he's done nothing for me." Myron similarly refused to disparage Carole personally, and privately blamed Clark Gable for estranging him from his favorite client. It was the first known case of an actor suing for release from his own agent, so it became the precedent example for Hollywood.

Both sides claimed victory in the settlement; but viewed as precedent, the decision favored the agent. Carole won her release but she had to pay for it. In addition to costs of a distended court proceeding, she was ordered to yield a sum of $27,500 to Myron, based on unpaid agent commissions and his percentage of her income as projected through 1943. According to the resolution, the money Myron collected included his commission for one picture Carole never made, and his percentage of her theoretical income over a two-year period in which she was not even alive. Carole was disappointed by the decision but not overcome by it. She was happy to be free of the man who, many years ago and before she deserved it, had got her into the big money. Myron, on the other hand, was convinced that the legal action had damaged his reputation irreparably, and used it as further justification for drowning himself in liquor. In 1944 he was dead, victim of his own excesses at age forty-five.

Nat Wolff, a friend of Clark's, became Carole's agent in 1941 and negotiated her last two contract agreements, both of them as a free-lance artist. The final commitment was never fulfilled.

The last of her four RKO pictures, and her only comedy there, was *Mr. and Mrs. Smith,* filmed late in 1940 and released in the early spring of 1941. This was the Norman Krasna story referenced obliquely in the opening sentence of David Selznick's touching letter to Carole. It also had a Selznick connection: it was directed by an extravagantly talented Englishman brought over by Selznick to preside over *Rebecca,* the project that followed *Gone With the Wind* on Selznick's schedule. He was a chubby, acerbic chap, by name of Alfred Hitchcock; and *Mr. and Mrs. Smith* is the least representative of his American films. Without so much as an elusive shading of melodrama, its objective was screwball farce.

RKO paid the purchase price of the script on Carole's behalf, but without nominal credit Carole nevertheless accomplished one of her capricious objectives: she became the operative producer. She chose the director, cast the picture, selected virtually the entire crew, and oversaw adherence to the budget.

Harry Stradling, again her lensman, endorsed Carole's extraordinary notion that Alfred Hitchcock should direct. Carole met Hitchcock socially through David Selznick shortly after Hitchcock's arrival in Hollywood, and he rented her house in Bel-Air when Carole occupied the Encino ranch with Gable. She had been enjoying Hitchcock's British melodramas for years, but in all of them she detected an adroitness for humor that was the match for his bag of suspense tricks. In 1940 two classic American films bore his signature, with *Rebecca* followed by *Foreign Correspondent.* He was engaged on the latter venture and not yet committed to a third U.S. project when Carole asked if he'd like to do a screwball comedy. Hitchcock said not particularly, but that her participation might make him more enthusiastic. She asked Hitchcock if he would direct *Mr. and Mrs. Smith.* He replied that he was a gentleman, and that he acquiesced a lady whenever it was within his power.

They both wanted Cary Grant. Wanting Cary had become the reflex notion of anyone making a comedy, but they found they'd have to wait two years to get him. Carole and Hitchcock agreed that the only other Hollywood actor in Cary's class as a light comedian was Robert Montgomery. Hitchcock thought it remarkable that Lombard and Montgomery could both have been in Hollywood so long without having worked together. He suspected they might have been one of the all-time great teams, at the Tracy-Hepburn level. *Mr. and Mrs. Smith* was the sort of verbal sparring match that subsequently would represent the Tracy-Hepburn partnership. Carole and Montgomery enacted a married couple, irresistibly in love but bred for battle. The gimmick, not so shopworn *then,* was the discovery after so many years that there was a legal slip-up and they weren't officially married. Since the disclosure occurred while they were on the outs, there would be a parting until their capitulation to the happy ending dictated by formula. But even formula comedy could spell fun when engaging clowns were plying their craft.

The Smiths' romantic triangle had a third side, for which Carole reached into her professional past to restore a fading career—Gene Raymond's. A "new" Gene Raymond: this blondest of leading men dyed his hair black for the occasion and emerged an entirely new personality, farcically able and a rather tolerable "other man" under Hitchcock's administration.

The farce atmosphere inspired Carole to reclaim her behind-the-scenes jester's scepter. An unhappy actor's remark that Hitchcock "herded his actors like cattle" had made the traffic of gossip; so when the *Smith* production commenced, Carole had a tiny corral rigged up setside, with three young heiffers contained therein, bearing the labels of Lombard, Montgomery, and Raymond.

Carole also had fun at Montgomery's expense. It was an election year, and Franklin Roosevelt was victorious in his third-term bid for President while the picture was in mid-production. Carole was for Roosevelt, but Montgomery was just then beginning to work his way into strategic responsibility in California's Republican Party organization, and was a strong supporter of the Wendell Willkie candidacy. Carole would lurk in the dark brush of the studio lot; and after Bob had parked his car and reported in for his working day, she would plaster his Rolls-Royce with Roosevelt bumper stickers that proved difficult to remove. Somehow they would get removed, but Carole would have another supply ready.

In the published record of his famous extended interview with France's Francois Truffaut, Hitchcock shows no real interest in *Mr. and Mrs. Smith* and makes no claim for its excellence. He says he took the job only as a favor to Carole Lombard. Like everyone else, he admired her as person and artist, and said she was one of those special people who was destined to succeed in whatever endeavor she had undertaken.

Although not really deserving of scorn, *Mr. and Mrs. Smith* has also been knocked about by adherents of the *auteur* theory of film criticism. The contemporary reviews, too, were only lukewarm. The comedy ignited, but a good many critics believed Hitchcock was wasting his talent or his time or both. But the picture reversed the *Vigil in the Night* pattern. The box-office response was initially lively, and favorable word of mouth built a major commercial hit. Had *Mr. and Mrs. Smith* been in the earlier succession of premium Lombard vehicles—ideally as the follow project for *True Confession* that *Fools for Scandal* wrongly was—it might have looked right in place and have given her career added momentum. As it was, the belated happy news was that Carole Lombard was a screwball once more, and she felt she'd turned a corner and was headed back home.

Earlier Carole had agreed to extend her RKO pact by one year, for two additional pictures. Then there was an administrative upheaval. Pandro Berman, who had been in charge of RKO production, elected to become a smaller animal in a larger zoo, moving over to M-G-M as a producer with the Mayer team. Carole was not impressed by the men who took control of the studio. She thought that Charles Koerner, who took Berman's job, knew nothing about the movie game except how to operate a theater. Koerner was economy-minded and couldn't understand why Carole Lombard was entitled to so much of the studio's money. So Carole found herself released from commitment to the studio at the same time that she purchased her freedom from her old agent.

Despite indications that the *Smith* picture was rehabilitating her as a commercial draw, her established price was regarded as too luxurious. No more than half a dozen bona fide stars were then functioning exclusively as free lancers without at least a partial studio tie-in, and not even a Cary Grant commanded a per-picture fee in six figures. At about the same time, M-G-M paid Fredric March $100,000 to hold Joan Crawford's coat in *Susan and God* and L. B. Mayer's extravagance was criticized throughout the industry, whose pendulum again was swinging toward economy. Scripts kept coming Carole's way; there were some interesting feelers but no firm offers. The way Nat Wolff read the meter, Carole couldn't expect to obtain much work unless her price came down.

Carole's own assessment was that she had her RKO fling at precisely the wrong time. The studio had known better days; and later, in the mid-forties, it would experience another bountiful era. But she hit it on a downslide, when it made some good pictures and didn't know how to sell them; when it signed on some promising talent but didn't know how to develop it; and when it was rather at a loss for effective marketing of the star power it did possess.

Carole said the remarkable thing about both M-G-M and Warner Brothers was that for all the infighting that went on in those places, the people in charge stayed in charge. As a result, there was job security at every level, which translated onto the screen as consistent studio "styles." The turmoil of the turnovers she survived at Paramount could drive a person dizzy, and she knew it was much the same story at Fox—or at least it had been prior to the big studio's capitulative merger with Darryl Zanuck's 20th Century company.

M-G-M, Warners, Paramount, and 20th-Fox were the undisputed

Big Four; but by extension RKO-Radio made it a legitimate Big Five. Exhibitors had become quite vocal about their preference for Columbia product, but neither Columbia nor Universal could challenge for supremacy because they lacked the theatrical holdings such as RKO possessed in abundance. Yet RKO had been a suspiciously unstable scene from the time of Carole's arrival there. In two years she failed to recognize a characteristic studio style, and she often said she wished they'd put her in charge of the place for just a few months.

She thought that in a better-articulated studio operation, some of the young people under RKO contract could have been brought along to major stardom almost effortlessly—particularly the likes of Anne Shirley, Dennis O'Keefe, and Charles Laughton's new discovery, the incredibly beautiful Maureen O'Hara. Most of all Carole was smitten by the virtuoso skill she detected in a saucy, unmistakably individual girl named Lucille Ball. Carole asked Pandro Berman if the company was unable to recognize champion stock when it winked right at them. Berman said they all knew the Ball girl was talented, and that was why they kept her on. Why, everybody *loved* Lucy, but she obviously wasn't star material or it would have been found out. The thinking obviously was that a girl was going to make it pretty quickly or not make it at all. For an ingenue, Lucille Ball was an old war-horse—she'd been at the studio five or six years and was taken for granted, a sort of amiable commodity.

While Carole was filming *They Knew What They Wanted,* the Rodgers & Hart *Too Many Girls* was getting its screen treatment on an adjacent RKO sound stage. Carole had several opportunities to slip over and watch the exuberant doings at Pottawottamie College. Brought in from the stage company to repeat his role on the screen was a Cuban boy named Desi Arnaz. He was almost a threat to steal the picture from such a trained thief as Lucy, but not quite. Carole saw that Señor Arnaz had a crush on Miss Ball; but no one could have foreseen that hardly more than a dozen years later, Lucy and Desi would own the studio.

Only a matter of months later, another newcomer from Broadway would stir up RKO and its environs as never before or again. Orson Welles, that young Man from Mars, got himself and his Mercury Players into a group contract to make some RKO pictures under his own direction. The Welles egomania proved more captivating than terrifying, and Carole endorsed the consensus that Orson was a likely genius. She could meet him conversationally at his own level. They liked one another.

That was when Carole was trying to decide on renewing her RKO pact or pursuing the dubious liberty of free-lancing. Orson Welles almost talked her into staying at RKO and joining his Mercury core. He had a melodramatic script that she rather liked. She hesitated accepting even an alluring opportunity that would keep her from such frolicsome business as she thought was her immediate need. The Welles project was *Smiler with a Knife* and Orson said he couldn't do it as a picture unless it had Carole Lombard, whose personality was strategic to its design. Otherwise, he'd have to find another property or write something himself. Carole thanked him for the flattery but opted for the Smiths of screwball country as her RKO swan song. Thus was the course of cinema history altered significantly by Carole's whim, for Orson Welles abandoned *Smiler with a Knife* and thought of something else to do.

He and Herman Mankiewicz devised *Citizen Kane*.

Carole was not dismayed by the absence of other lush offers. She reasoned that an extended holiday from movie making might be beneficial all the way around. She noted that both Norma Shearer and Greta Garbo had been off the screen for two years at a time, then had made trumpeted returns—one as Marie Antoinette, the other as Ninotchka—amid intimations of enhanced prestige. Carole was not contemplating retirement, but the strategic thing was to bide her time and come storming back in something that was really first-rate. Upon completing *Mr. and Mrs. Smith,* it would be almost a full year until she faced the cameras once more.

Well, she needed a rest. And since she had gotten back into steady work, things had fallen behind at the ranch. She had to determine her own priorities.

The most important consideration was saving her marriage.

❋ XIV ❋

Print the Legend

In THAT sunny, beguiling western land of most wishful fiction, they were Hollywood's own Great Love Story.

King and Queen were they, and their romance was made in heaven. Screenplay by William Shakespeare . . . with additional dialogue by *Photoplay, Modern Screen, Motion Picture, Silver Screen, Movie Mirror, Screenland,* and the *Readers' Digest.*

Amid all the broken dreams and marriages, theirs was the one that most desperately had to last. Well, it did last: a thousand-day royal union terminated only by death. And yes, it was a great love story, after all.

Hollywood has known more than a few. Mary Pickford and Douglas Fairbanks—that was a great love story. Laurence Olivier and Vivien Leigh. Elizabeth Taylor and Richard Burton. Of such is the stuff of legend, for being rich in drama as well as romance. What matter that they do not end happily ever after? The truth is that great loves, like all great lives, are never the easy ones. The greatest love stories are the most difficult ones, with a boldness to challenge the most formidable obstacles.

When fate sealed the legend and outlined the myth of Gable and Lombard, the obstacles were intact and the stability of their union was shrouded in doubt. Or what is truth? Talking about Clark and Carole, the people who knew them best often recited similar platitudes but with varying inflections. And sometimes the dialogue was not the same at all. Clark Gable's pals seldom disputed the legend of the ideal marriage; and Jean Garceau, the efficient business manager Gable shared with Carole and then inherited from her, enforces it with authority. But Mrs. Garceau more easily invokes the Gable perspective. She remained in Clark's employ to the end of his own life. The people who were closest to Carole tend to a more cynical view of the famous Hollywood marriage.

Shortly after Carole's death, Stuart Peters received a curtly worded message from Clark Gable. As Carole's primary heir, Gable held Stuart's I.O.U. to his sister—a matter of seventy-five dollars. He wanted to collect. The demand shattered the uneasy friendship that had existed between Carole's two brothers and Gable, permanently estranging them from him. Years after Stuart's own death as well as Gable's, the surviving Fred Peters made his position perfectly clear to hopeful interviewers. He would talk about his sister; but he would not discuss her marriage to Gable, or talk about Clark in any way. Madalynne Fields Lang also shunned invitations to comment on the fabled union.

Carole's longtime friend William Haines said frankly that the marriage could not have endured. Despite her great spirit of tolerance, he said, she would finally have refused "to give and not receive." Ernst Lubitsch, who was about as fond of Clark as were, say, the brothers Selznick, was quoted in Hazel Flynn's column shortly after Carole's death: "The romance had ended, but the marriage lingered on." Mitchell Leisen also thought Carole had reached the end of her rope, while Marion Davies—always a devoted friend to Carole with loyalty also to Clark—said there had been some real problems but they hadn't been beyond solving.

Dixie Pantages Karlson, whose friendship with Carole was the longest in duration and the most intimate and confidential in character, said, "The marriage would have lasted because Carole would have made it last. Clark had things more or less as he wanted them and Carole knew he would never leave her. She had decided to make the best of things, even if it meant putting on a show. But the 'great love' you heard about . . . well, it was far from that."

Even Louella Parsons, whose reporting on the Gable-Lombard courtship and marriage never resembled anything other than a fairy tale, altered her stance during a fit of pique toward Gable while he was married to Sylvia Ashley. Parsons implied that Clark had been an errant husband to Carole, thus extracting some revenge for the broken promise of a "scoop" on their 1939 nuptials. (The old wound apparently never healed. In his dual biography *Hedda and Louella*, George Eels rather touchingly characterizes a pathetic, senile Parsons near the end of her days in nursing-home retirement, mumbling through tears while watching a Gable movie on TV: "Clark! Tell me—when are you and Carole going to tie the knot? Remember, I must be the first to know!")

Hedda Hopper's own memories suggested that the Gable-Lombard marriage was less than idyllic, but she had dutifully characterized it as that. Neither Hedda nor Louella encouraged or even acknowledged the separation rumors that plagued the Gables throughout 1941. Jimmy Fidler was the first to hint an impending breakup that never materialized, but Walter Winchell was the primary oracle for a "splituation." The rumors undoubtedly were fed by the Gables' suddenly putting their Encino ranch on the market in 1941. They showed the house to several prospective buyers, then withdrew it from the available list—thereby encouraging a "reconciliation" although there had been no separation. Carole explained that they had decided to sell because their house had become too well known, a showplace; but that they changed their minds when they realized how much the place had come to mean to them. Hearers were skeptical, even when Carole added guest rooms and a swimming pool—more to pacify Clark's friends than her own.

After Gable filmed *They Met in Bombay* with Rosalind Russell, he and Carole almost lost touch with the film community. During extended absences from the ranch they kept in contact only with Carole's mother and with Gable's reliable Man Friday, Otto Winkler; but even Winkler could not dissuade the speculative reporters from thinking all was not well with the Gables.

The Gables might take a long holiday to Oregon's Rogue River country, or shorter-term junkets to Lake Meade or Ensenada, in Baja California. Carole still derived pleasure from Clark's preferred pastimes, but he was less flexible than she: he still scorned the more intellectual life that she sometimes craved, and seemed increasingly jealous of Carole's relatively sophisticated circle from which he pointedly excluded himself.

Carole was not entirely successful at holding her own jealousies in check. Outwardly she tolerated Clark's rumored passing affairs as dalliances that meant nothing to him personally. He seemed to endorse the double-standard morality she loathed, and she knew Clark would not approve any messing around on her part. His blithely managed infidelities finally aroused her indignation. Although the stories involving Hedy Lamarr would subside, there would be new gossip. It might involve girls who were almost anonymous, or someone as topical as M-G-M's latest hard-sell project, the blond Lana Turner.

Perhaps Carole believed that a baby would serve as the only adhesive her marriage required. Early in 1941 she accompanied Clark Gable to Baltimore's Johns Hopkins Medical Center, where Gable ostensibly was going to have a shoulder ailment studied—one dating several years back, to a movie-making accident. Their primary reason for going was physical examinations for both of them— probing Carole's fertility and Clark's potency. Previously Carole had denied vigorously, but "with regret," occasional rumors that she was pregnant. The Johns Hopkins visit established that there was no physical reason for their inability to conceive. Being able to carry to full duration might have been foreseen as Carole's likely problem, and she had neither confirmed nor convincingly denied persistent reports of early miscarriage. She did say that on a trip to Mexico following the checkups at Johns Hopkins, she spent most of her and Clark's time trying to become pregnant.

Carole attributed her barrenness to a growing tension, of which she was especially aware after M-G-M got Clark into the *Honky Tonk* assignment with Lana Turner as his costar. Gable was reported enthusiastic about the western yarn with a he-man role made to order for him, but the chatter was that he was interested in the picture's fringe benefits—the same ones responsible for Carole's tension. Carole's assessment was that *Honky Tonk* was warmed-over stuff, a lame script.

Both *Strange Cargo* with Crawford and *Comrade X* with Hedy Lamarr had failed to perform at the box office as Gable pictures usually did, and not much was expected of *They Met in Bombay*. M-G-M had a whopping hit with *Boom Town* but multiple star power was cited, and there was renewed speculation that The King might be slipping. He needed a strong picture, and Carole thought he should be doing better than *Honky Tonk*. She found a script that Clark had brought home to read, and decided that *Woman of the Year* was a terrific property for Clark Gable and an agile actress —why not herself? Subsequent revelation that Katharine Hepburn had owned the property and sold it to M-G-M with herself in the package as star was briefly a personal disappointment to Carole, but Carole held to the opinion that it augured a good part for Gable.

Clark didn't think so. Although the screenplay reportedly had been fashioned for both Miss Hepburn *and* Spencer Tracy, he thought the woman's role was much the stronger. Besides, he didn't want to have anything to do with Hepburn. The part was available to him because Spencer Tracy couldn't do it—he was committed to *The Yearling,* which had just been put into production for a long schedule. Despite the urging of his studio and encouragement from Carole, Gable said he'd stick with *Honky Tonk.*

After *The Yearling* was canceled—although it was filmed years later with Gregory Peck in the role originally intended for Tracy— *Woman of the Year* got under way and initiated the famous Tracy-Hepburn team that most people prejudged as cockeyed. Soon it was also obvious that Tracy and Miss Hepburn, who previously had not been acquainted, already were more than mere costars to one another. When Carole accompanied Gable to M-G-M for the first studio screening of *Woman of the Year,* Gable reprised his enormous admiration of Tracy, who by canny underplaying had easily held his own against the prodigious Hepburn talent. Carole thought the picture was a humdinger, and when Gable said, "See? I could never have done with that part the things Spence does for it," she disagreed. "Hell yes, you could. You'd deliver for George Stevens [the director] in your own way, not Spence's, and if you worked with Kate you'd be great. The part was made for you. And it could have been written for me as easily as for her. It's the kind of picture we should be doing together."

Publicly she insisted that the Gables would not appear as costars, because "I think a husband and wife working together would be seeing too damn much of each other. It might do something to a swell relationship." Yet she continued to audit the story department's inventory for something agreeable to the two of them. Although she had little chance of blocking the *Honky Tonk* venture that only she disparaged, Carole almost engineered a Gable-Lombard occasion at M-G-M in *Miss Achilles' Heel,* later transmuted into a mildly screwballian *Design for Scandal* with Rosalind Russell and Walter Pidgeon. Now and then she even hinted that only a picture with Gable was likely to end the longest period of inactivity she had known in Hollywood.

When Clark completed *Honky Tonk* in the early fall of 1941, he and Carole went off to hunt duck and pheasant in the vague marshes and meadows of South Dakota. The exile prodded new intimations of marital unrest, with Winchell again the leading doomsayer. In an anthology of inaccurate reporting, Gable was thought to be doing the Dakota badlands as a solo, while Carole pined alone, at home in bed where she was also possibly dying of some dreadful and mysterious malady. They were alone together in Watertown, South Dakota, when they heard the Winchell testament. Another newscaster contradicted Winchell's revelation that the Gables were 2,000 miles apart, indicating that they were together after all but were "fighting, fighting, fighting." Carole could hatch her own contradictions. She told one group of newsmen that when Gable heard the reports, he smashed the portable radio against some rocks; and on another occasion she said he blasted the radio to smithereens with a shotgun.

Gable resented any invasion of privacy and never adjusted to having his personal life served up for public consumption. Carole played the Hollywood game more adroitly, often feigning anger when she was more accurately only amused. She would be exasperated, however, by telephone calls to the ranch at all hours, inquiring if the Gable marriage was still intact. Once she raged over the phone at a personal friend whose call to check out the troublesome rumors had interrupted a connubial adventure.

Upon their return to California, Carole issued a playful statement to the effect that "I ain't dying and I ain't divorcing Clark. I simply ain't any of the things they say." A severe attack of poison oak was Carole's nearest brush with the specter of death in 1941, but she remained prone to head colds and a creeping anemia. These she privately attributed to a general tension. Her prospects for recovery were hardly improved by reports that the M-G-M bosses were so taken with the Gable-Turner showing in *Honky Tonk* that they wanted to get Lana in another picture with The King right away. And The King thought it was a great idea, since it was his own. M-G-M was developing a romance-and-action yarn called *Somewhere I'll Find You* as a Gable vehicle, with the likelihood of promoting one of the newer studio actresses—perhaps Laraine Day or Ruth Hussey—as the love interest. Gable said he'd much prefer Lana Turner, and that settled it.

Rather suddenly, Carole got back to work before Clark did.

During a year-long layoff she had investigated scores of scripts without finding the sure things she knew her instincts could detect. She was thinking comeback, although there was no popular notion of her having been away. Counting all the films of her big-star period, she rated only *Fools for Scandal* as a total failure and did not regard her RKO tenure as a fatal mistake. But it had been too long since she had starred in an unqualified smash hit, and she held firm that only a venture offering that expectation would get her before the cameras once more. Over at Columbia, Harry Cohn was making interesting talk about a contract. He said frankly that he couldn't meet Carole's flat price, but could favor her with participation in the profits. Cohn had a comedy script called *He Kissed the Bride* and Carole liked it—but not enough. She said it would serve nicely as a follow-up picture to a successfully launched comeback, but that her immediate need was something more substantial than a diverting trifle. Then she heard about *To Be or Not to Be.*

It was a Lubitsch picture, and the way she became a part of it recalled her formative years at Paramount, when she was a sort of benchwarmer for Miriam Hopkins. Ever the Hopkins admirer, Ernst Lubitsch had envisioned *To Be or Not to Be* as *her* comeback picture. Actually it was a vehicle for a male star, and Lubitsch wanted Jack Benny. The nation's foremost radio comedian was then at the crest of his brief celebrity as a movie regular, having delivered a devastating *Charley's Aunt.* Broadly cartooning Germany's Nazis, *To Be or Not to Be* offered Benny the richly farcical role of "that great, *great* Polish actor, Joseph Tura." The Turas were a troupe of ham actors who would somehow turn the tables on Hitler's lunkheads, with Maria Tura essentially serving as decorative straight man for her husband.

Lubitsch was making *To Be or Not to Be* independently because none of the likely studios wished to get involved in a Nazified slapstick. It was more than two years since *Confessions of a Nazi Spy* had knocked the props from Hollywood's pose of international neutrality, and anti-Nazi propaganda had become a common ingredient of many dramatic American films. But in late 1941 the thinking in Hollywood as elsewhere was that the U.S. was moving inevitably toward all-out war with Hitler's Germany, and that a spoofing of the Nazis might well be the untimeliest thing. Lubitsch was having difficulty obtaining financing for the venture, and there were personality problems as well. Jack Benny and Miriam Hopkins had an uneasy relationship, and Miriam was fretting to have her part built up.

Carole learned of Lubitsch's predicament from Edna Best, the English actress who was then married to Nat Wolff, agent for Carole's dormant career. Wolff did not see *To Be or Not to Be* as a Lombard possibility; but Carole trusted Lubitsch's judgment. If he liked something enough to want to make it independently, it must be pretty funny. The quality of the picture ultimately would be more important than the size of her role, she reckoned. Besides, she had always wanted to do a Lubitsch film, and never had.

Lubitsch was delighted—flattered, he said—by Carole's interest, but did not expect her to remain enamored of the project after reading the script. He explained that Maria Tura was hardly more than a foil—very nearly a supporting role, but not quite. But in a quick reading Carole sensed discovery of the great comedy she'd been scouting. She thought Lubitsch's notion of using Jack Benny was sheer genius; and while the Maria Tura role was less showy, she found it challenging and also strategic to the design of a comedy that worked on several levels. She contacted Miriam Hopkins personally, and after Miriam's official withdrawal everything fell into place. With Carole Lombard included in his package, Lubitsch had no difficulty obtaining complete financing. That factor enabled Jack Benny to swallow his pride and yield top billing to Carole. She said, "Isn't it only fair, Jack, since you already have all the lines?"

Shooting began in October, 1941, on a tight schedule that would have the principal photography completed by Thanksgiving. Most of the filming was accomplished at the old United Artists studio, enabling Carole to boast of having worked at every major movie-making installation in Hollywood. *To Be or Not to Be* was the happiest experience of her career—the one time, she said, when everything began right, stayed right, and ended right. It was joy and relief to her just to be working again; but the fellowship with Lubitsch and his hand-picked company, which included many of the old Lombard crew at Paramount, was indeed sublime. Lubitsch later acknowledged that Carole had become a sort of unofficial co-director of the picture at his own invitation, because she obviously made an important cerebral contribution both as on-camera performer and sidelines observer. Mystified that he had never personally directed Carole during their long years of studio association, Lubitsch said he and Carole were in early accord that they should make many more pictures together. When Carole confided a hankering to play farce in period costume, Lubitsch intrigued her with intimations of a droll, sexually adventurous Catherine the Great.

An adjunct reward of *To Be or Not to Be* was Carole's belated kinship with the great German actor, Sig (for Siegfried) Rumann. He had come to New York before the Hitler takeover in Germany, to enact the Preysing role in the stage production of *Grand Hotel* that preceded the famous movie. As an eloquent anti-Nazi, Rumann took political asylum in the U.S. and found ample employment in Hollywood, but his wide-ranging seriocomic talent was rarely exploited in worthwhile films. Lubitsch had employed Rumann smartly as a bumbling Russian in *Ninotchka* but he was more in his element in the wienerschnitzel atmosphere of *To Be or Not to Be*. Rumann was a man of abundant good humor, but also morose about the nightmare that engulfed all of Europe. He was a mine of information about the Nazi terror and the holocaust aimed at European Jewry, and his tales put Carole's casual liberalism into a strong patriotic focus.

Also taking an important role in *To Be or Not to Be* was the young Robert Stack, whom Lubitsch cast on Carole's recommendation. Stack was then best known for having bestowed Deanna Durbin's first screen kiss, and Carole suspected that his serious good looks were suppressing an aptitude for comedy. On the *To Be or Not to Be* set it was apparent that Carole had made yet another conquest. He was the novice, Carole the model and inspiration—the John Barrymore situation in paraphrase, nearly eight years after *Twentieth Century,* although it seemed much longer than that.

While *To Be or Not to Be* was nearing completion, Carole told Hedda Hopper that she wanted to continue working "as long as I have my looks and my sanity," and that she expected to do two pictures a year as a minimum. At about that same time, she reached agreement with Harry Cohn to star in *He Kissed the Bride* for Columbia. She was not ready to commit herself to a contract, but one lay in the offing if the test picture gave her satisfaction. She approved of Cohn's choice of Alexander Hall as director of *He Kissed the Bride*. Carole wasn't acquainted with Hall, but he was coming off a Columbia smash, the farcical *Here Comes Mr. Jordan* with Robert Montgomery. Carole would have welcomed another teaming with Montgomery, but he had recently enlisted in the Navy —becoming, with James Stewart, the only major stars to enter military service before the country's formal entry into World War II. Cohn wanted Melvyn Douglas as Carole's costar and that was fine with her. Douglas had revealed a masterful drawing-room style in a number of Columbia's winning efforts, and for Lubitsch he had been superb opposite Garbo's Ninotchka. Cohn slotted *He Kissed the Bride* for an early 1942 shooting start, and Carole reduced her starting fee to $112,500. Her schedule would be coordinated with Clark's; he would begin filming *Somewhere I'll Find You* after the Christmas holidays.

Gable maintained a detachment toward Carole's negotiations with Harry Cohn, whom he despised for reasons of his own. But he could marvel at Carole's resourcefulness in getting along with Cohn when no one else could. Clark seldom exhibited interest in Carole's career except for the income it represented. He did not share Carole's enthusiasm for *To Be or Not to Be,* or for either Jack Benny or Ernst Lubitsch. He had difficulty pronouncing Lubitsch's name and often referred to him as "that horny hun" instead. Certainly Clark did not share Carole's interest in international affairs, and tended to discount "scare talk" about a likely war. Carole had given vocal sympathy to the Loyalists during the Spanish civil war that Gable ignored out of disinterest. And when Carole gave volunteer service to Bundles for Britain, Clark said that while the whole business between Hitler and Churchill was unfortunate, it was none of our affair. But all of that changed on December 7.

The Gables were watching a Sunday football game when they heard the first reports of the Japanese attack on Pearl Harbor. They left Gilmore Stadium at halftime and drove to the ranch—Gable icily silent in shock, while Carole sputtered every obscenity against imperial Japan. They joined the rest of the American people at radioside, and stayed home the next day to hear President Roosevelt ask Congress to declare war against Japan, Germany, Italy, and the lesser axis powers. During the dark days that followed, Clark began to digest the newspapers that previously had commanded only Carole's attention.

Hollywood responded quickly to the sudden turn of events. Dozens of projected films were scratched in favor of topical, patriotic movie stories. The Pacific-based *Somewhere I'll Find You* was one of the scripts altered in accordance with the headlines. Official Hollywood also joined in the war effort. L. B. Mayer, a longtime foe of Roosevelt's New Deal, personally volunteered M-G-M's resources to the President. Just before Christmas, Clark Gable was named to one of the President's "victory committees."

Two years of watching from the sidelines had prepared the nation psychologically for war. Throughout the nation young men were enlisting by the hundreds of thousands in every branch of the armed services. But the country was desperately unprepared industrially, and the prerequisite of planning a war was the financing of one. An immediate measure would be the sale of U.S. bonds—"defense bonds" in the early going, and "war bonds" after the initiative shifted to the Allies. Remembering Mary Pickford's remarkable effectiveness selling Liberty Bonds during the first World War, the President's counselors reasoned that a movie star would be the logical spearhead for launching the first national bond drive. L. B. Mayer proposed either Mickey Rooney or Clark Gable from his own studio, and Mickey actually rated as the nation's top box-office attraction. But as a son of Ohio, Gable represented the great Midwest; and Harry Hopkins, the Presidential adviser who was calling the shots, thought it essential that the drive begin in the American heartland. Besides, President Roosevelt was said to have suggested that Gable's sex appeal would sell more bonds than Mickey Rooney's juvenile charm. So Clark was invited to initiate the bond campaign in Columbus, Ohio.

But Clark didn't want to sell bonds, and he could be stubborn. He begged off, explaining that he would be shooting a picture in mid-January, when the bond drive was targeted. Mayer argued that he could close down the picture for a few days, or "shoot around" its star; but Gable disliked the studio boss and did not want him to have the satisfaction. To Harry Hopkins, Clark said, "I'll help you any way I can, other than personal appearances. But I hate crowds and don't know how to act when I'm in one. Besides, I'm no salesman." Carole told Harry Hopkins she could talk Clark into it, but she overestimated her influence. She prodded Clark on his patriotic duty, and said that if he'd go East to kick off the bond drive, she'd go with him and help out. When she said she would have considered it an honor just to be asked, Clark said, "All right, Maw, consider yourself asked!" As a member of the Victory Committee, he proposed his wife as much the better choice for the assignment.

Roosevelt and Hopkins were both delighted. They had met both

Carole and Clark during a Washington stopover the Gables made after their visit to the Johns Hopkins clinic in Baltimore. Franklin Roosevelt, besides having long been a Carole Lombard fan, was still eloquent in expressing his gratitude of her famous advocacy of the income tax. Harry Hopkins's opinion was that women were the more effective salesmen of patriotism among other things, and Clark said his wife could outperform anybody selling anything. Carole accepted the assignment without hesitation; but she still thought she could prevail on Clark to accompany *her.* Since Carole Lombard was Indiana's foremost standard bearer in Hollywood, the decision was to inaugurate the bond drive in Indianapolis— actually the center of gravity for the U.S. population in 1942.

January 15 was confirmed as the climactic event of the drive, with Carole slotted for a formal appearance at the Indiana state auditorium following a day of bond-selling at the state capitol. Once she was convinced that Clark would not change his mind about making the trip, Carole asked her mother to accompany her. Bess was, after all, the true Hoosier; and it was an extraordinary opportunity for Carole to enjoy a long visit with her mother, whom she felt she had neglected during the recent years that had been given almost entirely to Gable. Bess Peters did not hesitate to accept; Carole's itinerary prior to Indianapolis was somewhat complicated, but they agreed that Bess could take a detour to Fort Wayne before rejoining Carole in Indianapolis for the final event before their homeward return.

Carole and her mother went on an all-day shopping spree in Beverly Hills before their departure. Carole outfitted Bess with a complete new wardrobe for the trip, assuring her that "now you're the sexiest sixty-five-year-old woman in America." Bess joked about catching herself a millionaire husband when they started selling bonds.

They left Los Angeles by train on Monday morning, January 12. They were accompanied by Otto Winkler, Gable's own shadow in his capacity as M-G-M press agent. Carole told Clark that as much as she liked Otto, she didn't think it necessary that he go along—she and her mother had proved before that they could take care of themselves. But the M-G-M policy was to engage a studio functionary as buffer between its popular stars and the wild public during junkets away from Hollywood; and while Carole had no official connection with M-G-M, Clark arranged Winkler's assignment through the studio. Eddie Mannix heard Clark say, "Honey, Otto has to go along to keep an eye on you so you don't get into any mischief." Carole's reply, with an unmistakable serious edge, was "Yeah, but who's going to be keeping an eye on *you?*"

Clark had fitful streaks of unreasonable jealousy, and during Carole's filming of *To Be or Not to Be* he suspected her of an affair with the fiftyish Ernst Lubitsch, one of Hollywood's renowned womanizers; and he was also distrustful of Carole's interest in Robert Stack, who was considerably younger than herself. A report of tension between the married stars when Carole began the eastward journey would evolve into minor Hollywood legend; but Carole was probably the one most worried about the separation of more than a week, not having been away from Clark for more than a day or two at a time during their three-year marriage. The return trip was not yet scheduled, but Carole wanted to be back in southern California no later than January 21, when the first preview screening of *To Be or Not to Be* was slated. She was to begin costume fittings for *He Kissed the Bride* the following week.

The Chicago-bound train stopped at Salt Lake City, where Carole worked into training as a salesman of patriotism, making an impromptu but eloquent pitch for defense bonds and stamps before a crowd that gathered at the train station just to get a glimpse of her. She spoke of the heroic Allied defenses of Manila and Singapore, and vowed that a united America would prove to its foes that such heroism had not been in vain. They cheered lustily when she said, "This is our great chance to prove what we've been saying all our lives—that ours is the greatest nation in the history of mankind." Elbert Dickey of Salt Lake City remembered that her tears were real.

In Chicago she was introduced as the honorary national chairman of the defense drive, and responded with an unrehearsed pep rally, erupting from a scheduled formal press conference. From Chicago she tried unsuccessfully to reach Gable by telephone, while Otto Winkler wired the studio that Carole was doing a super job.

Bess Peters took another train for the quick ride to Fort Wayne, while Carole and Winkler remained in Chicago for other meetings pertaining to the sales effort. Carole told officials that upon returning to Hollywood she would enlist "every star with any glitter at all" into the campaign. On Wednesday, January 14, she and Otto

Winkler flew to Indianapolis and Bess rejoined them the next day. Carole placed a call to Clark Gable at M-G-M, having failed to contact him at home; but he also couldn't be found at the studio. Winkler dispatched progress reports regularly to the studio, and Clark was assured that everything was going well. He tried to contact Carole in Indianapolis on Thursday, but she had already left her hotel for the state capitol.

She started the day selling bonds in a crowded corridor, then moved into the rotunda and mounted a table. Her personal appearance was an unquestioned success but there was early lethargy in the bond buying. Then Carole decided against giving autographs unless the recipient had made a bond purchase. The orders started coming in and Carole got the salesmanship fever; she gave large red, white, and blue receipts to the new investors and signed "Carole Lombard Gable" on every one. The herd psychology triumphed, and orders poured in faster than they could be processed. Carole kept a battery of salesgirls hopping with excited instructions: "The man on the balcony railing will buy a thousand dollar bond—get him quick. The fellow in the brown suit will go five hundred—kiss his bald head and tell him it's from me!"

That night she donned a strapless, black velvet formal and made her final pitch before 12,000 persons crowded into the auditorium at the Cadle Tabernacle. It was a stately occasion, more sentimental than frenzied, and some of Carole's relatives were among the assembly. They sensed that perhaps above all, it was Bess Peters's moment of proud triumph. Her daughter simply owned the audience, and could give a crowd of any size an assurance of intimacy. Carole said she was proud to be an American, and more grateful than she'd ever been that Indiana had bred her. They had sung "The Star-Spangled Banner" at the start of the program, before Indiana's Governor Henry Schricker introduced the glowing star; but at the end of the festivities Carole decided she wanted to sing it again. She led the throng in an *a capella* rendering of the national anthem, while dignitaries from every corner of the state (including Elwood's Wendell Willkie) made bond pledges.

In the afterglow of her triumph, while the crowd was leaving the auditorium in patriotic euphoria, Carole learned that she had sold two million dollars in bonds—surely the single-day record. Carole was pleased, but she quickly rejected an overture to put in a Friday appearance at Wasson's department store for additional bond subscriptions. Carole said thanks, but she was going home to California. She told her mother to get packed for their journey, and asked Otto Winkler to find out what planes were going to California.

Bess Peters, who feared air travel and in fact had never flown, was startled. They had Saturday-morning train reservations and expected to arrive in Los Angeles on Monday evening. Otto Winkler also had anticipated a relaxing train ride, and supposed the issue was settled when the few scheduled flights from Indianapolis to Los Angeles all showed full passenger lists. But Carole was distressed. Possibly she had lingering worries about Lana Turner, or perhaps she was only anxious to be with Clark again. But she wanted to get home, and over her mother's protests she began phoning the airlines and pleading for accommodation. The Transcontinental & Western Airlines had just received cancellation requests from three passengers on Flight No. 3 to Los Angeles. Departure was at 4:00 A.M.—just three hours away. And Carole wanted to go.

She usually got her way. This time Bess Peters carried a stiff argument. Although Winkler's own preference was clearly seen, he took a discreetly neutral position and suggested they let the toss of a coin decide between flying or taking the train. Carole agreed. She called tails while Otto's quarter was in the air. It landed tails; they'd take the plane.

At the Indianapolis Municipal Airport they boarded a 1942 version of a luxury liner of the air—a twenty-one-passenger Douglas transport christened the Skyclub for its TWA flights. New York had been the point of origin for a multiple-stop flight that would end at the Lockheed Air Terminal in Los Angeles. Flying time from Indianapolis would be almost seventeen hours, but by gaining three hours westbound on time changes, they figured to arrive in Los Angeles shortly before 6:00 P.M. on Friday. That was the information Otto Winkler wired to Clark Gable and also to M-G-M. Carole sent her own wire to Clark: "Hey, Pappy, you'd better get in this man's army."

The James Todds of Indianapolis, friends of Bess who watched her and Carole board the plane, related that even at the last minute the star's mother was trying to talk her out of flying. Bess took a fast pulse-reading of fate and found the vibrations didn't favor a safe journey. Carole usually indulged her mother's faith in numerology, but this time she scorned it and coaxed her mother aboard.

Most of the passengers ticketed all the way to Los Angeles were in military uniform—fliers in the Army Ferry Command. As civilian passengers departed at interim stops, their seats were taken by other officers. The logistics of boarding men on military orders caused ground delays that put the flight behind schedule; and at Amarillo, Texas, Otto Winkler wired the information that they would not arrive in Los Angeles before 8:00 P.M. It was the last message Otto sent.

There was one other scheduled stop prior to Los Angeles. The Skyclub put down in Albuquerque, New Mexico to discharge two passengers and receive others. At Albuquerque nine pilots with military orders were waiting to board, and all had to be accommodated. In addition to the two civilians scheduled to deplane there (one of whom was the novelist Harvey Fergusson), seven passengers were nonmilitary, including Carole's party. Airport officials apologized for having to bump all seven, who would have an option to take a train to Los Angeles almost immediately, or fly the following day. The other passengers were compliant, but Carole put up a fuss. Didn't she qualify as some kind of military officer since she'd just sold two million dollars' worth of defense bonds? Once again she charmed them. Since the plane wasn't overloaded for weight, officials decided three extra passengers would not be a safety hazard. Three fliers who boarded at Albuquerque simply would not have seats. Carole was heard to apologize to the officers for "pulling rank." The four other civilians were briefly stranded in Albuquerque; and one was the concert violinist Joseph Szigeti, a newcomer to the United States.

What happened after that was mostly speculation, into which was sifted some conflicting accounts of what the pilot reported in his last radio report, received at 7:07 P.M. There was no anxiety in pilot Wayne Williams's voice as he reported that he was slightly off course, flying about thirty-five miles west of Las Vegas, Nevada. But several eyewitness accounts given later by residents of the Blue Diamond mine area, only fifteen miles from Las Vegas, were in agreement that it was surely no later than 7:07 when the plane burst into flames. Some thought it exploded before the actual crash into Olcott Mountain—also called Table Rock and Double-Up Peak—just five miles from the Blue Diamond. The plane had made an unscheduled stop at Las Vegas, before taking off again at 6:50 P.M. A popular theory was that the passengers were probably aware of the impending crash seconds before the actual impact.

The Las Vegas police received word of the apparent crash almost instantly, and dispatched ambulances with doctors to the area of the mine. But it was the season of early darkness, and the rugged terrain would render it impossible for a search party to reach the scene of the crash before daybreak on Saturday.

Clark Gable had planned a surprise homecoming party for his wife and mother-in-law. The Peters brothers were at the ranch, with only the full corps of servants to round out the welcoming committee. The servants said they had never seen Clark in such a state of nervous excitement. He kept rubbing his hands together and saying he was certainly glad that Maw was finally going to be home again.

Knowing that the plane would arrive late, Clark had not left the ranch for the Lockheed Air Terminal when he received the phone call from Eddie Mannix. Carole's plane was believed to be down in Nevada. First reports were only fragmentary, and Clark chartered a plane for Las Vegas, still hoping to find his wife alive. Mannix and Buster Collier accompanied him, and by the time they reached Nevada it was no longer a doubtful issue; there were no survivors. But Clark trudged dutifully up the mountainside, supported also by Spencer Tracy who had taken another plane to Las Vegas immediately upon hearing of the tragedy.

Five military passengers were hurled clear of the wreckage, their broken bodies strewn hundreds of feet apart. All other passengers and crew had been trapped in the cabin and were burned beyond recognition. Positive identification was a later formality, based primarily on dental records.

Clark Gable was a tragic figure, heroic in his manly grief, while morosely expressing a conviction of personal guilt. For reasons never probed, but long subjected to speculation both reasonable and wild, he held himself responsible for Carole's death.

But her death sealed and protected for all time the legend of Hollywood's greatest love story.

❋ XV ❋

The Melody Lingers On

SOME PEOPLE are remembered for their deaths. It is a tribute to Carole Lombard's personality that her own community nourishes the memory of her life.

It seems fair to say that no American performer in any medium was so deeply mourned in this century, or so sorely missed. Yet she has continued to inhabit the film colony during every cycle of its stark change—a happy, irrepressible ghost, still a part of the Hollywood atmosphere where fact and fable commingle.

Mention her name in the film colony environs and senior citizens light up. A third of a century has passed, but they speak of her with vivid recall and a sense of immediacy; why, it seems like only yesterday . . .

People who could not possibly remember her, and some who were not even born during her lifetime, tend toward cynical embrace of Hollywood's ongoing legends; but her vitality persuades them. Young people stabilize the legend by swallowing it whole. They are interested in the Gable romance, but their fascination for Carole Lombard exists quite apart from it.

The Lombard allure is rooted in personality, but the passing of years has yielded a positive revaluation of her artistry. She belongs to a brief but vibrant chapter of film history when the luminous stars were indeed much larger than life, and the popular belief has been that the times made them "big" in a way that stars can never be so big again. But we are also coming to appreciate that the great stars of the Age of the Movies were also *better* . . . if only because the system brought the unmistakable cream inevitably to the top. Some of the great stars were brilliant only as personalities especially right for the motion picture medium. Undoubtedly a few were splendid actors and actresses, often exhibiting astonishing range within the confinement of their formulated screen images. A very small number revealed steady growth as performers while also exhibiting ever stronger command as personalities, and Carole Lombard was one of these.

Yet she was always an artist, even if her own awareness came only belatedly. Her singular naturalness will stand as her historical vindication. Her earliest extant performances reveal this. Time has tarnished the work of many of her contemporaries, but on film Carole simply is getting better.

In 1942, when the nation that mourned her was united in a patriotic cause, Carole Lombard was saluted as a heroine who had given her life in the service of her country. She was a statistic of tragedy, but the aftermath of her life had ironic intimations of happy ending.

More than having simply loved Clark Gable, she had endeavored to be an influence on him—to make him a man to match his mountainous charm. This she apparently accomplished posthumously. Gable, who was too old for military conscription, nevertheless enlisted in the Army Air Corps and served with commissioned distinction. During the postwar years he was romanticized as one in love with a ghost, vainly seeking another Lombard; but his friends also saw a gentleness that had not existed before, and a sensitive and considerate man where once there had been only a selfish one. The public quietly rejoiced when a more settled Clark Gable entered into a blissful final marriage with his longtime friend Kay Williams, and rejoiced again but with mixed emotions when Kay Gable delivered a son—John Clark Gable, born months after his father's death at age fifty-nine. The public was also grateful to Kay Gable for carrying out Clark's long-expressed wish to be buried beside his third wife, Carole Lombard.

Historically at least, Carole's saga also had a happy ending along professional lines. *To Be or Not to Be,* released two months after her death, did not display her virtuosity so much as her maturity as comedienne, but it was the finest picture of her career. Conforming to expectation, it was both ill-timed and ahead of its time as a spoofing of a national enemy, when the war news was still mostly bad and Hitler's Germany was not acceptable to most people as a laughing matter. Like most Lubitschean masterworks, it is both hilarious and provocative and has aged like good vintage wine. It is Jack Benny's film, but there is a beauty in the very generosity of the Lombard performance. Time and again she sets up Benny perfectly, and in no small way is responsible for Benny's only attainment of cinematic grandeur. Certainly it was a good one to go out with—far more worthy of a beloved star than the scheduled Columbia comedy would have been. Retitled *They All Kissed the Bride,* it caused no ripples, nor does it stir the memory. Its gentle irony was that Carole's replacement as star was the dancing rival of their teen years, M-G-M's Joan Crawford.

In June, 1942, Irene Dunne christened the Liberty ship *Carole Lombard,* which served in the Pacific theater throughout the duration of the war. In 1944 it was commended by England's George VI for rescuing survivors of a sunken British freighter and landing them safely at Ceylon.

Also in 1942, a series of inquiries determined that the plane that carried Carole, her mother, her acting press agent, sixteen servicemen, and a crew of three to their deaths had been flying off course through restricted air territory—a foolish short-cut maneuver to regain lost time. The hearings revealed that the pilot had a tainted record and had been reprimanded several times for disregarding regulations. It was a matter of years before final compensation was made to the heirs of all the crash victims, but "the Carole Lombard disaster" is often cited as one of the classic cases that brought about a more rigid discipline of air-travel safety.

The Allies won the war, and Hollywood and America got back to their old business, but the old business would never be the same. Except for the film colony that kept the flame of her personality, the world almost forgot about Carole Lombard for a while.

But then an unforeseen phenomenon of the Age of Television was the birth and growth of the Film Generation. Its important discovery was that Hollywood's much-maligned legacy of old pictures was a treasure chest of myriad jewels. They found new poetry in old westerns; and in simple program films they found *relevance* that the pictures' modest creators probably never suspected. But the screwball comedy emerged many-splendored, as the most distinctively American gem of the bountiful prewar years; and they found Carole Lombard.

Screwball comedy would have had its shining hour without her. The premium farces would and will endure as a vigorous justification of America's movies in their finest era. But interest in a form intensifies when attention polarizes around a central illustration of the form. If a movie is an orchestration of component parts, then Carole Lombard is the glamorous conductor of the screwball concerto.

She defined the screwball comedy's style and progression, and its character mirrored her own. By extension, it is no less true that Carole Lombard, while a self-liberated oracle of the "new woman" on the one hand, was an irrepressible creature for her own time.

It was an idealistic time. Optimism fed a naïve America and healed its wounds, even as a storm was brewing that would tear the world asunder. We slogged through the Depression determined to prevail, and confident that we *would* prevail if only we could keep our sense of humor. Clowning broadly but without vulgarity, hoydenishly glamorous, always exhibiting the most remarkable balance of brashness and innocence, Carole cheered us on.

When the war came, we were united in a way we haven't been since. Now we long for that unity again, and the yearning is the tap root of nostalgia. No less remarkable for being naïve, it was a unity that trumpeted an exhilarated American spirit in its most admirable aspects.

And on film for all time, that spirit is inhabited in the soul of this woman.

The Films of Carole Lombard

Included are all feature-length motion pictures in which Carole Lombard is known, or reasonably believed, to have appeared. Not included are the fourteen Mack Sennett one-reel and two-reel comedies in which she participated in 1927 and 1928.

1. A PERFECT CRIME (Associated)

March, 1921. Five reels. Director, Allan Dwan. Scenario and titles, Allan Dwan, from a magazine story by Carl Clausen.

Cast: Monte Blue, Jacqueline Logan, Stanton Heck, Hardee Kirkland. *(Unbilled, the young Jane Peters played a small role.)*

2. DICK TURPIN (Fox)

February, 1925. 72 minutes. Director, John G. Blystone. Story, scenario, and titles, Charles Kenyon and Charles Darnton.

Cast: Tom Mix, Kathleen Myers, Philo McCullough, Alan Hale, James Marcus, Fred Kohler, Bull Montana, Lucille Hutton, Fay Holderness. *(Carole Lombard's scene with Tom Mix and Kathleen Myers was cut from the release print, but she was visible in a group scene.)*

3. GOLD AND THE GIRL (Fox)

April, 1925. 53 minutes. Director, Edmund Mortimer. Story, scenario and titles, John Stone.

Cast: Buck Jones, Elinor Fair, Bruce Gordon, Lucien Littlefield, Claude Peyton, Carol Lombard, Alphonz Ethier.

4. MARRIAGE IN TRANSIT (Fox)

April, 1925. 53 minutes. Director, Roy William Neill. Scenario and titles by Dorothy Yost, from a novel by Grace Livingston Hill.

Cast: Edmund Lowe, Carol Lombard, Adolph Milar, Frank Beal, Harvey Clark, Wade Boteler.

5. HEARTS AND SPURS (Fox)

June, 1925. 52 minutes. Director, W. S. Van Dyke. Story, scenario and titles, John Stone.

Cast: Buck Jones, Carol Lombard, William Davidson, Freeman Wood, Jean LaMotte, Gordon Russell.

6. DURAND OF THE BADLANDS (Fox)

October, 1925. 62 minutes. Director, Lynn Reynolds. Scenario and titles, Lynn Reynolds, from a story by Maibelle Justice.

Cast: Buck Jones, Marion Nixon, Malcolm Waite, Luke Cosgrave, George Lessey, Carol Lombard, Buck Black, Fred DeSilva.

7. THE ROAD TO GLORY (Fox)

January, 1926. 66 minutes. Director, Howard Hawks. Story, scenario and titles, by Howard Hawks and L. G. Rigby.

Cast: May McAvoy, Leslie Fenton, Ford Sterling, Rockcliffe Fellowes, Freedman Wood, Milla Davenport, John MacSweeney. *(Carole Lombard had begun work in this film when she was injured in an automobile accident. She was replaced in her minor role, but remained in two scenes, her character unidentified.)*

8. THE FIGHTING EAGLE (Pathé)

September, 1927. 85 minutes. Director, Donald Crisp. Scenario, Douglas Doty, and titles, John Kraft, from Sir Arthur Conan Doyle's story, *The Exploits of Brigadier Gerard.*

Cast: Rod La Rocque, Phyllis Haver, Sam DeGrasse, Julia Faye, Sally Rand, Max Barwyn, Clarence Burton.

(Rod La Rocque insisted that Carole Lombard had played a small part in this costume film produced by Cecil B. DeMille's unit. Mitchell Leisen, the art director, doubted Carole's participation, but Donald Crisp verified that he had once directed Carole Lombard in a silent feature, so presumably this was it.)

9. HALF A BRIDE (Paramount)

June, 1928. 70 minutes. Director, Gregory LaCava. Original story and scenario, Doris Anderson and Percy Heath, titles by Julian Johnson.

Cast: Esther Ralston, Gary Cooper, William Worthington, Freeman Wood, Mary Doran, Guy Oliver, Ray Gallagher.

(Whether any of Carole Lombard's limited footage remained in the release print is unknown. No print is believed to exist now.)

10. THE DIVINE SINNER (Rayart)

July, 1928. 60 minutes. Producer, Trem Carr. Director, Scott Pembroke. Original story, scenario, and titles, Robert Dillon.

Cast: Vera Reynolds, Nigel de Brulier, Bernard Siegel, Ernest Hilliard, Carol Lombard, John Peters, Harry Northrup.

11. POWER (Pathé)

September, 1928. 65 minutes. Producer, Ralph Block. Director, Howard Higgin. Original story and scenario, Tay Garnett. Titles, John Kraft.

Cast: William Boyd, Alan Hale, Jacqueline Logan, Jerry Drew.

(Carole Lombard and Joan Bennett appeared together in one scene.)

12. ME, GANGSTER (Fox)

October, 1928. 64 minutes. Director, Raoul Walsh. Scenario, Raoul Walsh, and titles, William Kernell, from the novel by Charles Francis Coe.

Cast: June Collyer, Don Terry, Anders Randolph, Stella Adams, Gustav von Seyffertitz, Carol Lombard, Burr McIntosh, Walter James, Nigel de Brulier, Al Hill, Bob Perry.

13. SHOW FOLKS (Pathé)

November, 1928. Silent film with sound effects, musical score, and one song; 73 minutes. Director, Paul Stein. Scenario, Jack Jungmeyer and George Dromgold, and titles, John Kraft, from an idea by Ralph Block.

Cast: Eddie Quillan, Lina Basquette, Robert Armstrong, Carol Lombard, Bessie Barriscale.

14. NED McCOBB'S DAUGHTER (Pathé)

January, 1929. Silent film with sound effects; 68 minutes. Director, William J. Cowen. Screenplay, Beulah Marie Dix (scenario) and Edwin Justus Mayer (titles), from the play by Sidney Howard.

Cast: Irene Rich, Theodore Roberts, Robert Armstrong, George Barraud, Carol Lombard, Edward Hearn, Louis Natheaux.

15. HIGH VOLTAGE (Pathé)

July, 1929. All-talking film; 57 minutes. (All subsequent titles are talkies.) Director, Howard Higgin. Original story and screenplay, Elliot Clawson, with additional dialogue by James Gleason.

Cast: William Boyd, Carol Lombard, Diane Ellis, Owen Moore, Billy Bevan, Phillips Smalley, Lee Shumway.

16. BIG NEWS (Pathé)

September, 1929. 61 minutes. Director, Gregory LaCava. Screenplay,

Walter DeLeon and Jack Jungmeyer (scenario), and Frank Reicher (dialogue), from an original story by George Brooks.

Cast: Robert Armstrong, Carol Lombard, Tom Kennedy, Sam Hardy, Warner Richmond, Robert Dudley, Louis Payne, Gertrude Sutton.

17. THE RACKETEER (Pathé)

November, 1929. 66 minutes. Director, Howard Higgin. Screenplay, Paul Gangelin (original story and scenario) and A. A. Kline (dialogue).

Cast: Robert Armstrong, Carol Lombard, Roland Drew, Paul Hurst, Hedda Hopper, Jeanette Loff, John Loder, Winter Hall, Winifred Harris.

18. DYNAMITE (Pathé)

December, 1929. 118 minutes. Director, Cecil B. DeMille. Story and screenplay, Jeanie MacPherson, with additional dialogue by John Lawson and Gladys Unger.

Cast: Conrad Nagel, Kay Johnson, Charles Bickford, Julia Faye, Joel McCrea, Muriel McCormick, Robert Edeson, Leslie Fenton, Barton Hepburn, Tyler Brooke. *(Carole Lombard began the filming and was replaced, but is visible in the release print, without her character identified.)*

19. THE ARIZONA KID (Fox)

April, 1930. 83 minutes. Director, Alfred Santell. Screenplay, Ralph Block and Joseph Wright, from Block's original story.

Cast: Warner Baxter, Mona Maris, Carol Lombard, Theodore Von Eltz, Mrs. Soledad Jimenez, Walter Lewis, Hank Mann, Wilfred Lucas, Arthur Stone.

20. SAFETY IN NUMBERS (Paramount)

July, 1930. 78 minutes. Director, Victor Schertzinger. Screenplay, Beulah Marie Dix (scenario) and George Marion Jr. (dialogue), from an original story by George Marion, Jr., and Percy Heath.

Cast: Charles Buddy Rogers, Josephine Dunn, Roscoe Karns, Virginia Bruce, Carol Lombard, Kathryn Crawford, Francis McDonald, Geneva Mitchell, Louise Beavers, Lawrence Grant.

21. FAST AND LOOSE (Paramount)

November, 1930. 87 minutes. Director, Fred Newmeyer. Screenplay, Doris Anderson and Jack Kirkland (scenario) and Preston Sturges (dialogue) from David Gray's adaptation of Avery Hopwood's play, *The Best People.*

Cast: Miriam Hopkins, Carole Lombard, Frank Morgan, Charles Starrett, Henry Wadsworth, Ilka Chase, Winifred Harris, Herbert Yost.

22. IT PAYS TO ADVERTISE (Paramount)

February, 1931. 75 minutes. Director, Frank Tuttle. Screenplay, Arthur Kober and Ethel Doherty, from an original story by Roi Cooper Megrue and Walter Hackett.

Cast: Skeets Gallagher, Norman Foster, Carole Lombard, Helen Johnson, Eugene Pallette, Lucien Littlefield, Louise Brooks, Morgan Wallace, Marcia Manners, Junior Coughlan.

23. MAN OF THE WORLD (Paramount)

April, 1931. 71 minutes. Director, Richard Wallace. Original story and screenplay, Herman Mankiewicz.

Cast: William Powell, Carole Lombard, Wynne Gibson, Guy Kibbee, Lawrence Gray, Tom Ricketts, Andre Cheron, George Chandler, Tom Costello.

24. LADIES' MAN (Paramount)

May, 1931. 70 minutes. Director, Lothar Mendes. Screenplay, Herman Mankiewicz, from a story by Rupert Hughes.

Cast: William Powell, Kay Francis, Carole Lombard, Gilbert Emery, Olive Tell, John Holland, Martin Burton, Frank Atkinson.

25. UP POPS THE DEVIL (Paramount)

June, 1931. 86 minutes. Director, Edward Sutherland. Screenplay, Arthur Kober and Eve Unsell, from the play by Frances Goodrich and Albert Hackett. Additional dialogue by Preston Sturges.

Cast: Stuart Erwin, Carole Lombard, Norman Foster, Skeets Gallagher, Lilyan Tashman, Edward Nugent, Joyce Compton, Theodore von Eltz, Harry Beresford, Eulalie Jenson.

26. I TAKE THIS WOMAN (Paramount)

August, 1931. 73 minutes. Directors, Marion Gering and Slavko Vorkapich. Screenplay, Vincent Lawrence, from the story, *Lost Ecstasy,* by Mary Roberts Rinehart.

Cast: Gary Cooper, Carole Lombard, Lester Vail, Helen Ware, Charles Trowbridge, Helen Jerome Eddy.

27. NO ONE MAN (Paramount)

January, 1932. 72 minutes. Director, Lloyd Corrigan. Screenplay, Percy Heath, Sidney Buchman and Agnes Brand Leahy, from a story by Rupert Hughes.

Cast: Carole Lombard, Ricardo Cortez, Paul Lukas, George Barbier, Juliette Compton, Virginia Hammond, Irving Bacon, Pat Moriarty.

28. SINNERS IN THE SUN (Paramount)

May, 1932. 71 minutes. Director, Alexander Hall. Screenplay, Vincent

Lawrence, Waldemar Young and Samuel Hoffenstein, from the story, *Beachcomber,* by Mildred Cram.

Cast: Carole Lombard, Chester Morris, Adrienne Ames, Alison Skipworth, Walter Byron, Cary Grant, Reginald Barlow, Rita LaRoy, Frances Moffett, Luke Cosgrave.

29. VIRTUE (Columbia)

October, 1932. 87 minutes. Director, Edward Buzzell. Screenplay, Robert Riskin, from an original story by Ethel Hill.

Cast: Carole Lombard, Pat O'Brien, Jack LaRue, Mayo Methot, Ward Bond, Shirley Grey, Willard Robertson, Ed LeSaint.

30. NO MORE ORCHIDS (Columbia)

December, 1932. 72 minutes. Director, Walter Lang. Screenplay, Gertrude Purcell, from an original story by Grace Perkins.

Cast: Carole Lombard, Walter Connolly, Lyle Talbot, Louise Closser Hale, C. Aubrey Smith, Allen Vincent, Ruthelma Stevens, Ed LeSaint, Jameson Thomas.

31. NO MAN OF HER OWN (Paramount)

December, 1932. 86 minutes. Director, Wesley Ruggles. Screenplay, Maurine Watkins and Milton Gropper, from an original story by Edmund Goulding and Benjamin Glazer.

Cast: Clark Gable, Carole Lombard, Dorothy Mackaill, Grant Mitchell, George Barbier, Elizabeth Patterson, J. Farrell MacDonald, Walter Walker, Paul Ellis, Lillian Harmer, Frank McGlynn, Sr.

32. FROM HELL TO HEAVEN (Paramount)

March, 1933. 68 minutes. Director, Erle C. Kenton. Screenplay, Sidney Buchman and Percy Heath, from a story by Lawrence Hazard.

Cast: Jack Oakie, Carole Lombard, Adrienne Ames, David Manners, Sidney Blackmer, Verna Hillie, James C. Eagles, Shirley Grey, Bradley Page, Berton Churchill, Nydia Westman, Cecil Cunningham, Clarence Muse, Walter Walker, Donald Kerr.

33. SUPERNATURAL (Paramount)

April, 1933. 60 minutes. Director, Victor Halperin. Screenplay, Harvey Thew and Brian Marlow, from an original story by Garnett Weston.

Cast: Carole Lombard, Randolph Scott, Vivienne Osborne, Alan Dinehart, Beryl Mercer, H. B. Warner, William Farnum, Willard Robertson.

34. BRIEF MOMENT (Columbia)

August, 1933. 72 minutes. Director, David Burton. Screenplay, Brian Marlow, from the play by S. N. Behrman.

Cast: Carole Lombard, Gene Raymond, Monroe Owsley, Donald Cook, Reginald Mason, Theresa Maxwell Conover, Florence Britton, Jameson Thomas, Arthur Hohl, Herbert Evans.

35. THE EAGLE AND THE HAWK (Paramount)

August, 1933. 70 minutes. Director, Stuart Walker. Screenplay, Bogart Rogers and Seton I. Miller, from a story by John Monk Saunders.

Cast: Fredric March, Cary Grant, Jack Oakie, Carole Lombard, Guy Sterling, Forrester Harvey, Kenneth Howell, Douglas Scott, Leland Hodgson, Crauford Kent, Russell Scott.

36. WHITE WOMAN (Paramount)

November, 1933. 69 minutes. Director, Stuart Walker. Screenplay, Samuel Hoffenstein, Gladys Lehman and Jane Loring, from an original story by Norman Reilly Raine and Frank Butler.

Cast: Charles Laughton, Carole Lombard, Charles Bickford, Kent Taylor, Percy Kilbride, James Bell, Ethel Griffies, Marc Laurence, Noble Johnson, Claude King, Charles Middleton.

37. BOLERO (Paramount)

February, 1934. 85 minutes. Director, Wesley Ruggles. Screenplay, Horace Jackson, from a story by Carey Wilson, Kubec Glasmon, and Ruth Ridenour.

Cast: George Raft, Carole Lombard, Frances Drake, William Frawley, Ray Milland, Sally Rand, Gertrude Michael, Del Henderson, John Irwin, Gloria Shea, Phillips Smalley.

38. WE'RE NOT DRESSING (Paramount)

April, 1934. 65 minutes. Director, Norman Taurog. Screenplay, Horace Jackson, Francis Martin, and George Marion, Jr., from Benjamin Glazer's story adaptation of Sir James M. Barrie's play, *The Admirable Crichton.*

Cast: Bing Crosby, Carole Lombard, George Burns, Gracie Allen, Ethel Merman, Leon Errol, Ray Milland, Jay Henry, John Irwin, Charles Morris, Ted Oliver.

39. TWENTIETH CENTURY (Columbia)

May, 1934. 91 minutes. Director, Howard Hawks. Screenplay, Ben Hecht and Charles MacArthur, from their play.

Cast: John Barrymore, Carole Lombard, Walter Connolly, Roscoe Karns, Etienne Girardot, Charles Levison, Ralph Forbes, Billie Seward, Dale Fuller, Edgar Kennedy.

40. NOW AND FOREVER (Paramount)

October, 1934. 80 minutes. Director, Henry Hathaway. Screenplay,

Vincent Lawrence and Sylvia Thalberg, from a story by Jack Kirkland and Melville Baker.

Cast: Gary Cooper, Carole Lombard, Shirley Temple, Sir Guy Standing, Charlotte Granville, Gilbert Emery, Henry Kolker, Jameson Thomas, Egon Brecher.

41. LADY BY CHOICE (Columbia)

October, 1934. 78 minutes. Director, David Burton. Screenplay, Jo Swerling. Story, Dwight Taylor, suggested by characters created by Damon Runyon.

Cast: Carole Lombard, May Robson, Walter Connolly, Roger Pryor, Arthur Hohl, Raymond Walburn, James Burke, Henry Kolker, John Boyle.

42. THE GAY BRIDE (M-G-M)

January, 1935. 80 minutes. Producer, Harry Rapf. Director, Jack Conway. Screenplay, Charles Francis Coe, from his play, *Repeal.*

Cast: Carole Lombard, Chester Morris, Zasu Pitts, Nat Pendleton, Leo Carrillo, Sam Hardy, Walter Walker.

43. RUMBA (Paramount)

February, 1935. 77 minutes. Producer, William LeBaron. Director, Marion Gering. Screenplay, Howard J. Green, from a story by Guy Endore and Seena Owen.

Cast: George Raft, Carole Lombard, Margo, Lynne Overman, Monroe Owsley, Iris Adrian, Akim Tamiroff, Gail Patrick.

44. HANDS ACROSS THE TABLE (Paramount)

October, 1935. 81 minutes. Producer, E. Lloyd Sheldon. Director, Mitchell Leisen. Screenplay, Vincent Lawrence, Norman Krasna, and Herbert Fields, from a story by Vina Delmar.

Cast: Carole Lombard, Fred MacMurray, Ralph Bellamy, Astrid Allwyn, Marie Prevost, Ruth Donnelly, William Demarest, Edward Gargan, Marcelle Corday, Joseph Tozer, Albert Conti, Herman Bing.

45. LOVE BEFORE BREAKFAST (Universal)

March, 1936. 70 minutes. Producer, Edmund Grainger. Director, Walter Lang. Screenplay, Herbert Fields, from a novel by Faith Baldwin.

Cast: Carole Lombard, Preston Foster, Cesar Romero, Janet Beecher, Betty Lawford, Douglas Blackley, Don Briggs, Bert Roach, E. E. Clive, Andre Beranger.

46. MY MAN GODFREY (Universal)

July, 1936. 95 minutes. Producer, Charles R. Rogers. Director, Gregory LaCava. Screenplay, Morrie Ryskind and Eric Hatch, from the novel, *1011 Fifth Avenue,* by Eric Hatch.

Cast: William Powell, Carole Lombard, Alice Brady, Gail Patrick, Mischa Auer, Eugene Pallette, Alan Mowbray, Jean Dixon.

47. THE PRINCESS COMES ACROSS (Paramount)

August, 1936. 77 minutes. Producer, Arthur Hornblow, Jr. Director, William K. Howard. Screenplay, Walter DeLeon, Francis Martin, Frank Butler and Don Hartman, from a story by Philip MacDonald and Louis Lucien Rogyer.

Cast: Carole Lombard, Fred MacMurray, Douglas Dumbrille, Alison Skipworth, William Frawley, Porter Hall, George Barbier, Sig Rumann, Lumsden Hare, Mischa Auer, Bradley Page, Milburn Stone.

48. SWING HIGH, SWING LOW (Paramount)

March, 1937. 98 minutes. Producer, Arthur Hornblow, Jr. Director, Mitchell Leisen. Screenplay, Virginia Van Upp and Oscar Hammerstein II, from the play *Burlesque,* by George Manker Watters and Arthur Hopkins.

Cast: Carole Lombard, Fred MacMurray, Charles Butterworth, Jean Dixon, Dorothy Lamour, Cecil Cunningham, Franklin Pangborn, Harvey Stephens, Charles Arnt, Anthony Quinn, Dennis O'Keefe, Charles Judels.

49. NOTHING SACRED (United Artists)

November, 1937. 77 minutes. Producer, David O. Selznick. Director, William Wellman. Screenplay, Ben Hecht, from a story by James Street.

Cast: Carole Lombard, Fredric March, Walter Connolly, Charles Winninger, Frank Fay, Sig Rumann, Maxie Rosenbloom, Aileen Pringle, Margaret Hamilton, Hedda Hopper, John Qualen, Olin Howland. *(This was Carole Lombard's only film photographed in Technicolor.)*

50. TRUE CONFESSION (Paramount)

November, 1937. 76 minutes. Producer, Albert Lewin. Director, Wesley Ruggles. Screenplay, Claude Binyon, from a play by Louis Verneuil and Georges Berr.

Cast: Carole Lombard, Fred MacMurray, John Barrymore, Una Merkel, Porter Hall, Edgar Kennedy, Lynne Overman, Fritz Feld, Toby Wing, Hattie McDaniel, Tommy Dugan.

51. FOOLS FOR SCANDAL (Warner Brothers)

April, 1938. 82 minutes. Producer-Director, Mervyn LeRoy. Screenplay, Herbert Fields and Joseph Fields, from an original story by Nancy Hamilton, James Shute, and Rosemary Casey.

Cast: Carole Lombard, Fernand Gravet, Ralph Bellamy, Allen Jenkins, Marie Wilson, Isabel Jeans, Marcia Ralston, Heather Thatcher.

52. MADE FOR EACH OTHER (United Artists)

February, 1939. 95 minutes. Producer, David O. Selznick. Director, John Cromwell. Screenplay, Jo Swerling, from his own original story.

Cast: Carole Lombard, James Stewart, Charles Coburn, Lucile Watson, Eddie Quillan, Alma Kruger, Ruth Weston, Donald Briggs, Harry Davenport, Esther Dale, Louise Beavers, Ward Bond, Olin Howland.

53. IN NAME ONLY (RKO Radio)

August 1939. 102 minutes. Producer, George Haight. Director, John Cromwell. Screenplay, Richard Sherman, from a novel by Bessie Breuer.

Cast: Carole Lombard, Cary Grant, Kay Francis, Charles Coburn, Helen Vinson, Katharine Alexander, Jonathan Hale, Peggy Ann Garner.

54. VIGIL IN THE NIGHT (RKO Radio)

February, 1940. 96 minutes. Producer-Director, George Stevens. Screenplay, Fred Guiol, P. J. Wolfson, and Rowland Leigh, from the novel by A. J. Cronin.

Cast: Carole Lombard, Brian Aherne, Anne Shirley, Julien Mitchell, Robert Coote, Brenda Forbes, Rita Page, Peter Cushing, Ethel Griffies, Doris Lloyd, Emily Fitzroy.

55. THEY KNEW WHAT THEY WANTED (RKO Radio)

October, 1940. 96 minutes. Producer, Erich Pommer. Director, Garson Kanin. Screenplay, Robert Ardrey, from the play by Sidney Howard.

Cast: Carole Lombard, Charles Laughton, William Gargan, Harry Carey, Frank Fay, Joe Bernard, Janet Fox, Karl Malden, Victor Kilian, Lee Tung-Foo.

56. MR. AND MRS. SMITH (RKO Radio)

February, 1941. 95 minutes. Producer, Harry Edington. Director, Alfred Hitchcock. Original story and screenplay, Norman Krasna.

Cast: Carole Lombard, Robert Montgomery, Gene Raymond, Jack Carson, Lucile Watson, Philip Merivale, William Tracy, Esther Dale, Emma Dunn, Betty Compson, Charles Halton.

57. TO BE OR NOT TO BE (United Artists)

February, 1942. 100 minutes. Producer-Director, Ernst Lubitsch. Screenplay, Edwin Justus Mayer, from an original story by Ernst Lubitsch and Melchior Lengyel.

Cast: Carole Lombard, Jack Benny, Robert Stack, Felix Bressart, Sig Rumann, Stanley Ridges, Lionel Atwill, Tom Dugan, Miles Mander, Henry Victor, Maude Eburne, Helmut Dantine, Charles Halton, James Finlayson.

Index